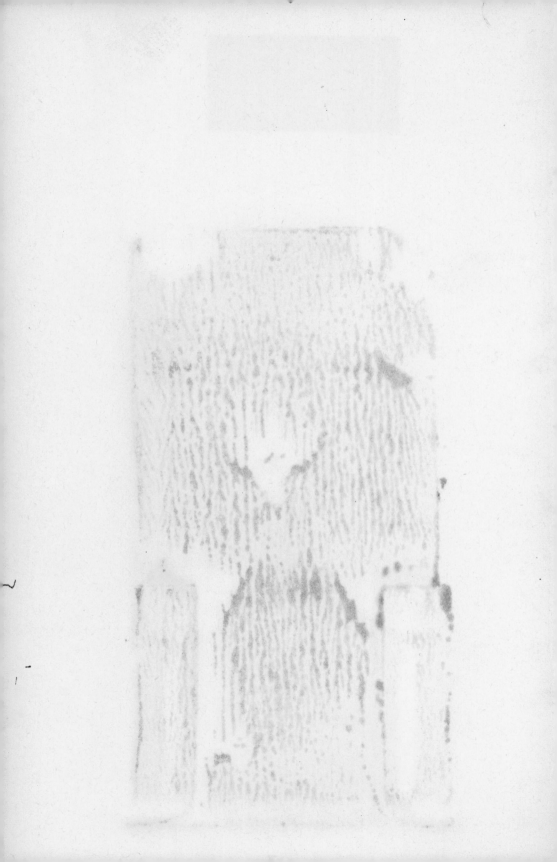

THE FIRST & THE FIFTH

A Da Capo Press Reprint Series

CIVIL LIBERTIES IN AMERICAN HISTORY

GENERAL EDITOR: LEONARD W. LEVY

Claremont Graduate School

THE FIRST
&
THE FIFTH

With Some Excursions into Others

By O. John Rogge

DA CAPO PRESS · NEW YORK · 1971

A Da Capo Press Reprint Edition

This Da Capo Press edition of
The First and the Fifth
is an unabridged republication of the first edition
published in 1960. It is reprinted by
special arrangement with Thomas Nelson, Inc.

Library of Congress Catalog Card Number 71-140377
SBN 306-70087-5

Published by Da Capo Press
A Division of Plenum Publishing Corporation
227 West 17th Street, New York, N.Y. 10011
All Rights Reserved

Manufactured in the United States of America

THE FIRST

and

THE FIFTH

BY O. JOHN ROGGE

Our Vanishing Civil Liberties. 1949
Why Men Confess. 1959

THE FIRST

AND

THE FIFTH

With Some Excursions Into Others

BY

O. JOHN ROGGE, A.B., LL.B., S.J.D.

Formerly Assistant United States Attorney General
in Charge of the Criminal Division of the Department of Justice

THOMAS NELSON & SONS

Edinburgh   NEW YORK   *Toronto*

TYPOGRAPHY BY FRANK KARPELES

Library of Congress Catalog Card No.: 60–7292

MANUFACTURED IN THE UNITED STATES OF AMERICA

TO THE

United States Supreme Court

AUTHOR'S NOTE

I gratefully acknowledge permission of the *California, Michigan* and *New York University Law Reviews* to use material in these articles of mine: *The New Federal Immunity Act and The Judicial Function*, 45 *Calif. L. Rev.* 109 (1957); *"Concept of Ordered Liberty"—A New Case*, 47 *Calif. L. Rev.* 238 (1959); *Compelling the Testimony of Political Deviants*, 55 Mich. L. Rev. 163, 375 (1956–57); *"Congress Shall Make No Law * * *"*; 56 *Mich. L. Rev.* 331, 579 (1958); *State Power Over Sedition, Obscenity and Picketing*, 34 N.Y.U.L. Rev. 817 (1959).

The material has been brought down to date. This book speaks as of October 1959. It carries through the term of the United States Supreme Court which ended in June 1959; and the first session of the 86th Congress, which adjourned in September.

I am indebted for aid in the preparation of the manuscript to my secretary, Miss Pauline Chakonas.

O.J.R.

CONTENTS

THE FIRST

and

THE FIFTH

CHAPTER I

ENDURING BIRTHRIGHTS

By a fortuitous combination of circumstances the Anglo-American peoples developed a set of individual rights which secure to the individual a certain area free from the state's intrusion. This was one of the factors that helped to produce a fairly independent citizenry in the West and relatively a more mature one than in the East.

Two of these individual rights, which are in a sense opposites, are those to freedom of utterance on the one hand and to silence on the other. The latter right the bench and bar know generally as the privilege against self-incrimination. The right to freedom of utterance is protected against federal action by the First Amendment, and that to silence by the Fifth. Both of these amendments secure yet other individual rights. The First guarantees as well freedom of religion, and the Fifth Amendment also contains the important due process clause.

I

Congress shall make no law respecting an establishment of religion, or prohibiting the free exercise thereof; or abridging the freedom of speech, or of the press; or the right of the people peaceably to assemble, and to petition the Government for a redress of grievances.

V

No person shall be held to answer for a capital, or otherwise infamous crime, unless on a presentment or indictment of a Grand Jury, except in cases arising in the land or naval forces, or in the Militia, when in actual service in time of War or public danger; nor shall any person be subject for the same offence to be twice put in jeopardy of life or limb; nor shall be compelled in any criminal case to be a witness against himself, nor be deprived of life, liberty, or property, without due process of law; nor shall private property be taken for public use, without just compensation.

However, the framers of the first ten amendments did not intend them to be applicable to state action. On the contrary, they intended the states to have certain powers over utterances which they denied to the federal government. They sought to make doubly certain of confining the federal government to its delegated powers by the provisions of the Tenth Amendment.

X

The powers not delegated to the United States by the Constitution, nor prohibited by it to the States are reserved to the States respectively, or to the people.

The restraints on state action against the individual dèpend first of all on the relevant provisions of state constitutions. Next they depend on the interpretation to be given to the privileges and immunities and the due process clauses of the first section of the Fourteenth Amendment to the federal Constitution. This amendment was ratified in 1868, after the Civil War.

XIV

Section 1. All persons born or naturalized in the United States, and subject to the jurisdiction thereof, are citizens of the United States and of the State wherein they reside. No State shall make or enforce any law which shall abridge the privileges or immunities of citizens of the United States; nor shall any State deprive any person of life, liberty, or property, without due process of law; nor deny to any person within its jurisdiction the equal protection of the laws.

Does this section make the first eight amendments, and particularly the First Amendment, applicable to the states? Or, to put in question form Justice Jackson's negative answer in his dissenting opinion in *Beauharnais* v. *Illinois*: Does the Fourteenth Amendment incorporate the First?

In *Adamson* v. *California*, involving the contention that a California statute which permitted comment on a defendant's failure in a criminal case to take the stand, violated the Fifth Amendment by way of the Fourteenth, Justice Black with the concurrence of Justice Douglas and the agreement on this point of Justices Murphy and Rutledge, expressed the view that historically "one of the chief objects that the provisions of the Amendment's first section, separately, and as a whole were intended to accomplish was to make the Bill of Rights, applicable to the States." Two years later these four justices adhered to this view in *Wolf* v. *Colorado*, where the Court affirmed a state court conviction based on evidence obtained as a result of an unreasonable search, although Justice Black concurred with the majority on the ground that "the federal exclusionary rule is not a command of the Fourth Amendment but is a judicially created rule of evidence which Congress might negate." Is the view of the four dissenters in these two cases correct?

The answer to this question will depend on the intent of the framers of the Fourteenth Amendment. It is the position of the writer that they did not intend, either by the privileges and immunities clause or the due process clause of that amendment, to make the first eight amendments applicable to the states.

What then did the framers of the Fourteenth Amendment mean by these clauses? There are two privileges and immunities clauses in the Constitution, as there are two due process clauses. The other privileges and immunities clause is in article IV, section 2 of the body of the Constitution; and the other due process clause is in the Fifth Amendment. Although the privileges and immunities which the Fourteenth Amendment protects are of citizens of the United States whereas those of Article IV, section 2 are of citizens in the several states, the framers of the Fourteenth Amendment in their use of the phrase did not mean anything expansively different than did the framers of the body of the Constitution in their use of it. Article IV, section 2 provides: "The Citizens of each State shall be entitled to all Privileges and Immunities of Citizens in the several States." By this provision its framers meant no more than that all citizens were to have the local measure of legal protection plus the local measure of freedom to cross state lines. The privileges and immunities clause of the Fourteenth Amendment means somewhat but not greatly more.

With the due process clauses the story is different. These clauses have a continuous history with the Anglo-American peoples of more than seven centuries. They go back to clause 39 of the Magna Carta of King John in 1215. Over the centuries they have been applied not only in procedural but also in substantive ways. Today the Fourteenth Amendment's due process clause safeguards to the individual as against state action all those rights which, in the apt phrasing of Justice Benjamin N. Cardozo in the Supreme Court's opinion in *Palko* v. *Connecticut*, "have been found to be implicit in the concept of ordered liberty."

In order to determine such rights one will bear in mind the specific provisions not only of the First and Fifth Amendments, but of the Fourth, Sixth and Eighth Amendments as well. One will do so, not because the Fourteenth Amendment incorporates the first eight amendments and thus makes them applicable to the states, but rather as a handy yardstick to help one give content to the concept of ordered liberty. The Fourth Amendment forbids unreasonable searches and seizures and general warrants. The Sixth secures public trial by jury, confrontation, witnesses in one's favor, and counsel. The Eighth protects against excessive bail.

IV

The right of the people to be secure in their persons, houses, papers, and effects, against unreasonable searches and seizures, shall not be violated, and no Warrants shall issue, but upon probable cause, supported by Oath or affirmation, and particularly describing the place to be searched, and the persons or things to be seized.

VI

In all criminal prosecutions, the accused shall enjoy the right to a speedy and public trial, by an impartial jury of the State and district wherein the crime shall have been committed, which district shall have been previously ascertained by law, and to be informed of the nature and cause of the accusation; to be confronted with the witnesses against him; to have compulsory process for obtaining Witnesses in his favor, and to have the Assistance of Counsel for his defence.

VIII

Excessive bail shall not be required, nor excessive fines imposed, nor cruel and unusual punishments inflicted.

Besides the specific individual rights which the first eight amendments protect, there are others which developed after the adoption of the federal Bill of Rights. These include: the right to privacy; the right to engage in political activity; the right of freedom of movement across national boundaries; the right to knowledge; the right of confrontation in other than criminal cases; the right to a jury trial in criminal contempt of court cases; the right to use the mails; and the right to engage in peaceful picketing. If there are invasions of these or yet other unenumerated rights at the hands of the state, counsel will look to the due process clause of the Fourteenth Amendment. If such invasions come from federal action, counsel will look first to the provisions of the federal Bill of Rights. Counsel will look there first in order to see whether any of such provisions can be construed to cover the unenumerated right whose recognition counsel will urge. Counsel will do this for the reason that constitutions must be interpreted to apply if possible to new situations: constitutions must be made as timeless as possible. For instance, if one wishes to contend that wiretapping is unconstitutional as an invasion of one's right to privacy, one will argue that it falls within the Fourth Amendment's prohibition against unreasonable searches. But counsel will also wonder about the provisions of the Ninth Amendment.

IX

The enumeration in the Constitution, of certain rights, shall not be construed to deny or disparage others retained by the people.

However, we shall find that those who seek the protection of unenumerated rights will usually have to rely on the due process clauses.

Our survey will thus cover some of the least understood as well as some of the most used parts of the Constitution. Among the least understood are the privileges and immunities clauses and the Ninth Amendment. Among the most used are the due process clauses, the First Amendment's guarantee of freedom of utterance, and the Fifth Amendment's provision for a right of silence. Primarily this book is about the last two guarantees. Hence its title.

The First Amendment's guarantee of freedom of speech and of the press and the Fifth Amendment's protection of the right of silence have been before the Supreme Court repeatedly in recent years. The world situation accounts for this, more particularly the threats of an aggressive international Communist movement.

This century has witnessed not only two world wars but also a cold war, which came crowding on the heels of the second hot one. Hardly had the Nazis been defeated when the Communists began their course of aggrandizement. In 1945 they engaged in guerrilla fighting in Greece, and took to Moscow and put on trial there the sixteen Polish leaders in the underground fight against the Nazis. The latter act enabled Russia to proceed with its Lublin Committee and ultimately a Communist government for Poland. In 1946 came the so-called cultural decrees, and the next year the establishment of the Cominform, five years after the dissolution of the Comintern. The year 1948 saw the Communist coup in Czechoslovakia and the year 1950 saw Communist aggression in Korea.

To the cold war one must add a century and more of background. In 1825 Robert Owen founded New Harmony, Indiana, a Communist community on the banks of the Wabash. A decade and a half later Pierre Joseph Proudhon in his first famous book asserted: "What is Property? Theft." In January of the revolutionary year 1848 in Europe *The Communist Manifesto* proclaimed: "The Communists disdain to conceal their views and aims. They openly declare that their ends can be attained only by the forcible overthrow of all existing social conditions. Let the ruling classes tremble at a Communist revolution. The proletarians have nothing to lose but their chains. They have a world to win.

"Working men of all countries, Unite!"

The next month there was an uprising in France followed by rioting everywhere in Germany. Within a few weeks the old ministries in Baden, Württemberg, Bavaria, Hanover, Brunswick, Hesse, Nassau,

Thuringia, and Saxony fell. In Vienna, Metternich had to resign and leave. Then the Hungarians, Bohemians, Southern Slavs, and Italians in Lombardy and Venetia simultaneously demanded autonomy and constitutions for their provinces. Within three decades, with the shot which Vera Zasulich fired at General Trepov, the nihilists in Russia started on a long series of assassinations. There were also assassinations in other countries. In 1881 Charles J. Guiteau, a disgruntled office seeker, shot President James A. Garfield. Twenty years later Leon Czolgosz, a Polish anarchist, fatally wounded President William Mc-Kinley. At the time President McKinley was attending the Pan-American exposition at Buffalo, New York. In between there was the Haymarket Square bomb-throwing riot of 1886 in Chicago. The assassination in 1914 of the Austrian Archduke Francis Ferdinand at Sarajevo in what is now Yugoslavia precipitated World War I. Before the war was over the Communists had staged their coup d'état in Russia and murdered Czar Nicholas II and his entire family, his wife, and their son and four daughters.

In the early part of 1917, the year of the Communist coup d'état in Russia, several of the Russian Bolshevik leaders were in New York city, among them both Leon Trotsky and Nikolai I. Bukharin. Trotsky was here for two months beginning the middle of January. Bukharin was here even longer. He arrived in November 1916 and left after Trotsky did. Two years later the Communists in the world formed the Communist International, the Comintern, in Moscow, and organized the Communist labor party in this country in Chicago.

That year the Socialist party met in convention on August 30 in Machinists' Hall in Chicago. In order to ready themselves for it, some Socialist party members held a Left Wing conference in New York city, June 21–24, 1919, which adopted a resolution urging all revolutionary socialists to send delegates to the forthcoming convention. These delegates were to be prepared to form a new party if the Socialist party refused to reinstate all suspended and expelled members. The conference also instructed its executive committee to draft and publish the *Left Wing Manifesto* and adopted *Revolutionary Age* as the Left Wing's official newspaper. The *Manifesto* appeared in the July 5, 1919 issue of *Revolutionary Age* and furnished the basis for the conviction of its business manager, Benjamin Gitlow, of criminal anarchy in New York.

At the convention the Left Wingers created a disturbance and were thrown out by the conservative Socialists, assisted by the police. The next day the Left Wingers met in an ante-room, and later adjourned to the IWW Hall. There they founded the Communist Labor party, and voted to take steps to affiliate with the Comintern. They also pledged agreement with the Comintern's principles. One of the participants in this founding convention was William Bross Lloyd. After it he and seventeen other participants were convicted for sedition in Illinois.

International Communism embarked upon a proselytizing as well as an aggressive course. Fascism was to do likewise. Both made use of a coup d'état to come to power, the Nazis in Germany fifteen years after the Communists in Russia. Hitler became chancellor on January 30, 1933. Both were totalitarian in nature and both made use of fifth columns in other countries, the one in the form of local Communist groups and their sympathizers and the other of various organizations and individuals. The report in 1955 by the Australian commission on Soviet espionage, the defecting Vladimir Petrov's revelations, and the subsequent surfacing in Moscow of the long missing British diplomats Donald Maclean and Guy Burgess emphasized once again the conspiratorial and international characteristics of communism. Maclean and Burgess had become communists in their student days at Cambridge University.

Various of these events made us begin to consider the problem of subversion. We began to do so more than fifty years ago. At the turn of the century there was much discussion of anarchism, socialism and nihilism. After President McKinley's assassination New York passed a criminal anarchy act. Fourteen other states followed in its lead. Congress excluded from admission into this country aliens who were "anarchists, or persons who believe in or advocate the overthrow by force or violence of the Government of the United States or of all government."

Immediately after World War I seventeen states adopted criminal syndicalism laws. In a single year, 1919, twenty-six states, more than half, passed laws against the display of red flags. In the same year both the United States Senate and the state of New York began to investigate communist propaganda in this country. The New York legislature created the Joint Committee Investigating Seditious Activities, often called the Lusk Committee, after Senator Clayton R. Lusk, who headed it. Since then there have been many investigations by many committees, state as well as federal, of individuals regarded as communists or communist sympathizers and groups and organizations thought to be communist or communist dominated. Since then there have been many measures against subversion. These investigations and these measures produced numerous claims by political deviants as well as others of invasions of their rights to freedom of utterance or to silence or both. A substantial number of the cases arising out of such claims ultimately reached the Supreme Court of the United States.

Among the early cases to come before the Supreme Court were *Schenck* v. *United States* (1919), and *Gitlow* v. *New York* (1925). It was in the *Schenck* case that Justice Holmes in the Court's opinion enunciated his famous clear and present danger test, a test which Judge Learned Hand has recently come to doubt. In that case the Court sustained a conviction under the federal Espionage Act of 1917. In the *Gitlow* case the Court upheld the validity of New York's criminal anarchy act of 1902. However, some language in the Court's opinion became the basis for the assertion that the Fourteenth Amendment incorporated the First. In the writer's view this language was misinterpreted.

Five years after the decision in the *Gitlow* case, Charles Evans Hughes became Chief Justice (1930–41), to be followed by Harlan Fiske Stone (1941–46). In the decade and a half of these two chief justices, freedom of speech and of the press received the Court's strong support. In these years the Court applied the approach of Jefferson and Madison and of Justices Brandeis and Holmes, the approach which is today that of Justices Black and Douglas and in substance that of Chief Justice Warren.

Stone's successor was Fred M. Vinson. Then in the summer of 1949 Justices Frank Murphy and Wiley Rutledge both died. It was at the hands of the Court as headed by Vinson from the fall of 1949 until his death four years later and the appointment of Chief Justice Warren that individual rights fared worst.

Under Chief Justice Warren the rights of the individual are again in the ascendant. This comes at a most opportune juncture; for we are in a period when the president of this country calls upon us to observe May 1 as Law Day; when on occasion throughout the world expectant eyes turn to our Supreme Court; when other countries, Greece, France, Western Germany, India, Italy, and yet others have adapted to their own needs our practice of judicial review; and when international meetings, in the West, in the East, and in India, have considered ways of fostering the extension of the rule of law throughout the world.

The time has come, indeed it is overdue, for a reexamination of the circumstances leading to the adoption of the federal Bill of Rights, the framers' intent in drafting the First Amendment, its subsequent construction, particularly the development and application of Justice Holmes's clear and present danger test, and the respective areas of federal and state power. It is the position of the writer that, at least so far as Congress is concerned, speech is as free as thought, and that unless and until speech becomes a part of a course of conduct which Congress can restrain or regulate no federal legislative power over it exists. State power, despite the due process clause of the Fourteenth Amendment, is somewhat more extensive. This is the way the framers of the first ten amendments clearly intended it to be. We will begin with a consideration of federal power over speech. Here we will deal with what Justice Holmes in his dissenting opinion in *Abrams* v. *United States* correctly described as "the sweeping command" of the First Amendment.

CHAPTER II

"CONGRESS SHALL MAKE NO LAW"

Founders' Assurances on Freedom

The Constitution originally did not have a bill of rights because the delegates to the federal Convention which proposed it did not feel that one was necessary. They had assembled in order to meet the need for strengthening the national government. They did not regard individual rights in danger, certainly not from that source. Besides, they thought that the states would protect individual rights. The first recognition of such rights by the Convention was an emendation in the handwriting of John Rutledge of South Carolina to the report of the Committee of Detail. This called for a jury trial in criminal cases in the state where the offense was committed, and became article III, section 2, clause 3. In the closing weeks provisions were added against bills of attainder, ex post facto laws, and religious tests for federal office holders, and for the protection of the writ of habeas corpus. These are to be found in article I, sections 9 and 10, and article VI, clause 3. But that was all. Three days before the Convention adjourned Charles Pinckney of South Carolina, whose original draft of a plan for a federal constitution did not contain a bill of rights, and Elbridge Gerry of Massachusetts moved to insert a declaration "that the liberty of the Press should be inviolably observed. . . ." Roger Sherman of Connecticut answered: "It is unnecessary—The power of Congress does not extend to the Press." The record continues: "On the question, it passed in the negative."

However, the absence of a bill of rights became the strongest objection to the ratification of the Constitution. Its supporters countered with the argument that since the federal government was one of enumerated powers a bill of rights was unnecessary; indeed, it might even be dangerous, for it would furnish some ground for a contention that such an enumeration was exhaustive. The earliest and leading protagonist of this double-barreled position was James Wilson of Pennsylvania. In October 1787, less than a month after the federal convention had adjourned, he stated to a gathering in Philadelphia:

12

. . . for it would have been superfluous and absurd, to have stipulated with a federal body of our own creation, that we should enjoy those privileges, of which we are not divested either by the intention or the act that has brought that body into existence. For instance, the liberty of the press, which has been a copious subject of declamation and opposition: what control can proceed from the federal government, to shackle or destroy that sacred palladium of national freedom? If, indeed, a power similar to that which has been granted for the regulation of commerce, had been granted to regulate literary publications, it would have been as necessary to stipulate that the liberty of the press should be preserved inviolate, as that the impost should be general in its operation. . . .

The next month in the Pennsylvania convention on the ratification of the Constitution he contended:

. . . But in a government consisting of enumerated powers, such as is proposed for the United States, a bill of rights would not only be unnecessary, but, in my humble judgment, highly imprudent. In all societies, there are many powers and rights which cannot be particularly enumerated. A bill of rights annexed to a constitution is an enumeration of the powers reserved. If we attempt an enumeration, every thing that is not enumerated is presumed to be given. The consequence is, that an imperfect enumeration would throw all implied power into the scale of the government, and the rights of the people would be rendered incomplete. On the other hand, an imperfect enumeration of the powers of government reserves all implied power to the people; and by that means the constitution becomes incomplete. But of the two, it is much safer to run the risk on the side of the constitution; for an omission in the enumeration of the powers of government is neither so dangerous nor important as an omission in the enumeration of the rights of the people.

The following year Alexander Hamilton of New York in *The Federalist*, No. 84, put Wilson's argument in its best-known form, although the last instalment of this number did not come from the press until after New York, the eleventh state, had ratified the Constitution. Thus, this number had little actual effect on the political course of events. Hamilton reasoned:

I go further, and affirm that bills of rights, in the sense and to the extent in which they are contended for, are not only unnecessary in the proposed Constitution, but would even be dangerous. They would contain various exceptions to powers not granted; and, on this very account, would afford a colorable pretext to claim more than were granted. For why declare that things shall not be done which there is no power to do? Why, for instance, should it be said that the liberty of the press shall not be restrained, when no power is given by which restrictions may be imposed? I will not contend that such a provision would confer a regulating power; but it is evident that it would furnish, to men disposed to usurp, a plausible pretence for claiming that power. They might urge with a semblance of reason, that the Constitution ought not to be charged with the absurdity of providing against the abuse of an authority which was not given, and that the provision against restraining the liberty of the press afforded a clear implication, that a power to prescribe proper regulations concerning it was intended to be vested in the national government. This may serve as a specimen of the numerous handles which would be given to the doctrine of constructive powers, by the indulgence of an injudicious zeal for bills of rights.

Thomas Jefferson, who was then our minister to France, in a letter of December 20, 1787, from Paris, to his friend James Madison, answered Wilson's argument:

. . . I will now add what I do not like. First the omission of a bill of rights providing clearly and without the aid of sophisms for freedom of religion, freedom of the press, protection against standing armies, restrictions against monopolies, the eternal and unremitting force of the habeas corpus laws, and trials by jury in all matters of fact triable by the laws of the land and not by the law of Nations. To say, as Mr. Wilson does that a bill of rights was not necessary because all is reserved in the case of the general government which is not given, while in the particular ones all is given which is not reserved might do for the Audience to whom it was addressed, but is surely gratis dictum, opposed by strong inferences from the body of the instrument, as well as from the omission of the clause of our present confederation which had declared that in express terms. . . .

Madison at first espoused Wilson's thesis. In the Virginia convention in June 1788 on the ratification of the Constitution he argued: ". . . Can the general government exercise any power not delegated? If an enumeration be made of our rights, will it not be implied that everything omitted is given to the general government? Has not the honorable gentleman [Patrick Henry] himself admitted that an imperfect enumeration is dangerous? . . ."

After further debate he took the position that while he was not against amendments he was opposed to a bill of rights:

Mr. Madison conceived that what defects might be in the Constitution might be removed by the amendatory mode in itself. As to a solemn declaration of our essential rights, he thought it unnecessary and dangerous—unnecessary, because it was evident that the general government had no power but what was given it, and that the delegation alone warranted the exercise of power; dangerous, because an enumeration which is not complete is not safe. Such an enumeration could not be made, within any compass of time, as would be equal to a general negation, such as his honorable friend [Mr. Wythe] had proposed. He declared that such amendments as seemed, in his judgment, to be without danger, he would readily admit, and that he would be the last to oppose any such amendment as would give satisfaction to any gentleman, unless it were dangerous.

However, on October 17, 1788 he wrote to Jefferson:

. . . My own opinion has always been in favor of a bill of rights; provided it be so framed as not to imply powers not meant to be included in the enumeration. At the same time I have never thought the omission a material defect, nor been anxious to supply it even by *subsequent* amendment, for any other reason than that it is anxiously desired by others. I have favored it because I supposed it might be of use, and if properly executed could not be of disservice. I have not viewed it in an important light— 1. because I concede that in a certain degree, though not in the extent argued by Mr. Wilson, the rights in question are reserved by the manner in which the federal powers are granted. 2. because there is great reason to fear that a positive declaration of some of the most essential rights could not be obtained in the requisite latitude. I am sure that the rights of conscience in particular, if submitted to public definition, would be narrowed much more than they are likely ever to be by an assumed power. . . . 3. because the limited powers of the federal Government and the jealousy of the subordinate Governments, afford a security which has not existed in the case of the State Governments, and exists in no other. . . .

Jefferson in a letter of March 15, 1789 from Paris answered him. As to his second point he countered: "Half a loaf is better than no bread. If we cannot secure all our rights, let us secure what we can." And as to his third, that a bill of rights would furnish a text whereby the state governments "will try all the acts of the federal government." In the beginning of his letter he stated: "In the arguments in favor of a declaration of rights, you omit one which has great weight with me, the legal check which it puts into the hands of the judiciary. This is a body, which if rendered independent and kept strictly to their own department merits great confidence for their learning and integrity. In fact what degree of confidence would be too much for a body composed of such men as Wythe, Blair and Pendleton? On characters like these the 'civium ardor prava jubentium' [frenzy of the citizens bidding what is wrong] would make no impression."

Madison, under the impact of his correspondence with his friend Jefferson and the general demands for a bill of rights, changed his position, and became the principal draftsman of the first Ten Amendments. After studying the proposals of the various states he prepared his own set of amendments, which he laid before the first Congress on June 8, 1789. In doing so he explained:

The first of these amendments relates to what may be called a bill of rights. I will own that I never considered this provision so essential to the federal constitution, as to make it improper to ratify it, until such an amendment was added; at the same time, I always conceived, that in a certain form, and to a certain extent, such a provision was neither improper nor altogether unless. . . .

. . . The people of many States have thought it necessary to raise barriers against power in all forms and departments of Government, and I am inclined to believe, if once bills of rights are established in all the States, as well as the federal constitution, we shall find that although some of them are rather unimportant, yet, upon the whole, they will have a salutary tendency. . . .

But whatever may be the form which the several States have adopted in making declarations in favor of particular rights, the great object in view is to limit and qualify the powers of Government, by excepting out of the grant of power those cases in which the Government ought not to act, or to act only in a particular mode. . . .

. . . It has been said, that in the Federal Government they [declarations of rights] are unnecessary, because the powers are enumerated, and it follows, that all that are not granted by the constitution are retained; that the constitution is a bill of powers, the great residuum being the rights of the people; and, therefore, a bill of rights cannot be so necessary as if the residuum was thrown into the hands of the Government. I admit that these arguments are not entirely without foundation; but they are not conclusive to the extent which has been supposed. It is true, the powers of the General Government are circumscribed, they are directed to particular objects; but even if Government keeps within those limits, it has certain discretionary powers with respect to the means, which may admit of abuse to a certain extent, in the same manner as the powers of the State Governments under their constitutions may to an indefinite extent; because in the constitution of the United States, there is a clause granting to Congress the power to make all laws which shall be necessary and proper for carrying into execution all the powers vested in the Government of the United States, or in any department or officer thereof; this enables them to fulfil every purpose for which the Government was established. Now, may not laws be considered necessary and proper by Congress for it is for them to judge of the necessity and propriety to accomplish those special purposes which they may have in contemplation, which laws in themselves are neither necessary nor proper; as well as improper laws could be enacted by the State Legislatures, for fulfilling the more extended objects of those Governments. I will state an instance, which I think in point, and proves that this might be the case. The General Government has a right to pass all laws which shall be necessary to collect its revenue; the means for enforcing the collection are within the direction of the Legislature: may not general warrants be considered necessary for the purpose . . .

In other words, in certain areas the federal government was not to act at all, and in other areas to act only in a particular manner. In the instances of freedom of speech and of the press it was not to act at all. During the course of the debates on his proposals he pointed out: ". . . The right of freedom of speech is secured; the liberty of the press is expressly declared to be beyond the reach of this Government. . . ."

When he submitted his proposals in June he took occasion to meet the argument that bills of rights were ineffective:

. . . It is true, there are a few particular States in which some of the most valuable articles have not, at one time or other, been violated; but it does not follow but they may have, to a certain degree, a salutary effect against the abuse of power. If they are incorporated into the constitution, independent tribunals of justice will consider themselves in a peculiar manner the guardians of those rights; they will be an impenetrable bulwark against every assumption of power in the legislative or executive; they will be naturally led to resist every encroachment upon rights expressly stipulated for in the constitution by the declaration of rights. Besides this security there is a great probability that such a declaration in the federal system would be enforced; because the State Legislatures will jealously and closely watch the operations of this Government, and be able to resist with more effect every assumption of power, than any other power on earth can do; and the greatest opponents to a Federal Government admit the State Legislatures to be sure guardians of the people's liberty. . . .

"Here," in the words of Irving Brant, "was not only the doctrine of judicial review but the lusty germ of the Virginia and Kentucky Resolutions. . . ."

Framers' Intent

By the unqualified prohibitions of the First Amendment the framers intended to accomplish a double purpose: they "sought," in the words of Professor Zechariah Chafee, "to preserve the fruits of the old victory abolishing the censorship, and to achieve a new victory abolishing sedition prosecutions." The struggle against censorship and prior restraint, in the form of licensing, had been won in England in 1695. One would like to feel that John Milton's *Areopagitica* contributed to this result. According to Macaulay, however, the end of licensing was due to the petty grievances involved in enforcing it.

Yet as early as 1609 Edward Coke had ruled that thought was free: ". . . And so long as a man does not offend neither in act nor in word any law established, there is no reason that he should be examined of his thought or cogitation: for as it hath been said in the proverb, *thought is free; . . . .*"

Toward the middle of the same century Milton made his classic presentation for freedom of the press. Appropriately enough he addressed it to the Long Parliament. With an eloquence that has never been surpassed he argued: "And though all the winds of doctrine were let loose to play upon the earth, so Truth be in the field, we do injuriously by licensing and prohibiting to misdoubt her strength. Let her and Falsehood grapple; who ever knew Truth put to the worse, in a free and open encounter."

He was contending against a parliamentary censorship and for unlicensed printing. However, his views did not then prevail. Governmental censorship continued for over fifty years. The Licensing Act of 1662, after the Restoration, not only prohibited seditious and heretical books and pamphlets, but also forbade any person to print any material unless it was first entered with the Stationers' Company, a government monopoly, and duly licensed by the appropriate state or clerical functionary. No book was to be imported without a license; no person was permitted to sell books without a license; all printing presses had to be registered with the Stationers' Company; and the number of master printers was limited to twenty, who were to be licensed and to furnish bond. Furthermore, the act granted sweeping powers to search for suspect printed matter in houses and shops, except the houses of peers. In this form governmental censorship, renewed and augmented from time to time, continued through most of the latter half of the century. Finally in 1695, when the then existing licensing law expired, the House of Commons declined to extend it. The House of Lords voted for renewal but, when the Commons insisted, acquiesced. Thus the licensing system, in all important respects, lapsed. It was never revived.

But prosecutions for seditious libel remained. Blackstone explained in his *Commentaries* (1769):

. . . The liberty of the press is, indeed, essential to the nature of a free state; but this consists in laying no *previous* restraints upon publications, and not in freedom from censure for criminal matter when published. Every freeman has an undoubted right to lay what sentiments he pleases before the public; to forbid this, is to destroy the freedom of the press; but if he publishes what is improper, mischievous, or illegal, he must take the consequence of his own temerity. To subject the press to the restrictive power of a licenser, as was formerly done, both before and since the revolution, is to subject all freedom of sentiment to the prejudices of one man, and make him the arbitrary and infallible judge of all controverted points in learning, religion, and government. But to punish (as the law does at present) any dangerous or offensive writings, which, when published, shall, on a fair and impartial trial, be adjudged of a pernicious tendency, is necessary for the preservation of peace and good order, of government and religion, the only solid foundations of civil liberty. . . .

Thus the crown found such prosecutions a fairly good substitute for the old censorship.

Blackstone explained, too, the theory underlying these prosecutions:

. . . The direct tendency of these libels is the breach of the public peace, by stirring up the objects of them to revenge, and perhaps to bloodshed. The communication of a libel to any one person is a publication in the eye of the law; and, therefore, the sending an abusive private letter to a man is as much a libel as if it were openly printed, for it equally tends to a breach of the peace. For the same reason, it is immaterial, with respect to the essence of a libel, whether the matter of it be true or false; since the provocation, and not the falsity, is the thing to be punished criminally; though, doubtless, the falsehood of it may aggravate its guilt and enhance its punishment. In a civil action, we may remember, a libel must appear to be false, as well as scandalous; for, if the charge be true, the plaintiff has received no private injury, and has no ground to demand a compensation for himself, whatever offense it may be against the public peace; and, therefore, upon a civil action, the truth of the accusation may be pleaded in bar of the suit. But, in a criminal prosecution, the tendency which all libels have to create animosities, and to disturb the public peace, is the whole that the law considers. . . .

Hence arose the explanation in criminal libel prosecutions as distinct from civil suits for libel that "the greater the truth the greater the libel."

One's position on the crime of seditious libel depended on one's view of the nature of the relationship between those in positions of governmental authority and the people. In England, despite the victory over censorship in 1695, the people generally continued to regard the rulers as their superiors who could not be subjected to any censure that would tend to diminish their authority. The people could not criticize them directly in newspapers or pamphlets, but only through their lawful representatives in Parliament, who might be petitioned in an orderly manner.

But the framers of the First Amendment regarded those in positions of governmental authority as the servants of the people. Accordingly the people might find fault with them as they saw fit, as well as discuss freely questions of governmental policy. As Madison explained in the Third Congress, "If we advert to the nature of Republican Government, we shall find that the censorial power is in the people over the Government, and not in the Government over the people." Under this view the crime of seditious libel was a thing of the past. Sir James Fitzjames Stephen pointed out in his *History of the Criminal Law of England:* "To those who hold this view fully and carry it out to all its consequences there can be no such offense as sedition. There may indeed be breaches of the peace which may destroy or endanger life, limb, or property, and there may be incitements to such offenses, but no imaginable censure of the government, short of a censure which has an immediate tendency to produce such a breach of the peace, ought to be regarded as criminal." It was this view which was embodied in the unqualified prohibitions of the First Amendment.

A few years after its adoption when Talleyrand, the French foreign minister, complained to the American envoys Charles Cotesworth Pinckney, John Marshall and Elbridge Gerry about the insults and calumnies in the American press against the French Government, they replied in a memorial drafted by Marshall:

The genius of the Constitution, and the opinions of the people of the United States, cannot be overruled by those who administer the Government. Among those principles deemed sacred in America; among those sacred rights considered as forming the bulwark of their liberty, which the Government contemplates with awful reverence, and would approach only with the most cautious circumspection, there is no one of which the importance is more deeply impressed on the public mind than the liberty of the press. That this liberty is often carried to excess, that it has sometimes degenerated into licentiousness, is seen and lamented; but the remedy has not yet been discovered. Perhaps it is an evil inseparable from the good with which it is allied: perhaps it is a shoot which cannot be stripped from the stalk, without wounding vitally the plant from which it is torn. However desirable those measures might be which might correct without enslaving the press, they have never yet been devised in America. No regulations exist which enable the Government to suppress whatever calumnies or invectives any individual may choose to offer to the public eye; or to punish such calumnies and invectives, otherwise than by a legal prosecution in courts which are alike open to all who consider themselves as injured.

Sedition Act of 1798

In *Dennis* v. *United States* Chief Justice Vinson, in an opinion in which Justices Reed, Burton, and Minton joined, commented: "No important case involving free speech was decided by this Court prior to *Schenck* v. *United States*." However, there were two great prior occasions when the scope of the First Amendment's proscriptions against any law abridging freedom of speech and of the press were thoroughly debated, and a conclusion finally and generally reached against any exceptions: at the time of the Sedition Act of 1798; and after President Andrew Jackson in December 1835 proposed to Congress the passage of a law which would prohibit the use of the mails for "incendiary publications intended to instigate the slaves to insurrection."

The Sedition Act of 1798 was passed during the course of what President John Adams later called "the half War with France." This act made it a penal offense to publish any false, scandalous and malicious writings against the government, the president or either house of Congress with the intent to bring them into disrepute or stir up hatred against them. However, the act entrusted the determination of criminality to the jury, thus adopting the reform embodied in Fox's Libel Act in England, and in addition allowed truth as a defense.

The focal points of the opposition to this act were the Virginia Resolutions, drafted by Madison, and the Kentucky Resolutions, the first of which were drafted by Jefferson and the second of which may have been. The Kentucky Resolutions of 1798 declared that the act "is not law, but is altogether void, and of no force" because it violated the First and Tenth Amendments: the First in "that libels, falsehood, and defamation, equally with heresy and false religion, are withheld from the cognizance of federal tribunals."

Kentucky concluded with the resolve "that it does also believe, that, to take from the states all the powers of self-government, without regard to the special government, and reservations solemnly agreed to in that compact, is not for the peace, happiness, or prosperity of these states; and that, therefore, this commonwealth is determined, as it doubts not its co-states are, to submit to undelegated and consequently unlimited powers in no man, or body of men, on earth. . . ."

The Kentucky Resolutions of 1799 added, ". . . That, if those who administer the general government be permitted to transgress the limits fixed by that compact, by a total disregard to the special delegations of power therein contained, an annihiliation of the state governments, and the creation, upon their ruins, of a general consolidated government, will be the inevitable consequence . . . ," and suggested as a rightful remedy a nullification by the states.

Madison prepared not only the Virginia Resolutions but also an *Address of the General Assembly to the People of the Commonwealth of Virginia* to accompany those of 1798, and a *Report* which contained a point-by-point defense of them. He drew up the *Report* because the replies of the various states to the Kentucky and Virginia Resolutions of 1798 were generally unfavorable. In the *Address* he quoted from the reply which Marshall drafted for himself and his fellow envoys to Talleyrand. He further explained that steps had already been taken which might lead to a consolidated government, standing armies and even a form of monarchy: ". . . They consist— . . . In destroying, by the sedition act, the responsibility of public servants and public measures to the people, thus retrograding towards the exploded doctrine 'that the administrators of the Government are the masters, and not the servants, of the people,' and exposing America, which acquired the honour of taking the lead among nations towards perfecting political principles, to the disgrace of returning first to ancient ignorance and barbarism."

In the *Report* Madison assailed the two arguments which the Federalists advanced in support of the act: that Congress had power to punish crimes under the common law of England; and that the First Amendment in prohibiting Congress from making any law impairing freedom of the press had created a power to punish the licentiousness of the press. He took the contention that under the express power of Congress to "suppress Insurrections" one could "imply the power to *prevent* insurrections, by punishing whatever may *lead* or *tend* to them," and in answer suggested that if libels tended to insurrections, then the thing to do was to pass and execute laws for the suppression of insurrections, but not for the punishment of libels:

> . . . But it surely cannot, with the least plausibility, be said, that the regulation of the press, and a punishment of libels, are exercises of a power to suppress insurrections. The most that could be said would be that the punishment of libels, if it had the tendency ascribed to it, might prevent the occasion of passing or executing laws necessary and proper for the suppression of insurrections.
>
> . . . for if the power to *suppress insurrections* includes a power to *punish libels*, or if the power to punish includes a power to *prevent*, by all the means that may have that *tendency*, such is the relation and influence among the most remote subjects of legislation, that a power over a very few would carry with it a power over all. And it must be wholly immaterial whether unlimited powers be exercised under the name of unlimited powers, or be exercised under the name of unlimited means of carrying into execution limited powers.

He explained at length that the First Amendment's prohibition included not only the Blackstonian concept of previous restraint but subsequent punishment as well: it included any law. In this country the people were the masters, not the government, and hence had a greater freedom of animadversion. Especially in the case of the press the bad had to be taken with the good:

> The freedom of the press under the common law is, in the defenses of the Sedition Act, made to consist in an exemption from all *previous* restraint on printed publications by persons authorized to inspect and prohibit them. It appears to the committee that this idea of the freedom of the press can never be admitted to be the American idea of it; since a law inflicting penalties on printed publications would have a similar effect with a law authorizing a previous restraint on them. It would seem a mockery to say

that no laws should be passed preventing publications from being made, but that laws might be passed for punishing them in case they should be made.

The essential difference between the British Government and the American Constitutions will place this subject in the clearest light.

In the British Government the danger of encroachments on the rights of the people is understood to be confined to the executive magistrate. The representatives of the people in the Legislature are not only exempt themselves from distrust, but are considered as sufficient guardians of the rights of their constituents against the danger from the Executive. Hence it is a principle, that the Parliament is unlimited in its power; or, in their own language, is omnipotent. Hence, too, all the ramparts for protecting the rights of the people—such as their Magna Charta, their Bill of Rights, etc.—are not reared against the Parliament, but against the royal prerogative. They are merely legislative precautions against executive usurpations. Under such a Government as this, an exemption of the press from previous restraint, by licensers appointed by the King, is all the freedom that can be secured to it.

In the United States the case is all together different. The People, not the Government, possess the absolute sovereignty. The Legislature, no less than the Executive, is under limitations of power. Encroachments are regarded as possible from the one as well as from the other. Hence, in the United States the great and essential rights of the people are secured against legislative as well as against executive ambition. They are secured, not by laws paramount to prerogative, but by constitutions paramount to laws. This security of the freedom of the press requires that it should be exempt not only from previous restraint by the Executive, as in Great Britain, but from legislative restraint also; and this exemption, to be effectual, must be an exemption not only from the previous inspection of licensers, but from the subsequent penalty of laws.

The state of the press, therefore, under the common law, cannot, in this point of view, be the standard of its freedom in the United States. . . .

The nature of governments elective, limited, and responsible in all their branches, may well be supposed to require a greater freedom of animadversion than might be tolerated by the genius of such a government as that of Great Britain. . . .

. . . Some degree of abuse is inseparable from the proper use of every thing, and in no instance is this more true than in that of the press. It has accordingly been decided by the practice of the States, that it is better to leave a few of its noxious branches to their luxuriant growth, than, by pruning them away, to injure the vigour of those yielding the proper fruits. And can the wisdom of this policy be doubted by any who reflect that to the press alone, chequered as it is with abuses, the world is indebted for all the triumphs which have been gained by reason and humanity over error and oppression; who reflect that to the same beneficent source the United States owe much of the lights which conducted them to the ranks of a free and independent nation, and which have improved their political system into a shape so auspicious to their happiness? . . . The article of amendment, instead of supposing in Congress a power that might be exercised over the press, provided its freedom was not abridged, was meant as a positive denial to Congress of any power whatever on the subject. . . .

Is, then, the Federal Government, it will be asked, destitute of every authority for restraining the licentiousness of the press, and for shielding itself against the libelous attacks which may be made on those who administer it?

The Constitution alone can answer this question. If no such power be expressly delegated, and if it be not both necessary and proper to carry into execution an express power—above all, if it be expressly forbidden, by a declaratory amendment to the Constitution—the answer must be, that the Federal Government is destitute of all such authority.

. . . The peculiar magnitude of some of the powers necessarily committed to the Federal Government; the peculiar duration required for the functions of some of its departments; the peculiar distance of the seat of its proceedings from the great body of its constituents; and the peculiar difficulty of circulating an adequate knowledge of them through any other channel; will not these considerations, some or other of which produced other exceptions from the powers of ordinary governments, all together, account for the policy of binding the hand of the Federal Government from touching the channel which alone can give efficacy to its responsibility to its constituents, and of leaving those who administer it to a remedy for their injured reputations, under the same laws, and in the same tribunals, which protect their lives, their liberties, and their properties?

On the floor of Congress, John Nicholas of Virginia pointed out the fallacy of the bad tendency doctrine and the danger in the position which gave Congress the power to punish other than acts. The occasion was the debate on the report of a select committee on petitions praying for a repeal of the alien and sedition laws. Nicholas cautioned:

The suggestion on which the authority over the press is founded, is, that seditious writings have a tendency to produce opposition to Government. What has a greater tendency to fit men for insurrection and resistance to Government, than dissolute, immoral habits, at once destroying love of order, and dissipating the fortune which gives an interest in society?

The doctrine that Congress can punish any act which has a tendency to hinder the execution of the laws, as well as acts which do hinder it, will, therefore, clearly entitle them to assume a general guardianship over the morals of the people of the United States.

Such a result was of course contrary to anything this country's founders had in mind.

The best contemporary estimate of the Sedition Act of 1798 came from John Taylor of Caroline:

> . . . The design of substituting political for religious heresy, is visible in the visage of sedition laws. A civil priesthood or government, hunting after political heresy, is an humble imitator of the inquisition, which fines, imprisons, tortures and murders, sometimes mind, at others, body. It affects the same piety, feigned by priestcraft at the burning of an heretick; and its party supplies such exultations, as those exhibited at an auto da fe, by a populace. . . .

The Federalists, although they used this act against their opponents, nevertheless lost the election of 1800; but it is impossible to say that the act contributed appreciably to the result. However, the attempt of the Federalists to renew the act in the closing days of the Adams administration failed and the act expired by its own terms on March 3, 1801. The next day Jefferson declared in his first inaugural address:

> If there be any among us who would wish to dissolve this Union or to change its republican form, let them stand undisturbed as monuments of the safety with which error of opinion may be tolerated where reason is left free to combat it. I know, indeed, that some honest men fear that a republican government can not be strong, that this Government is not strong enough; but would the honest patriot, in the full tide of successful experiment, abandon a government which has so far kept us free and firm on the theoretic and visionary fear that this Government, the world's best hope, may by possibility want energy to preserve itself? I trust not. I believe this, on the contrary, the strongest Government on earth. I believe it the only one where every man, at the call of the law, would fly to the standard of the law, and would meet invasions of the public order as his own personal concern. Sometimes it is said that man can not be trusted with the government of himself. Can he, then, be trusted with the government of others? Or have we found angels in the forms of kings to govern him? Let history answer this question.

The general opinion, at least until the cold war period, was that the Sedition Act of 1798 violated the First Amendment. After he became president, Jefferson pardoned all prisoners who were convicted under it and Congress eventually repaid all fines. Justice Holmes in his dissenting opinion in *Abrams* v. *United States,* in which Justice Brandeis joined, wrote: ". . . I wholly disagree with the argument of the Government that the First Amendment left the common law as to seditious libel in force. History seems to me against the notion. I had conceived that the United States through many years had shown its repentence for the Sedition Act of 1798, by repaying fines that it imposed." President

Woodrow Wilson concluded that the act "cut perilously near the root of freedom of speech and of the press."

"Incendiary Publications"

The second great occasion which called for a full discussion of the scope of the First Amendment was President Jackson's proposal for barring the use of the mails to what were then called "incendiary publications." The Senate referred President Jackson's proposal to a Special Committee with John C. Calhoun of South Carolina as Chairman and two Southern and two Northern members—the Senate Committee on the Post Office and Post Roads had but one Southern member. The Special Committee, despite its majority of Southern members, despite the vehemence of Northern antislavery agitation and the dissemination from the North of a volume of abolitionist literature throughout the South, and despite Calhoun's bitter antagonism to abolitionist literature and his intense desire for the enactment of some measure to avoid the horrible insurrection which he feared those activities were engendering, reported adversely on President Jackson's proposal on the ground that the First Amendment forbade any such measure. In support of its conclusions the Committee cited Madison's Report on the Sedition Act of 1798. The Committee stated:

. . . while they agree . . . as to the evil and its highly dangerous tendency, and the necessity of arresting it, they have not been able to assent to the measure of redress which he recommends.

After the most careful and deliberate investigation they have been constrained to adopt the conclusion that Congress has not the power to pass such a law. . . .

In the discussion on the point, the Committee do not deem it necessary to inquire whether the right to pass such a law can be derived from the power to establish post offices and post roads, or from the trust "of preserving the relation created by the constitution between the States," as supposed by the President. However ingenious or plausible the arguments may be to derive the right from these, or any other sources, they must fall short of their object. The jealous spirit of liberty which characterized our ancestors at the period when the constitution was adopted, forever closed the door by which the right might be implied from any of the granted powers, or any other source, if there be any other. The committee refer to the amended article of the constitution which, among other things, provides that Congress shall pass no law which shall abridge the liberty of the press—a provision which interposes, as will be hereafter shown, an insuperable objection to the measure recommended by the President. . . .

That it was the object of this provision to place the freedom of the press beyond the possible interference of Congress, is a doctrine not now advanced for the first time. It is the ground taken, and so ably sustained by Mr. Madison, in his celebrated report to the Virginia Legislature, in 1799, against the alien and sedition law, and which conclusively settled the principle that Congress has no right, in any form, or in any manner, to interfere with the freedom of the press. The establishment of this principle not only overthrew the sedition act, but was the cause of the great political revolution which, in 1801, brought the republican party, with Mr. Jefferson as its head, into power. . . .

. . . Nothing is more clear than that the admission of the right, on the part of Congress, to determining what papers are incendiary, and as such to prohibit their circulation through the mail, necessarily involves the right to determine what are not incendiary, and to enforce their circulation. . . . It would give Congress, without regard to the prohibition laws of the States, the authority to open the gates to the flood of incendiary publications which are ready to break into those States, and to punish all who dare resist as criminals. Fortunately, Congress has no such right. . . .

However, Calhoun as chairman prepared a bill which in its first section, as amended, made it unlawful "for any deputy postmaster, in any State, Territory, or District of the United States, knowingly to deliver to any person whatever, any pamphlet, newspaper, handbill, or other printed matter or pictorial representation touching the subject of slavery, where, by the laws of the said State, Territory, or District, their circulation is prohibited; and any deputy postmaster who shall be guilty thereof, shall be forthwith removed from office." The Calhoun bill was likewise defeated: the vote against it was 25 to 19. In opposing Calhoun's bill, Senator John Davis of Massachusetts reminded his colleagues: "The liberty of the press was not like the other reserved rights, reserved by implication, but was reserved in express terms; it could not be touched in any manner." He had this further comment, which is even more pertinent today than when it was uttered: "The public morals were said to be in danger; it was necessary to prevent licentiousness, tumult, and sedition; and the public good required that the licentiousness should be restrained. All these were the plausible pretenses under which the freedom of the press had been violated in all ages. . . ."

Senator Henry Clay of Kentucky considered this bill "unconstitutional; and if not so, that it contained a principle of a most dangerous and alarming character. . . . After much reflection he had come to the conclusion that they could not pass any law interfering with the subject in any shape or form whatsoever. . . . The States alone had the power, and their power was ample for the purpose . . . the bill was calculated to destroy all the landmarks of the constitution, establish a precedent for dangerous legislation, and to lead to incalculable mischief. . . ."

Finally Daniel Webster, whose influence on the early development of our constitutional principles was second only to that of Chief Justice Marshall, vehemently attacked the measure. He declared that the freedom of the press included "the liberty of printing as well as the liberty of publishing, in all the ordinary modes of publication; and was not the circulation of papers through the mails an ordinary mode of publication?" Further: "Now against the objects of this bill he had not a word to say; but with constitutional lawyers there was a great difference between the object and the means to carry it into effect . . . Congress had not the power, drawn from the character of the paper, to decide whether it should be carried in the mail or not; for such decision would be a direct abridgment of the freedom of the press. He confessed that he was shocked at the doctrine. He looked back to the alien and sedition laws which were so universally condemned throughout the country. . . ."

Meanwhile the House Committee on the Post Office and Post Roads brought in a bill which took an opposite position to that in Calhoun's bill: the House Committee's bill, as finally enacted, made it a penal offense if any postmaster should "unlawfully detain in his office any letter, package, pamphlet, or newspaper, with intent to prevent the arrival and delivery of the same to the person or persons to whom such letter, package, pamphlet or newspaper may be addressed or directed. . . ." The House passed the bill in June. The Senate, after defeating Calhoun's bill, accepted the House bill, with a few minor changes; and in July the two houses were brought into agreement. This act in principle prohibited the post office department from censoring the mail: its job was simply that of carrying it. Years later Judge Thurman W. Arnold in the concluding paragraph of his opinion in the *Esquire* case aptly stated:

We believe that the Post Office officials should experience a feeling of relief if they are limited to the more prosaic function of seeing to it that "neither snow or rain nor heat nor gloom of night strays these couriers from the swift completion of their appointed rounds."

The Supreme Court in *Ex parte Jackson* in an opinion by Justice Field, in the course of a review of the proceedings in the Senate on President Jackson's proposal and Calhoun's bill, commented:

. . . In the Senate, that portion of the message was referred to a select committee, of which Mr. Calhoun was chairman; and he made an elaborate report on the subject, in which he contended that it belonged to the States, and not to Congress, to determine what is and what is not calculated to disturb their security, and that to hold otherwise would be fatal to the States; for if Congress might determine what papers were incendiary, and as such prohibit their circulation through the mails, it might also determine what were not incendiary, and enforce their circulation.

Two days before President Jackson made his proposal the Richmond Compiler set forth the First Amendment together with comparable provisions from state constitutions with this introduction: "The following are extracts from the constitutions of the United States and the several states of the union, from which it will be seen that no law can constitutionally be passed for the purpose of restraining the fanatics of the north in their crusade against our rights."

Thus on two great occasions prior to *Schenck* v. *United States* this country's leaders refused to read exceptions into the First Amendment's unqualified prohibitions. On the first occasion, at the time of the Sedition Act of 1798, those leaders included the framers of the first ten amendments. On the second occasion, at the time of President Jackson's proposal of December 1835, those leaders included men who were already past their early childhood when the first ten amendments were adopted. It would be difficult to suggest more authoritative interpretations.

Deeds Not Words

Madison's criticism in his *Report* of the bad tendency doctrine and his suggestion that federal power was limited to acts and could not apply to speech alone, Jefferson had made earlier and in a more direct and even stronger fashion. In his draft of *A Bill for Establishing Religious Freedom*, which he introduced into the Virginia Assembly in 1779, and which passed that body in 1785, he stated: ". . . that to suffer the civil magistrate to intrude his powers into the field of opinion, and to restrain the profession or propagation of principles on supposition of their ill tendency is a dangerous fallacy, which at once destroys all religious liberty, because he being of course judge of that tendency will make his opinions the rule of judgment, and approve or condemn the sentiments of others only as they shall square with or differ from his own; that it is time enough for the rightful purposes of civil government, for its officers to interfere when principles break out into overt acts against peace and good order. . . ."

And before Jefferson drafted this bill the Rev. Philip Furneaux, a dissenting divine, in one of a series of famous letters to Blackstone, which were published in book form in London in 1770, and in Philadelphia three years later, had eloquently urged the same approach:

If it be objected, that when the tendency of principles is unfavourable to the peace and good order of society, as it may be, it is the magistrate's duty then, and for that reason, to restrain them by penal laws: I reply, that the tendency of principles, though it be *unfavourable*, is not *prejudicial* to society, till it issues in some *overt acts* against the public peace and order; and when it does, *then* the magistrate's authority to punish commences; that is, he may punish the *overt acts*, but not the tendency, which is not actually hurtful; and, therefore, his penal laws should be directed against *overt acts only*, which are detrimental to the peace and good will; and not against principles, or the tendency of principles.

The distinction between the tendency of principles, and the overt acts arising from them, is, and cannot but be, observed in many cases of a civil *nature*; in order to determine the bounds of the magistrate's power, or at least to limit the exercise of it, in such cases. It would not be difficult to mention customs and manners, as well as principles, which have a tendency unfavourable to society, and which, nevertheless, cannot be restrained by penal laws, except with the total destruction of civil liberty. And here, the magistrate must be contented with pointing his penal laws against the evil overt acts resulting from them. . . . Punishing a man for the *tendency* of his principles, is punishing him *before* he is guilty, for fear he *should be* guilty.

So, too, had Montesquieu, the oracle of the founding fathers, and Jeremy Bentham; although Montesquieu had added a nullifying qualification. Montesquieu in his *L'Esprit des Lois* (1748) in a chapter entitled, *Of Indiscreet Speeches*, had written:

Words do not constitute an overt act. . . . Words carried into action assume the nature of that action. Thus a man who goes into a public market-place to incite the subject to revolt, incurs the guilt of high treason, because the words are joined to the action, and partake of its nature. It is not the words that are punished, but an action in which words are employed. They do not become criminal, but when they are annexed to a criminal action: everything is confounded, if words are construed into a capital crime, instead of considering them only as a mark of that crime.

Bentham in his *A Fragment on Government* (1776), which was a criticism of Blackstone's exposition in his *Commentaries* on the nature of sovereignty, in explaining the difference between a free and a despotic government, stated that one of the distinguishing circumstances lay in "the security with which malcontents may communicate their sentiments, concert their plans, and practise every mode of opposition short of actual revolt, before the executive power can be legally justified in disturbing them."

But Montesquieu's exception for the advocacy of violence blurs the workable distinction between speech and criminal deeds, with the double result that the exception not only is difficult of application but also provides the basis for stultifying restrictions on speech. A striking idea is just as moving to action whether stated philosophically in a seminar or shouted from the rostrum. As Justice Holmes admitted in his dissenting opinion in *Gitlow* v. *New York*: "Every idea is an incitement." Besides, in Mark Antony fashion, the advocacy of an immediate resort to violence may be couched in peaceful and submissive terms. Jefferson and Madison were wise enough not to follow Montesquieu's exception.

The Court, however, in the application of Justice Holmes's clear and present danger test, did make an exception under certain circumstances for the advocacy of violence. As a result even the Warren Court found itself recently in *Yates* v. *United States* drawing a distinction between the advocacy of the violent overthrow of the government as "a rule or principle of action," proscribed in the charge in *Dennis* v. *United States*, and the advocacy of such overthrow as a "necessity" and a "duty," proscribed in the charge in the *Yates* case. The Court itself admitted that such distinctions "are often subtle and difficult to grasp." Justice Clark found them, and rightly so, "too 'subtle and difficult to grasp.' "

The *Dennis* case arose out of the first Foley Square conspiracy prosecution against leaders of the American Communist party. They were charged with conspiring to teach and advocate the overthrow of the government by force and violence. This was in violation of the advocacy provisions of Title I of the Alien Registration Act, 1940, this country's third sedition law, commonly known as the Smith Act after its principal draftsman, Congressman Howard W. Smith of Virginia. The trial judge, Harold R. Medina, instructed the jury that the charged teaching and advocacy had to "be of a rule or principle of action and by language reasonably and ordinarily calculated to incite persons to such action, all with the intent to cause the overthrow or destruction of the Government of the United States by force and violence as speedily as circumstances will permit." The jury convicted, the Court of Appeals for the Second Circuit affirmed in August 1950, and the Supreme Court in June 1951.

The *Yates* case involved a judgment of conviction against fourteen persons in the Los Angeles conspiracy prosecution under the Smith Act against American Communist party leaders. This time the Supreme Court reversed, ordering an acquittal as to five of the defendants and a new trial as to the remaining nine. One of the grounds of reversal was the trial court's refusal to instruct the jury in the words of Judge Medina in the *Dennis* case. Instead he told them:

The kind of advocacy and teaching which is charged and upon which your verdict must be reached is not merely a desirability but a necessity that the Government of the United States be overthrown and destroyed by force and violence and not merely a propriety but a duty to overthrow and destroy the Government of the United States by force and violence.

The Court felt that this instruction defined advocacy too much in terms of the teaching of abstract doctrine rather than incitement to illegal action: "The distinction between advocacy of abstract doctrine and advocacy directed at promoting unlawful action is one that has been consistently recognized in the opinions of this Court, beginning with *Fox* v. *Washington* . . . and *Schenck* v. *United States*. . . ." Justice Clark could not draw the distinctions which the Court did between the charge in the *Dennis* case and that in the *Yates* case: "While there may be some distinctions between the charges, as I view them they are without material difference. I find, as the majority intimates, that the distinctions are too 'subtle and difficult to grasp.' "

Jefferson's classic statement from his draft of A *Bill for Establishing Religious Freedom* has not gone wholly unnoticed. The idea that it is time enough for the government to step in when advocacy breaks out into criminal conduct other than advocacy has been stressed; but in dissenting opinions. Justice Black in his concurring and dissenting opinion in the *Yates* case, in which Justice Douglas joined (they would have directed the acquittal of all of the defendants), and Justice Douglas in his dissenting opinion in the *Dennis* case both quoted from Jefferson's statement. Justice Douglas also quoted from it in his dissenting opinion, with the concurrence of Justice Black, in *Lerner* v. *Casey* and *Beilan* v. *Board of Education*. In the *Lerner* case the Court held that the discharge of a subway conductor by the New York City Transit Authority and in *Beilan* of a teacher in the public schools by the Philadelphia Board of Education for refusal to answer questions about Communist affiliations did not violate the Fourteenth Amendment's due process clause. Justice Black, prefatory to quoting Jefferson in the *Yates* case, stated: "I believe that the First Amendment forbids Congress to punish people for talking about public affairs, whether or not such discussion incites to action, legal or illegal."

These two justices expressed this idea in yet other recent cases. In *First Unit. Church* v. *Los Angeles* and *Speiser* v. *Randall*, Justice Douglas, in a concurring opinion in which Justice Black joined, said: "Advocacy which is in no way brigaded with action should always be protected by the First Amendment." In these cases the Court, under the Fourteenth Amendment's due process clause, invalidated a California statute which as applied required tax exemption claimants to sign a loyalty statement on their tax returns and thereafter to assume the burden of proving loyalty.

Justice Douglas, again with the concurrence of Justice Black, said the same thing in a dissenting opinion in two recent obscenity cases, *Roth* v. *United States* and *Alberts* v. *California:* "Freedom of expression can be suppressed if, and to the extent that, it is so closely brigaded with illegal action as to be an inseparable part of it." In the *Roth* case the Court sustained the constitutionality of a federal obscenity statute and in the *Alberts* case a California one.

He expressed the same view, this time with the concurrence not only of Justice Black but also of Chief Justice Warren, in a dissenting opinion in an anti-picketing case, *Teamsters Union* v. *Vogt, Inc.:* "I would return to the test enunciated in *Giboney*—that this form of expression can be regulated or prohibited only to the extent that it forms an essential part of a course of conduct which the State can regulate or prohibit." In that case the Court sustained the validity of a Wisconsin statute which prohibited even peaceful picketing when done for organizational purposes.

Chief Justice Warren tends toward the position of Justices Black and Douglas that the First Amendment protects advocacy unless it is connected with criminal conduct other than advocacy. He joined with them in Justice Douglas's dissenting opinion in the *Vogt* case. He wrote in his concurring opinion in the *Roth* case: "* * * It is not the book that is on trial; it is a person. The conduct of the defendant is the central issue, not the obscenity of a book or picture. * * *" He added in his dissenting opinion in *Kingsley Books, Inc.* v. *Brown,* another obscenity case decided the same day as the *Roth* and *Alberts* cases: "* * * It is the manner of use that should determine obscenity. It is the conduct of the individual that should be judged, not the quality of art or literature. * * *" There the Court upheld a New York statute which provided for civil non-jury injunctive proceedings against obscene publications.

The approach of Jefferson and Madison, and of Justices Black and Douglas, is a farsighted one. If prevailing social structures provide a fair measure of equal justice, opportunity and freedom for all, speech will not overthrow them. On the other hand, if such structures are arbitrary and unjust, the suppression of speech will not save them. The measures of the czars of Russia left nothing to be desired in the way of suppression. Yet their government came to a violent and bloody end.

Under Madison and Jefferson's and Black and Douglas's view of the First Amendment, the advocacy of the violent overthrow of the government and even a conspiracy to advocate its violent overthrow would be entitled to protection. Under this view the *Dennis* case was wrongly decided. The advocacy provisions of the Smith Act, under which over

130 leaders of the American Communist party were indicted and more than 100 convicted and sentenced to prison terms (although only 29 so far have served their prison sentences), violate the First Amendment. A fortiori, so does the provision of that act which makes it a crime to be a member of an organization that advocates the forcible overthrow of the government, "knowing the purposes thereof." To date, however, at least as to the advocacy provisions, the law has developed to the contrary.

CHAPTER III

STATE POWER

Early State Power

By the First and Tenth Amendments the framers of the federal Bill of Rights intended that whatever governmental power existed over utterances was to reside in the states rather than the federal government. The proceedings of the first Congress on the first ten amendments show this; the opposition to the Sedition Act of 1798 stressed it; and the defeat of President Jackson's proposal for barring "incendiary publications" from the mails reaffirmed the point.

Specifically the framers of the federal Bill of Rights intended the states and not the federal government to have jurisdiction over the offense of seditious libel. Had the questions presented themselves they would have taken the same position with reference to the offenses of blasphemy, profanity and obscenity. In the case of obscenity the question could not have arisen, for the first reported decision in this country sustaining a conviction for it did not occur until more than a quarter of a century after the first Congress proposed the first ten amendments.

One of the proposed amendments which Madison put before the first Congress on June 8, 1789 provided: "No State shall violate the equal rights of conscience, or the freedom of the press, or the trial by jury in criminal cases." This proposed amendment came from Madison alone. No state convention asked for it. In offering it he explained: ". . . it is proper that every Government should be disarmed of powers which trench upon those particular rights. I know, in some of the State constitutions, the power of the Government is controlled by such a declaration; but others are not. I cannot see any reason against obtaining even a double security on those points; and nothing can give a more sincere proof of the attachment of those who oppose this constitution of these great and important rights than to see them join in obtaining the security I have now proposed; because it must be admitted, on all hands, that the State Governments are as liable to attack these invaluable privileges as the General Government is, and therefore ought to be as cautiously guarded against."

35

The House sent Madison's proposals to a special committee of which he was one of the members. The special committee revised this proposal to read: "No State shall infringe the equal rights of conscience, nor the freedom of speech, or of the press, nor of the right of trial by jury in criminal cases."

Representative Thomas Tucker of South Carolina objected to it: "This is offered, I presume, as an amendment to the constitution of the United States, but it goes only to the alterations of the constitutions of particular States. It will be much better, I apprehend, to leave the State Governments to themselves, and not to interfere with them more than we already do; and that is thought by many to be rather too much. I therefore move, sir, to strike out these words."

But: "Mr. Madison conceived this to be the most valuable amendment in the whole list. If there was any reason to restrain the Government of the United States from infringing upon these essential rights, it was equally necessary that they should be secured against the State Governments. He thought that if they provided against the one, it was as necessary to provide against the other, and was satisfied that it would be equally grateful to the people."

Madison won out in the House. After a further minor revision this proposal went to the Senate in this form: "No State shall infringe the right of trial by Jury in criminal cases, nor the rights of conscience, nor the freedom of speech, or of the press." But in the Senate the position which Tucker took in the House won out, and this proposal was rejected.

The national debate on the Sedition Act of 1798 underlined the point that the states had a certain amount of power over utterances which was denied the federal government. In the debates in Congress, Nicholas of Virginia, Nathaniel Macon of North Carolina and Edward Livingston of New York all drew a distinction between state and federal power. Nicholas: ". . . He had heard it said that all the States take cognizance of offenses of this sort. But does that give the power to the General Government? Because the States declare certain things offences, have the General Government power over the like offences? If so, it would have a concurrent power with all the State Governments, which, he believed, would be a novel idea. Indeed, he was utterly at a loss to find any ground upon which to found a law of this kind. He was confident there was none."

Macon: ". . . He thought this subject of the liberty of the press was sacred, and ought to be left where the Constitution had left it. The States have complete power on the subject, and when Congress legislates, it ought to have confidence in the States, as the States ought also to have confidence in Congress, or our Government is gone. . . ."

Livingston: ". . . Every man's character is protected by law, and every man who shall publish a libel on any part of the Government, is liable to punishment. Not, said Mr. L., by laws which we ourselves have made, but by laws passed by the several States. And is not this most proper? . . ."

Madison took the same position in his *Address* and subsequent *Report* on the Virginia Resolutions of 1798. In his *Address* he stated: ". . . But the laws for the correction of calumny were not defective. Every libellous writing or expression might receive its punishment in the State courts. . . ." In his *Report* he added that libelled federal officials had to seek redress "under the same laws, and in the same tribunals, which protect their lives, their liberties, and their properties."

A few months before his second inauguration Jefferson wrote to Mrs. John (Abigail) Adams, the wife of his political opponent in the presidential campaign of 1800:

. . . Nor does the opinion of the unconstitutionality, & consequent nullity of that law [Sedition Act of 1798], remove all restraint from the overwhelming torrent of slander, which is confounding all vice and virtue, all truth and falsehood, in the U.S. The power to do that is fully possessed by the several State Legislatures. It was reserved to them, & was denied to the General Government, by the Constitution, according to our construction of it. While we deny that Congress have a right to control the freedom of the press, we have ever asserted, the right of the States, and their exclusive right, to do so.

In his second inaugural he took occasion to restate his position:

During this course of administration and in order to disturb it, the artillery of the press has been levelled against us, charged with whatsoever its licentiousness could devise or dare. These abuses of an institution so important to freedom and science, are deeply to be regretted, inasmuch as they tend to lessen its usefulness, and to sap its safety; they might, indeed, have been corrected by the wholesome punishments reserved and provided by the laws of the several States against falsehood and defamation; but public duties more urgent press on the time of public servants, and the offenders have therefore been left to find their punishment in the public indignation.

The defeat of President Jackson's proposal demonstrated once again that the only power that existed over utterances, as such, resided in the states. In the words of Clay, "The States alone had the power, and their power was ample for the purpose."

In order to make doubly certain that the federal government did not have or exercise any powers other than those which the Constitution either expressly or by implication delegated to it, the framers of the federal Bill of Rights added the Tenth Amendment. Madison had originally proposed: "The powers not delegated by this Constitution, nor prohibited by it to the States, are reserved to the States respectively." As revised this became the Tenth Amendment. An effort was twice made, once by Tucker and again by Gerry, to carry the idea embodied in this amendment still further by inserting the word "expressly" before the word "delegated." This was the way it had been in the Articles of Confederation. Madison opposed Tucker's proposal "because it was impossible to confine a Government to the exercise of express powers; there must necessarily be admitted powers by implication, unless the Constitution descended to recount every minutiae." Madison's view prevailed. However, in the area covered by the First Amendment the Tenth Amendment meant that whatever power there was over utterances, as such, resided, not in the federal government, but in the states or in the people.

In accordance with the framers' intent the Supreme Court in Chief Justice Marshall's time and speaking through him in the leading case of *Barron* v. *Baltimore* ruled, referring to the first Ten Amendments: ". . . These amendments contain no expression indicating an intention to apply them to the state governments. This court cannot so apply them." That case involved a claim by an individual that city officials had taken his property for a public use without just compensation in violation of the Fifth Amendment. Chief Justice Marshall in the Court's opinion denied the amendment's applicability. Later at the same term the Court followed this ruling in *Livingston* v. *Moore*, involving a claim by an individual of a denial of the right to a jury trial in violation of the Seventh Amendment. The Court held: "* * * it is now settled that those amendments do not extend to the states. * * *" The Court, both before and after the adoption of the Fourteenth Amendment, has consistently and correctly followed these early rulings.

Fourteenth Amendment Privileges

But did the adoption of the Fourteenth Amendment restrict state power over utterances? The answer to this question will depend on just what one means by it. Justices Black, Douglas, Murphy and Rutledge, and many others, have asserted that the proscriptions of the first section of the Fourteenth Amendment, primarily the provision forbidding any state to "make or enforce any law which shall abridge the privileges or immunities of citizens of the United States," and secondarily the command, "nor shall any State deprive any person of life, liberty, or property, without due process of law," make the first eight amendments applicable to the states. This proposition has become known as the incorporation theory. The writer does not subscribe to this theory. If therefore one asks, Did the Fourteenth Amendment incorporate the first eight and thus make them applicable to state action?, the writer's answer is that historically it did not. However, the Fourteenth Amendment's due process clause does place restrictions on state action, not because it incorporates the first eight amendments, but rather by reason of its own inner meaning and without the benefit of the incorporation theory. We will consider the incorporation theory, and first take up whether the Fourteenth Amendment's privileges and immunities clause furnishes any basis for it.

Without pressing the nice distinctions of former Professor Wesley N. Hohfeld of the Yale Law School between privilege and no-right, immunity and disability, and right and duty as jural correlatives, and privilege and duty, immunity and liability, and right and no-right as jural opposites, it would nevertheless seem that the phrase privileges and immunities is not itself an apt one to cover the various individual rights which the first eight amendments secure. The word privilege connotes inequality. It derives from the Latin *privilegium* (*privus*, private plus *lex*, *legis*, law), and originally meant a measure relating to a particular individual. It could be either against or for. It could inflict penalties on a particular citizen by name without any previous trial. Or it could exempt an individual from the operation of a law.

It was often in the latter sense that the word privilege came into use in our law. It denoted an advantage enjoyed by a person or class of persons beyond the common advantages of others. A frequent use of the word prior to the drafting of the federal Bill of Rights was in connection with the British Parliament. During the struggle between Parliament and the first two Stuarts, James I (1603–1625) and Charles I (1625–1649), while the king held forth about his prerogative the Commons insisted on their privileges. Blackstone in the first volume of his *Commentaries*, originally published in 1765, described these privileges as "very large and indefinite," and explained: "Privilege of Parliament was principally established, in order to protect its members not only from being molested by their fellow subjects, but also more especially from being oppressed by the power of the crown." Two principal privileges were freedom from arrest in civil matters and freedom of speech.

However, with one exception, the word privilege has not come into general use to denote the various rights which the first eight amendments guarantee to all individuals here. The exception is the right not to be one's own accuser, or as it is put in the Fifth Amendment: ". . . nor shall [any person] be compelled in any criminal case to be a witness against himself." This right has come to be generally known as the privilege against self-incrimination, although some judges with a deep understanding of this right have more aptly described it as a right of silence. The word privilege probably came into use for this right because of the application of this word to confidential communications, such as those between attorney and client, which the law early protected. A judicial grant of silence to an attorney in order to protect a communication to him from his client was called a privilege as early as 1740.

Nor did the framers of the federal Constitution intend the phrase privileges and immunities as a composite of such individual rights as those later embodied in the first eight amendments. Their use of the phrase in Art. IV, section 2 derived from the first paragraph of Art. IV of the Articles of Confederation 1777: "The better to secure and perpetuate mutual friendship and intercourse among the people of the different States in this Union, the free inhabitants of each of these States, paupers, vagabonds and fugitives from justice excepted, shall be entitled to all privileges and immunities of free citizens in the several States; and the people of each State shall have free ingress and regress to and from any other State, and shall enjoy therein all the privileges of trade and commerce, subject to the same duties, impositions and restrictions as the inhabitants thereof respectively, provided that such restrictions shall not extend so far as to prevent the removal of property imported into any State, to any other State of which the owner is an inhabitant; provided also that no imposition, duties or restrictions shall be laid by any State, on the property of the United States, or either of them."

Charles Pinckney of South Carolina later stated that he was the one who first proposed Art. IV, section 2 of the Constitution to the Convention; and his original draft of a plan for a federal constitution did contain such a provision. There was virtually no discussion of it. The only reference in Madison's account reads: "Gen. Pinckney was not satisfied with it. He seemed to wish some provision should be included in favor of property in slaves." Some notes in the handwriting of George Mason of Virginia indicate that he felt that more language should have been taken from Art. IV of the Articles of Confederation and that he wished to amend Art. IV, section 2 of the Constitution by adding, "and every citizen having an estate in two or more States shall have a right to remove his property from one State to another," but he never proposed such an amendment.

At the time Pinckney said that he was the one who first proposed Art. IV, section 2 of the Constitution, he also explained to the best of his ability what the privileges of South Carolina citizens were. This was in February 1821. The occasion was a debate in the federal House of Representatives on the admission of Missouri as a state. Congress, as one of the two measures which came to be known as the Missouri Compromise, had passed an act the preceding year authorizing "the people of the Missouri territory to form a constitution and state government." The people of Missouri promptly did so, and in their constitution provided, with reference to their General Assembly: "It shall be their duty, as soon as may be, to pass such laws as may be necessary, *First*. To prevent free negroes and mulattoes from coming to, and settling in this state, under any pretext whatsoever. . . ."

Congress met again in November 1820, and the anti-slavery people protested against this clause as a violation of Art. IV, section 2. They argued that in some states free Negroes were citizens and thus had the privilege to cross state lines. Their opponents contended that Negroes were not citizens within the meaning of the Constitution. This was Pinckney's position.

Preliminarily he took note of "the frequent calls made upon me in this House, and references in.the other, as to the true meaning of" Art. IV, section 2. After some comments on the excellencies of the Missouri constitution, he made plain that Art. IV, section 2 did not include Negroes: ". . . the article . . . having been made by me, it is supposed I must know, or perfectly recollect, what I meant by it. In answer, I say, that, at the time I drew that constitution, I perfectly knew that there did not exist such a thing in the Union as a black or colored citizen. . . ."

Then after explaining who were citizens of South Carolina, he sought to describe their privileges: ". . . Their privileges vary according to their sex and situation. Females are wholly excluded from a right to vote, or to office, and are confined to their proper sphere; but all males born in the State, or in the United States, after a certain residence in that State, or adopted according to law, are equal, except clergymen, who, on account of their office, are excluded from the Legislature. At the age of eighteen they are all enrolled into the militia, and serve as the defenders of their country. At twenty-one they are, from our general suffrage law, qualified to vote, to serve on juries, and to be eligible to the Legislature, and all offices except two, which require greater age. They have a right to sue, and are liable to be sued; to take a freehold, and hold property. They are all entitled to the trial by jury, and intermarry at any age."

Two years later Circuit Justice Washington in the much cited case of *Corfield* v. *Coryell*, after an introductory flourish, ended up with a similar description as to the ground which the phrase privileges and immunities covered: ". . . Protection by the government; the enjoyment of life and liberty, with the right to acquire and possess property of every kind, and to pursue and obtain happiness and safety; subject nevertheless to such restraints as the government may justly prescribe for the general good of the whole. The right of a citizen of one state to pass through, or to reside in any other state, for purposes of trade, agriculture, professional pursuits, or otherwise; to claim the benefit of the writ of habeas corpus; to institute and maintain actions of any kind in the courts of the state; to take, hold and dispose of property, either real or personal; and an exemption from higher taxes or impositions than are paid by the other citizens of the state; may be mentioned as some of the particular privileges and immunities of citizens, which are clearly embraced by the general description of privileges deemed to be fundamental: to which may be added, the elective franchise, as regulated and established by the laws or constitution of the state in which it is to be exercised. These, and many others which might be mentioned, are, strictly speaking, privileges and immunities, and the enjoyment of them by the citizens of each state, in every other state, was manifestly calculated (to use the expressions of the preamble of the corresponding provision in the old articles of confederation) 'the better to secure and perpetuate mutual friendship and intercourse among the people of the different states of the Union.'"

A decade thereafter Story in his *Commentaries*, citing this case, gave this concise statement: ". . . It is obvious, that, if the citizens of each state were to be deemed aliens to each other, they could not take, or hold real estate, or other privileges, except as other aliens. The intention of this clause was to confer on them, if one may so say, a general citizenship; and to commmunicate all the privileges and immunities, which the citizens of the same state would be entitled to under the like circumstances."

Did the framers of the Fourteenth Amendment by "privileges or immunities of citizens of the United States" mean anything expansively different than did the framers of the Constitution by "Privileges and Immunities of Citizens in the several states"? It would appear not.

Indeed Congressman John A. Bingham of Ohio, whom Justice Black in his dissenting opinion in *Adamson* v. *California* stated "may without extravagance be called the Madison of the first section of the Fourteenth Amendment," specifically showed on several occasions that in his thinking he tied the two provisions together. He did so when he proposed his draft of a constitutional amendment on February 3, 1866 to the Joint Committee on Reconstruction, of which he was one of the fifteen members. He did so in his opening speech in the House on his draft. He did so in the last major speech in the House on it. His draft provided: "The Congress shall have power to make all laws which shall be necessary and proper to secure to citizens of each State all privileges and immunities of citizens in the several States (Art. IV, sec. 2); and to all persons in the several States equal protection in the rights of life, liberty and property (5th Amendment)." The Committee adopted his proposal, and on February 13 it was introduced, minus the references in parentheses, in the House and the Senate.

In his opening speech on it he explained that it was in "the language of the second section of the fourth article, and of a portion of the fifth amendment," and quoted Art. IV, section 2 and the due process clause of the Fifth Amendment. It is true that a little later he said: "And, sir, it is equally clear by every construction of the Constitution, its contemporaneous construction, its continued construction, legislative, executive, and judicial, that these great provisions of the Constitution, this immortal bill of rights embodied in the Constitution, rested for its execution and enforcement hitherto upon the fidelity of the States." But he had previously twice shown and was to show again that his draft rested on Art. IV, section 2 plus the due process clause of the Fifth Amendment.

In the last major speech on his draft he again quoted Art. IV, section 2 and the due process clause of the Fifth Amendment, and soon asserted: "Gentlemen admit the force of the provisions in the bill of rights, that the citizens of the United States shall be entitled to all the privileges and immunities of citizens of the United States in the several States, and that no person shall be deprived of life, liberty, or property without due process of law * * *."

However, his draft came to naught. The House after this debate postponed further consideration, which never came; and the Senate ordered it to lie on the table.

One will note that when Congressman Bingham last addressed himself to his draft he spoke of privileges and immunities of citizens of the United States rather than citizens in the several states, as it is in Art. IV, section 2. In this respect he forecast the form of a new section which he proposed on April 21, 1866 to the Joint Committee on Reconstruction for insertion in a pending draft amendment. His new section provided: "No state shall make or enforce any law which shall abridge the privileges or immunities of citizens of the United States; nor shall any state deprive any person of life, liberty or property without due process of law, nor deny to any person within its jurisdiction the equal protection of the laws." This section, with the subsequent addition of the definition of citizenship, became the first section of the Fourteenth Amendment.

With reference to his new section Congressman Bingham said in the House: ". . . But, sir, it has been suggested, not here, but elsewhere, if this section does not confer suffrage the need of it is not perceived. To all such I beg leave again to say, that many instances of State injustice and oppression have already occurred in the State legislation of this Union, of flagrant violations of the guarantied privileges of citizens of the United States, for which the national Government furnished and could furnish by law no remedy whatever. Contrary to the express letter of your Constitution, cruel and unusual punishments have been inflicted under State laws within this Union upon citizens, not only for crimes committed, but for sacred duty done, for which and against which the Government of the United States had provided no remedy and could provide none.

"Sir, the words of the Constitution that 'the citizens of each State shall be entitled to all privileges and immunities of citizens in several States' include, among other privileges, the right to bear true allegiance to the Constitution and laws of the United States, and to be protected in life, liberty and property. Next, sir, to the allegiance which we all owe to God our Creator, is the allegiance which we owe to our common country."

Although his quoted language, "cruel and unusual punishments," is to be found in the Eighth Amendment, he did not say, in 1866, that this section made the first eight amendments applicable to the states.

During the summer in a speech at Bowerstown, Ohio, while he was campaigning for re-election, he gave this explanation of the Fourteenth Amendment's first section: ". . . It is the spirit of Christianity embodied in your legislation. It is a simple, strong, plain declaration that equal laws and equal and exact justice shall hereafter be secured within every State of this Union by the combined power of all the people of every State. . . . Hereafter the American people can not have peace, if, as in the past, States are permitted to take away freedom of speech, and to condemn men, as felons, to the penitentiary for teaching their fellow men that there is a hereafter, and a reward for those who learn to do well." But he did not refer specifically either to the First Amendment or to the first eight amendments.

Nearly five years later, in March 1871, he did. He was arguing in favor of a civil rights measure, a key provision of which, in section 2 and which became R.S. §5519, the Supreme Court subsequently held unconstitutional in *United States* v. *Harris*. During the course of his argument he contended "that the privileges and immunities of citizens of the United States, as contradistinguished from citizens of a State, are chiefly defined in the first eight amendments to the Constitution of the United States," and proceeded to read these amendments.

But Congressman (later President) James A. Garfield of Ohio and Congressman John F. Farnsworth of Illinois, who had participated in 1866 in the debates in the House on the Fourteenth Amendment, challenged the correctness of his contention. At one point Congressman Garfield was about to read portions of what Congressman Thaddeus Stevens of Pennsylvania, chairman of the delegation from the House to the Joint Committee on Reconstruction, had said when he began debate in the House on the Fourteenth Amendment. Stevens had said:

This proposition is not all that the committee desired. It falls short of my wishes, but it fulfills my hopes. I believe it is all that can be obtained in the present state of public opinion. . . .

*   *   *

The first section prohibits the States from abridging the privileges and immunities of citizens of the United States, or unlawfully depriving them of life, liberty, or property, or of denying to any person within their jurisdiction the "equal" protection of the laws.

I can hardly believe that any person can be found who will not admit that every one of these provisions is just. They are all asserted, in some form or other, in our DECLARATION or organic law. But the Constitution limits only the action of Congress, and is not a limitation on the States. This amendment supplies that defect, and allows Congress to correct the unjust legislation of the States, so far that the law which operates upon one man shall operate *equally* upon all. Whatever law punishes a white man for a crime shall punish the black man precisely in the same way and to the same degree. Whatever law protects the white man shall afford "equal" protection to the black man. Whatever means of redress is afforded to one shall be afforded to all. Whatever law allows the white man to testify in court shall allow the man of color to do the same. These are great advantages over their present codes. Now different degrees of punishment are inflicted, not on account of the magnitude of the crime, but according to the color of the skin. Now color disqualifies a man from testifying in the courts, or being tried in the same way as white men. I need not enumerate these partial and oppressive laws. Unless the Constitution should restrain them, those States will all, I fear, keep up this discrimination and crush to death the hated freedmen. . . .

Before Garfield could get to read his quotation from Stevens, Bingham interrupted him with the comment: ". . . The remark of Mr. Stevens had no relation to that provision, none at all . . ."

To which Garfield responded: "My colleague can make but he cannot unmake history. . . ."

However, one important voice did say in 1866 that the privileges and immunities of citizens of the United States included the individual rights which the first eight amendments secured, that of Senator Howard of Michigan, who presented the Fourteenth Amendment to the Senate. This was to have been done by Senator William F. Fessenden of Maine, Chairman on the part of the Senate of the Joint Committee on Reconstruction, but Senator Fessenden was ill and Senator Howard substituted for him. The depth of his approach may be gathered from these excerpts of his presentation:

It would be a curious question to solve what are the privileges and immunities of citizens of each of the States in the several States. I do not propose to go at any length into that question at this time. It would be a somewhat barren discussion. But it is certain the clause was inserted in the Constitution for some good purpose. It has in view some results beneficial to the citizens of the several States, or it would not be found there; yet I am not aware that the Supreme Court have ever undertaken to define either the nature or extent of the privileges and immunities thus guarantied. Indeed, if my recollection serves me, that court, on a certain occasion not many years since, when this question seemed to present itself to them, very modestly declined to go into a definition of them, leaving questions arising under the clause to be discussed and adjudicated when they should happen practically to arise. But we may gather some intimation of what probably will be the opinion of the judiciary by referring to a case adjudged many years ago by Judge Washington in one of the circuit courts of the United States, and I will trouble the Senate but for a moment by reading what that very learned and excellent judge says about these privileges and immunities of the citizens of each State in the several States. It is the case of Corfield vs. Coryell. . . .

                        *   *   *

Such is the character of the privileges and immunities spoken of in the second section of the fourth article of the Constitution. To these privileges and immunities, whatever they may be—for they are not and cannot be fully defined in their entire extent and precise nature—to these should be added the personal rights guarantied and secured by the first eight amendments of the Constitution; such as the freedom of speech and of the press; the right of the people peaceably to assemble and petition the Government for a redress of grievances, a right appertaining to each and all the people; the right to keep and to bear arms; the right to be exempted from the quartering of soldiers in a house without the consent of the owner; the right to be exempt from unreasonable searches and seizures, and from any search or seizure except by virtue of a warrant issued upon a formal oath or affidavit; the right of an accused person to be informed of the nature of the accusation against him, and his right to be tried by an impartial jury of the vicinage; and also the right to be secured against excessive bail and against cruel and unusual punishments.

But such an understanding of the Fourteenth Amendment's first section would have caused difficulties in Senator Howard's own state, for Michigan had already made grand juries unnecessary unless a judge in writing directed otherwise, whereas the Fifth Amendment began: "No person shall be held to answer for a capital, or otherwise infamous crime, unless on a presentment or indictment of a Grand Jury. . . ." Michigan's constitution of 1850 did not require a grand jury and a Michigan statute of 1859 gave the courts of that state "the same power and jurisdiction to hear, try, and determine prosecutions upon information for crimes, misdemeanors and offenses . . . as they possess and may exercise in cases of like prosecutions upon indictment." Grand juries were not to be drawn "at the sittings of any court . . . unless the judge thereof shall so direct by writing."

Moreover, lawyers in prosecutions upon information in Michigan did not raise the point that such prosecutions violated the Fifth Amendment by virtue of the Fourteenth. They were unaware of any incorporation idea. A number of years after the adoption of the Fourteenth Amendment counsel did urge, but not in a criminal case, that a Michigan statute violated the unreasonable searches and seizures provision of the Fourth Amendment and the due process clause of the Fifth, but not on the basis of the incorporation idea. Rather they apparently made the same contention as counsel had in the early case of *Barron* v. *Baltimore*, and with the same result. The Michigan case was *Weiner* v. *Bunbury*. The statute in question authorized summary proceedings against delinquent tax collectors. Judge Cooley speaking for a unanimous court stated that the statute did not violate the federal Constitution: ". . . It is settled beyond controversy, and without dissent, that these amendments [the Fourth and Fifth, and inferentially the rest of the first eight] are limitations upon federal, and not upon state power.—*Barron* v. *Baltimore* . . ."

Nor did Judge Cooley in his *Constitutional Limitations*, which first came out in the same year as the ratification of the Fourteenth Amendment, 1868, say anything about this amendment incorporating the first eight.

Other provisions in these amendments which would have caused difficulties in many states if the Fourteenth Amendment incorporated them are those of the Seventh Amendment: "In Suits at common law, where the value in controversy shall exceed twenty dollars, the right of trial by jury shall be preserved, and no fact tried by a jury shall be otherwise re-examined in any Court of the United States, than according to the rules of the common law."

Yet another difficulty with the incorporation theory is that it leaves us with poor draftsmanship, for under it there are two due process clauses applicable to the states, that of the Fifth and that of the Fourteenth Amendment. Of course one can say, as Senator Howard did: "The last two clauses of the first section of the amendment disable a State from depriving not merely a citizen of the United States, but any person whoever he may be of life, liberty, or property without due process of law, or from denying to him the equal protection of the laws of the State. . . ." And this is an answer, although not a very satisfactory one.

One will find corroboration for the estimate one will have formed from a reading of Senator Howard's remarks in the Senate on the Fourteenth Amendment of the quality of his legal reasoning in these words of Chief Justice James V. Campbell of the Supreme Court of Michigan on the occasion of memorial proceedings before it for Howard: "If he did not, as has been suggested, possess that sort of an intellect that would enable him to wield the slender scimeter [sic] of saladin to sever the gauzy veil that was not worth severing, he was able to wield the ponderous battle ax of the Lion-Hearted, before which iron and steel went down like wood."

So far we have dealt with the statements that most strongly support Justice Black's incorporation argument. Nearly all of the balance of the evidence, which Professor Charles Fairman voluminously set forth in an article, amply supports his conclusion with reference to Justice Black's position: "In his contention that Section 1 was intended and understood to impose Amendments I to VIII upon the states, the record of history is overwhelmingly against him."

Not long after the ratification of the Fourteenth Amendment the bench and bar in the *Slaughter-House Cases* expended upon the privileges or immunities clause of the Fourteenth Amendment's first section considerably more hard thinking than had the amendment's draftsmen and sponsors, and Justice Miller speaking for the Court gave this description of such privileges or immunities:

One of these is well described in the case of *Crandall* v. *Nevada*. It is said to be the right of the citizen of this great country, protected by implied guaranties of its Constitution, "to come to the seat of government, to transact any business he may have with it, to seek its protection, to share its offices, to engage in administering its functions. He has the right of free access to its seaports, through which all operations of foreign commerce are conducted, to the sub-treasuries, landoffices, and courts of justice in the Several States." And quoting from the language of Chief Justice Taney in another case, it is said "that *for all the great purposes for which the Federal Government was established* we are one people, with one common country, *we are all citizens of the United States*"; and it is, as such citizens, that their rights are supported in this court in *Crandall* v. *Nevada.*

Another privilege of a citizen of the United States is to demand the care and protection of the Federal government over his life, liberty, and property when on the high seas or within the jurisdiction of a foreign government. Of this there can be no doubt, nor that the right depends upon his character as a citizen of the United States. The right to peaceably assemble and petition for redress of grievances, the privilege of the writ of *habeas corpus,* are rights of the citizen guarantied by the Federal Constitution. The right to use the navigable waters of the United States, however they may penetrate the territory of the several States, and all rights secured to our citizens by treaties with foreign nations, are dependent upon citizenship of the United States, and not citizenship of a State. One of these privileges is conferred by the very article under consideration. It is that a citizen of the United States can, of his own volition, become a citizen of any State of the Union by a *bona fide* residence therein, with the same rights as other citizens of that State. To these may be added the rights secured by the thirteenth and fifteenth articles of amendment, and by the other clause of the fourteenth, next to be considered.

This still represents the law. As Justice Frankfurter remarked parenthetically in *Adamson* v. *California:* ". . . (This opinion is concerned solely with a discussion of the Due Process Clause of the Fourteenth Amendment. I put to one side the Privileges or Immunities Clause of that Amendment. For the mischievous uses to which what clause would lend itself if its scope were not confined to that given it by all but one of the decisions beginning with the *Slaughter-House Cases,* 16 Wall. 36, see the deviation in *Colgate* v. *Harvey,* 296 U.S. 404, overruled in *Madden* v. *Kentucky,* 309 U.S. 83.)"

Freedom to cross state lines as a privilege of federal citizens was the basis of Justice Douglas's concurring opinion, in which Justices Black and Murphy joined, in *Edwards* v. *California,* where the Court under the commerce clause invalidated a state statute that made it a misdemeanor knowingly to bring or assist in bringing a non-resident "indigent person" into the state; and freedom peaceably to assemble and to discuss national issues as a privilege of such citizens was the basis of Justice Roberts' opinion, in which Justice Black concurred, in *Hague* v. *C.I.O.,* where the Court voided two ordinances of Jersey City, New Jersey, one of which forbade public meetings without a permit and the other of which prohibited the distribution of pamphlets.

In view of the emphasis, in constitutional provisions, in Congress and in the courts, on freedom to cross state lines, for example, in Art. IV of the Articles of Confederation 1777, in the debates in Congress on the Missouri constitution of 1820 and in *Crandall* v. *Nevada*, it is an interesting speculation whether egress and ingress across national boundaries is an implied constitutional privilege of federal citizens. In the *Crandall* case, which arose before the adoption of the Fourteenth Amendment, the Court invalidated a state "capitation tax of one dollar upon every person leaving the State by any railroad, stage coach, or other vehicle engaged or employed in the business of transporting passengers for hire" on the ground that freedom to cross state lines was to be inferred "from the Constitution itself, and from the decisions of this court in exposition of that instrument." Although Stone in his dissenting opinion in *Colgate* v. *Harvey*, citing a statement in *Helson and Randolph* v. *Kentucky*, stated that the *Crandall* case to the extent that it relied on privileges and immunities rather than on the commerce clause had been overruled, it is submitted that Justice Douglas in his concurring opinion in *Edwards* v. *California* is right in his insistence that the *Crandall* case should continue to rest "on the broader ground of rights of *national* citizenship."

Freedom to cross national boundaries was before the Supreme Court in three recent passport cases: those of Rockwell Kent, an artist, Dr. Walter Briehl, a Los Angeles psychiatrist, and Weldon Bruce Dayton, a cosmic ray physicist. However, the government in its brief in the *Kent* and *Briehl* cases conceded that under the due process clause of the Fifth Amendment individuals had a constitutional right to travel:

On that point, there is no controversy between the parties. For, while this Court has not yet decided whether the Constitution protects the travel of citizens across the boundaries of the nation as it protects their travel across state boundaries, we do not challenge, but readily accept, the existence of a general "natural" or "constitutional" right to depart from or enter the country as an aspect of the "liberty" subject to the protections of the Constitution. We fully accede to the definitive ruling of Shachtman v. Dulles, * * *—confirmed in substance in the opinions below—that there is a "right to travel" and that restraints on that right must conform to the Fifth Amendment. . . .

In these two cases the Court in a five to four decision, although not reaching any constitutional issue, accordingly commented through Justice Douglas: "The right to travel is a part of the 'liberty' of which the citizen cannot be deprived without the due process of law of the Fifth Amendment." The Court did cite *Crandall* v. *Nevada*, *Williams*

v. *Fears* and *Edwards* v. *California* as support for the statement: "Freedom of movement is basic in our scheme of values." But it did not refer specifically to the privileges of American citizens.

Neither historically nor judicially will the privileges or immunities clause of the Fourteenth Amendment's first section sustain the contention that this section either was intended to, or did, make the first eight amendments applicable to the states. There remains the due process clause of that amendment.

Fourteenth Amendment Due Process

There is no historical evidence to support the contention that the due process of the Fourteenth Amendment was intended to make the first eight amendments applicable to the states. Moreover, if such was the intention there would then be two due process clauses applicable to the states, that of the Fifth as well as that of the Fourteenth Amendment, and both would extend their protection to "any person."

However, a comment in *Gitlow* v. *New York*, where the Court sustained the constitutionality of New York's criminal anarchy act of 1902, has been the starting-point for a number of statements by the Court to the effect that the due process clause of the Fourteenth Amendment does make the First Amendment applicable to the States. Referring to such statements Justice Black in his dissenting opinion in *Beauharnais* v. *Illinois*, in which Justice Douglas joined, stated: "And we have held in a number of prior cases that the Fourteenth Amendment makes the specific prohibitions of the First Amendment equally applicable to the states."

But the Court in the *Gitlow* case did not say that the due process clause of the Fourteenth Amendment made the First Amendment applicable to the states. What the Court said was this: "For present purposes we may and do assume that freedom of speech and of the press—which are protected by the First Amendment from abridgment by Congress —are among the fundamental personal rights and 'liberties' protected by the due process clause of the Fourteenth Amendment from impairment by the States. . . ." This is something quite different from saying that the First Amendment was now applicable to the states. And Justice Holmes in a dissenting opinion in which Justice Brandeis joined emphasized the difference:

. . . The general principle of free speech, it seems to me, must be taken to be included in the Fourteenth Amendment, in view of the scope that has been given to the word "liberty" as there used, although perhaps it may be accepted with a somewhat larger latitude of interpretation than is allowed to Congress by the sweeping language that governs or ought to govern the laws of the United States.

Unfortunately, however, the language in the *Gitlow* case lent itself to being misunderstood. Individuals could read into it what they wanted to see, but what was not there. A similar thing happened to Justice Holmes's language in *Schenck* v. *United States* about shouting fire in a crowded theatre, although with more justification than in the instance of the language in the *Gitlow* case. Just as those who wanted restrictions on speech, cited Holmes's hypothetical case as a prime illustration for their argument; so those who wanted the First Amendment applicable to the states, cited the *Gitlow* case as so saying. Thus the difference between what the Court said and what it was taken to have said in that case became obscure.

Finally Justice Jackson in his dissenting opinion in *Beauharnais* v. *Illinois* critically re-examined the contention that the due process clause of the Fourteenth Amendment incorporated the First Amendment. In that case the Court sustained the validity of an Illinois group libel law. Justice Jackson, although dissenting, vigorously rejected the incorporation theory: ". . . The history of criminal libel in America convinces me that the Fourteenth Amendment did not 'incorporate' the First, that the powers of Congress and of the States over this subject are not of the same dimensions, and that because Congress probably could not enact this law it does not follow that the States may not." He set forth with some emphasis the quoted language from the Holmes and Brandeis dissent in the *Gitlow* case, and prefaced it with this comment: ". . . What they wrote, with care and circumspection, I accept as the wise and historically correct view of the Fourteenth Amendment."

Justice Jackson's re-examination of the incorporation theory in the *Beauharnais* case finally bore fruit. In June 1958 the Court in *NAACP* v. *Alabama* was careful not to say that the due process clause of the Fourteenth Amendment made the First applicable to the states. There the Court held that an Alabama court order which required the NAACP to produce its Alabama membership lists violated that clause, but not by reason of any incorporation theory. Justice Harlan for a unanimous court said:

Effective advocacy of both public and private points of view, particularly controversial ones, is undeniably enhanced by group association, as this Court has more than once recognized by remarking upon the close nexus between the freedoms of speech and assembly. * * * It is beyond debate that freedom to engage in association for the advancement of beliefs and ideas is an inseparable aspect of the "liberty" assured by the Due Process Clause of the Fourteenth Amendment which embraces freedom of speech. * * *

The due process clause of the Fourteenth Amendment furnishes even less support for the incorporation theory than the privileges or immunities clause of that amendment. It supplies no basis for that theory historically and an erroneous one judicially.

Three Molding Developments

We thus have this constitutional picture: there is no federal power over speech unless connected with criminal conduct other than speech; state power exists, but it is limited by the due process clause of the Fourteenth Amendment. However, that is the only limitation on state power over speech so far as the federal Constitution is concerned.

Three developments took place which operated to change this picture in practice. These developments restricted state power, and gave and enlarged federal power over utterances. One of these was the Supreme Court's extended and expansive application of the federal Constitution's due process clauses. This development was a natural one, for it was in accord with the historical origin and role of these clauses. It was this application of the Fourteenth Amendment's due process clause which mostly accounted for the restrictions on state power over speech. Indeed, it accounted for these restrictions to such an extent that it seemed to give some support for the incorporation theory.

The other two developments were: the great growth of what may be termed a federal police power; and the enunciation and development of Justice Holmes's clear and present danger test. The former of these two was inevitable. The latter was a mistaken application of the criminal law of attempt and conspiracy to the field of speech. These two developments gave and enlarged federal power over speech. We will take up each of these three developments in turn.

CHAPTER IV

"CONCEPT OF ORDERED LIBERTY"

A New Case

The extended use which the Supreme Court made of the due process clauses, especially that of the Fourteenth Amendment, is but a part of the continuous history of these clauses, a continuous history which extends back more than seven centuries. Furthermore, such extended use reflects the approach of the Anglo-American peoples and of their bench and bar to the individual. Whenever, for instance, an American lawyer has a case in the state courts in which he feels that his client has not been given the consideration which our current standards of fairness and decency and our regard for the individual human being require, he turns to the due process clause of the Fourteenth Amendment. A recent case on the writer's desk is illustrative.

A mother came into the office on behalf of her son, an epileptic, who, when he was but a few months over thirteen years of age, was permitted to plead guilty to murder in the second degree. The year was 1943. The place was Poughkeepsie, New York. He was sentenced to prison for an indeterminate term of from thirty years to life. He had been in custody, at the Dutchess County jail, at Sing Sing, at Elmira Reformatory, in the Dannemora State Hospital, again at Elmira, at the Great Meadow Correctional Institution and at Clinton Prison, Dannemora, for over fifteen years.

Today such a result is not possible in New York. A series of six measures, five of which were enacted as a group in 1948 and one in 1949, brought to an end the classification of any child under the age of fifteen as a criminal. Governor Thomas E. Dewey in approving the group of five bills stated:

These five measures bring about a major advance in our legal concepts of crime and of juvenile delinquency. By redefinition they bring to an end the classification of any child under the age of 15 as a criminal.

With regard to children 15 years of age, a flexible procedure analogized to that of the youthful offender is made applicable. Discretion is left with the courts as to whether the fifteen year old charged with a crime punishable by death or life imprisonment should be treated as a criminal or as a juvenile delinquent in the Children's Court or the Domestic Relations Court, whichever is appropriate.

It is a shocking thought that under our criminal statutes a child of seven may be guilty of crime and conceivably could be electrocuted for the crime of murder. Of course, no enlightened community would permit such a situation to occur. The fact is, however, that within the very recent past children of 13 and 14 have been indicted for Murder in the First Degree and have pleaded guilty to homicide in the lesser degrees in connection with killings for which they had been the causative agents. The time is well overdue to state in the law in no uncertain terms that a child under the age of 15 has no criminal responsibility irrespective of the act involved.

*   *   *

It is particularly gratifying to me that we in the State of New York are making this important advance in our laws, an advance which recognizes and proclaims the dignity of human beings, in a period in which it is frequently difficult to separate the institutions of barbarism from those of civilization.

Ironically enough, although Governor Dewey's mention of the fact "that within the very recent past children of 13 and 14 have been indicted for Murder in the First Degree and have pleaded guilty to homicide in the lesser degrees" included a reference to the boy in question, Edwin Codarre, the new legislation was of little or no help to him: the New York Court of Appeals in *People* v. *Oliver*, in which it held that this legislation applied to any subsequent trial even though for an offense committed before its enactment, pointed out by way of dictum "that the construction that we are here according to the amendment cannot be applied in favor of an offender tried and sentenced to imprisonment before its enactment."

Edwin Codarre became thirteen on July 7. Two weeks later he went to the Kiwanis Boys' Camp at East Fishkill, New York. He was to stay only two weeks. However, he obtained a job in the camp's kitchen and stayed on.

Almost from the beginning of his time there, he became friends with a local farm boy. In the ensuing period he entered into a sexual relationship with the boy's sister, who was ten. Several days before her death he stayed all night at her home. Her brother was there. The parents were away. That night the two boys broke into a local gasoline station and pilfered some candy and cigarettes.

A few days later, on August 13, Edwin and the girl were walking along a dirt road which bordered a cornfield. He made advances to her. She

threatened in a loud tone of voice to disclose, not the sexual relationship, but the pilfering. Edwin, panic-stricken lest someone overhear her
confession of the pilfering, put his hands to her throat in order to
silence her loud talk and crushed her larynx. But he had no intention
to kill her. He wanted merely to shut her up.

Edwin was an epileptic; and Dr. Ralph S. Banay, one of the four
doctors who examined Edwin, so advised the court at an evening conference which occurred the day before Edwin pleaded guilty. Those
present were the judge, the district attorney, Edwin's counsel, the four
doctors, and a stenographer. Edwin himself was not there. Dr. Banay
told the judge that at the time of the commission of the offense Edwin
"was experiencing a psychomotor epileptic attack."

At this conference the judge showed that his guilding considerations
were to avoid the state winning a conviction of murder in the first
degree on the one hand and Edwin winning an acquittal on an insanity
plea on the other. As to the former the minutes of the conference show:

The Court: I don't want to see this boy burned. I never have. He is too
young at the age of 13, and I don't want to see that lad convicted of
murder first. I don't say he will. I don't know, but I don't want to see that
chance taken if I can help it, and that's my feeling.

And as to the latter:

The Court: * * * Suppose they committed him to Matteawan, with very
good treatment, he was released in a year, under the very capable care of
Dr. MacNeill, he is a free man, isn't he?
Dr. Banay: He would be released if it is testified he has recovered.
The Court: Then he would be out at the age of 14 and with no provision
for parole, and then we are in a hot spot. * * *

The only way out as the judge saw it was to have Edwin Codarre
plead guilty to murder in the second degree. This was what happened
the next morning. Here are the minutes of that plea:

The Court: Edwin Codarre, will you come to the bench, please, and Mrs.
Bishop [Edwin's mother], will you come up?
Mr. Dow [Edwin's counsel], may I have the privilege of talking with this
young man and his mother?
Mr. Dow: Yes.
The Court: Mrs. Bishop, I direct my remarks to you first. I assume you have
talked with your counsel appointed to defend your son?
Mrs. Bishop: Yes, sir.
The Court: Have you discussed this question of a plea?
Mrs. Bishop: Yes sir.

The Court: You have heard the suggestion from Mr. Dow that your son be permitted to withdraw his plea of not guilty to murder in the first degree and plead guilty to murder in the second degree? You have heard that, have you?

Mrs. Bishop: Yes, sir.

The Court: Do you acquiesce in that request?

Mrs. Bishop: I do to this extent, that I am convinced beyond a doubt that he needs some medical attention.

The Court: The question is, do you acquiesce in your son taking a plea to murder in the second degree?

Mrs. Bishop: If that saves him from the electric chair, that's agreeable.

The Court: I can say as a matter of law that it does. Do you desire to acquiesce in that plea and have your son plead to murder in the second degree?

Mrs. Bishop: Yes, sir.

The Court: Now, Edwin, you have also heard the counsel appointed to defend you in this plea this morning, have you not?

Edwin Codarre: Yes, sir.

The Court: And did you understand what Mr. Dow said?

Edwin Codarre: Yes, sir.

The Court: Did you understand him to say that it was your desire to withdraw your plea to murder in the first degree and to plead guilty to murder in the second degree? Did you hear him so state that?

Edwin Codarre: Yes, sir.

The Court: Do you know what that means?

Edwin Codarre: Yes.

The Court: It means that it is a lower or reduced charge. In fact, the only reduced charge that I know of that you could plead to. Do you want to plead guilty to murder in the second degree, and do you want to withdraw your plea of not guilty to murder in the first degree?

Edwin Codarre: I will take the one that Mr. Dow said.

The Court: That is murder in the second degree, is that correct?

Edwin Codarre: Yes, sir.

The Court: I am glad that this has happened. I don't know whether you are innocent or guilty. That's not for me to decide. That's the province of the jury, but I join in with the District Attorney and your counsel because of your age, Edwin. I don't think that the people of Dutchess County and I don't think the jury that is sitting in your case, and I cannot be sure, but I think I can speak for them, I don't think the District Attorney or authorities or the State Police or anyone wanted to see you convicted of murder in the first degree. If you had been, I am satisfied that there is a great Court of Appeals that might still have given assistance. I am also satisfied that we have a type of law in this Country and this State where the Governor has a right to exercise Executive Clemency, and I am sure that that Governor would have done just that in your case, but it won't be necessary for that to happen, and I am glad that this case is winding up as it is, because it would be no pleasure for anyone to send a boy of your age, thirteen years, to the electric chair, and thank God it is not on my shoulders to do that.

I am also mindful of the fact there is a little girl of ten. She won't be here any more. All that may be done won't bring her back, but she has a mother and a father too and they won't have that little girl any more because she will never come back.

I consent and accept that plea of murder in the second degree, and I will sentence you after I get a probation report. I will sentence you on December 6th at ten o'clock.

I want to say further about this matter, that before accepting this plea, it is no secret that last night we were here until ten o'clock, without your knowledge, which it should be, and I want to express grateful appreciation to Dr. Cheney, Dr. Grover, Dr. Laidlaw and Dr. Banay because we conferred with them at length until ten o'clock. It was a plea of insanity originally. Certainly I wouldn't want to sentence any boy to a Correction Institution if he were insane, and through the good offices of these doctors that have come here, two representing one side and two representing the other, we came to a conclusion which we hope and feel is correct, and it was after that lengthy discussion that we really came to that conclusion of this plea which I still think is the proper thing myself. I want to thank those doctors for their help because it was a help to make a decision.

Events were to prove that Dr. Banay's diagnosis of epilepsy, which the other three doctors disputed, was correct. On July 23, 1954 Dr. Leo A. Thume, senior physician at the Great Meadow Correctional Institution, wrote Edwin's mother concerning him:

In regards to his Epilepsy, he is progressing rather well. His last admission for any major seizure was in August 1953. Upon questioning him this morning he states: he had about ten minor seizures within the past year, but these must have been quite slight as we have no record of the nurse or doctor attending him at these times.

He is on Hibicon which is a specific for Epilepsy, and I would say he is doing well for anyone in his position.

A few days later Mr. William E. Leonard, acting commissioner of the state of New York Department of Correction, wrote her:

* * * It is reported that your son was received at Great Meadow from Elmira Reformatory on May 24, 1951 and classified in Group III due to Epilepsy. There is also a history of his being in Dannemora State Hospital from April 6, 1946 to June 10, 1949 * * *. * * * His record shows an encephalogram was taken on July 7, 1949 at Elmira with the following results: "There is an increase of sharp waves after hyperventilation, and the whole graph is strongly indicative for an epilepsia of the grand mal type. Conclusion: This man should be placed on anti-convulsive medication." Since your son has been confined in Great Meadow Correctional Institu-

tion he has received medication for Epilepsy, and has been admitted to the hospital on several occasions with a grand mal type of epileptic seizure. On being questioned by the institution physician under date of July 23, 1954, your son stated he has had approximately ten minor attacks during the past year. However, there is no record of a nurse attending him, or admissions to the hospital since August 18, 1953.

There have been two applications on Edwin's behalf for a writ of error coram nobis. They raised the points that: (1) he was insane at the time of the commission of the offense, at the time of the plea of guilty and at the time of sentencing; (2) he was not adequately represented by counsel; and (3) by reason of his illness and his extreme youth he was incompetent to plead guilty. Both applications were denied without a hearing. Both denials were affirmed on appeal.

There have been various applications for executive clemency, first to Governor Dewey, then to Governor Averill Harriman, and now to Governor Nelson A. Rockefeller. All so far have been denied.

In a case like this, where state court remedies have been exhausted, defendant's counsel seeks a last recourse. He has it. It is the Fourteenth Amendment's due process clause.

Per Legem Terrae

The extended use which the Supreme Court made of the Constitution's due process clauses to protect individual rights began late in the last century with some cases in the area of economic regulation. The turning-point is usually regarded as the *Minnesota Rate* case in 1890, where the Court invalidated a Minnesota act establishing a railroad and warehouse commission because the act as construed by the Supreme Court of Minnesota, made the commission's recommendations as to rates final. Before that in *Munn* v. *Illinois* the Court had sustained an Illinois statute which fixed maximum charges for the storage of grain in warehouses at Chicago, and in *Peik* v. *Chicago & N.W. Ry. Co.*, a Wisconsin act which fixed maximum domestic passenger fares and intrastate freight rates for railroads operating in that state. And more than a decade and a half after the *Minnesota Rate* case the Court in *Patterson* v. *Colorado* let stand a contempt conviction for the publication of certain articles and a cartoon which dealt with the Supreme Court of Colorado. In that case Justice Holmes speaking for the Court said: ". . . We leave undecided the question whether there is to be found in the Fourteenth Amendment a prohibition similar to that in the First. . . ." Still later he and Justice Brandeis joined in the Court's opinion in *Prudential Insurance Co.* v. *Cheek*, which stated: ". . . neither the Fourteenth Amendment nor any other provision of the Constitution of the United States imposes upon the States any restrictions about 'freedom of speech' or the 'liberty of silence' . . ."

But the change which came in the area of economic regulation with the *Minnesota Rate* case came to that of utterance after *Gitlow* v. *New York*. With reference to the change in views of Justices Holmes and Brandeis in the half decade between the *Prudential Insurance Co.* decision and their dissent in the *Gitlow* case, Justice Jackson in his dissenting opinion in *Beauharnais* v. *Illinois* commented: "However, these two Justices, who made the only original contribution to legal thought on the difficult problems bound up in these Amendments, soon reversed and took the view that the Fourteenth Amendment did impose some restrictions upon the States. But it was not premised upon the First Amendment nor upon any theory that it was incorporated in the Fourteenth."

Not long after the *Gitlow* case the Court made various applications of the Fourteenth Amendment's due process clause in the field of human rights. It held, in *Moore* v. *Dempsey*, that a defendant was entitled to a trial free from mob domination, and, in *Tumey* v. *Ohio*, to a fair trial before a fair tribunal. It held, in *Powell* v. *Alabama*, arising out of the Scottsboro prosecution, that he was entitled to counsel. It invalidated, in *Brown* v. *Mississippi*, coerced confessions. Since these decisions there have been a multitude of others like them.

The Court's expanded application of the due process clause produced the division of due process requirements into procedural and substantive due process. One of the most striking treatments of due process requirements under procedural and substantive due process headings occurs in Justice Jackson's dissenting opinion in *Shaughnessy* v. *United States ex rel. Mezei*. There the Court sustained the attorney general's commitment of an alien to Ellis Island without a hearing. The alien had lived peaceably in this country for a quarter of a century and was returning to his wife and home in Buffalo, New York after a trip to Hungary to visit his ailing mother. Justice Jackson concluded that the alien had been accorded substantive but not procedural due process:

II. Substantive Due Process.

*   *   *

I conclude that detention of an alien would not be inconsistent with substantive due process, provided,—and this is where my dissent begins—he is accorded procedural due process of law.

III. Procedural Due Process.

Procedural fairness, if not all that originally was meant by due process of law, is at least what it most uncompromisingly requires. Procedural due process is more elemental and less flexible than substantive due process. It yields less to the times, varies less with conditions, and defers much less to legislative judgment. Insofar as it is technical law, it must be a specialized responsibility within the competence of the judiciary on which they do not bend before political branches of the Government, as they should on matters of policy which comprise substantive law.

If it be conceded that in some way this alien could be confined, does it matter what the procedure is? Only the untaught layman or the charlatan lawyer can answer that procedures matter not. Procedural fairness and regularity are of the indispensable essence of liberty. Severe substantive laws can be endured if they are fairly and impartially applied. Indeed, if put to the choice, one might well prefer to live under Soviet substantive law applied in good faith by our common law procedures than under our substantive law enforced by Soviet procedural practices * * *

However, the Court's expanded use of the due process clause did not go unchallenged, particularly with reference to cases in the area of economic regulation. Some, who enthusiastically welcomed such use in the area of human rights, condemned it without measure in that of economic regulation. For instance, Justices Black, Douglas and Murphy in their concurring opinion in *Federal Power Comm'n* v. *Natural Gas Pipeline Co.*, declared in a footnote: "To hold that the Fourteenth Amendment was intended to and did provide protection from state invasions of the right of free speech and other clearly defined protections contained in the Bill of Rights, *Drivers Union* v. *Meadowmoor Co.*, 312 U.S. 287, 301–302, is quite different from holding that "due process," an historical expression relating to procedure, *Chambers* v. *Florida, supra,* confers a broad judicial power to invalidate all legislation which seems "unreasonable" to courts. In the one instance, courts proceeding within clearly marked constitutional boundaries seek to execute policies written into the Constitution; in the other, they roam at will in the limitless area of their own beliefs as to reasonableness and actually select policies, a responsibility which the Constitution entrusts to the legislative representatives of the people." Then they continued in the text:

We shall not attempt now to set out at length the reasons for our belief that acceptance of such a meaning is historically unjustified and that it transfers to courts powers which, under the Constitution, belong to the legislative branch of government. But we feel that we must record our disagreement from an opinion which, although upholding the action of the Commission on these particular facts, nevertheless gives renewed vitality to a "constitutional" doctrine which we are convinced has no support in the Constitution.

The doctrine which makes of "due process" an unlimited grant to courts to approve or reject policies selected by legislatures in accordance with the judges' notion of reasonableness had its origin in connection with legislative attempts to fix the prices charged by public utilities. And in no field has it had more paralyzing effects.

Recently Justice Douglas writing for the Court in *Williamson* v. *Lee Optical Co.* stated: "The day is gone when this Court uses the Due Process Clause of the Fourteenth Amendment to strike down state laws, regulatory of business and industrial conditions, because they may be unwise, improvident, or out of harmony with a particular school of thought.* * *" Some writers have been troubled at the extent to which state courts have not followed the Supreme Court in this regard.

Those who questioned the use of substantive due process in the economic area stressed the procedural aspects of this concept. For instance, in the *Natural Gas Pipeline Co.* case, Justices Black, Douglas and Murphy in their concurring opinion referred to Mr. Justice Black's statement for the Court in *Chambers* v. *Florida* that "the due process provision of the Fourteenth Amendment—just as that in the Fifth—has led few to doubt that it was intended to guarantee procedural standards adequate and appropriate then and thereafter, to protect, at all times people charged with or suspected of crime by those holding positions of power and authority." One writer suggested that there was a gap between procedural and substantive due process which the doctrine of the separation of powers in a somewhat strained fashion had to bridge: ". . . by the end of the eighteenth century the orthodox procedural meaning of due process was too thoroughly established semantically, contextually and historically to accommodate a radically new, i.e. substantive, meaning without some respectable constitutional go-between; namely, the separation of powers."

But the concept underlying due process of law began in the phrase, per legem terrae, by the law of the land. In the Magna Carta's clause 39 King John promised: "No freeman shall be taken or imprisoned or disseized or exiled or in any way destroyed, nor will we go upon him nor send upon him except by the lawful judgment of his peers or [per legem terrae] by the law of the land."

King John's successors confirmed and reissued the Magna Carta, sometimes repeatedly. Edward III (1327-77), in addition to his frequent confirmations of it, further provided: "That no man of what estate or condition that he be, shall be put out of land or tenement, or taken, nor imprisoned, nor disinherited, nor put to death, without being brought in answer [par due proces de lei] by due process of law." Thus the phrase due process of law came into being.

Coke equated the two: ". . . by the law of the land (that is, to speak it once for all) by the due course, and process of law." We in this country have made the same identification. Our earlier state constitutions usually used the phrase, by the law of the land. Daniel Webster in his argument in the Supreme Court in the *Dartmouth College* case identified the law of the land provision in the New Hampshire Constitution with due process: ". . . One prohibition is 'that no person shall be . . . deprived of his life, liberty or estate, but by judgment of his peers, or the law of the land.' . . . Have the plaintiffs lost their francises by 'due course and process of law?' . . . By the law of the land, is most clearly intended, the general law . . . The meaning is, that every citizen shall hold his life, liberty, property and immunities, under the protection of the general rules which govern society. . . ." Conversely, the Supreme Court in *Murray's Lessee* v. *Hoboken Land & Improvement Co.*, its first major decision under the due process clause of the Fifth Amendment in a case challenging action of the federal government, equated that clause with the law of the land: "The words, 'due process of law,' were undoubtedly intended to convey the same meaning as the words, 'by the law of the land,' in Magna Charta. Lord Coke in his commentary on those words (2 Inst. 50,), says they mean due process of law. The constitutions which have been adopted by the several States before the formation of the federal constitution, following the language of the great charter more closely, generally contained the words, 'but by the judgment of his peers, or the law of the land. * * *'"

Historically, therefore, it is not correct to confine due process clauses to procedure. These clauses have always had their law of the land meaning as well. In a time when there was an emphasis on procedure, they may seem to have been limited to procedure. But in a later time when there was an emphasis on property rights the champions of such rights also relied on the due process clause. Chief Justice Taney, regarding slaves as property, used the due process clause to support his conclusion in the *Dred Scott* case that the provision of one of the two acts known as the Missouri Compromise which prohibited slavery north of 36 degrees 30 minutes north latitude except in Missouri was unconstitutional.

However, his opponents also relied on due process clauses: they used such clauses in their arguments against slavery. In 1856, the same year as the *Dred Scott* case, the Republican party in its first national platform declared: ". . . that, as our republican fathers, when they had abolished slavery in all our national territory, ordained that no person should be deprived of life, liberty, or property without due process of law, it becomes our duty to maintain this provision of the Constitution against all attempts to violate it for the purpose of establishing slavery in any Territory of the United States, by positive legislation prohibiting its existence or extension therein * * *."

With the change in emphasis from property rights to human rights the due process clause of the Fourteenth Amendment has tended to become identified with the protection of such rights against state action. But whatever the emphasis, we have not confined our due process clauses to procedure alone.

Outlines of Due Process

The use of the due process clause of the Fourteenth Amendment to protect human rights has given rise to another type of objection than that to the extended application of this clause in the area of economic regulation, namely, that such use produces results which are too indefinite. Justice Black would remedy this situation by having the Fourteenth Amendment incorporate, certainly the entire First Amendment, and various parts of the rest of the first eight. For example, in his dissenting opinion in *Beauharnais* v. *Illinois* he quoted this language from Justice Jackson's earlier opinion for the Court in *West Virginia Board of Education* v. *Barnette*:

In weighing arguments of the parties it is important to distinguish between the due process clause of the Fourteenth Amendment as an instrument for transmitting the principles of the First Amendment and those cases in which it is applied for its own sake. The test of legislation which collides with the Fourteenth Amendment, because it also collides with the principles of the First, is much more definite than the test when only the Fourteenth is involved. Much of the vagueness of the due process clause disappears when the specific prohibitions of the First become its standard. The right of a State to regulate, for example, a public utility may well include, so far as the due process test is concerned, power to impose all of the restrictions which a legislature may have a "rational basis" for adopting. But freedoms of speech and of press, of assembly, and of worship may not be infringed on such slender grounds. * * *

More recently Justice Clark gave a comparable reason for his concurrence in *Irvine* v. *California*, where the Court sustained a state court conviction based on evidence resulting from an illegal breaking and entering and an illegally secreted microphone:

Had I been here in 1949 when *Wolf* was decided, I would have applied the doctrine of *Weeks* v. *United States*, 232 U.S. 383 (1914), to the states. * * *
Of course, we could sterilize the rule announced in Wolf by adopting a case-by-case approach to due process in which inchoate notions of propriety concerning local police conduct guide our decisions. But this makes for such uncertainty and unpredictability that it would be impossible to foretell—other than by guesswork—just how brazen the invasion of the intimate

privacies of one's home must be in order to shock itself into the protective arms of the Constitution. In truth, the practical result of this *ad hoc* approach is simply that when five Justices are sufficiently revolted by local police action a conviction is overturned and a guilty man may go free. *Rochin* bears witness to this. We may thus vindicate the abstract principle of due process, but we do not shape the conduct of local police one whit; unpredictable reversals on dissimilar fact situations are not likely to curb the zeal of those police and prosecutors who may be intent on racking up a high percentage of successful prosecutions. I do not believe that the extension of such a vacillating course beyond the clear cases of physical coercion and brutality, such as *Rochin*, would serve a useful purpose.

In the area of economic regulation Justice Black would meet the problem of indefiniteness by restricting the power of the Court under the due process clauses of the Fifth and the Fourteenth Amendments. In the area of human rights he would solve it by having the Fourteenth Amendment incorporate various parts of the first eight amendments. As he stated in his concurring opinion in *Rochin* v. *California*, where the Court upset a state court conviction based on evidence obtained by pumping the defendant's stomach against his will:

In the view of a majority of the Court, however, the Fifth Amendment imposes no restraint of any kind on the states. They nevertheless hold that California's use of this evidence violated the Due Process Clause of the Fourteenth Amendment. Since they hold as I do in this case, I regret my inability to accept their interpretation without protest. But I believe that faithful adherence to the specific guarantees in the Bill of Rights insures a more permanent protection of individual liberty than that which can be afforded by the nebulous standards stated by the majority.

What the majority hold is that the Due Process Clause empowers this Court to nullify any state law if its application "shocks the conscience," offends "a sense of justice" or runs counter to the "decencies of civilized conduct." * * *

* * * I long ago concluded that the accordion-like qualities of this philosophy must inevitably imperil all the individual liberty safeguards specifically enumerated in the Bill of Rights. Reflection and recent decisions of this Court sanctioning abridgment of the freedom of speech and press have strengthened this conclusion.

Especially would Mr. Justice Black have the Fourteenth Amendment incorporate the first. But there are no reasons historically or interpretatively why due process clauses apply to human rights and not to property rights. Nor is there any reason why the due process clause of the fourteenth amendment incorporates the First and not, let us say, the Fifth or Seventh amendments. On the other hand, if there were a selective incorporation, this would still leave us with somewhat the same feeling of indefiniteness as the expanded application of the Fourteenth Amendment's due process clause without the benefit of the incorporation theory. As Mr. Justice Frankfurter commented in his concurring opinion in *Adamson* v. *California:*

Indeed, the suggestion that the Fourteenth Amendment incorporates the first eight Amendments as such is not unambiguously urged. Even the boldest innovator would shrink from suggesting to more than half the States that they may no longer initiate prosecutions without indictment by grand jury, or that thereafter all the States of the Union must furnish a jury of twelve for every case involving a claim above twenty dollars. There is suggested merely a selective incorporation of the first eight Amendments into the Fourteenth Amendment. Some are in and some are out, but we are left in the dark as to which are in and which are out. Nor are we given the calculus for determining which go in and which stay out. * * *

Besides, even if the due process clause of the Fourteenth Amendment did incorporate the first eight amendments, there still would not be all the certainty that one could desire; for the justices of the Court have disagreed and will continue to disagree as to the meaning and application of various of the provisions of these amendments under a substantial number of circumstances. More conclusive than all these considerations is the fact that this clause simply does not incorporate the first eight amendments.

Let us therefore take this clause as it stands. Moreover, let us take it on the basis of Justice Clark's suggestion in his concurring opinion in *Irvine* v. *California* that the clause means what five justices of the Court say it does. Even so, the Court has done a necessary and acceptable piece of work. We need some final arbiter for the questions which the Court has decided under the due process clauses. We have been able to devise no better institution than this for this purpose. As Justice Frankfurter explained in the recent case of *Bartkus* v. *Illinois*, where the Court in a five to four decision sustained a federal prosecution of the same acts on which there had already been a state court conviction:

* * * Decisions under the Due Process Clause require close and perceptive inquiry into fundamental principles of our society. The Anglo-American system of law is based not upon transcendental revelation but upon the conscience of society ascertained as best it may be by a tribunal disciplined for the task and environed by the best safeguards for disinterestedness and detachment.

Under this system nine trained laywers apply their disciplined minds to these questions on a case by case basis. They consider the presentations of counsel, deliberate among themselves, and give us their reasoned conclusions. From these opinions one can get a pretty good idea of the human rights that the Court will protect against state action, and in general to what extent. The broad outlines will be there.

In *Davidson* v. *New Orleans*, which Justice Frankfurter in his dissenting opinion in *Irvine* v. *California* described as containing the Court's "first full-dress discussion of the Due Process Clause of the Fourteenth Amendment," the Court through Justice Miller indicated what its course in the construction and application of this clause would be, namely, "the gradual process of judicial inclusion and exclusion, as the cases presented for decision shall require, with the reasoning on which such decisions may be founded." Justice Cardozo speaking for the Court in *Palko* v. *Connecticut* added, with reference to human rights cases: "The line of division may seem to be wavering and broken if there is a hasty catalogue of the cases on the one side and the other. Reflection and analysis will induce a different view. There emerges the perception of a rationalizing principle which gives to discrete instances a proper order and coherence. . . . The exclusion . . . [of certain claimed protections] has not been arbitrary or casual. It has been dictated by a study and appreciation of the meaning, the essential implications, of liberty itself."

Thus a long line of cases from *Brown* v. *Mississippi* and *Chambers* v. *Florida* to the recent case of *Payne* v. *Arkansas* tells us that forced confessions are violative of due process and that state court convictions based on them will be reversed. In the *Payne* case the Court held: "The use in a state criminal trial of a defendant's confession obtained by coercion—whether physical or mental—is forbidden by the Fourteenth Amendment." In June 1949 on the last day of the term the Court threw out confessions in three different cases from three different states.

But in the application of the rule against coerced confessions, cases will fall on one side of the line and on the other. Occasionally the results will be difficult to reconcile. Often the members of the Court will disagree among themselves, in cases on both sides of the line, with frequent concurring as well as dissenting opinions. In the three cases from three different states in which the Court invalidated confessions in June 1949 the majority was unable to reach a common opinion in any one of them. Yet the main outlines will be clear enough, and concurring and dissenting opinions but show the vigor and the individuality of the judicial process.

Another long line of cases from *Powell* v. *Alabama* to the recent case of *Chandler* v. *Fretag* makes plain that every defendant in every state criminal case, whether capital or noncapital, is entitled to be represented by counsel of his own choosing. As the Court said in the leading case of

Powell v. *Alabama:* "If in any case, civil or criminal, a state or federal court were arbitrarily to refuse to hear a party by counsel, employed by or appearing for him, it reasonably may not be doubted that such a refusal would be a denial of a hearing, and, therefore, of due process in the constitutional sense." Moreover a defendant is entitled to a reasonable amount of time to obtain counsel and to consult with him. As the Court held in *Powell* v. *Alabama:* "It is hardly necessary to say that, the right to counsel being conceded, a defendant should be afforded a fair opportunity to secure counsel of his own choice. . . . The prompt disposition of criminal cases is to be commended and encouraged. But in reaching that result a defendant, charged with a serious crime, must not be stripped of his right to have sufficient time to advise with counsel and prepare his defense." In *Chandler* v. *Fretag* the Court through Chief Justice Warren added: ". . . a defendant must be given a reasonable opportunity to employ and consult with counsel; otherwise the right to be heard by counsel would be of little worth." In addition, counsel must have an adequate time and opportunity to prepare his client's defense.

Furthermore, every defendant in every state capital case is entitled to have the "effective appointment of counsel" whether he requests it or not. So is every defendant in every state noncapital case where he "has not intelligently and understandably waived the benefit of counsel and where the circumstances show that his rights could not have been fairly protected without counsel." Whether a refusal or failure to appoint counsel in a state noncapital case results in fundamental unfairness violative of due process depends on the circumstances of each case. Again, as in the application of the rule against coerced confessions, cases will fall on one side of the line and on the other. But the main outlines of the right to counsel are clear enough. Indeed they are abundantly clear.

The Court in *Powell* v. *Alabama* reached its conclusions about the necessity of the effective assistance of counsel, not because, but in spite, of the Sixth Amendment's provision that "the accused shall enjoy the right . . . to have the Assistance of Counsel for his defence." Earlier, in *Hurtado* v. *California,* in holding that a state could proceed against deviants by way of information rather than indictment, the Court reasoned that the Fifth Amendment's inclusion of a provision for indictment along with a due process clause meant that the due process clause of the Fourteenth Amendment did not require states to keep the grand jury method. But later, in *Chicago, B. & Q.R.R. Co.* v. *Chicago,* during the period of the stress on property rights, in holding that a state could not authorize the taking of private property for a public use without just compensation because of the Fourteenth Amendment's due process clause, the Court reached its conclusion despite the fact that the Fifth Amendment also provides, "nor shall private property be taken for public use, without just compensation." Subsequently Justice Moody speaking for the Court in *Twining* v. *New Jersey*, where the Court sustained a state court practice permitting comment on a defendant's failing to take the stand, observed by way of dictum: ". . . it is possible that some of the personal rights safeguarded by the first eight Amendments against national action may also be safeguarded against state action, because a denial of them would be a denial of due process of law. *Chicago, Burlington & Quincy Railroad* v. *Chicago* * * *. If this is so, it is not because those rights are enumerated in the first eight amendments, but because they are of such a nature that they are included in the conception of due process of law." In *Powell* v. *Alabama* the Court through Justice Sutherland quoted this language with approval and continued: "While the question has never been categorically determined by this court, a consideration of the nature of the right and a review of the expressions of this and other courts, makes it clear that the aid of counsel is of this fundamental character."

The Court has held or indicated that various other human claims are of this fundamental character, and as such are entitled to protection against state action under the Fourteenth Amendment's due process clause. Thus under this clause an individual is entitled to be free against state action from unreasonable searches and seizures. In *Wolf* v. *Colorado* the Court by way of dictum observed: "The security of one's privacy against arbitrary intrusion by the police—which is at the core of the Fourth Amendment—is basic to a free society. It is therefore implicit in 'the concept of ordered liberty' and as such enforceable against the States through the Due Process Clause. . . . Accordingly, we have no hesitation in saying that were a State affirmatively to sanction such police intrusion into privacy it would run counter to the guaranty of the Fourteenth Amendment."

One accused is entitled to be advised of the charges against him as well as an adequate opportunity to defend against them. As the Court in *Snyder* v. *Massachusetts* observed by way of dictum through Justice Cardozo: ". . . What may not be taken away is notice of the charge and an adequate opportunity to be heard in defense of it. . . ." There the Court held that the refusal of a state court judge to permit a defendant to be present while the jury took a view of the murder scene did not constitute a denial of due process. The decision was five to four. Justice Roberts wrote a dissenting opinion in which Justices Brandeis, Sutherland and Butler concurred.

An accused has a fundamental right to a public trial. In a leading case,

In re Oliver, the Court held violative of due process a contempt sentence imposed in a secret proceeding by a state court judge sitting as part of what Justice Black characterized as "Michigan's unique one-man grand jury system." Speaking for the Court he said: ". . . Whatever other benefits the guarantee to an accused that his trial be conducted in public may confer upon our society, the guarantee has always been recognized as a safeguard against any attempt to employ our courts as instruments of persecution. The knowledge that every criminal trial is subject to contemporaneous review in the forum of public opinion is an effective restraint on possible abuse of judicial power. . . ."

In another leading case which came up from Michigan, *In re Murchison*, the Court again emphasized that a defendant was entitled to a fair trial before a fair tribunal. Specifically the Court ruled that a Michigan judge sitting as a one-man grand jury could not, consistent with due process, pass judgment even in a public hearing on a charge of contempt committed before him in a secret hearing. The Court, again speaking through Justice Black, said: "A fair trial in a fair tribunal is a basic requirement of due process. Fairness of course requires an absence of actual bias in the trial of cases. But our system of law has always endeavored to prevent even the probability of unfairness. To this end no man can be a judge in his own case and no man is permitted to try cases where he has an interest in the outcome. . . . Such a stringent rule may sometimes bar trial by judges who have no actual bias and who would do their very best to weigh the scales of justice equally between contending parties. But to perform its high function in the best way 'justice must satisfy the appearance of justice.' . . ."

A person accused is entitled to be confronted with the witnesses against him and to cross-examine them. As the Court in *Snyder* v. *Massachusetts* further observed by way of dictum through Justice Cardozo: ". . . Thus, the privilege to confront one's accusers and cross-examine them face to face is assured to a defendant by the Sixth Amendment in prosecutions in the federal courts (*Gaines* v. *Washington*, * * *), and in prosecutions in the state courts is assured very often by the constitutions of the states. For present purposes we assume that the privilege is reinforced by the Fourteenth Amendment, though this has not been squarely held. . . ."

The members of the Court would probably also agree that a state may not twice place a person in jeopardy for the same offense; nor execute a convicted defendant "in a cruel manner." In addition, the Court will invalidate under the Fourteenth Amendment's due process clause any shocking state action. A good recent example is *Rochin* v. *California*, where the state obtained evidence in a narcotics case by pumping the defendant's stomach against his will. The Court upset the resulting conviction.

Again, as in the application of the rule against coerced confessions or the determination of whether the refusal or failure to appoint counsel in a state noncapital case has resulted in fundamental unfairness, close questions will arise. What constitutes proscribed double jeopardy under the Fourteenth Amendment's due process clause? And does it include collateral estoppel, that is, does due process require that the determination of an essential fact in a criminal case be binding in another proceeding in which the issues are different? In the federal courts under the Fifth Amendment's provision, "nor shall any person be subject for the same offence to be twice put in jeopardy of life or limb," an acquittal is final. Recently in *Green* v. *United States* the Court stated through Justice Black: ". . . Thus it is one of the elemental principles of our criminal law that the Government cannot secure a new trial by means of an appeal even though an acquittal may appear to be erroneous. . . ." Nor, in the federal courts, may a defendant be tried again if a jury has once been selected and sworn and then discharged on the government's motion without the defendant's consent. As the Court further stated in *Green* v. *United States:* ". . . This Court, as well as most others, has taken the position that a defendant is placed in jeopardy once he is put to trial before a jury so that if the jury is discharged without his consent he cannot be tried again. . . ." Also, collateral estoppel is applicable to federal criminal cases. In another case at the same term, *Hoag* v. *New Jersey*, the Court through Justice Harlan commented: ". . . Although the rule [collateral estoppel] was originally developed in connection with civil litigation it has been widely employed in criminal cases in both state and federal courts. . . ." In the fourth place, a federal defendant indicted for a greater offense and convicted of a lesser one, in the event he obtains a reversal on appeal, may not be retried for the greater offense. The Court so held in *Green* v. *United States*, involving an indictment for first degree murder, a conviction for second degree murder, a successful appeal and a retrial and conviction for first degree murder. The Court reversed the second conviction.

On all four points the results would probably be different as to state action under the due process clause of the Fourteenth Amendment. In *Palko* v. *Connecticut* the Court sustained a Connecticut statute which gave the state an appeal in criminal cases. In a recent case, *Brock* v. *North Carolina*, the Court permitted a state court in a criminal case to withdraw a juror and declare a mistrial on the motion of the prosecution and over the objection of the defendant, and at a later time to try him again. The prosecution moved for a mistrial when two of the state's witnesses refused to testify on the ground that their answers might tend to incriminate them. On collateral estoppel the Court stated in *Hoag* v. *New Jersey:* "Despite its wide employment, we entertain grave doubts whether collateral estoppel can be regarded as a constitutional requirement. . . ." On the fourth point the Court in *Palko* v. *Connecticut* not only upheld a state statute which gave the state an appeal but also permitted the prosecution to appeal a conviction of second degree murder and on retrial secure a conviction of first degree murder.

A fifth close double jeopardy question arises out of multiple prosecutions based on the same occurrence. In multiple federal prosecutions it can arise under the Fifth Amendment, and in multiple state prosecutions it has arisen under the due process clause of the Fourteenth Amendment. What the result would be in a multiple federal prosecution is problematical. The present Court would probably decide the question by a five to four vote, but in which direction it would go is hard to say. Multiple state prosecutions were sustained at the last term in two cases: *Hoag* v. *New Jersey,* involving a robbery, five victims, four indictments and two trials; and *Ciucci* v. *Illinois,* involving a murder, four victims, four indictments, and three trials. The decision in one case was five to three and in the other five to four. Justice Brennan did not take part in the case which came up from New Jersey.

On two other important points the safeguards against state action under the due process clause of the Fourteenth Amendment are less than against the federal government under the first eight amendments. A state may proceed by way of an information of a prosecutor rather than an indictment of a grand jury: this was *Hurtado* v. *California*. A state may also restrict the privilege against self-incrimination: such were the holdings in *Adamson* v. *California* and *Twining* v. *New Jersey*. In *Snyder* v. *Massachusetts* the Court stated by way of dictum: "The privilege against self-incrimination may be withdrawn and the accused put upon the stand as a witness for the state." However, neither the *Adamson* nor the *Twining* case had to go this far. All that was involved in the one was a state statute and in the other a state practice permitting comment on the failure of an accused to take the stand. A state statute which specifically provided that the state could compel a defendant in a criminal trial to take the stand would have greater difficulty surviving the due process clause.

Not only close questions, but also new questions will arise. Involuntary confessions in state court proceedings violate the Fourteenth Amendment's due process clause. This clause also entitles one in such proceedings to counsel of one's own choice. But suppose during the period that one is giving a voluntary confession to state authorities, one asks to consult with counsel and this request is denied. Has there been a violation of due process? In two recent cases, *Cicenia* v. *LaGay* and *Crooker* v. *California*, the Court held that there had not been. Both decisions were handed down on the last day of the term. The vote in the one was five to three and in the other five to four. The *Cicenia* case arose out of a New Jersey conviction, and again Justice Brennan did not sit.

Also, how far does the right to counsel extend? The Court stated in the *Crooker* case that it extended to pretrial proceedings if its denial so prejudiced an accused "as to infect his subsequent trial with an absence of 'that fundamental fairness essential to the very concept of justice.'" At the preceding term in *In Re Groban* the Court held that the right did not extend to the secret investigative proceeding of a state fire marshal to determine the cause of a fire. Once again the vote was five to four.

From time to time new claims produce new due process clause protections. Recently in *Lambert* v. *California* the Court held, despite the rule that "ignorance of the law will not excuse," frequently repeated, that a Los Angeles felon registration ordinance violated "Due Process where it is applied to a person who has no actual knowledge of his duty to register, and where no showing is made of the probability of such knowledge." The vote, as so often happens in these cases, was five to four. In two other recent cases, *Griffin* v. *Illinois* and *Eskridge* v. *Washington Prison Bd.*, the Court held that indigent defendants in criminal cases were entitled to a free copy of the trial transcript where this was necessary for them to "be afforded as adequate appellate review as defendants who have money enough to buy transcripts." In the *Griffin* case Justice Frankfurter in a concurring opinion aptly characterized the expanding nature of due process: "'Due process' is, perhaps, the least frozen concept of our law—the least confined to history and the most absorptive of powerful social standards of a progressive society." The vote in this ecase was the almost characteristic five to four. Also there was no opinion in which a majority of the Court could join.

In 1959 in *Burns* v. *Ohio* the Court held that a state may not constitutionally require an indigent defendant in a criminal case to pay a filing fee before permitting him to file a motion for leave to appeal in one of its courts. Chief Justice Warren said for the Court; ". . . The imposition by the State of financial barriers restricting the availability of appellate review for indigent criminal defendants has no place in our heritage of Equal Justice Under Law."

Recent cases further provided some good instances of the uncertainty that exists when the first eight amendments are applied to the federal government. *Green* v. *United States*, which involved the constitutional defense of double jeopardy, was decided by a five to four vote.

Another good illustration is *Knapp* v. *Schweitzer*, announced on the last day of the term. That case involved a state grand jury witness in New York who was under a compulsion to testify because of a state immunity act and who claimed that his testimony would incriminate him under the provisions of a federal statute, §302 of the Labor-Management Relations Act, 1947, commonly known as the Taft-Hartley Act. The New York Appellate Division ruled against the witness, concluding its opinion with the statement that there was no "real and substantial danger that the testimony compelled by the State will be used in a subsequent Federal prosecution." The Court of Appeals of New York and the federal Supreme Court both affirmed, the former without opinion, and the latter with four opinions, the Court's opinion by Justice Frankfurter, a concurring opinion by Justice Brennan, a dissenting opinion by Chief Justice Warren, and a dissenting opinion by Justice Black in which Justice Douglas joined. The three dissenters and Justice Brennan also cast doubt on *Feldman* v. *United States*, where the Court held that testimony given by a debtor in a discovery proceeding in a state court in New York, most of which was given under a limited immunity provision which simply forbade the use of such testimony in a subsequent criminal proceeding against the debtor, was admissible against him in a federal court on the trial of a mail fraud indictment despite the Fifth Amendment's privilege against self-incrimination. Justice Brennan ended his concurring opinion with the words: ". . . I should not be understood as believing that our decision today forecloses reconsideration of the *Feldman* holding in a case requiring our decision of that question." Chief Justice Warren concluded his dissenting opinion similarly: ". . . At all events, the unsettling influence that *Feldman* has had upon the course of this litigation indicates that a satisfactory solution cannot be reached without a reconsideration of that decision." Justice Black, who wrote a dissenting opinion in the *Feldman* case in which Justices Douglas and Rutledge joined, left no doubt but that in his opinion the *Feldman* case should be overruled. In the *Knapp* case he wrote, referring to the *Feldman* decision: ". . . In that case a minority of this Court held, 4–3, that information extracted from a person by state authorities under threat of punishment could be used to convict him of a federal crime. The passage of time has only strengthened my conviction that this result is thoroughly contrary to the guarantee of the Fifth Amendment that no person shall be compelled to be a witness against himself, at least in a federal prosecution."

The *Feldman* case was a four to three decision, with two justices not participating. What the law now is with reference to the applicability of the Fifth Amendment's privilege against self-incrimination and its due process clause to the offer by a federal prosecutor in a federal criminal proceeding of testimony obtained by state officials under a state immunity statute is in the realm of speculation. However, neither federal prosecutors nor attorneys for accused persons will have any doubt as to their respective courses. Prosecutors will continue to rely on the *Feldman* case. Attorneys for defendants will argue on the one hand that the *Feldman* case is distinguishable and on the other that it should be overruled. If an attorney for a defendant is able to prove that there was a course of cooperation between federal and state authorities he may succeed in having the *Feldman* case at least distinguished. And if there was no such cooperation he may still be able to have it overruled. The Court will be divided, very likely five to four. If an attorney for a defendant loses, he will make the point again the next time an opportunity presents itself.

As With Equity

The objection that the Fourteenth Amendment's due process clause without the incorporation theory produces results which are too indefinite reminds one of a comparable objection in an earlier time to equity: equitable relief was said to be as variable as the length of the chancellor's foot. But equity did a needed and creditable job. So has the Supreme Court under the Fourteenth Amendment's due process clause. Let us hope that it will continue to do so, a hope that finds support in the current emphasis on accomplishing the rule of law throughout the world.

CHAPTER V

FEDERAL POLICE POWER

One of the developments which helped to provide the basis for an emerging and expanding federal power over speech was the great growth of an undefined federal police power. This occurred largely under the commerce and postal clauses. It began over a century ago. As early as 1838 Congress passed a law requiring the installation of safety devices upon steam vessels. Beginning in 1842 Congress enacted a long series of statutes proscribing obscene material. The first such act prohibited the importation of "indecent and obscene prints, paintings, lithographs, engravings, and transparencies." In 1848 Congress prohibited the importation of spurious and adulterated drugs and provided a system of inspection to make the prohibition effective. In 1865 Congress made it a misdemeanor to mail an "obscene book, pamphlet, picture, print, or other publication of a vulgar and indecent character." The next year Congress controlled the transportation on land and water of explosives. In 1868 Congress made it unlawful to use the mails for lottery literature and paraphernalia.

In 1872 Congress codified the various postal laws, and added to its proscription of obscene material "disloyal devices printed or engraved." In the succeeding section it forbade "letters or circulars concerning illegal lotteries" and prohibited in addition those "concerning schemes devised and intended to deceive and defraud the public for the purpose of obtaining money under false pretences." The next year material relating to contraception was added to the proscribed list. However, this same act eliminated the phrase about disloyal devices. In 1876 the provisions against lottery literature were broadened by eliminating the word "illegal." In 1895 Congress prohibited the introduction or carriage of lottery tickets in the mails or in interstate commerce. This act was held constitutional in the *Lottery Case, Champion* v. *Ames.* Earlier measures against lotteries were sustained in *Ex parte Jackson* and *In re Rapier.* In the *Jackson* case the Court announced that under the postal clause Congress could refuse the facilities of the mails "for the distribution of matter deemed injurious to the public morals." In *Public*

76

Clearing House v. *Coyne* the Court upheld the postmaster general in the issuance of a fraud order authorizing the interception and return to the sender of all mail addressed to a company engaged in operating an endless chain scheme. The Court stated that Congress could "forbid the delivery of letters to such persons or corporations as in its judgment are making use of the mails for the purpose of fraud or deception or the dissemination among its citizens of information of a character calculated to debauch the public morality."

In 1893 Congress began to enact the safety appliance acts now applicable to interstate railroads. The first of these was the Automatic Coupler Act. In 1906 Congress forbade the distribution or sale of impure foods and drugs by means of interstate commerce: it passed two comprehensive statutes known as the Meat Inspection Act and the Pure Food Act. Two years later Congress passed legislation regulating the employment of children in the District of Columbia, and in 1916 prohibited the movement in interstate commerce of the products of child labor. In 1918 Congress enacted minimum wage legislation for women and children in the District of Columbia. This act was held unconstitutional in *Adkins* v. *Children's Hospital*; but the *Adkins* case was subsequently overruled in *West Coast Hotel Co.* v. *Parrish*, involving a minimum wage statute of the state of Washington.

In 1910 Congress enacted the Mann Act, which bore the title "An Act To further regulate interstate and foreign commerce by prohibiting the transportation therein for immoral purposes of women and girls, and for other purposes." This act was sustained in *Hoke* v. *United States*, and pushed to disturbing lengths in *Caminetti* v. *United States*.

By an act of 1912 Congress made it an offense to import from abroad or transport in interstate commerce or send through the mails, for exhibition purposes, prize fight films. In the same year Congress provided that advertisements in second class mail had to be labelled as such. In 1919 Congress passed the National Motor Vehicle Theft Act. In the last year of the Hoover administration it legislated against labor injunctions and "yellow dog" contracts, as well as against kidnaping. The former is popularly known as the Norris-LaGuardia Act, and the latter as the Lindbergh Act.

Then came the New Deal, and with it many new statutes which greatly expanded the exercise of federal power. These included the Securities Act of 1933, the Securities Exchange Act of 1934, the Public Utility Holding Company Act of 1935, and the National Labor Relations Act, enacted in the same year. There was federal legislation on such diverse subjects as cosmetics and racketeering. One act made it an offense to transport dentures if the impression for them was taken by one who was not licensed to practice dentistry. The constitutionality of most of the securities legislation was settled in *Electric Bond & Share Co. v. SEC*, and *North American Co. v. SEC*; and that of the main provisions of the National Labor Relations Act in *NLRB v. Jones & Laughlin Steel Corp*.

More recently the Congress sought to restrain gambling by placing an occupational tax on gamblers. This tax was sustained in two Supreme Court decisions.

In 1959 in *F.T.C. v. Mandel Brothers* the Court assumed the validity of the Fur Products Labeling Act without discussing federal power.

Thus the federal government has expanded into a little bit of almost everything, from obscenity to prostitution, from cosmetics to contraception, from labor relations to securities, from theft and fraud to food and drugs, from safety appliances to lotteries, racketeering and gambling.

By way of contrast federal legislation when our Constitution was new placed much greater reliance on state governments. An act of 1799 directed federal coastal officials duly to observe "the quarantines and other restraints, which shall be required and established by the health laws of any state" with respect to any incoming vessels and "faithfully to aid in the execution of such quarantines and health laws." An act of 1803 told customs officers "to notice and be governed by the provisions of the laws now existing of the several states prohibiting the admission or importation of any negro, mulatto, or other person of colour." The Special Committee which reported adversely on President Jackson's proposal for barring the use of the mails to "incendiary publications" cited these acts to show the respect which Congress had been wont to give to state laws.

The federal government also branched out into sedition again, as well as into subversion generally. During World War I Congress enacted the country's second major sedition act; and with the struggle against international communism and Russian nationalism, a third, the Smith Act, as well as a volume of legislation against subversion. The second sedition act was passed in 1918 as an amendment of the Espionage Act of 1917; and the latter act in turn added new offenses to those established during the Civil War.

During the Civil War, Congress passed an act making it a crime for two or more persons in any state or territory to "conspire together to overthrow, or to put down, or to destroy by force, the Government of the United States." A derivative of this act is still on the statute books. There was also a general federal conspiracy statute, which became section 37 of the Criminal Code of 1909. In addition, section 332 of this code included in its definition of a principal anyone who counselled or induced another to commit an offense against the United States. It was under a combination of the latter two provisions that Emma Goldman and Alexander Berkman were convicted during World War I for conspiring by means of speeches and publications to induce men to evade the draft.

It was not an offense, however, to persuade a man not to enlist voluntarily. Nor was it a crime if a lone individual made a deliberate but unsuccessful attempt to obstruct the draft, unless there were additional facts which made his conduct amount to treason. In the Espionage Act of 1917 Congress accordingly made it a crime willfully to "cause or attempt to cause insubordination" among members of our armed forces or willfully to "obstruct the recruiting or enlistment service of the United States." These provisions were involved in the *Schenck*, *Frohwerk*, and *Debs* cases.

The 1918 amendment inserted "attempt to obstruct" in the clause just quoted, and further proscribed various kinds of utterances. For instance, it was an offense, when the United States was at war, willfully to "utter, print, write, or publish any disloyal, profane, scurrilous, or abusive language about the form of government of the United States, or the Constitution of the United States, or the military or naval forces of the United States, or the flag of the United States, or the uniform of the Army or Navy of the United States, or any language intended to bring the form of government to the United States, or the Constitution of the United States, or the military or naval forces of the United States, or the flag of the United States, or the uniform of the Army or Navy of the United States into contempt, scorn, contumely, or disrepute." The *Abrams* case arose under the provisions of this act. It was repealed on March 3, 1921.

The Espionage Act of 1917 also declared publications and other matter in violation of its provisions to be non-mailable. The 1918 amendment added a section which empowered the postmaster general "upon evidence satisfactory to him that any person or concern" was using the mails in violation of the act to cause mail addressed to any such person or concern to be returned to the senders.

In 1940 came the Smith Act. Then under the impact of the cold war, which followed close on the heels of World War II, Congress passed numerous measures against subversion. These included the Labor-Management Relations Act, 1947, commonly known as the Taft-Hartley Act after Senator Robert A. Taft of Ohio and Representative Fred A. Hartley, Jr., of New Jersey, the Internal Security Act of 1950, known as well as the McCarran Act, after Senator Pat McCarran of Nevada, and the Communist Control Act of 1954. The Taft-Hartley Act in section 9(h) requires the officers of any labor union wishing to use the machinery of the National Labor Relations Board to file with the Board non-communist affidavits. Title I of the Internal Security Act of 1950 is officially designated as the Subversive Activities Control Act of 1950. This title requires "Communist-action" and "Communist-front" organizations to register with the attorney general. The Communist Control Act of 1954 provides that membership in the Communist Party, with knowledge of the party's purpose, subjects one "to all the provisions and penalties of the Internal Security Act of 1950, as amended, as a member of a 'Communist-action' organization." Just what this means is a matter of doubt. As a result of this measure, there is now legislation aimed at three types of communist organizations: communist action, communist front, and communist infiltrated. A labor union which is determined to be any of these three types is ineligible to act as an employee's bargaining representative under the National Labor Relations Act. When President Eisenhower signed this measure he issued a statement in which he said: ". . . I am proud that in this battle against the subversive elements in this country we have been able to preserve the rights of the accused in accordance with our traditions and the Bill of Rights."

The Supreme Court sustained the validity of section 9(h) of the Taft-Hartley Act in *American Communications Assn.* v. *Douds,* and of the advocacy provisions of the Smith Act in *Dennis* v. *United States.* The constitutionality of the Subversive Activities Control Act of 1950 was argued before it in *Communist Party* v. *Subversive Activities Control Board,* but the Court did not reach the issue. Instead it sent the case back to the Subversive Activities Control Board for reconsideration because of the alleged false testimony of three government witnesses: Harvey Matusow, Paul Crouch, and Manning Johnson.

CHAPTER VI

JUSTICE HOLMES'S TEST

Intent, Attempt, Solicitation and Conspiracy

The second development which made for the emergence and extension of federal power over speech, and helped as well to prepare the way for the Supreme Court's affirmation of the constitutionality of the advocacy provisions of the Smith Act in the *Dennis* case was Justice Holmes's extension in his "clear and present danger" test of the approach in the law of attempts and of conspiracy to the field of speech. This was what Chief Justice Vinson in the *Dennis* case described as Justice Holmes's "classic dictum" in the *Schenck* case. By this test Justice Holmes made an exception to the First Amendment for words which "are used in such circumstances and are of such a nature as to create a clear and present danger that they will bring about the substantive evils that Congress had the right to prevent." This test has been commended, as one "of great value," by Professor Chafee, and condemned as "both unintelligible in practice and baseless in theory," by Alexander Meiklejohn. A little earlier Meiklejohn described it "as a peculiarly inept and unsuccessful attempt to formulate an exception to the principle of freedom of speech." Recently Judge Learned Hand, who in the *Dennis* case turned Justice Holmes's test into its converse, questioned its survival. In 1958 in the last of his three Holmes Lectures at the Harvard Law School he said: "I doubt that the doctrine will persist, and I cannot help thinking that for once Homer nodded."

The law of attempts, although now largely governed by statute, began as an exercise by courts of a common law power to punish dangerous conduct not proscribed by statute. On a federal level there is not supposed to be any such power. As Justice Douglas put it for the Court in *Jerome* v. *United States*: "* * * There is no common law offense against the United States." * * *. Hence an attempt to commit a federal crime would not itself be criminal federally unless a federal statute made it so.

As for the common law power, although one can find early instances

81

of its exercise, the law of attempts received its formulation and development under the guiding hand of Lord Mansfield. A leading case is *Rex v. Scofield*. There the defendant was charged with having put a lighted candle among matches and small pieces of wood under the stairway of a house with the intent to burn the house. But there was neither allegation nor proof that the house was burned. The defendant's counsel argued that an attempt to commit a misdemeanor was not an indictable offense. Lord Mansfield and Justice Bullard answered: "It makes a great difference, whether an act was done; as in this case putting fire to a candle in the midst of combustible matter (which was the only act necessary to commit a misdemeanor), and where no act at all is done. The *intent* may make an act, innocent in itself, criminal; nor is the *completion* of an act, criminal in itself, necessary to constitute criminality. Is it no offence to set fire to a train of gunpowder with intent to burn a house, because by accident, or the interposition of another the mischief is prevented?"

It was the law of attempts which Justice Holmes discussed as a judge of the Supreme Judicial Court of Massachusetts in *Commonwealth v. Kennedy*, and as chief justice of that court in *Commonwealth v. Peaslee*, before going to the federal Supreme Court. The *Kennedy* case involved an attempt to kill by placing poison in the victim's cup. In sustaining a conviction Justice Holmes writing for the court said:

. . . As the aim of the law is not to punish sins, but is to prevent certain external results, the act done must come pretty near to accomplishing that result before the law will notice it. . . . Every question of proximity must be determined by its own circumstances, and analogy is too imperfect to give much help. Any unlawful application of poison is an evil which threatens death, according to common apprehension, and the gravity of the crime, the uncertainty of the result, and the seriousness of the apprehension, coupled with the great harm likely to result from poison even if not enough to kill, would warrant holding the liability for an attempt to begin at a point more remote from the possibility of accomplishing what is expected and might be the case with lighter crimes. . . .

In the *Peaslee* case the indictment charged simply that the defendant had put combustible material in a building with intent to burn it. The court held the indictment insufficient. In the course of the court's opinion Chief Justice Holmes pointed out that in order to constitute an indictable attempt, more than preparation was necessary. The difference between them, however, was only one of degree. He said:

. . . [P]reparation is not an attempt. But some preparations may amount to an attempt. It is a question of degree. If the preparation comes very near to the accomplishment of the act, the intent to complete it renders the crime so probable that the act will be a misdemeanor although there is still a *locus penitentiae* in the need of a further execution of the will to complete the crime. As was observed in a recent case, the degree of proximity held sufficient may vary with circumstances, including among other things the apprehension which the particular crime is calculated to excite. . . .

A recent illustrative federal case is *United States* v. *Coplon*. Judith Coplon was convicted of an attempt to deliver defense information to a Russian confederate, Gubitchev. She had the material in her purse but before she could hand it over to him they were arrested. The Court of Appeals for the Second Circuit, although reversing the conviction, nevertheless held that the facts were sufficient to constitute an attempt. Chief Judge Learned Hand wrote for the court: "There can be no doubt in the case at bar that 'preparation' had become 'attempt.' "

Justice Holmes also dealt with the law of attempts in his *The Common Law*:

Some acts may be attempts or misdemeanors which could not have effected the crime unless followed by other acts on the part of the wrongdoer. For instance, lighting a match with intent to set fire to a haystack has been held to amount to a criminal attempt to burn it, although the defendant blew out the match on seeing that he was watched. So the purchase of dies for making counterfeit coin is a misdemeanor, although of course the coin would not be counterfeited unless the dies were used. . . .

It will be readily seen that there are limits to this kind of liability. The law does not punish every act which is done with the intent to bring about a crime. If a man starts from Boston to Cambridge for the purpose of committing a murder when he gets there, but is stopped by the draw and goes home, he is no more punishable than if he had sat in his chair and resolved to shoot somebody, but on second thoughts had given up the notion. . . . We have seen what amounts to an attempt to burn a haystack; but it was said in the same case, that, if the defendant had gone no further than to buy a box of matches for the purpose, he would not have been liable.

Eminent judges have been puzzled where to draw the line, or even to state the principle on which it should be drawn, between the two sets of cases. But the principle is believed to be similar to that on which all other lines are drawn by the law. Public policy, that is to say, legislative considerations, are at the bottom of the matter; the considerations being, in this case, the nearness of the danger, the greatness of the harm, and the degree of apprehension felt. When a man buys matches to fire a haystack, or starts on a journey meaning to murder at the end of it, there is still a considerable chance that he will change his mind before he comes to the point. But when he has struck the match, or cocked and aimed the pistol, there is very little chance that he will not persist to the end, and the danger becomes so great that the law steps in. With an object which could not be used innocently, the point of intervention might be put further back, as in the case of the purchase of a die for coining.

The degree of apprehension may affect the decision, as well as the degree of probability that the crime will be accomplished. . . .

In judging whether conduct is sufficiently dangerous to constitute a criminal attempt, intent, as Lord Mansfield and Justice Holmes made plain, is a relevant factor. In *Swift & Co.* v. *United States*, a Sherman Anti-Trust Act case, Justice Holmes as a member of the United States Supreme Court in writing the Court's opinion further explained:

. . . The statute gives this proceeding against combinations in restraint of commerce among the States and against attempts to monopolize the same. Intent is almost essential to such a combination and is essential to such an attempt. Where acts are not sufficient in themselves to produce a result which the law seeks to prevent—for instance, the monopoly—but require further acts in addition to the mere forces of nature to bring that result to pass, an intent to bring it to pass is necessary in order to produce a dangerous probability that it will happen. *Commonwealth* v. *Peaslee.* . . . But when that intent and the consequent dangerous probability exist, this statute, like many others and like the common law in some cases, directs itself against that dangerous probability as well as against the completed result. . . .

Years earlier in *The Common Law* he wrote:

There is another class of cases in which intent plays an important part, for quite different reasons from those which have been offered to account for the laws of malicious mischief. The most obvious example of this class are criminal attempts. Attempt and intent, of course, are two distinct things. Intent to commit a crime is not itself criminal. There is no law against a man's intending to commit a murder the day after tomorrow. The law only deals with conduct. An attempt is an overt act. . . .

. . . The importance of the intent is not to show that the act was wicked, but to show that it was likely to be followed by hurtful consequence.

For example, the conduct of one who on a hunting trip shoots at a bear and accidentally hits a companion is less dangerous than that of one who with intent to kill shoots at a person and misses; for on an overall basis the conduct of those who act with an intent to kill another will result in many more homicides than the conduct of those who have no such intent.

The crime of solicitation rests on the same basis and began in the same way as that of attempt. A little over a decade and a half after the *Scofield* case came *Rex* v. *Higgins*. There the defendant was indicted for soliciting the servant of another to steal his master's goods but the indictment contained no charge that the servant either agreed to, or did, steal the goods. The Court of King's Bench, relying heavily upon the *Scofield* case, affirmed a judgment of conviction. Justice Lawrence in the course of his opinion said:

. . . [A]ll offences of a public nature, that is, all such acts or attempts as tend to the prejudice of the community, are indictable. Then the question is, whether an attempt to get another to steal is not prejudicial to the community? Of which there can be no doubt. The whole argument for the defendant turns upon a fallacy in assuming that no act is charged to have been done by him; for a solicitation is an act. . . .

As in the law of attempts, again there was a case before the Supreme Judicial Court of Massachusetts while Justice Holmes was a member of that court, *Commonwealth* v. *Flagg*. The indictment charged that the defendant offered ten dollars to another to burn a certain barn. This was held sufficient. Chief Justice Morton wrote for the court: "It is an indictable offence at common law for one to counsel and solicit another to commit a felony or other aggravated offence, although the solicitation is of no effect, and the crime counselled is not in fact committed. . . ."

Legal writers and courts have differed as to whether a solicitation should be treated as a distinct crime from an attempt. Professor Francis B. Sayre wrote:

. . . Although in some jurisdictions solicitations are treated as indictable attempts, either by virtue of judicial decisions failing to distinguish them, or statutory provisions, the great weight of authority is otherwise. Analytically the two crimes are distinct. Each has its own peculiar features; clearly not every indictable solicitation can be considered as an indictable attempt. The one who attempts to commit a felony becomes a principal if the attempt succeeds, and he who solicits becomes an accessory before the fact. An indictable solicitation may not come close enough to the crime to constitute an indictable attempt. For instance, where A urges B to murder C in another town, and B is persuaded to do so but, because of A's conversation having been overheard, is arrested when entering a store to purchase a revolver, B's acts have not gone beyond the stage of mere preparation, and neither A nor B should be convicted for an attempt. A should, nevertheless, be liable for the crime of solicitation, and both A and B for the crime of conspiracy. In spite of their many similarities, therefore, these two crimes should not be confused.

On the other hand Thurman W. Arnold argued:

Solicitation involves the same considerations as attempts. The conduct simply consists of hiring or inducing someone to act instead of acting oneself. Courts should assume the same kind of power to extend the limits of a given rule to cover persuasion and inducements, as well as conduct, where the policy of the particular rule seems to require it. There is no object in treating it differently from attempt. This distinction between solicitation and attempt leads to an occasional absurd result, but usually it is a harmless device for relieving a defendant of liability under an attempt indictment when his conduct seems not sufficiently serious to merit court action.

So far as treating a solicitation as an attempt is concerned, it would seem that Arnold has the better of the argument. In the supposititious case which Professor Sayre puts there is no reason why A, if deemed to be guilty of an offense in addition to that of conspiracy, should not be held liable for the crime of attempt.

However, if A solicits B to commit an offense and B refuses, A should no more be held guilty of an attempt than if he had gone to a store to buy a revolver in order to murder somebody or a box of matches in order to burn a building and the storekeeper refused to sell to him. A fortiori should this result apply to the general advocacy of illegal action? As Francis Wharton wisely reasoned in his *Criminal Law*:

For we would be forced to admit, if we hold that solicitations to criminality are generally indictable, that the propagandists, even in conversation, of agrarian or communistic theories are liable to criminal prosecutions; and hence the necessary freedom of speech and of the press would be greatly infringed. It would be hard, also, we must agree, if we maintain such general responsibility, to defend, in prosecutions for soliciting crime, the publishers of Byron's *Don Juan*, of Rousseau's *Emile*, or of Goethe's *Elective Affinities*. Lord Chesterfield in his letters to his son, directly advises the latter to form illicit connections with married women; Lord Chesterfield, on the reasoning here contested, would be indictable for solicitation to adultery. Undoubtedly, when such solicitations are so publicly and indecently made as to produce public scandal, they are indictable as nuisances or as libels. But to make bare solicitations or allurements indictable as attempts, not only unduly and perilously extends the scope of penal adjudication, but forces on the courts psychological questions which they are incompetent to decide, and a branch of business which would make them despots of every intellect in the land.

From the standpoint of arresting probably dangerous conduct the crime of conspiracy involves the same considerations as that of attempt, but, unlike that of attempt, it did not begin as a general offense at common law. Rather it originated in a series of statutes dating from the time of Edward I enacted to remedy specific abuses: at first only combinations to procure false indictments, bring false appeals, or maintain vexatious suits constituted criminal conspiracies.

Whereas the crime of solicitation should be treated as part of that of attempt the crime of conspiracy should not be so treated; for the very fact that persons have entered into a conspiracy to do a certain act increases the chances that the act will be done. As Chief Justice Vinson wrote in the *Dennis* case, "It is the existence of the conspiracy which creates the danger." Thus the crime consists in the conspiracy. As Judge Justin Miller stated in his *Handbook of Criminal Law*, "The reason for finding criminal liability in case of a combination to effect an unlawful end or to use unlawful means, where none would exist, even though the act contemplated were actually committed by an individual, is that a combination of persons to commit a wrong, either as an end or as a means to an end, is so much more dangerous, because of its increased power to do wrong, because it is more difficult to guard against and prevent the evil designs of a group of persons than of a single person, and because of the terror which fear of such a combination tends to create in the minds of people."

An overt act might or might not be required. It was not at common law. The general federal conspiracy statute, first enacted in 1867, calls for an overt act; but the act making it a crime to conspire to overthrow the government of the United States by force, first enacted during the Civil War, and the Sherman Anti-Trust Act do not. Neither did the Smith Act. Even if an overt act is necessary, it need not be dangerous enough to constitute an attempt; indeed, in and of itself it need not be dangerous at all, for the danger lies in the act of conspiring. As Justice Holmes pointed out in his dissenting opinion in *Hyde* v. *United States:*

. . . conspiracy is not an attempt. . . . An attempt, in the strictest sense, is an act expected to bring about a substantive wrong by the forces of nature. With it is classed the kindred offence where the act and the natural conditions present or supposed to be present are not enough to do the harm without a further act, but where it is so near to the result that if coupled with an intent to produce that result, the danger is very great. *Swift & Co.* v. *United States.* . . . But combination, intention, and overt act may all be present without amounting to a criminal attempt—as if all that were done should be an agreement to murder a man fifty miles away and the purchase of a pistol for the purpose. There must be dangerous proximity to success. But when that exists the overt act is the essence of the offence [of attempt]. On the other hand, the essence of the conspiracy is being combined for an unlawful purpose; and if an overt act is required, it does not matter how remote the act may be from accomplishing the purpose, if done to effect it; that is, I suppose, in furtherance of it in any degree. . . .

Or as Justice Harlan wrote in the Court's opinion in the *Yates*, *Schneiderman* and *Richmond* cases concerning the overt act: "Nor, indeed, need such an act, taken by itself, even be criminal in character. *Braverman* v. *United States* * * *. The function of the overt act in a conspiracy prosecution is simply to manifest 'that the conspiracy is at work,' *Carlson* v. *United States*, . . ."

If one applies the law of attempt and conspiracy, with the suggested approach of treating solicitation as an attempt, to the field of speech and of the press one should arrive at the conclusion that the exhortation or incitement of another to do an illegal act should not, without more, amount to a crime. The same result should follow if there is no more than the advocacy by an individual of the overthrow of the government by force and violence. The question becomes more difficult of resolution if there is a conspiracy to advocate such overthrow, for such conduct is more dangerous than the advocacy of violence by a lone individual. Thus Justice Jackson in his concurring opinion in the *Dennis* case placed his approval of the constitutionality of the advocacy provisions of the Smith Act on the strongest possible ground, that of conspiracy. Nevertheless, even a conspiracy to advocate the violent overthrow of the government should not be regarded as sufficiently dangerous to suffer proscription. Moreover to treat such conduct as criminal is not an effective remedy for it. To this point too, Justice Jackson addressed himself in his concurring opinion in the *Dennis* case. In his concluding paragraph he wrote: "While I think there was power in Congress to enact this statute and that, as applied in this case, it cannot be held unconstitutional, I add that I have little faith in the long-range effectiveness of this conviction to stop the rise of the Communist movement. Communism will not go to jail with these Communists. No decision by this Court can forestall revolution whenever the existing government fails to command the respect and loyalty of the people and sufficient distress and discontent is allowed to grow up among the masses. Many failures by fallen governments attest that no government can long prevent revolution by outlawry. . . ."

In any event a conspiracy to advocate violence as well as the individual advocacy of violence, without more, should be held to be within the protection of the First Amendment. However, the law started on another course.

"A Clear and Present Danger"

The points of departure for that other course were *Fox* v. *Washington* and *Goldman* v. *United States*. The *Fox* case involved a statute of the state of Washington which made the advocacy of the commission of any crime an offense. The printed matter in question was an article entitled "The Nude and the Prudes." Apparently some nudists had been arrested and convicted for indecent exposure. The article predicted and encouraged the boycott of those who had been responsible for this, and concluded: "The boycott will be pushed until these invaders will come to see the brutal mistake of their action and so inform the people." The Supreme Court sustained a conviction under the state statute for these utterances. Justice Holmes delivered the Court's opinion. He took the article in question to advocate a breach of the state laws against indecent exposure. Without referring to *Commonwealth* v. *Flagg* he wrote concerning the Washington statute: ". . . It lays hold of encouragements that, apart from statute, if directed to a particular person's conduct, generally would make him who uttered them guilty of a misdemeanor if not an accomplice or a principal in the crime encouraged, and deals with the publication of them to a wider and less selected audience. Laws of this description are not unfamiliar. . . ."

However, apart from the constitutional question whether the states under the Fourteenth Amendment's requirement that no state shall "deprive any person of life, liberty, or property, without due process of law" have a greater power over utterances than the federal government under the First Amendment's injunction that "Congress shall make no law," it would seem clear that as a matter of good government the utterances in question should not have been punished.

In the *Goldman* case Emma Goldman and Alexander Berkman for their utterances were convicted of a conspiracy to induce resistance to the Selective Draft Law of 1917. The Supreme Court sustained their conviction. Chief Justice White wrote for the Court: ". . . an unlawful conspiracy under §37 of the Criminal Code to bring about an illegal act and the doing of overt acts in furtherance of such conspiracy is in and of itself inherently and substantially a crime punishable as such irrespective of whether the result of the conspiracy has been to accomplish its illegal end. *United States* v. *Rabinowich* . . . and the authorities there cited."

The stage was now set for the *Schenck, Frohwerk* and *Debs* cases, the first cases which the Court decided under the Espionage Act of 1917. Eugene V. Debs and the defendants in the *Schenck* case were socialists. The defendants in the *Frohwerk* case were German sympathizers who put out a German language newspaper, the *Missouri Staats Zeitung*. Debs was indicted under the 1917 act, as amended in 1918, for obstructing and attempting to obstruct the draft by making a speech in which he advocated socialism and advanced the Marxist thesis that capitalism caused wars. The defendants in the other two cases were indicted, among other things, for conspiring to obstruct the draft; in the *Schenck* case by circulating a socialist leaflet, and in the *Frohwerk* case by distributing a newspaper. In the *Schenck* case there was also evidence that the defendants mailed their leaflet to draftees. The Court unanimously affirmed judgments of conviction in all three cases. In each instance Justice Holmes delivered the Court's opinion.

It was in the *Schenck* case that he laid down his clear and present danger test:

. . . The question in every case is whether the words are used in such circumstances and are of such a nature as to create a clear and present danger that they will bring about the substantive evils that Congress has a right to prevent. It is a question of proximity and degree. . . . The Statute of 1917, in §4 punishes conspiracies to obstruct as well as actual obstruction. If the act (speaking, or circulating a paper), its tendency and the intent with which it is done are the same, we perceive no ground for saying that success alone warrants making the act a crime. *Goldman* v. *United States.* . . .

In the *Frohwerk* case he added:

. . . We venture to believe that neither Hamilton nor Madison, nor any other competent person then or later, ever supposed that to make criminal the counselling of a murder within the jurisdiction of Congress would be an unconstitutional interference with free speech. . . .
It is said that the first count is bad because it does not allege the means by which the conspiracy was to be carried out. But a conspiracy to obstruct recruiting would be criminal even if no means were agreed upon specifically by which to accomplish the intent. It is enough if the parties agreed to set to work for that common purpose. That purpose could be accomplished or aided by persuasion as well as by false statements. . . . The conspiracy is the crime, and that is one, however diverse its objects. . . .

However, it is submitted that in none of these cases, nor in the *Fox* and *Goldman* cases, was sufficient consideration given, from a legislative standpoint, to the lack of danger in the proscribed conduct, and, from a judicial standpoint, in view of the First Amendment, to the lack, apart from speech, of criminal conduct. Neither legislatively nor judicially was there an adequate distinction between the word and the criminal deed. In the *Fox* and *Goldman* cases the First Amendment was not discussed at all. In the other three cases it was considered in too cursory a fashion. Justice Holmes bears out this observation in a comment he made about the *Debs* case in a letter to Sir Frederick Pollock: ". . . There was a lot of jaw about free speech, which I dealt with somewhat summarily in an earlier case—*Schenck* v. *U.S.* . . . also *Frohwerk* v. *U.S.* . . . As it happens I should go farther probably than the majority in favor of it, and I daresay it was partly on that account that the C.J. assigned the case to me."

Chief Justice Vinson was thus correct when in his opinion in the *Dennis* case he referred, in connection with the *Schenck* case, to "the summary treatment accorded an argument based upon an individual's claim that the First Amendment protected certain utterances." He was also right in his appraisal of what he called "the Holmes-Brandeis rationale," which became the Court's approach. After discussing *Gitlow v. New York*, he stated: "Justices Holmes and Brandeis, then, made no distinction between a federal statute which made certain acts unlawful, the evidence to support the conviction being speech, and a statute which made speech itself the crime. This approach was emphasized in *Whitney v. People of State of California*. . . ."

But Debs should not have gone to prison for making what Chief Justice Vinson described in the *Dennis* case as "one speech attacking United States' participation in the war"; nor the defendants in the *Frohwerk* case for what Chief Justice Vinson in the same case called the "publication of twelve newspaper articles attacking the war." The *Schenck* case is somewhat more difficult of resolution, for the defendants mailed their leaflets to draftees; but they, too, should have been permitted to go their way unmolested.

A lone individual should be free to advocate anything, even a violation of the law. It is too difficult to draw a distinction between advocacy of a change in the law and incitement to a violation of it. Besides, such advocacy is of little consequence in a sound society; its proscription, at least by Congress, violates the First Amendment; and its suppression is not an effective countermeasure. A conspiracy to advocate a violation of the law may involve more danger than such advocacy by an unattached individual, but the same considerations apply and the same result should follow.

One closer case remains, a conspiracy to cause a violation of the law, to be carried out by advocacy: this was the *Schenck* case. As Justice Holmes pointed out in the *Frohwerk* case, the conspiracy was the crime. However, again and especially at this juncture, a distinction should have been drawn between speech and other conduct. It should have made a determining difference in the *Schenck* case whether the conspiracy to obstruct the draft was to be carried out by advocacy, or by some physical means, such as, let us say, the abduction of a draftee. It is only in the latter instance that the conspiracy should have been punishable.

It was in the *Schenck* case that Justice Holmes made his famous statement about shouting fire in a crowded theatre. What he actually said was: "The most stringent protection of free speech would not protect a man in falsely shouting fire in a theatre and causing a panic." But this is not advocacy. Shouting fire under such circumstances is as much an act as firing a gun or lighting a fire. It is the same as if by a shout one intentionally detonated an infernal machine. This is criminal conduct; not speech.

A conspiracy to cause a violation of the law by means of advocacy was the problem which concerned the writer the most when he took charge of the so-called sedition case of World War II, known on the third indictment as *United States* v. *McWilliams*. At the outset the writer read Chafee's *Free Speech in the United States*, (1941), just as he had read Chafee's *Freedom of Speech*, in his law school days; this was probably the book which stimulated him the most during his entire academic period.

In order to make sure that Americans had their full measure of freedom of speech, the writer passed by the advocacy provisions of the Smith Act—he had criticized them at a meeting of the states' attorneys general at the Department of Justice in 1940, the year the Smith Act was adopted, as appearing to him to be in violation of the First Amendment. (For this, one of the attorneys general suggested that the writer must be a communist or its equivalent.) Instead he selected those provisions which made it a crime to conspire to cause insubordination among members of our armed forces and to distribute written or printed matter counseling such insubordination—some of the literature of the defendants had turned up at army posts. But he still had his misgivings, and accordingly narrowed the application of even those provisions by seeking an indictment only against those individuals who additionally had some form of Nazi connections such as the Nazi party, the Nazi propaganda ministry, the Nazi foreign office, various Nazi organizations in touch with deviant groups in other countries, the German Library of Information, the German embassy in Washington, D.C., various German consulates in this country, the German-American Bund, and yet others. The third indictment thus alleged that the defendants conspired "with each other and with officials of the Government of the German Reich and leaders and members of the said Nazi Party."

During the midst of the trial the Supreme Court decided *Hartzel* v. *United States*, reversing a conviction against an individual whose literature was similar to that of the defendants in the sedition case. The ground of the decision was the insufficiency of the evidence to show intent. The defendants in the sedition case promptly made the decision the basis of a new motion to dismiss. But Justice Murphy in the Court's opinion in the *Hartzel* case had this sentence, referring to the defendant: "There was no evidence of his having been associated in any way with any foreign or subversive organization." The writer used it as the basis for an argument that he had anticipated the Court's decision, and that the *Hartzel* case was accordingly distinguishable. The trial judge, Edward C. Eicher, agreed.

However, several months later Judge Eicher died, and the sedition case ended in a mistrial. The following year the Supreme Court in *Keegan* v. *United States* reversed the conviction of members of the German-American Bund on a charge of conspiracy to counsel evasion of military service. At the end of February 1946 the writer made use of both the *Hartzel* and *Keegan* cases to recommend that the Department of Justice should nol-pros all three sedition indictments. The department did not accept his recommendation. A few weeks later the writer went to Germany at the request of Attorney General, now Justice, Tom C. Clark, to look for additional evidence. He found some, but in September 1946 he nevertheless repeated his recommendation that the three sedition prosecutions be nol-prossed. Again the department failed to follow his recommendation. However, various of the defendants made motions to dismiss and these were granted. As a result of his experiences in the sedition case and his reflections on the Frist Amendment since then, the writer tends to the conclusion that even a conspiracy to cause a violation of the law, if the means to be employed consist of advocacy, should go unpunished. Legislatively the proscription of such a conspiracy is both unwise and ineffective; and constitutionally, at least so far as the Congress is concerned, it violates the First Amendment. From a federal standpoint, only those conspiracies should be punished where the defendants intend to effectuate them either with acts or with acts as well as advocacy.

As this analysis premonishes on hindsight, Justice Holmes's clear and present danger test was to bring unwelcome results to him and Justice Brandeis. It soon did. Before the year in which it was enunciated was out, come *Abrams* v. *United States*, where Justice Holmes in the course of his eloquent dissenting opinion, in which Justice Brandeis concurred, stated: "In this case sentences of twenty years imprisonment have been imposed for the publishing of two leaflets that I believe the defendants had as much right to publish as the government has to publish the Constitution of the United States now vainly invoked by them." The two leaflets opposed sending American troops to Vladivostok and Murmansk in the summer of 1918.

In the same opinion, however, Justice Holmes also wrote:

94 THETHE FIRST AND THE FIFTH

I never have seen any reason to doubt that the questions of law that alone were before this court in the cases of *Schenck, Frohwerk* and *Debs* . . . , were rightly decided. I do not doubt for a moment that by the same reasoning that would justify punishing persuasion to murder, the United States constitutionally may punish speech that produces or is intended to produce a clear and imminent danger that it will bring about forthwith certain substantive evils that the United States constitutionally may seek to prevent. The power undoubtedly is greater in time of war than in time of peace because war opens dangers that do not exist at other times.

He further made plain that what he had done in his clear and present danger test had been to apply to the field of advocacy the approach of the law of attempts. He additionally said in the *Abrams* case: ". . . Now nobody can suppose that the surreptitious publishing of a silly leaflet by an unknown man, without more, would present any immediate danger that its opinions would hinder the success of the government arms or have any appreciable tendency to do so. Publishing those opinions for the very purpose of obstructing however, might indicate a greater danger and at any rate would have the quality of an attempt. . . ."

But the results in the *Abrams* and other advocacy cases in which he and Justice Brandeis dissented stemmed from the application of the approach in the law of attempt and of conspiracy to the field of speech. Once it is conceded that advocacy, without more, is not always protected by the First Amendment, then in times of stress neither the restrictive scope of a statute nor the clear and present danger test will be of great value in limiting suppression of speech. Concerning the prosecutions arising during World War I, Professor Chafee in discussing *Masses Publishing Co.* v. *Patten* had to conclude:

As a result of this and similar decisions, the district judges ignored entirely the first element of criminal attempt and solicitation, that the effort, though unsuccessful, must approach dangerously near success. . . . A few judges, notably Amidon of North Dakota, swam against the tide, but of most Espionage Act decisions what Jefferson and Stephen and Schofield said about the prosecutions under George III and the Sedition Act of 1798 can be said once more, that men were punished without overt acts, with only a presumed intention to cause overt acts, merely for the utterance of words which judge and jury thought to have a tendency to injure the state. Judge Rogers was right in saying that the words of the Espionage Act of 1917 bear slight resemblance to the Sedition Law of 1798, but the judicial construction is much the same, except that under the Sedition Law truth was a defense.

On truth as a defense in the prosecutions under this country's first sedition act James M. Smith, in *Freedom's Fetters*, wrote:

The interpretation which the courts put on the truth provision made it worse than useless as an aid to the defendant. Under the rulings handed down by the judges of the Supreme Court on circuit, this supposed safeguard actually reversed the normal criminal law presumption of innocence. Instead of the government's having to prove that the words of the accused were false, scandalous, and malicious, the defendant had to prove that they were true. As Judge Samuel Chase put it, the accused had to prove all of his statements "to the marrow. If he asserts three things and proves but two," the jurist said, "he fails in his defense, for he must prove the whole of his assertions to be true." This is a clear illustration of the doctrine of presumptive guilt; in practice, the courts presumed the defendant guilty until he proved himself innocent.

Moreover, the accused was required not only to prove the truth of every word in every statement but, in one instance, to prove an entire count in an indictment by the same witness. Even though the statement contained more than one point, the defendant could not introduce different witnesses to prove different points. According to Judge Chase, this practice would have been irregular and subversive of every principle of law.

The court also refused to distinguish between a false statement of facts and erroneous opinions. Indeed, the expression of any opinion on future events could be condemned as false under the interpretation given section three of the law. Although the prosecutor could no more prove the falsity of a prediction than the defendant could prove its truth, the statement was considered false because the defendant had failed to carry the burden of proof.

The exception to the First Amendment which Justice Holmes sanctioned in his clear and present danger test was to help produce still other unwanted results to him and especially to Justice Brandeis. At the term following the one at which the opinion in the *Abrams* case came down, the Court ruled in *Milwaukee·Pub. Co.* v. *Burleson* not only that the provisions of the Espionage Act of 1917 declaring certain matter to be nonmailable were constitutional but also that the postmaster general had the power to deny the use of second-class mail to a newspaper publisher who in the opinion of the postmaster general had violated the act's provisions. Both justices dissented.

In addition, the Court sustained convictions under state statutes restricting utterances: under a Minnesota sedition act in *Gilbert* v. *Minnesota*; New York's criminal anarchy act in *Gitlow* v. *New York*; and California's criminal syndicalism act in *Whitney* v. *California*. Justice Brandeis dissented in the *Gilbert* case and both he and Justice Holmes in the *Gitlow* case. However, in the latter case Justice Holmes concluded his dissenting opinion, in which Justice Brandeis joined, with this paragraph:

If the publication of this document had been laid as an attempt to induce an uprising against government at once and not at some indefinite time in the future it would have presented a different question. The object would have been one with which the law might deal, subject to the doubt whether there was any danger that the publication could produce any result, or in other words, whether it was not futile and too remote from possible consequences. But the indictment alleges the publication and nothing more.

Concerning this dissent Justice Holmes wrote Pollock: "My last performance during the term, on the last day, was a dissent (in which Brandeis joined) in favor of the rights of an anarchist (so-called) to talk drool in favor of the proletarian dictatorship." Actually Gitlow was a Communist.

The writer is aware that what he is about to say will be regarded by many as lese majesty, but he does wish to suggest that Justice Holmes's approach to freedom of utterance, at least in some measure, at times had a light quality to it. His use in his letters to Pollock of the words "jaw" and "drool" in his references to the *Debs* and *Gitlow* cases attests to this. Further along the same road came the Supreme Court's decision in the *Dennis* case sustaining the validity of the advocacy provisions of the Smith Act.

CHAPTER VII

SEDITION AND OBSCENITY

Dennis v. United States

The approach in the *Fox, Goldman, Schenck, Frohwerk* and *Debs* cases laid the basis for the Court's decision in the *Dennis* case, in which it sustained the validity of the advocacy provisions of this country's third sedition law, the Smith Act. Chief Justice Vinson, relying on the phrasing of Chief Judge Learned Hand in the court's opinion below, modified the clear and present danger test into its converse: "Chief Judge Learned Hand, writing for the majority below, interpreted the phrase as follows: 'In each case [courts] must ask whether the gravity of the "evil," discounted by its improbability, justifies such invasion of free speech as is necessary to avoid the danger.' . . . We adopt this statement of the rule."

Dennis Case Dilemma

Besides resulting in a certain measure of suppression of speech which it is submitted the First Amendment protects, the clear and present danger test as applied in the *Dennis* case involves the Court in this dilemma: either the Court has increased its legislative functions; or it has transferred to the courts the determination of a question of fact which should have been left with the jury. It was the first horn of this dilemma which led Justice Jackson in his concurring opinion in the *Dennis* case to refuse to apply the clear and present danger test in reaching his conclusion as to the validity of the advocacy provisions of the Smith Act.

Let us take these provisions. The Court sustained them because of the threats with which international communism confronts us. As Chief Justice Vinson explained in his opinion in the Dennis case, "The situation with which Justices Holmes and Brandeis were concerned in Gitlow was a comparatively isolated event, bearing little relation in their minds to any substantial threat to the safety of the community. . . . They were not confronted with any situation comparable to the instant one—the development of an apparatus designed and dedicated to the overthrow of the Government, in the context of world crisis after crisis." But suppose the communist danger lessens. Suppose communism changes industrially into various separate and fairly autonomous corporate entities and that in communist countries groups of engineers, scientists, writers, artists, professional people and industrial managers arise who are successful in demanding from the governing structures greater freedom for themselves. What happens if the government now obtains a conviction on a conspiracy indictment under the advocacy provisions of the Smith Act against the leaders of American communism? What happens to such a conviction once international communism no longer exists as a threatening force in the world?

After the *Dennis* decision the courts in Smith Act prosecutions fell into the practice of examining the international situation. They concluded that bad as it was when the prosecution began in the *Dennis* case, it had not lessened: if anything, it had become worse. The Court of Appeals for the Second Circuit in *United States* v. *Flynn*, the second Foley Square Smith Act conspiracy prosecution, stated: ". . . if the danger was clear and present in 1948, it can hardly be thought to have been less in 1951, when the Korean conflict was raging and our relations with the communist world had moved from cold to hot war." The Court of Appeals for the Third Circuit in *United States* v. *Mesarosh* and for the Sixth Circuit in *Wellman* v. *United States* quoted this language with approval. The Court of Appeals for the Seventh Circuit in *United States* v. *Lightfoot* cited it similarly. In the *Lightfoot* case the defendant pointed to the end of the Korean war. Also, in the words of the court, "defendant's counsel seemed to be deeply impressed by the Spirit of Geneva, and he professed to believe that the Geneva Conference had resulted in a complete relaxation of International tensions." The court responded: "The period covered by the indictment is, of course, the critical period for us to consider. However, in any case, whether a clear and present danger existed cannot depend on whether the faces of the Communist Leaders in Russia are suffused with smiles. We need only make passing mention of the fact that at the time of the writing of this opinion, the smiles have been replaced with scowls, and the sugary words of such leaders have been supplanted by words of vituperative condemnation."

Suppose, however, that internationl communism loses its momentum and power, and the Court so finds. Will the Court then hold that the advocacy provisions of the Smith Act cannot constitutionally be applied on the ground that there is no longer a clear and present danger that advocacy of the overthrow of the government by force and violence will bring about this result? But surely that will be legislating just as much as if Congress were to pass an act repealing the advocacy provisions of the Smith Act. It was this difficulty which Justice Jackson had in mind when he wrote in his concurring opinion:

> If we must decide that this Act and its application are constitutional only if we are convinced that petitioner's conduct creates a "clear and present danger" of violent overthrow, we must appraise imponderables, including international and national phenomena which baffle the best informed foreign offices and our most experienced politicians. We would have to foresee and predict the effectiveness of Communist propaganda, opportunities for infiltration, whether, and when, a time will come that they consider propitious for action, and whether and how fast our existing government will deteriorate. And we would have to speculate as to whether an approaching Communist coup would not be anticipated by a nationalistic fascist movement. No doctrine can be sound whose application requires us to make a prophecy of that sort in the guise of a legal decision. The judicial process simply is not adequate to a trial of such farflung issues. The answers given would reflect our own political predilections and nothing more.
>
> The authors of the clear and present danger test never applied it to a case like this, nor would I. . . .

The other horn of the dilemma in the clear and present danger test as applied in the *Dennis* case is the removal from the jury of the determination of an issue of fact which that body properly should decide. In the ordinary case the jury determines whether there has been a criminal attempt or conspiracy. At first when the approach of the law of attempt and conspiracy was applied to the field of speech, this seemed to be the law there too. Justice Brandeis in his concurring and dissenting opinion in *Schaefer* v. *United States,* in which Justice Holmes joined, after explaining that the newly announced clear and present danger test was a rule of reason which involved a question of degree, continued: ". . . And because it is a question of degree the field in which the jury may exercise its judgment is, necessarily, a wide one. But its field is not unlimited. The trial provided for is one by judge *and* jury; and the judge may not abdicate his function. If the words were of such a nature and were used under such circumstances that men, judging in calmness, could not reasonably say that they created a clear and present danger that they would bring about the evil which Congress sought and had a right to prevent, then it is the duty of the trial judge to withdraw the case from the consideration of the jury; and if he fails to do so, it is the duty of the appellate court to correct the error. . . ."

And such seemed to be the ruling of the Court in *Pierce* v. *United*

States. In sustaining the overruling of a demurrer to the indictment Justice Pitney in the Court's opinion said: ". . . Whether the statements contained in the pamphlet had a natural tendency to produce the forbidden consequences, as alleged, was a question to be determined not upon demurrer but by the jury at the trial. There was no error in overruling the demurrer."

The defendants took the stand and testified that their sole purpose in distributing the pamphlet in question was to gain converts for socialism. Justice Pitney for the Court responded: "What interpretation ought to be placed upon the pamphlet, what would be the probable effect of distributing it in the mode adopted, and what were defendants' motives in doing this, were questions for the jury, not the court, to decide."

But District Judge Medina in the *Dennis* case instructed the jury that the application of the clear and present danger test presented a question of law for the determination of the court: "This is a matter of law about which you have no concern. It is a finding on a matter of law which I deem essential to support my ruling that the case should be submitted to you to pass upon the guilt or innocence of the defendants. . . ." And the Supreme Court affirmed a judgment of conviction under this instruction. Chief Justice Vinson wrote:

> The question in this case is whether the statute which the legislature has enacted may be constitutionally applied. In other words, the Court must examine judicially the application of the statute to the particular situation, to ascertain if the Constitution prohibits the conviction. We hold that the statute may be applied where there is a "clear and present danger" of the substantive evil which the legislature had the right to prevent. Bearing, as it does, the marks of a "question of law," the issue is properly one for the judge to decide.

Justice Douglas in his dissent observed: "I had assumed that the question of the clear and present danger, being so critical an issue in the case, would be a matter for submission to the jury. It was squarely held in *Pierce* v. *United States* . . . to be a jury question. . . ." But the Court in the *Dennis* case ruled otherwise.

Due Process Restrictions

Justice Holmes's clear and present danger test operated to create a developing federal power over utterances. By way of contrast the Fourteenth Amendment's due process clause operated to establish an increasing body of constitutional restrictions on state power over utterances. Federal power over utterances grew; state power diminished.

After the Supreme Court's opinion in 1925 in the *Gitlow* case a long line of its decisions safeguarded to the individual as against state action freedom of utterance, association and assembly. This line runs from *Stromberg* v. *California*, *Near* v. *Minnesota*, and *De Jonge* v. *Oregon*, in all of which Chief Justice Hughes wrote the Court's opinions, to the recent case of *NAACP* v. *Alabama*. It includes many additional cases which cover almost every type of expression. Indeed the line is so long and the cases are so numerous and so strong that they have lent weight to the erroneous contention that the Fourteenth Amendment incorporates the First.

However, as Justice Jackson made plain in his dissenting opinion in *Beauharnais* v. *Illinois* and as the Court itself recently seemed to recognize, at least tacitly, in *NAACP* v. *Alabama* the Fourteenth Amendment does not incorporate the First. Accordingly, as Justices Holmes and Brandeis indicated in their dissent in *Gitlow* v. *New York* and as Justice Jackson spelled out in his dissenting opinion in the *Beauharnais* case, the states under the due process clause of the Fourteenth Amendment still have more extensive powers over speech, press and assembly than the federal government constitutionally has under the unqualified prohibitions of the First Amendment. Justice Jackson, after considering state libel laws, concluded: "For these reasons I should not, unless clearly required, confirm to the Federal Government such latitude as I think a State reasonably may require for orderly government of its manifold concerns. The converse of the proposition is that I would not limit the power of the State with the severity appropriately prescribed for federal power."

Thus states may constitutionally have libel laws with criminal as well as civil sanctions. This the Court conceded in *Near* v. *Minnesota*: ". . . But it is recognized that punishment for the abuse of the liberty accorded to the press is essential to the protection of the public, and that the common law rules that subject the libeler to responsibility for the public offense, as well as for the private injury, are not abolished by the protection extended in our constitutions, . . . The law of criminal libel rests upon that secure foundation. . . ." States may experiment with group libel laws. So the Court held in the *Beauharnais* case. States may punish "fighting words," as the Court held, unanimously be it noted, in *Chaplinsky* v. *New Hampshire*: ". . . There are certain well-defined and narrowly limited classes of speech, the prevention and punishment of which have never been thought to raise any Constitutional problem. These include the lewd and obscene, the profane, the libelous, and the insulting or 'fighting' words—those which by their very utterance inflict injury or tend to incite an immediate breach of the peace. . . ."

States and municipalities may take further steps for the comfort and welfare of their inhabitants. As incident to regulating streets for traffic purposes, they may in a similar fashion regulate parades, requiring a permit and compensable license fees for them, as the Court held, again unanimously, in *Cox* v. *New Hampshire*. They may prohibit on the streets the operation of sound trucks and loud speakers, *Kovacs* v. *Cooper*, as well as the distribution of commercial advertising handbills, *Valentine* v. *Chrestensen*. They may forbid door-to-door canvassing by salesmen, including salesmen for publications, *Breard* v. *Alexandria*. A state may also protect its children by a child labor law which it may apply to the distribution by a child of religious literature on the public streets, *Prince* v. *Massachusetts*.

In two recent cases, *Poulos* v. *New Hampshire* and *Feiner* v. *New York* the Court carried forward the approach in the *Cox* and *Chaplinsky* cases. In the *Poulos* case the Court accepted as valid another provision of the same ordinance it approved in the *Cox* case, this time one requiring a permit for a park meeting. However, the issuance of a permit as the New Hampshire Supreme Court construed the ordinance, involved a ministerial rather than a discretionary act. In the *Feiner* case the Court sustained a conviction under a New York statute which made it an offense to engage in disorderly conduct which might occasion a breach of the peace. Feiner was making a soapbox speech at a street intersection in Syracuse by means of a loud speaker system attached to an automobile. After a time the police demanded that he stop. When he kept on talking they arrested him. According to the police they acted to keep the gathering "from resulting in a fight."

To test state legislation dealing with utterances by the application solely of the Fourteenth Amendment's due process clause rather than the unqualified prohibitions of the Frist Amendment will tend to trouble those who emphasize individual rights, for the states will thus have somewhat more leeway with such legislation than the federal government. However, the leeway which the states will have will be small. Nevertheless, small though it be, the Court in determining its range should temper its desire to secure to the individual a full measure of freedom of utterance on any question with a little of the Holmes-Brandeis concept of the states as laboratories for social and economic experimentation. The states should accordingly be allowed some room in which to experiment.

Thus without any incorporation theory the general outlines of what the states may and may not do under the Fourteenth Amendment's due process clause are clear enough. In only one area is there any disturbing amount of uncertainty, that of subversion, and here it is due to two factors, neither of which can be attributed to the due process clause, whether with or without incorporation: the clear and present danger test; and pre-emption. The former we have already considered; the latter we will take up presently.

Prurient Interest Test

By the application of Justice Holmes's clear and present danger test the Court erroneously restricted the absolute prohibitions of the First Amendment and blurred the workable distinction between speech and conduct other than speech. Recently in four of a series of five cases the Court complicated the free speech picture still further by holding that so-called obscene utterances did not fall within .the protection of the First Amendent at all. In the process the Court gave us a new test, the prurient interest test. This test was for the purpose of determining obscenity. In the writer's view this test will prove to be of even less use than Justice Holmes's clear and present danger test, and, like it, ultimately will have to be abandoned.

Two of the four cases were *Roth* v. *United States* and *Alberts* v. *California,* where the Court sustained federal and state criminal obscenity statutes. The Court in an opinion by Justice Brennan held "that obscenity is not within the area of constitutionally protected speech or press." Justices Black and Douglas dissented in both cases, and Justice Harlan as well in the *Roth* case. Justices Black and Douglas drew the distinction of Madison and Jefferson between utterances and criminal conduct other than utterances. Justice Harlan rested his dissent on the ground that the First Amendment's prohibitions placed a greater restriction on federal power than the Fourteenth Amendment's due process clause placed on state power. A third case was *Kingsley Books* v. *Brown,* where the Court sustained a New York statute which provided for civil non-jury injunctive proceedings against obscene publications. The vote this time was five to four. Justice Frankfurter delivered the Court's opinion. He did not think that the statute constituted proscribed prior restraint. Justices Black and Douglas thought that it did. Chief Justice Warren made the point that it was the manner of use that should determine obscenity. Justice Brennan dissented on the ground that "the absence in this New York obscenity statute of a right to jury trial is a fatal defect." The fourth case was *Adams Newark Theater Co.* v. *City of Newark.* Here the Court on the authority of the preceding three cases in a per curiam decision sustained the validity of a Newark ordinance which forbade stage performers to expose certain parts of their bodies and to use profane, lewd or lascivious language.

The basis for the Court's establishment in the *Roth* and *Alberts* cases of an exception to the First Amendment for so-called obscenity was this: "The guarantees of freedom of expression in effect in 10 of the 14 States which by 1792 had ratified the Constitution, gave no absolute protection for every utterance. Thirteen of the 14 States provided for the prosecution of libel, and all of those States made either blasphemy or profanity, or both, statutory crimes." But the framers of the federal Bill of Rights by the First and Tenth Amendments intended the states to have certain powers over speech which they expressly sought to deny to the federal government.

Especially should the goverance of obscenity be in hands of the states and their political subdivisions rather than the federal government. Under our federal system the prosecution of offenses, as the Court has more than once pointed out, and as it reiterated in 1958 in *Knapp* v. *Schweitzer*, is primarily the concern of the states. In the *Knapp* case the Court through Mr. Justice Frankfurter stated: ". . . Except insofar as penal remedies may be provided by Congress under the explicit authority to 'make all Laws which shall be necessary and proper for carrying into execution' the other powers granted in Art. I, §8, the bulk of authority to legislate on what may be compendiously described as criminal justice, which in other nations belongs to the central government, is under our system the responsibility of the individual States." In another recent case, *Rochin* v. *California*, this same justice wrote for the Court: "In our federal system the administration of criminal justice is predominantly committed to the care of the states. The power to define crime belongs to Congress only as an appropriate means of carrying into execution its limited grant of legislative powers. . . ." Justice Reed in his dissenting opinion in the *Nelson* case, in which Justices Burton and Minton joined, relied on this fact. He quoted a section of the federal criminal code which provides: "Nothing in this title shall be held to take away or impair the jurisdiction of the courts of the several States under the laws thereof." Then he commented: "That declaration springs from the federal character of our Nation. It recognizes the fact that maintenance of order and fairness rests primarily with the States."

Moreover, if we must have obscenity legislation at all, it is especially such legislation that should be confined to the states and their political subdivisions in order that we may have state diversity rather than federal conformity. As Justice Harlan, carrying forward the Holmes-Brandeis concept of the states as experimental laboratories, argued in his dissenting opinion in *Roth* v. *United States*:

Not only is the federal interest in protecting the Nation against pornography attenuated, but the dangers of federal censorship in this field are far greater than anything the States may do. It has often been said that one of the great strengths of our federal system is that we have, in the forty-eight States, forty-eight experimental social laboratories. "State statutory law reflects predominantly this capacity of a legislature to introduce novel techniques of social control. The federal system has the immense advantage of providing forty-eight separate centers for such experimentation." Different States will have different attitudes toward the same work of literature. The same book which is freely read in one State might be classed as obscene in another. And it seems to me that no overwhelming danger to our freedom to experiment and to gratify our tastes in literature is likely to result from the suppression of a border-line book in one of the States, so long as there is no uniform nation-wide suppression of the book, and so long as other States are free to experiment with the same or bolder books.

Quite a different situation is presented, however, where the Federal Government imposes the ban. The danger is perhaps not great if the people of one State, through their legislature, decide that *Lady Chatterley's Lover* goes so far beyond the acceptable standards of candor that it will be deemed offensive and non-sellable, for the State next door is still free to make its own choice. At least we do not have one uniform standard. But the dangers to free thought and expression are truly great if the Federal Government imposes a blanket ban over the Nation on such a book. The prerogative of the States to differ on their ideas of morality will be destroyed, the ability of States to experiment will be stunted. The fact that the people of one State cannot read some of the works of D. H. Lawrence seems to me, if not wise or desirable, at least acceptable. But that no person in the United States should be allowed to do so seems to me to be intolerable, and violative of both the letter and spirit of the First Amendment.

I judge this case, then, in view of what I think is the attentuated federal interest in this field, in view of the very real danger of a deadening uniformity which can result from nation-wide federal censorship, and in view of the fact that the constitutionality of this conviction must be weighed against the First and not the Fourteenth Amendment. . . .

Certain additional criticisms, although lesser ones, of the Court's statement are in order. The ten states to which the majority opinion refers are Delaware, Georgia, Maryland, Massachusetts, New Hampshire, North Carolina, Pennsylvania, South Carolina, Vermont and Virginia. These reduce to nine as of the date when the first Congress proposed the first ten amendments (September 25, 1789); for the cited constitution of one of them, Delaware, dates from 1792. In the second place these state constitutional provisions were not always in as sweeping terms as the First Amendment. For example, the Vermont constitution of

1786 expressly identified freedom of speech and of the press with discussions of "the transactions of government." In the third place these state constitutional provisions at times contained exceptions. The Pennsylvania constitution of 1790 and the Delaware constitution of 1792 had exceptions for seditious libel, that of South Carolina of 1790 for licentiousness, and that of Maryland of 1776 for immorality. The Pennsylvania constitution of 1790 provided that in seditious libel prosecutions truth was to be a defense and "the jury shall have a right to determine the law and the facts, under the direction of the court, as in other cases." The South Carolina constitution of 1790 in providing for religious freedom expressly stated: "That the liberty of conscience thereby declared shall not be so construed as to excuse acts of licentiousness, or justify practices inconsistent with the peace or safety of this State." The Maryland declaration of rights of 1776 had this exception: ". . . unless, under colour of religion, any man shall disturb the good order, peace or safety of the State, or shall infringe the laws of morality. . . ." By way of contrast the First Amendment provided without qualification: "Congress shall make no law . . . abridging the freedom of speech, or of the press. . . ."

In the fourth place the states did not always observe their own constitutional provisions. As Madison pointed out when he submitted his proposed amendments to the first Congress in June 1789: ". . . there are a few particular States in which some of the most valuable articles have not, at one time or other, been violated. . . ."

But the main difficulty with the Court's statement is the failure, as in the case of the application of Justice Holmes's clear and present danger test, to give effect to the intent of the framers of the federal Bill of Rights to deny to the federal government all power over speech unless connected with criminal conduct other than speech. As a result, the federal government, along with the states and their political subdivisions, is in the business of protecting us from obscenity.

In order to determine what is obscene we have a new test, the prurient interest test: "Obscene material is material which deals with sex in a manner appealing to prurient interest." The writer doubts its worth. He is aware of our concern about utterances allegedly obscene. Yet he feels that if there were no restrictions on utterances save such as are involved in prohibitions like those against disturbances or breaches of the peace, the pornographers would have their day and that would be the end of them.

However, the law developed in accordance with the people's fears. We now have the prurient interest test, whatever that may mean. Under it the Supreme Court has examined various utterances and advised us as to their findings on the point of obscenity. Under it the Supreme Court has become, to quote from a remark of Justice Jackson during the course of the argument in the case involving the question of the obscenity of Edmund Wilson's *Memoirs of Hecate County*, "the High Court of Obscenity."

At the term following the Court's decisions in the *Roth* and *Alberts* cases the Court considered the film, *The Game of Love*, two nudist periodicals *Sunshine & Health* and *Sun Magazine*, and a publication called *One*, aimed at homosexuals. The last publication contained a story about a Lesbian's influence on a young girl, described alleged homosexual activities of British peers, and had an article about other magazines containing similar material. The Court ruled them all to be not obscene.

In a fourth case at the same term, and one which also involved nudist periodicals as well as two publications which contained only reproductions of human nudes without any text at all, the Court, after a confession of error by the solicitor general, vacated the judgment of the court below and remanded the case to the district court for reconsideration in the light of the *Roth* case. The district judge had included in the standard of obscenity which he had applied that which "offends the sense of propriety, morality, and decency of" the average person of the community. The Court of Appeals for the Ninth Circuit had adopted the district court's standard. But the Supreme Court had laid down the prurient interest test. When this case returned to the district court, the judge held all the publications there involved, even those solely with pictures and without any text at all, to be not obscene.

In 1959 the Court had before it a ban on the film *Lady Chatterley's Lover*. This was the very work which Justice Harlan cited hypothetically in his dissenting opinion in the *Roth* case when he was arguing for state diversity as against federal conformity in support of his conclusion that the states rather than the federal government had jurisdiction over obscenity. The ban was in the state of New York, where a number of the previous bans to come before the Supreme Court originated. All the members of the Court except Justice Black saw the film and lifted the ban.

There is one consolation in the present arrangement: the Court will confine what it regards as obscene within very narrow limits. Following the term at which it decided the *Roth* and *Alberts* cases it has not found anything to be obscene, whether it be nudist magazines or a publication beamed at homosexuals. Also, beginning with *The Miracle* case the Court so far has lifted the ban on every film to come before it. In addition to *The Miracle*, the list includes: *Lady Chatterley's Lover;*

The Game of Love; The Moon Is Blue; La Ronde (a picture made from Arthur Schnitzler's *Reigen*); *Native Son* and *M*; and *Pinky*.

Although in the case of obscenity the Court created an exception to the First Amendment, obscenity statutes must still be drawn with care, for they must meet the requirements of the due process clauses: of the Fifth Amendment in case of federal, and of the Fourteenth in case of state legislation.

In this area, unlike that of sedition, where the First Amendment governs federal action and the Fourteenth Amendment's due process clause that of the state, the constitutional yardstick is the same, whether the legislation is federal or state.

By reason of the due process clauses, obscenity statutes must not be unreasonably restrictive and they must be reasonably certain in their meaning, especially if they contain criminal sanctions. Thus at the same term as the *Roth* and *Alberts* cases, the Court in *Butler* v. *Michigan* unanimously invalidated a state statute which made criminal the general sale or distribution of literature "tending to incite minors." In the Court's words through Justice Frankfurter: ". . . The incidence of this enactment is to reduce the adult population of Michigan to reading only what is fit for children. It thereby arbitrarily curtails one of those liberties of the individual, now enshrined in the Due Process Clause of the Fourteenth Amendment, that history has attested as the indispensable conditions for the maintenance and progress of a free society."

Also, such statutes must be reasonably definite. This is a general due process requirement for all legislation, whether federal or state, whether civil or criminal. Moreover, the standards of certainty in statutes with criminal sanctions are more exacting than those with civil ones only. As the Court pointed out many years ago in *United States* v. *Reese* through Chief Justice Waite: ". . . Every man should be able to know with certainty when he is committing a crime."

Or as the Court ruled more recently in *Winters* v. *New York* through Justice Reed: ". . . The standards of certainty in statutes punishing for offenses is higher than in those depending primarily upon civil sanction for enforcement. The crime 'must be defined with appropriate definiteness.' * * * There must be ascertainable standards of guilt. Men of common intelligence cannot be required to guess at the meaning of the enactment. . . ."

In the third place, a statute applying to utterances must be particularly clear and precise. If it could apply to a protected form of expression as well as unprotected ones, it must fall. As the Court also said in the *Winters* case: ". . . It is settled that a statute so vague and indefinite, in form and as interpreted, as to permit within the scope of its language the punishment of incidents fairly within the protection of the guarantee of free speech is void, on its face, as contrary to the Fourteenth Amendment. . . ."

Accordingly the Court has invalidated or cast doubt on much legislation dealing with obscenity and related matters: in *Holmby Productions* v. *Vaughn* reversing a denial of injunctive relief under a state statute using the words "cruel, obscene, indecent or immoral"; in *Superior Films* v. *Dep't of Education* invalidating an Ohio statute using the words "moral, educational or amusing and harmless character"; in *Commercial Pictures Corp.* v. *Board of Regents* invalidating a New York statute using the word "immoral"; in *Gelling* v. *Texas* an ordinance using the words "prejudicial to the best interests of the people"; in *Joseph Burstyn, Inc.* v. *Wilson* a New York statute using the word "sacrilegious"; in *Winters* v. *New York* a New York statute which as construed applied to "massed" stories of bloodshed and lust; and in *Musser* v. *Utah* vacating a judgment under a Utah statute which made it an offense to conspire to commit any action "injurious to public morals." The Utah defendants had conspired to advocate polygamy. After the federal Supreme Court's decision the Utah Supreme Court declared the statute void for vagueness.

But if obscenity statutes are along the lines of those which the Court sustained in the *Roth* and *Alberts* cases, or of the provisions of the American Law Institute's Model Penal Code, from which the Court quoted in the *Roth* case they will be approved. The Model Penal Code suggested this definition for obscenity: ". . . A thing is obscene if, considered as a whole, its predominant appeal is to prurient interest, i.e., a shameful or morbid interest in nudity, sex, or excretion, and if it goes substantially beyond customary limits of candor in description or representation of such matters. * * *"

The Warren Court

In forming an estimate of a country, one consideration is the amount of freedom, particularly freedom of utterance, that its governing structures secure to the individual. Freedom of utterance should be absolute unless it is connected with criminal conduct other than utterance or unless it amounts to a disturbance of the peace. Another consideration, in forming such an estimate, is the extent of the decentralization of governmental power. Under our federal system the writer is in favor of what we popularly know as States' rights, although it would be more accurate to speak of state power. The Tenth Amendment reads: "The powers * * * reserved to the States respectively, or to the people."

From the standpoint of state as against federal power, the Warren

Court has been as nationalist as any of its predecessors. But from the standpoint of freedom of utterance, this Court, in practice although not in words, has swung in the direction of the approach of Jefferson and Madison and of Justices Black and Douglas. It, too, at least in practice, has protected advocacy unless connected with criminal conduct other than advocacy. One can give no better example of this trend than the treatment which the Warren Court has accorded to the Smith Act prosecutions of leaders of the American Communist party.

The first such prosecution to reach the Court was in Chief Justice Vinson's time. It was the *Dennis* case, arising out of the first Foley Square Smith Act conspiracy indictment. In that case Eugene Dennis, general secretary, and ten other top leaders of the American Communist party went to trial. All were convicted. The Vinson Court affirmed in June 1951. The next such case to reach reviewing courts was the Baltimore Smith Act conspiracy indictment. Here there were six defendants, all of whom were convicted. The Court of Appeals for the Fourth Circuit affirmed, and the Vinson Court denied review.

The third such case which reviewing courts passed on arose out of the second Foley Square conspiracy prosecution. This prosecution was against Elizabeth Gurley Flynn, a member of the party's national committee, and twenty others. Of these, fifteen went to trial in 1952; thirteen were convicted and two acquitted, the latter two at the direction of the judge. The Court of Appeals for the Second Circuit affirmed in 1954 and the Supreme Court denied review in January 1955. Although this was the Warren Court, Chief Justice Warren had been on the bench but little more than a year.

Subsequently two of the thirteen convicted defendants in this prosecution, Alexander Trachtenberg and George Blake Charney, obtained new trials as a result of Harvey Matusow's recantations. The remaining eleven, plus the eleven convicted defendants in the first Foley Square conspiracy prosecution, the six defendants from the Baltimore conspiracy case, and Mrs. Barbara Hartle from the Seattle conspiracy case, for a total of 29, are the only convicted American Communist party leaders who so far have served their prison terms. Mrs. Hartle stood by her associates through the trial but then contacted the FBI and withdrew her appeal. Ironically enough, her co-defendants who appealed with her had their convictions reversed with a direction to enter a judgment in their favor. Of all the more than 100 American Communist party leaders who have been convicted in Smith Act prosecutions and sentenced to prison terms, these 29 are the only ones so far who have served their prison sentences. All the others have either obtained or are still seeking reversals of their convictions.

The next case to come before the Supreme Court was that of Stephen Mesarosh, also known as Steve Nelson. This case involved a judgment of conviction against five defendants in the Pittsburgh conspiracy prosecution. The Court directed the granting of a new trial after the government advised the Court that it had serious reason to doubt the truthfulness of one of its witnesses, Joseph D. Mazzei, who was a paid informer for the government. The solicitor general disclosed this situation to the Court in a motion to remand the case to the trial court for further proceedings. Instead the Court ordered a new trial. Mesarosh was also the successful defendant in another case, *Pennsylvania* v. *Nelson,* in which the Court invalidated a Pennsylvania sedition law, and cast doubt on such laws of other states, on the ground that the federal Smith Act pre-empted the field.

Then came the petitions for review involved in *Yates* v. *United States,* where the Court drew the unrealistic distinction between the advocacy of the violent overthrow of the government as a rule or principle of action and the advocacy of such overthrow as a necessity and a duty. These petitions arose out of the Los Angeles conspiracy indictment against fifteen defendants. The defendants included William Schneiderman, Loretta Starvus Stack, Oleta O'Connor Yates and Al Richmond. All of the defendants save one, who was severed because of ill-health, were convicted. The Court directed an acquittal as to five and a new trial as to the remaining nine. Thereafter the government procured the dismissal of the indictment on the ground that the prosecution "cannot satisfy the evidentiary requirements laid down by the Supreme Court in its opinions reversing the convictions."

At the same term as the *Yates* decision the Court in *Wellman* v. *United States,* arising out of the Detroit conspiracy prosecution, vacated the judgment of the Court of Appeals for the Sixth Circuit affirming a conviction, and remanded the case for further consideration in the light of the Court's decision in the *Yates* case. Since then the various courts of Appeals have so far reversed the Smith Act conspiracy convictions on which they have ruled. Sometimes they have sent the cases back for new trials, but in other instances they have ordered the dismissal of the indictments. Listed chronologically these decisions are:

Bary v. *United States* (Denver conspiracy prosecution). The Court of Appeals for the Tenth Circuit reversed and sent the case back for a new trial. One of the defendants was Patricia Blau. Prior to this prosecution she and her husband in separate cases successfully insisted on their right of silence or, as it is usually called, privilege against self-incrimination, in cases which went all the way to the Supreme Court. These cases helped to establish the right of silence for Communists.

United States v. *Silverman* (New Haven conspiracy case). The Court of Appeals for the Second Circuit reversed with directions to dismiss the indictment.

United States v. *Kuzma* (Philadelphia conspiracy case). The Court of Appeals for the Third Circuit reversed with directions to enter a judgment of acquittal as to four of the defendants and leave to take further proceedings as to the remaining five. Thereafter District Judge J. Cullen Ganey dismissed the indictment.

Fujimoto v. *United States* (Honolulu conspiracy prosecution); *Huff* v. *United States* (Seattle conspiracy case). The Court of Appeals for the Ninth Circuit reversed with instructions to enter judgments in favor of all defendants. It was in the Seattle conspiracy case that Mrs. Hartle abandoned her appeal and served her prison sentence. Circuit Judge Richard M. Chambers in writing the court's opinion complained that the Supreme Court's decision in the *Yates* case left the Smith Act a virtual shambles: "One may as well recognize that the Yates decision leaves the Smith Act, as to any further prosecution under it, a virtual shambles—unless the American Communist Party should witlessly set out to reconstitute itself again with a new 'organization'." But Circuit Judges William H. Hastie and Frederick G. Hamley said: "We concur in Judge Chambers' opinion, except in so far as it refers to the effect of the Yates decision upon future prosecutions under the Smith Act. In our view, this statement is unnecessary to the decision."

Sentner v. *United States; Forest* v. *United States* (St. Louis conspiracy conviction). The Court of Appeals for the Eighth Circuit reversed with directions to the court below to grant a new trial. Subsequently the government dropped the case on the ground that the *Yates* decision left it with no alternative.

Wellman v. *United States* (Detroit conspiracy conviction). The Court of Appeals for the Sixth Circuit, after the Supreme Court vacated that court's previous judgment of affirmance, reversed and remanded the case for a new trial.

Brandt v. *United States* (Cleveland conspiracy conviction). In this appeal, too, the Court of Appeals for the Sixth Circuit reversed and sent the case back for a new trial.

United States v. *Jackson* (third Foley Square conspiracy trial). This trial involved seven of the defendants in the second conspiracy indictment there, the *Flynn* case. They were: Sidney Stein, James E. Jackson, Jr., William Norman and Fred M. Fine, who staged a mass flight with four of the defendants in the first conspiracy indictment there, the *Dennis* case; Alexander Trachtenberg and George Blake Charney, who obtained a new trial because of Harvey Matusow's recantations, and Mrs. Marion Bachrach, who won a severance because she suffered from cancer. They went to trial in 1956. The judge directed an acquittal as to Mrs. Bachrach. The remaining six were convicted. However, on appeal the Court of Appeals for the Second Circuit reversed. The court was unanimous in reversing, and by a two to one vote directed the dismissal of the indictment.

In addition to these conspiracy prosecutions, there were separate indictments under the membership clause of the Smith Act against the defendants in the *Dennis* case and eight more individuals singly. The cases of two of the eight, Junius Irving Scales and Claude Mack Lightfoot, have been before the Supreme Court. Scales was North Carolina chairman, and Lightfoot a party functionary in Chicago. In each case the Court in a per curiam opinion ruled: "Upon consideration of the entire record and the confession of error by the Solicitor General, the judgment . . . is reversed. *Jencks* v. *United States*." It was in the *Jencks* case that the Court ruled that a defendant was entitled to an order directing the Government to produce for inspection all reports of its witnesses "in its possession, written and, when orally made, as recorded by the F.B.I., touching the events and activities as to which they testified at the trial." Scales has again been tried and convicted, his conviction has again been affirmed by the Court of Appeals for the Fourth Circuit, and the Supreme Court has again granted certiorari. One of the witnesses against him was Mrs. Hartle.

Three of the remaining six have been tried and convicted once. One of the three, John Francis Noto, has had his conviction affirmed on appeal, by the Court of Appeals for the Second Circuit. He has petitioned the Supreme Court to review his case, and the Court has agreed to do so.

It may well be that, besides Mrs. Hartle, the only American Communists to serve prison terms as the result of Smith Act convictions will be those in the first two Foley Square conspiracy prosecutions and the Baltimore conspiracy case, a total of 28. Enough has already occurred since Earl Warren has been Chief Justice to enable one to say that the Supreme Court, and the federal courts generally, in its lead (not always too happily), have turned toward the approach of Jefferson and Madison and Justices Black and Douglas: the results they have reached, in effect if not in words, have protected advocacy unless connected with criminal deeds other than advocacy.

Yet other decisions indicate this same trend. In two cases, *Maisenberg* v. *United States* and *Nowak* v. *United States*, the Supreme Court held that proof that a naturalized citizen had been a member and a functionary as well of the Communist party did not sustain the government's charges of fraud and lack of attachment to the principles of the Constitution. In *Rowoldt* v. *Perfetto* the Court ruled that Communist party membership in order to warrant deportation of an alien had to be a "meaningful association." In two more cases, *United States* v. *Witkovich* and *Barton* v. *Sentner,* the Court held that the attorney general's supervisory power over aliens ordered deported did not include power to ask questions about Communist affiliations. The Court limited his inquiries to those "reasonably calculated to keep the Attorney General advised regarding the continued availability for departure of aliens whose deportation is overdue."

In yet another group of cases the Court ruled in favor of individuals who refused to answer questions put to them by, or produce records for, governmental authorities inquiring into subversion; and this even though the individuals in question did not base their refusals on the Fifth Amendment's right of silence. In one case, *Watkins* v. *United States,* a labor union organizer admitted Communist associations but refused to name names. He acknowledged before a subcommittee of the House Committee on Un-American Activities: "I would like to make it clear that for a period of time from approximately 1942 to 1947 I cooperated with the Communist Party and participated in Communist activities to such a degree that some persons may honestly believe that I was a member of the party." Yet he refused to identify former Communists, saying: ". . . I do not believe that any law in this country requires me to testify about persons who may in the past have been Communist Party members or otherwise engaged in Communist Party activity but who to my best knowledge and belief have long since removed themselves from the Communist movement."

In another case, *Sweezy* v. *New Hampshire,* a socialist who lectured at the University of New Hampshire refused to answer the inquiries of the attorney general of New Hampshire about his lecture and about the activities of his wife and others in the formation of the Progressive Party in that state. The legislature of New Hampshire by a joint resolution had designated the attorney general as its agent for the investigation of subversive activities. In both cases the Court upset the sentences. In the *Watkins* case it also directed the dismissal of the indictment. Justice Clark dissented in both cases. Justice Burton joined him in the *Sweezy* case. In that case Justice Frankfurter in a concurring opinion quoted from a statement of a conference of senior scholars from the University of Cape Town and the University of the Witwatersrand. One of the quoted paragraphs reads:

In a university knowledge is its own end, not merely a means to an end. A university ceases to be true to its own nature if it becomes the tool of Church or State or any sectional interest. A university is characterized by the spirit of free inquiry, its ideal being the ideal of Socrates—"to follow the argument where it leads." This implies the right to examine, question, modify or reject traditional ideas and beliefs. Dogma and hypothesis are incompatible, and the concept of an immutable doctrine is repugnant to the spirit of a university. The concern of its scholars is not merely to add and revise facts in relation to an accepted framework, but to be ever examining and modifying the framework itself.

In three more of these cases, those of Abram Flaxer (president of United Public Workers), Lloyd Barenblatt (an instructor at Vassar College), and Harry Sacher (a New York lawyer), involving contempt convictions for refusals to answer questions or produce records at the request of congressional committees or subcommittees, the Court vacated judgments of affirmance by the Court of Appeals for the District of Columbia Circuit and remanded the cases to that court for consideration in the light of the Court's decision in the *Watkins* case. Flaxer refused to produce a membership list of his union to the Senate Internal Security Subcommittee. Sacher refused to answer questions of this subcommittee, and Barenblatt of a subcommittee of the House Committee on Un-American Activities.

In a sixth such case, *Uphaus* v. *Wyman*, the Court vacated a contempt judgment against Willard Uphaus, the executive director of the New Hampshire World Fellowship Center, for refusing to answer questions of the attorney general of New Hampshire, and remanded the case to the Supreme Court of that state for consideration in the light of the federal Supreme Court's decision in the *Sweezy* case.

The Court of Appeals for the District of Columbia Circuit and the Supreme Court of New Hampshire again affirmed judgments of conviction. The federal Supreme Court again took the cases. It first ruled in the cases of Sacher and Flaxer. In both it reversed. In Sacher's case the Court directed a dismissal of the indictment, and in Flaxer's an acquittal of the defendant.

In yet a third group of cases the Supreme Court held unconstitutional a California statute which as applied required tax exemption claimants to sign a loyalty statement on their tax returns and then to assume the burden of proving loyalty.

Lower federal courts, at times with reluctance, followed in the Supreme Court's lead. The best-known case was that of Marilyn Monroe's playwright husband, Arthur Miller, author of *Death of a Salesman* and *All My Sons*. He refused to tell a subcommittee of the House

Committee on Un-American Activities who was present at a meeting of Communist party writers in 1947. Instead he told the subcommittee: "My conscience will not permit me to use the name of another person and bring trouble to him." He was indicted and convicted for contempt, but the Court of Appeals for the District of Columbia Circuit, with the full court of nine judges sitting en banc, in a per curiam opinion reversed with directions to enter a judgment of acquittal. The Court cited the *Watkins* case.

There were others. One was that of Marcus Singer, a zoology professor at Cornell University. He also refused to name names before a subcommittee of the House Committee on Un-American Activities. Instead he explained: "I am prepared to speak fully about myself, but I could never, sir, in honor and conscience, trade some one else's career for my own." He was indicted and convicted and the Court of Appeals for the District of Columbia Circuit at first affirmed; but after the *Watkins* decision it reversed with instructions to enter a judgment of acquittal.

Another was that of Seymour Peck, an employee of the *New York Times*. Peck was a witness in the Senate Internal Security Subcommittee's investigation of Communist influence in the press. He answered all questions about himself but he refused to identify other persons as Communists, asserting his rights under the First Amendment. He was indicted and convicted but on appeal the Court of Appeals for the District of Columbia Circuit after the *Watkins* decision remanded the case to District Judge Luther W. Youngdahl with leave to entertain a motion to dismiss the indictment or for a new trial. At this point Judge Youngdahl granted a motion for an acquittal, saying:

. . . It is difficult to draw the line between investigations of the political beliefs of newspapermen and investigations of newspapers. For newspapers consist of news stories and editorials; and news stories and editorials are written by newspapermen. To inhibit the freeedom of thought and association of newspapermen is to infringe upon the freedom of the press. It is also a temptation to those investigating newspapermen to wander in the field of press content, and at times during these hearings the Subcommittee was unable to resist even this direct invasion. . . .

*   *   *

The questions which Peck refuse to answer infringed upon his basic First Amendment freedoms. . . .

*   *   *

. . . The infringement stems from the Subcommittee's action in summoning an individual, compelling him to disclose his past political associations, and insisting that he reveal the views and associations of his friends and colleagues. In so doing, the Subcommittee invaded the individual's protected freedoms of privacy, thought, and association. * * *

A fourth such case was that of Dr. Otto Nathan, the executor of Dr. Albert Einstein's estate. Nathan refused to answer questions of the House Committee on Un-American Activities. He was indicted and District Judge Edward M. Curran at first found him guilty; but after the *Watkins* decision he reversed himself and granted an acquittal motion. Judge Curran refused to "subscribe to the judgment of the Supreme Court." However, he ruled: "I cannot substitute my judgment for that of the Supreme Court. I am bound to follow it. I reluctantly grant the motion."

In June 1959, the last month of its 1958 term, the Warren Court continued on its course, but with some modifications. It ruled against the federal government in three cases arising out of security hearings of employees: *Vitarelli* v. *Seaton*; *Greene* v. *McElroy*; and *Taylor* v. *McElroy*. Vitarelli was a federal employee, and Greene and Taylor were employees of private contractors with the Defense Department. In all three cases the lower courts ruled against confrontation. In all three cases the Supreme Court reversed; but in two of the cases did not reach the issue of confrontation, and in the third said that it did not. In the *Vitarelli* case the Court rested its decision on the ground that the Secretary of the Interior had not followed his own regulations; and in the *Taylor* case on mootness (the Defense Department had notified all interested parties that the petitioner had been granted clearance). In the *Greene* case the Court held the procedures of the Defense Department to be unauthorized, but Chief Justice Warren in the Court's opinion further stated:

Certain principles have remained relatively immutable in our jurisprudence. One of these is that where governmental action seriously injures an individual, and the reasonableness of the action depends on fact findings the evidence used to prove the Government's case must be disclosed to the individual so that he has an opportunity to show that it is untrue. While this is important in the case of documentary evidence, it is even more important where the evidence consists of the testimony of individuals whose memory might be faulty or who, in fact, might be perjurers or persons motivated by malice, vindictiveness, intolerance, prejudice, or jealousy. We have formalized these protections in the requirements of confrontation and cross-examination. They have ancient roots. They find expression in the Sixth Amendment which provides that in all criminal cases the accused shall enjoy the right "to be confronted with the witnesses against him." This Court has been zealous to protect these rights from erosion. It has spoken out

not only in criminal cases. * * * but also in all types of cases where
administrative and regulatory action were under scrutiny. * * *"

During the course of the argument of this case Chief Justice Warren
said to counsel:

If my neighbor accuses me of anything else but this [that is, of being a
bad security risk] and they are going to put me in jail or deprive me of my
livelihood, I have a right to confront him. What is this different?

The language in Chief Justice Warren's opinion led Justice Clark
to feel that the Court had held that the due process clause of the Fifth
Amendment required confrontation and an opportunity for cross-examination in security hearings: ". . . While the Court disclaims deciding
this constitutional question, no one reading the opinion will doubt
that the explicit language of its broad sweep speaks in prophecy. Let
us hope that the winds may change. If they do not the present temporary debacle will turn into a rout of our internal security."

In *Kingsley Pictures Corp.* v. *Regents* the Court lifted the ban on
Lady Chatterley's Lover. The Court was unanimous in its conclusion
but expressed itself in six separate opinions. Justices Frankfurter and
Black again illustrated their differences in approach to the Fourteenth
Amendment's due process clause. Justice Frankfurter would apply this
clause in the field of obscenity in the same manner as in other areas, on
a case by case basis: "Unless I misread the opinion of the Court, it
strikes down the New York legislation in order to escape the task of
deciding whether a particular picture is entitled to the protection of
expression under the Fourteenth Amendment. Such an exercise of the
judicial function, however onerous or ungrateful, inheres in the very
nature of the judicial enforcement of the Due Process Clause. We
cannot escape such instance-by-instance, case-by-case application of
that clause in all the variety of situations that come before this Court.
It would be comfortable if, by a comprehensive formula, we could
decide when a confession is coerced so as to vitiate a state conviction.
There is no talismanic formula. Every Term we have to examine the
particular circumstances of a particular case in order to apply generali-
ties which no one disputes. It would be equally comfortable if a general
formula could determine the unfairness of a state trial for want of
counsel. But except in capital cases, we have to thread our way, Term
after Term, through the particular circumstances of a particular case
in relation to a particular defendant in order to ascertain whether due
process was denied in the unique situation before us."

Justice Harlan, in a separate concurring opinion in which Justices
Frankfurter and Whittaker joined, adopted Justice Frankfurter's ap-

proach of proceeding in obscenity questions as in other due process issues on a case by case basis, thus making of the Court, in Justice Jackson's language, "the High Court of Obscenity."

Justice Black, the only justice who did not see the film, in his search for certainty would have the Fourteenth incorporate the First and proscribe all prior restraint: "My view, is that stated by Mr. Justice Douglas, that prior censorship of moving pictures like prior censorship of newspapers and books violates the First and Fourteenth Amendments. * * * We are told that the only way we can decide whether a State or municipality can constitutionally bar movies is for this Court to view and appraise each movie on a case-by-case basis. Under these circumstances, every member of the Court must exercise his own judgment as to how bad a picture is, a judgment which is ultimately based at least in large part on his own standard of what is immoral. The end result of such decisions seems to me to be a purely personal determination by individual Justices as to whether a particular picture viewed is too bad to allow it to be seen by the public. Such an individualized determination cannot be guided by reasonably fixed and certain standards. Accordingly, neither States nor moving picture makers can possibly know in advance, with any fair degree of certainty, what can or cannot be done in the field of movie making and exhibiting. This uncertainty cannot easily be reconciled with the rule of law which our Constitution envisages."

Justice Douglas, in an opinion in which Justice Black joined, characterized Justice Harlan's dissent in the *Roth* case as an approach which would "apply to the States a watered-down version of the First Amendment."

In the same month the Court also invalidated a confession in a state court proceeding, *Spano* v. *New York*; held that an indigent defendant in a state court proceeding did not have to pay a filing fee in order to avail himself of appellate review, *Burns* v. *Ohio*; ruled in *Napue* v. *Illinois*: "The principle that a State may not knowingly use false evidence including false testimony, to obtain a tainted conviction, implicit in any concept of ordered liberty, does not cease to apply merely because the false testimony goes only to the credibility of the witness"; and reversed a one-year suspension from the practice of law of Harriet Bouslog Sawyer, one of the defense counsel in the Honolulu Smith Act conspiracy prosecution against communists. She had made a speech during the course of the trial in which she was quoted as saying: "There's no such thing as a fair trial in a Smith Act case. All rules of evidence have to be scrapped or the government can't make a case."

The Warren Court's modifications of its course occurred in *Uphaus* v.

Wyman, Raley v. *Ohio* and *Barenblatt* v. *United States*. In the *Uphaus* case the Court sustained a contempt finding by a New Hampshire state court for a refusal to answer questions of that state's attorney general. That official had been authorized by the state legislature to conduct an investigation with respect to violations of the state's attorney general. That official had been authorized by the state legislature to conduct an investigation with respect to violations of the state's Subversive Activities Act of 1951. Justice Clark in the Court's opinion, in ruling against the contention, based on *Pennsylvania* v. *Nelson*, that the federal Smith Act superseded New Hampshire's legislation against subversion, took pains to point out: "In *Nelson* itself we said that the precise holding of the court * * * is that the Smith Act * * * which prohibits the knowing advocacy of the overthrow of the Government of the United States by force and violence, supersedes the enforceability of the Pennsylvania Sedition Act which proscribes the *same conduct*." (Italics supplied.) In other words, all that the *Nelson* case held was that the Smith Act preempted the field only in so far as a state sedition act proscribed the same conduct as the Smith Act, namely, the overthrow of the United States government by force and violence as distinguished from a state government.

In the *Raley* case, involving four individuals, the Court, although reversing as to three, sustained an Ohio state court contempt conviction as to one of them for refusal to answer questions of the Ohio Un-American Activities Commission; and in Barenblatt upheld a federal court contempt conviction for refusal to answer questions of a subcommittee of the House Committee on Un-American Activities.

The *Raley* affirmance was by an evenly divided Court, Justice Potter Stewart not participating (his father is a member of the Ohio Supreme Court). In the *Barenblatt* and *Uphaus* cases the Court divided five to four, with Chief Justice Warren and Justices Black, Douglas and Brennan dissenting. Justice Brennan based his dissents on the ground that the First Amendment prohibited Congress and the Fourteenth Amendment's due process clause forbade a state legislature from engaging in exposure "purely for the sake of exposure." Chief Justice Warren and Justices Black and Douglas joined him in Uphaus.

The *Barenblatt* case was significant for yet another reason: Justice Black finally conceded that in the area of utterance the states might have greater power than Congress. In his dissenting opinion, in which Chief Justice Warren and Justice Douglas joined, he said: "Whatever the States were left free to do, the First Amendment sought to leave Congress devoid of any kind or quality of power to direct any type of national laws against the freedom of individuals to think what they please, advocate whatever policy they choose and join with others to bring about the social, religious, political and governmental changes which seem best to them."

After this decision Judge Curran, who had reluctantly followed the *Watkins* ruling in acquitting Dr. Nathan, imposed a $500 fine and six months' probation on Alden Whitman, a copy editor of *The New York Times*, for refusing to name names and answer other questions before the Senate Internal Security Subcommittee. A little earlier Carl Braden of Louisville, Kentucky, field secretary for the Southern Conference Educational Fund, and Frank Wilkinson of Los Angeles, secretary of the Citizens Committee to Preserve American Freedom, each drew one-year sentences for contempt of Congress.

But on an overall basis the Warren Court's modifications of its course shrink in significance. Besides, under the Tenth Amendment the *Nelson* case was wrongly decided anyway. Rather than limit this decision the Court should have overruled it. Beyond that, all that the *Uphaus, Raley* and *Barenblatt* decisions did was to give the state legislatures and Congress a certain amount of leeway in the performance of their functions: under the doctrine of the separation of powers they should have this leeway in any event.

Actions speak louder than words. Although the Warren Court still pays lip service to the language in the *Dennis* case, in practice it has protected advocacy when unconnected with criminal conduct other than advocacy. In similar fashion, although the Warren Court created a new exception to the First Amendment and gave us a new test to determine its extent, the prurient interest test for obscenity, in practice it has not found anything to be obscene since the term at which it gave us the new test. Despite the fact that semantically we now have two exceptions to the First Amendment where before we had one and before that none, measured in the one instance by the clear and present danger test and in the other by the prurient interest one, in practice an individual's right to freedom of utterance under the Warren Court is as great as, if not greater than, it was in the time of Chief Justices Hughes and Stone.

CHAPTER VIII

PICKETING

More Conduct Than Speech

By the clear and present danger and prurient interest tests the Supreme Court created exceptions to the First Amendment which the framers of the federal Bill of Rights did not intend. In between these two exceptions timewise, the Court again went against the framers' intent, but this time in the opposite direction. This time the Court treated conduct, namely, picketing, as protected under certain circumstances by the First Amendment because it also involved speech.

But picketing is conduct more than speech. This is true even if it is peaceful, as the Court itself recognized recently in *International Brotherhood of Teamsters* v. *Vogt, Inc.* Justice Frankfurter in the Court's opinion quoted with approval this language from the concurring opinion of Justice Douglas in *Bakery Drivers Local* v. *Wohl*: "Picketing by an organized group is more than free speech, since it involves patrol of a particular locality and since the very presence of a picket line may induce action of one kind or another, quite irrespective of the nature of the ideas that are being disseminated." Picket lines involve a concert of action in the same fashion as do combinations in restraint of trade or to fix prices. Their primary purpose is not the dissemination of ideas but to bring about certain action on the part of employers. It takes considerable courage in today's world for many people to cross a picket line. There are valid reasons for the protection of peaceful picketing, but it is submitted that the First Amendment is not among them. To base the protection of peaceful picketing on the First Amendment not only confuses the issues that are involved in the controversies between employers and employees, but also blurs still more the distinction that should be drawn between speech and conduct.

At one time peaceful picketing did not receive its fair share of judicial protection. As late as 1921 the Court ruled, in *Truax* v. *Corrigan*, a five to four decision with the Court's opinion by Chief Justice Taft, that an Arizona statute for the protection of peaceful picketing violated the equal protection clause of the Fourteenth Amendment.

But then came the Norris-LaGuardia Act and similar legislation, and the Court's decision in *Senn* v. *Tile Layers Protective Union*. In that case the Court held that a Wisconsin statute comparable to the Arizona one did not fall afoul either of the equal protection or the due process clause of the Fourteenth Amendment. The decision was again five to four but this time the Court's opinion was by Justice Brandeis. It is under the Fourteenth Amendment's due process clause that state legislation, aside from the question of pre-emption, should have continued to be determined.

However, in *Thornhill* v. *Alabama* the Court in an opinion by Justice Murphy identified peaceful picketing with freedom of speech and stated broadly: "In the circumstances of our times the dissemination of information concerning the facts of a labor dispute must be regarded as within the area of free discussion that is guaranteed by the Constitution." Soon thereafter the Court held in *American Federation of Labor* v. *Swing* that an injunction against peaceful organizational picketing, based on Illinois' common law policy against picketing, was unconstitutional, saying: "The right of free communication cannot therefore be mutilated by denying it to workers, in a dispute with an employer, even though they are not in his employ."

But the Court soon backed away somewhat from the *Thornhill* and *Swing* opinions. As the Court explained recently through Justice Frankfurter in the *Vogt* case: "Soon, however, the Court came to realize that the broad pronouncements, but not the specific holding of Thornhill had to yield 'to the impact of facts unforeseen,' or at least not sufficiently appreciated. . . . Cases reached the Court in which a State had designed a remedy to meet a specific situation or to accomplish a particular social policy. These cases made manifest that picketing, even though 'peaceful,' involved more than just communication of ideas and could not be immune from all state regulation. . . ."

The Court's retreat from the *Thornhill* and *Swing* opinions began at the very next term after the latter decision. In *Carpenters Union* v. *Ritter's Cafe* the Court held that Texas could enjoin as a violation of its antitrust law picketing by unions of a restaurant to bring pressure on its owner with respect to the use of nonunion labor by a contractor of the restaurant owner in the construction of a building having nothing to do with the restaurant. There followed in rather rapid succession, among others, *Giboney* v. *Empire Storage & Ice Co.*, *Teamsters Union* v. *Hanke* and *Plumbers Union* v. *Graham*. In the *Giboney* case the Court held that Missouri could enjoin picketing by a union, seeking to organize peddlers, of a wholesale dealer to induce it to refrain from selling to nonunion peddlers. In the *Hanke* case the Court decided that the State of Washington could enjoin the picketing of a business, conducted by the owners themselves without employees, in order to secure compliance with a demand to become a union shop. In the *Graham* case it held that Virginia could enjoin, as a violation of its right to work law, picketing which announced that nonunion men were employed on a building job. Then came the *Vogt* case, where the Court held that a Wisconsin statute applicable against even peaceful organizational picketing, a statute comparable to the common law policy of Illinois which the Court invalidated in the *Swing* case, was constitutional. As Justice Douglas pointed out in his dissenting opinion in the *Vogt* case, the "factual record" in the *Swing* case cannot be distinguished from that in the *Vogt* case. In both cases the Court's opinion was by Justice Frankfurter.

The result in the *Vogt* case led Justice Douglas, with the concurrence of Chief Justice Warren and Justice Black, to complain in his dissent: "Today, the Court signs the formal surrender. State courts and state legislatures cannot fashion blanket prohibitions on all picketing. But, for practical purposes, the situation now is as it was when *Senn* v. *Tile Layers Union* . . . was decided. State courts and state legislatures are free to decide whether to permit or suppress any particular picket line for any reason other than a blanket policy against all picketing." This is as the law ought to be. Much of the intermediate confusion could have been avoided had the First Amendment through the Fourteenth not been made the basis for the decisions in the *Thornhill* and *Swing* cases. It is precisely because the Court in the picketing cases blurred yet more the workable distinction between speech and non-verbal conduct that the Court in the last two decades, from *Senn* v. *Tile Layers Protective Union* to the *Vogt* case, has, to use the language of Justice Douglas in his dissent in the latter case, "come full circle."

Nevertheless, the dissenters in the *Vogt* case should take some comfort from the fact that in three recent decisions, one each year beginning with the year the *Vogt* case was decided, the Court set aside state court injunctions against picketing. In the most recent one, *Hotel Employees Union* v. *Sax Enterprises, Inc.* (1959), involving a consolidation of twelve cases, the Court held, per curiam, that the Florida courts lacked jurisdiction to enjoin organizational picketing at twelve Florida resort hotels.

The next preceding one was *Chauffeurs, Teamsters & Helpers Local* v. *Newell*, where the employer was an individual doing business as the El Dorado Dairy. He had three employees: a wholesale route driver, a retail route driver, and a third person who was a helper and a relief driver. The Court reversed, also per curiam, but based its decision on the limiting "Third" ground of the *Thornhill* case. In that ground the Court said, referring to the Alabama statute:

"*Third*. Section 3448 has been applied by the state courts so as to prohibit a single individual from walking slowly and peacefully back and forth on the public sidewalk in front of the premises of an employer, without speaking to anyone, carrying a sign or placard on a staff above his head stating only the fact that the employer did not employ union men affiliated with the American Federation of Labor; the purpose of the described activity was concededly to advise customers of the relationship existing between the employer and its employees and thereby to induce such customers not to patronize the employer. . . . The statute as thus authoritatively construed and applied leaves room for no exceptions based upon either the number of persons engaged in the proscribed activity, the peaceful character of their demeanor, the nature of their dispute with an employer, or the restrained character and the accurateness of the terminology used in notifying the public of the facts of the dispute."

The third case, and the one decided later in the same year as the *Vogt* case, was *Youngdahl* v. *Rainfair, Inc.* This case involved abusive as well as peaceful organizational picketing. While approving the latter the Court held as to the former: ". . . Petitioners urge that all of this abusive language was protected and that they could not, therefore, be enjoined from using it. We cannot agree. Words can readily be so coupled with conduct as to provoke violence. See *Chaplinsky* v. *New Hampshire*. . . ." However, the Court disapproved of an injunction in that case against all picketing: ". . . Nor can we say that a pattern of violence was established which would inevitably reappear in the event picketing were later resumed. Cf. *Milk Wagon Drivers Union* v. *Meadowmoor Dairies, Inc.,* . . ."

State Experimentation

From the standpoint of state power, picketing differs from sedition and obscenity in two respects. In the first place, it involves conduct more than speech. In the second place, a large part of the labor-management relations field falls within the scope of federal power by virtue of the commerce clause; and pre-emption, by reason of the National Labor Relations Act, enacted in 1935, the amendatory Labor-Management Relations Act, 1947, and the union shop provision of the Railway Labor Act, which was written into the law in 1951, has been great.

Nevertheless, aside from pre-emption, the Court in applying the Fourteenth Amendment's due process clause to state action should use a measure of the Holmes-Brandeis approach to the states as experimental social science laboratories. If, for instance, a state wants to try out a right to work law, and to that end to restrict even peaceful organizational picketing, it should be permitted within reasonable limits to do so. And recently in *Plumbers Union* v. *Graham* the Court did hold that Virginia could enjoin, as a violation of its right to work law, picketing, even though peaceful, which simply announced that nonunion men were employed on a building job.

Eighteen states in addition to Virginia have right to work laws. They are Alabama, Arizona, Arkansas, Florida, Georgia, Indiana, Iowa, Kansas, Mississippi, Nebraska, Nevada, North Carolina, North Dakota, South Dakota, South Carolina, Tennessee, Texas and Utah. Six states, including Kansas, held right to work referenda on November 4, 1958. The other five were California, Colorado, Idaho, Ohio and Washington. The measure passed only in Kansas. However, the addition of Kansas brings to 19 the number of states which now have such laws. One state, Louisiana, has repealed a right to work law.

CHAPTER IX

THE SHRINKING TENTH AMENDMENT

Pre-emption

By the clear and present danger and prurient interest exceptions to the First Amendment the Court extended federal power to utterances even when unconnected with non-verbal conduct. Once it has been determined that federal power exists in a certain area another question arises, and that is whether the exercise of federal power supersedes the exercise of state power in that area. A half decade after the decision in the *Dennis* case the Court held in *Pennsylvania* v. *Nelson* that the federal Smith Act pre-empted the field, and that for this reason a Pennsylvania sedition law was invalid. This decision also cast doubt on such laws of other states—thirty-three jurisdictions, including Alaska and Hawaii, have sedition statutes. Indeed, after the *Nelson* holding the highest courts of two states, Kentucky and Massachusetts, invalidated state sedition indictments, and the Supreme Court of Michigan held unconstitutional various provisions of the Michigan Communist Control Law, commonly referred to as the Trucks Act. State courts in Massachusetts quashed state sedition indictments against a total of eight persons, including Prof. Dirk Struik, Massachusetts Institute of Technology mathematician. It is almost needless to say at this point that this is just the opposite of what the framers of the First and Tenth Amendments intended. This result is also contrary to the intent of the principal draftsman of the Smith Act, Congressman Smith of Virginia.

The Court has insisted on pre-emption with especial vigor in the labor-management relations field. In the recent Florida picketing cases involved in *Hotel Employees Union* v. *Sax Enterprises, Inc.*, the Court rested its decision on the pre-emption ground: "The Florida courts were without jurisdiction to enjoin this organizational picketing, whether it was activity protected by §7 of the National Labor Relations Act, as amended, * * * *Hill* v. *Florida* * * * or prohibited by §8(b) (4) of the Act * * * *Garner* v. *Teamsters Union* * * *. This follows even

127

though the National Labor Relations Board refused to take jurisdiction, *Amalgamated Meat Cutters* v. *Fairlawn Meats* * * *."

In *Youngdahl* v. *Rainfair, Inc.*, the Court based part of its ruling on the concession: "* * * Respondent [employer] does not contend that the state court had power to enjoin peaceful organized activity, recognizing that generally the National Labor Relations Board has exclusive jurisdiction of such matters. *Weber* v. *Anheuser-Busch, Inc.* * * *."

There have been many comparable decisions. In the same month as the *Hotel Employees Union* decision the Court held in *Teamsters Local No. 24* v. *Oliver* that the Taft-Hartley Act precluded the application of Ohio's antitrust law to prevent interstate motor carriers and the Teamsters Union from carrying out their agreement establishing minimum rentals for trucks leased by carriers from owner operators who were union members: "* * * Since the federal law operates here, in an area where its authority is paramount, to leave the parties free, the inconsistent application of state law is necessarily outside the power of the State. * * *"

Yet more recently the Court held in the second case of *San Diego Building Trades Council* v. *Garmon* that pre-emption under the Taft-Hartley Act deprived a California state court of jurisdiction to award an employer damages under the state's general tort law for peaceful picketing in support of a demand for a union shop contract, and this even though the case arose in an area where the National Labor Relations Board had not exercised the full measure of its jurisdiction. Justice Frankfurter in a concluding paragraph wrote for the Court:

It is true that we have allowed the States to grant compensation for the consequences, as defined by the traditional law of torts, of conduct marked by violence and imminent threats to the public order. * * We have also allowed the States to enjoin such conduct. State jurisdiction has prevailed in these situations because the compelling state interest, in the scheme of our federalism, in the maintenance of domestic peace is not overridden in the absence of clearly expressed congressional direction. We recognize that the opinion in *United Construction Workers* v. *Laburnum* * * * found support in the fact that the state remedy had no federal counterpart. But that decision was determined, as is demonstrated by the question to which review was restricted, by the "type of conduct" involved, i.e., "intimidation and threats of violence." In the present case there is no such compelling state interest.

The following month, May 1959, on the basis of this case the Court in *Grocery Drivers Union* v. *Seven Up Bottling Co.*, vacated a judgment of a California state court which awarded damages to an employer for peaceful union picketing that violated California's jurisdictional strike act; and in *DeVries* v. *Baumgartner's Electric Construction Co.*, reversed a comparable South Dakota state court judgment.

In the same month in *Plumbers' Union* v. *Door County*, the Court held that the Taft-Hartley Act deprived a Wisconsin state court of jurisdiction of an injunction suit by a county in Wisconsin and its nonunion contractor against a union for peaceful picketing of a project for an addition to the county courthouse.

At the same term as the *Nelson* decision the Court ruled in *Railway Employees' Dept.* v. *Hanson* that the union shop provision of the Railway Labor Act, which was written into the law in 1951, superseded the right to work provision of the Nebraska constitution. This ruling affected the laws in seventeen states. In earlier cases in the labor field the Court determined that under the provisions of the National Labor Relations Act, and as amended by the Taft-Hartley Act, Wisconsin's Public Utility Anti-Strike Act, the strike vote provision of a Michigan labor mediation law, an order of the Wisconsin Employment Relations Board for the reinstatement of an employee discharged because of his failure to join a union even though his employment was not covered by a union shop or similar contract, a certification by the same board of a union as the collective bargaining representative, the provisions of a New York statute under which the New York Labor Relations Board permitted the unionization of foremen, and a Florida statute requiring a license for business agents of labor unions, were all invalid because of pre-emption. In the case involving the Michigan act the Court, after a review of the provisions of the National Labor Relations Act and the Taft-Hartley Act, ruled through Chief Justice Vinson: "None of these sections can be read as permitting concurrent state regulation of peaceful strikes for higher wages. Congress occupied this field and closed it to state regulation."

In *Alberts* v. *California*, the California obscenity case decided at the same time as the *Roth* case, counsel for petitioner, relying on federal obscenity legislation, argued: "The scheme of federal regulation is so pervasive as to make reasonable the inference that Congress left no room for the states to supplement it." The Court rejected the argument in that case, but federal power is now established. If Congress wishes to pre-empt the obscenity field it can do so Will Congress then add to the recently established Department of Health, Education, and Welfare yet another, a Department of Culture?

"A General Consolidated Government"

With the *Dennis, Nelson* and *Roth* decisions we are indeed in danger of becoming the "general and consolidated government" of which

Jefferson in the Kentucky Resolutions of 1798, and the "general consolidated government" of which the draftsman of the Kentucky Resolutions of 1799, expressed their fears. It was this problem which Justice
Harlan had in mind when he wrote his dissent in the *Roth* case.

It has been to this problem that President Eisenhower has repeatedly
given his attention during his two terms as our chief executive. In a
message to Congress in March 1953 he recommended "the creation of
a commission to study the means of achieving a sounder relationship
between Federal, State and local governments." Congress accordingly
established a Commission on Intergovernmental Relations "to study
the proper role of the Federal Government in relation to the States and
their political subdivisions . . . to the end that these relations may be
clearly defined and the functions concerned may be allocated to their
proper jurisdiction." The next month he told the 45th annual Conference of Governors, meeting in Seattle, that he had "asked for a commission that would study this proper division between state responsibility
and Federal responsibility."

The Commission on Intergovernmental Relations, with Meyer Kestnbaum as its chairman, submitted reports totalling over 2000 pages. The
index alone ran to almost 150 pages. In *A Report to the President for
Transmittal to the Congress* it mustered the admonition:

. . . Assuming efficient and responsible government at all levels—National,
State, and local—we should seek to divide our civic responsibilities so that
we:

*Leave to private initiative all the functions that citizens can perform
privately; use the level of government closest to the community for all public
functions it can handle; utilize cooperative intergovernmental arrangements
where appropriate to attain economical performance and popular approval;
reserve National action for residual participation where State and local
governments are not fully adequate, and for the continuing responsibilities
that only the National Government can undertake.*

President Eisenhower made the problem the subject of his address at
Williamsburg, Virginia at a state dinner of the 49th annual Conference
of State Governors. He cautioned that those who "would stay free must
stand eternal watch against excessive concentration of power in government." He pointed to the concentration of power in the hands of
the communists in Russia, and observed, with reference to recent efforts
there at decentralization, that even "Soviet rulers have felt compelled
to allow some small part of the Government to gravitate closer to the
people." He referred by way of contrast to our governmental system
of checks and balances, but continued: "Yet a distinguished American
scholar has only recently counseled us that in the measurable future,

if present trends continue, the states are sure to degenerate into power-less satellites of the National Government in Washington."

He stated the substance of the Tenth Amendment. With reference to a governor who wired Washington for help instead of asking the state legislature to act, he commented: "But does it not tend to encourage the still greater growth to the distant and impersonal centralized bureaucracy that Jefferson held in such dread and warned us about in such great and intense detail?"

He proposed the formation of a joint federal-state committee charged with these duties:

One—To designate functions which the states are ready and willing to assume and finance that are now performed or financed wholly or in part by the Federal Government;

Two—To recommend the Federal and State revenue adjustments required to enable the states to assume such functions, and

Three—To identify functions and responsibilities likely to require state or Federal attention in the future and to recommend the level of state effort, or Federal effort, or both, that will be needed to assure effective action.

Such a study group has since been created. It is known as the Joint Federal-State Action Committee, and consists of seven federal officials, including three Cabinet officers, and ten state governors.

Many people besides President Eisenhower and many bodies besides Congress have expressed concern about the growth of federal power at the expense of the states. In August 1956 at the 79th annual meeting of the American Bar Association the dominant note in the welcoming speech of Governor Allan Shivers of Texas and in the address of the association's then president, E. Smythe Gambrell, was that federal concentration of power threatened to destroy states' rights. Governor Shivers welcomed the members of the association "to a state whose people believe in the Tenth Amendment." Mr. Gambrell declared that in the "clamor of controversy" over the first eight amendments to the Constitution "our people seem to have overlooked the Ninth and Tenth Amendments." In the same month the speakers at the Conference of Chief Justices, composed of the highest judicial officers of the forty-eight states, took up the same theme. The latter body at its 1957 meeting authorized a special committee to study the role of the judiciary as it affected the distribution of power between the federal and state governments.

In addition to the President, the Conference of State Governors, the Conference of Chief Justices, and the American Bar Association, a Government Operations subcommittee of the House of Representatives in July 1957 gave attention to the continuing growth of federal power. It held a hearing. One of its witnesses was Meyer Kestnbaum. He said that the study to be conducted by the Joint Federal-State Action Committee as well as a series of regional meetings which the subcommittee planned to hold after Congress adjourned could do a great deal to focus attention on the problem.

In September 1957 the National Conference of Chief Justices set up two special committees to study means of slowing the "constant expansion" of federal governmental power. One of these was to study the judiciary's role in the growth of federal power at the expense of the states. It was called the Committee on Federal-State Relationships as Affected by Judicial Decisions. The following year this committee submitted a 31-page report to the next annual meeting of the Conference of Chief Justices in which it stated with reference to the federal Supreme Court: "It is our earnest hope which we respectfully express, that that great Court exercise to the full its power of judicial self-restraint by adhering firmly to its tremendous, strictly judicial powers and by eschewing, so far as possible, the exercise of essentially legislative powers when it is called upon to decide questions involving the validity of State action, whether it deems such action wise or unwise."

This committee also proposed a resolution which in part resolved: "5. That this conference hereby respectfully urges that the Supreme Court of the United States, in exercising the great powers confided to it for the determination of questions as to the allocation and extent of national and state powers, respectively, and as to the validity under the Federal Constitution of the exercise of powers reserved to the states, exercise one of the greatest of all judicial powers—the power of judicial self-restraint—by recognizing and giving effect to the difference between that which, on the one hand, the Constitution may prescribe or permit, and that which, on the other, a majority of the Supreme Court, as from time to time constituted, may deem desirable or undesirable, to the end that our system of federalism may continue to function with and through the preservation of local self-government." The resolution was adopted by a vote of 36 to 8.

Subsequently the magazine *U.S. News & World Report* conducted a poll of the 351 judges, active as well as retired, of the federal district courts and courts of appeals, asking them whether they agreed or disagreed "with the conclusions of the report by the Committee on Federal-State Relationships as Affected By Judicial Decisions." Of the judges replying, 128 in number, 46 per cent agreed, 39 per cent disagreed, and 15 per cent preferred not to express any view. Of those who did express an opinion, 54 per cent agreed and 46 per cent disagreed.

There was no great difference between those who replied from the South and those who replied from the rest of the country: of those who replied from the South, 55.5 per cent agreed; but of those who replied from the rest of the country, 42.4 per cent agreed. The greatest amount of agreement came from those in the District of Columbia who replied: 80 per cent agreed; 20 per cent disagreed; and none of those who replied declined to express an opinion.

A few weeks after the results of this poll were published Chief Judge Joseph C. Hutcheson, Jr., of the Court of Appeals for the Fifth Circuit in a speech before a meeting of the Fort Worth-Tarrant County Bar Association stated: "I think Congress ought to come in every now and then and limit the jurisdiction of the Supreme Court."

In the same month that the results of this poll were published Dean Erwin N. Griswold of the Harvard Law School, in a speech in California in which he defended the Court, nevertheless said that the Court could "do much to protect itself—and thus its essential function in our remarkable governmental structure—by hewing to the narrow line, by deciding only what it has to decide, and then only in precise terms limited to the particular case."

Remedial Efforts

So far little has been done about the growth of federal power at the expense of the states. Mr. Bennett B. Patterson of the Texas bar, who recently wrote a book entitled *The Forgotten Ninth Amendment*, would probably add to the forgotten Ninth the shrunken Tenth.

The Court has probably done the least of all. It has permitted a few state court actions: in *Hahn* v. *Ross Island Sand & Gravel Co.*, despite the federal Longshoremen's & Harbor Workers' Compensation Act's exclusive remedy clause, a barge worker's Oregon state court common law negligence suit against an employer who had elected not to be covered by Oregon's Workmen's Compensation Act; in *Automobile Workers* v. *Russell* a state court action by a nonunion employee against a union and its agent for preventing the nonunion employee by means of a close picket line from entering his employer's plant during a strike; in *International Ass'n of Machinists* v. *Gonzales* a state court suit by an expelled union member for restoration of his membership and for damages for his illegal expulsion; and in *United Construction Workers* v. *Laburnum Construction Corp.*, a tort action by a contractor against a labor union for compensatory and punitive damages although the conduct of which the contractor complained also constituted an unfair labor practice under the Taft-Hartley Act. With reference to the last decision the Court said in the *Russell* case: "This case is similar to

Laburnum in many respects. In each, a state court awarded compensatory and punitive damages against a union for conduct which was a tort and also assumed to be an unfair labor practice." But the Court has not gone beyond such holdings.

On one important issue the states did prevail: the ownership of tidelands oil. However, they did not win their victory before the Supreme Court, but in Congress. This but bears out the observation of the Commission on Intergovernmental Relations in its *Report to the President* that the Court, although the guardian of civil liberties, in comparison with, and contrast to, the other two branches of government, over the past century and a half "except when dealing with slavery, has probably taken the most consistently Nationalist position."

Even when there are specific proposals to let the states handle something there are objections on the ground that the federal government through one of its agencies should do the job. A good instance arises in a part of the labor-management relations field. The National Labor Relations Board, for budgetary and other reasons, has never exercised the full measure of its jurisdiction. The Taft-Hartley Act by an amendment of the National Labor Relations Act empowered the Board "by agreement with any agency of any State or Territory to cede to such agency jurisdiction over" certain cases in this area. However, the Board has not formally ceded any of its jurisdiction under this provision. The Court in a series of three recent cases held that under the circumstances the Board's jurisdiction was still exclusive. A bill before Congress would have given power in this area to the states. But there was objection to this course. The *New York Times* stated editorially that such a measure would produce results which "would fly in the face of one of the main objectives of the Taft-Hartley Law: a uniform national labor code." The *Times* concluded: "We think the N.L.R.B. should not only get enough funds to carry on its present operations better and more quickly, but enough more than that to cover the entire field—small and large companies alike—over which Congress has given it authority."

Nevertheless, Congress may not yet alter the results of the Court's ruling in the *Nelson* case. After the decision of the Pennsylvania Supreme Court in that case, Representative Smith of Virginia on the first day of the first session of the next Congress introduced a broad bill against pre-emption. It was H.R. 3. The next year at the second session of the same Congress, and nearly two months before the federal Supreme Court's decision in the *Nelson* case, Senator John L. McClellan of Arkansas did likewise. His bill was S. 3143. It had the co-sponsorship of eleven other senators. After the Court's decision Congressman Smith and other members of Congress who were members in 1940 and voted for the Smith Act stated publicly that they never intended supersession of state laws. Congressman Smith called for a law which would permit the states to proceed with prosecutions under their own sedition laws. The Subversive Activities Liaison Committee of the National Association of Attorneys General adopted a resolution urging amendatory legislation; and Senator Styles Bridges of New Hampshire introduced a bill, S. 3617, similar to, but more narrowly drawn than, H.R. 3 or S. 3143. So did Representative Francis E. Walter of Pennsylvania, H.R. 11341. Senator Bridges' bill had the co-sponsorship of fourteen other senators, eleven Republicans and three Democrats, and both his and Congressman Walter's bill had the endorsement of the Department of Justice. Deputy, later, Attorney. General William P. Rogers wrote to Senator James O. Eastland of Mississippi, chairman of the Senate Judiciary Committee, and to Congressman Emanuel Celler of New York, chairman of the House Judiciary Committee:

It is the view of the Department of Justice that in the fields of sedition and subversion, the Federal and State Governments can work together easily and well . . . This legislation would clearly express the congressional intent that such cooperation between the federal and State Governments in this field is to be encouraged.

The Department of Justice favors enactment of the bill.

The Senate Judiciary Committee reported favorably on Senator Bridges' bill, as well as that of Senator McClellan. The House Judiciary Committee amended Congressman Smith's bill into the form of that of Congressman Walter and took similar action. However, the Congress did not get to the passage of any of them.

But on January 3, 1957, at the beginning of the first session of the next Congress, Representatives Smith and Walter again introduced their bills. Smith's again was H.R. 3; Walter's became H.R. 977. Four days later Senator McClellan did likewise and ten days thereafter so did Senator Bridges. McClellan's bill became S. 337, and Bridges', S. 654. This time McClellan's bill had fourteen co-sponsors and Bridges', eleven. Many other similar bills were introduced, especially in the House. The House Judiciary Committee reported favorably on H.R. 977 and also on H.R. 3. The Senate Judiciary Committee did likewise as to both S. 654 and S. 337.

Congressman Smith's bill as amended by the House Judiciary Committee provided: "No Act of Congress shall be construed as indicating an intent on the part of Congress to occupy the field in which such Act operates, to the exclusion of all State laws on the same subject matter, unless such Act contains an express provision to that effect, or unless there is a direct and positive conflict between such Act and a State law so that the two cannot be reconciled or consistently stand together." Those of Senator Bridges and Congressman Walter confined themselves to the area of subversion.

On July 15–17, 1958 the House gave six hours of debate to H.R. 3. Congressman Walter offered his bill, H.R. 977, as a substitute for H.R. 3. Representative Edwin E. Willis of Louisiana offered H.R. 977 as an amendment to H.R. 3 as amended by the House Judiciary Committee. The House rejected Congressman Walter's offer of H.R. 977 as a substitute for H.R. 3 by a vote of 93 to 157, but accepted Congressman Willis' offer of H.R. 977 as an addition to H.R. 3 as amended. The vote was 249 to 147; thus giving us both H.R. 3 and H.R. 977, and showing us the temper of the House as well.

The following month in the last days of the session the Senate took up the narrower S. 654. But Senator McClellan for himself and on behalf of 33 of his colleagues offered an amendment in the way of a substitute which was a combination of S. 337 and S. 654, and which was substantially like the measure that passed the House. Senator Hennings moved to table this amendment, but his motion lost by a vote of 39 to 46. However, Senator John A. Carroll of Colorado moved to recommit S. 654 to the Judiciary Committee; and the following day his motion carried, albeit by the narrowest of margins, one vote, 41 to 40.

Nevertheless, a new Congress is in session, and not only did Congressman Smith once more introduce his H.R. 3 on the opening day, but also two days later Senator McClellan for himself and Senator Bridges as well as twenty-eight more of their colleagues introduced an S.3, identical with the H.R. 3 which passed the House of the 85th Congress. Congressman Walter again introduced his bill: this time it became H.R. 2368. He also introduced a bill, H.R. 2369, to alter the law as enunciated by the Supreme Court in the *Yates* case. So did Senator Keating, S. 527, on behalf of himself and eleven other senators. Still further bills were introduced to change the law as stated in Supreme Court decisions, and more will be.

H.R. 3 passed the House of the 86th Congress, but in the meantime the Supreme Court in the *Uphaus* case limited the opinion in *Pennsylvania* v. *Nelson* to the precise facts in that case, namely, state sedition legislation aimed, not at the overthrow of the state, but the federal government. This will remove the pressure for the passage of H.R. 3. Indeed, Congressman Walter told the House in June 1959 that the *Uphaus* ruling made H.R. 3 unnecessary. The House nevertheless passed it. Of course, the Senate has yet to act on it.

A better way to accomplish the objective of S. 654 and H.R. 977 of the 85th Congress is to have the Court overrule the *Dennis* case. With it will fall the *Nelson* case. Then power over sedition will again be with the states, where the framers of the federal Bill of Rights intended it to be. In a similar way the Court can give all power over obscenity to the states by overruling the *Roth* case. With reference to state power over picketing the Court can finally recognize that picketing involves conduct more than speech, and admit that the Fourteenth Amendment does not incorporate even the First Amendment; and the federal government generally can show somewhat more confidence in state governments when it comes to questions of pre-emption.

CHAPTER X

THE RIGHT OF SILENCE

Its Basis

The Anglo-American peoples are fortunate enough not only to have the right of freedom of utterance but its opposite as well, a right of silence. Indeed, the right of silence may be said to be even older than the right to freedom of utterance. The right of silence has origins which go back at least to 1246, when the English people first resisted a general inquisition into heresy.

The bench and bar usually refer to the right of silence as the privilege against self-incrimination. As we have noted, the use of the word privilege here is probably a borrowing from its use to describe certain confidential communications which the law early protected, such as those between attorney and client. An attorney's protected silence about his client's communications to him was called a privilege as early as 1740.

However, the Fifth Amendment does not use the word privilege. Rather it says: "* * * nor shall any person * * * be compelled in any criminal case to be a witness against himself * * *." And this is the true basis of the right of silence: under our system the individual does not have to confess his deviations. On the contrary, because of favoring circumstances we have developed a sufficiently equalitarian attitude toward deviants to permit them to stand mute. As Justice Douglas with the concurrence of Justice Black aptly put it in his dissenting opinion in *Ullmann* v. *United States:* "The Fifth Amendment protects the conscience and the dignity of the individual, as well as his safety and security, against the compulsion of government." Or as Justice Field, quoting with approval these words of counsel, James C. Carter, in his day the leader of the American bar, put it in his dissenting opinion in *Brown* v. *Walker,* ". . . both the safeguard of the Constitution and the common-law rule spring alike from that sentiment of *personal self-respect, liberty, independence, and dignity,* which has inhabited the breasts of English speaking peoples for centuries, and to save which they have always been ready to sacrifice many governmental facilities and

138

conveniences. . . ." A re-examination of the growth of this right in the light of the knowledge which has accumulated since Professor John Henry Wigmore first made his study of it, and a reappraisal of it in the light of the use that the communists have made of the inquisitional technique and the plethora of confessions they have obtained as a result, will enhance one's esteem of this right.

Each new period of human history to some extent makes its own restatement of the past. This does not mean that facts are altered, but rather that new events and the increase of knowledge make us give a new evaluation to some facts which were indifferently treated before and take note of others which were overlooked.

Over sixty years ago Professor Wigmore did a comprehensive survey of the growth of the right to remain silent. He concluded that the first few hundred years of the growth of this right represented purely a jurisdictional struggle between the state and the church and between the common law courts and the ecclesiastical courts. The later researches of Mary Hume Maguire and Professor E. M. Morgan showed that more was involved, even in the early history, than simply disputes over the scope of the authority of various officials. The most important element that was involved was an opposition to the inquisitional technique as such. But Professor Morgan's study came too late for him and that of Mrs. Maguire he refused to take seriously. It is time for a new examination.

When Justice Frankfurter in June 1949, on the occasion of the Supreme Court's invalidation of confessions in three different cases from three different states, South Carolina, Pennsylvania and Indiana, commented, "Ours is the accusatorial as opposed to the inquisitorial system," he was referring to the thousand years and more of history with which we are here concerned. In primitive societies the important agency in the regulation of human affairs was not the state, or a king, or a feudal lord. Rather it was the kinship group. A person's rights depended not on his relation to the state, or to a lord, but on his position in the kindred. Similarly, an offense was regarded not as against the state but as against the party injured or his kindred. If a life had been taken, the offense was against the slain person's kindred, and they were his avengers. Accordingly, in the centuries before the 1100's in England and the 1200's in France the prosecution of offenses (except where the offender was caught in the act or as a result of a chase on a hue and cry) was in most instances by the person who had been injured or by his kindred.

Also, in those early times the methods for determining issues were completely different, except for the survival to the present time of the use of oaths, from anything we know today. The early modes of proof were three-fold: the ordeal; oaths of one's self and one's kindred (or compurgation as later legal antiquaries, borrowing a term from ecclesiastical sources, were to call it); and trial by battle. All these modes of proof had one thing in common: they were irrational. They depended not on reasoning, but on a belief in magic. They all reflected primitive thinking. God would demonstrate where the truth lay. He would wreak his vengeance on those who swore falsely. He would choose the victor.

In the 800's and the following centuries in Western Europe two changes slowly occurred in the treatment of deviants. The state gradually took over the prosecution of offenses, and the older modes of proof became obsolete. It was the accusatorial and inquisitional systems which supplanted the older modes of proof. The accusatorial method was developed by the state. It owes much to Henry II, a wise administrator, and one of the greatest of English kings (1154–1189). He laid the basis for the survival and growth of the accusatorial system in England by his extension of an institution which the Frankish kings created in the 800's, the inquiry of neighbors, the ancestor of our grand and petit juries. The inquisitional technique was created by the church. It was devised by Innocent III, an outstanding papal legislator, and one of the greatest of popes (1198–1216). The two systems represent basically opposite approaches in the treatment of deviants and fundamentally different methods for the investigation and proof of offenses. Under the accusatorial method there is an insistence that the investigating authorities get their case from other sources than the mouth of the accused. Under the inquisitional system the investigators try to get their case from this very source. It is this difference which accounts for the fact that we do not have the quantity of confessions that communist regimes do.

Looked at in one way the accusatorial method was centuries older even than Henry II, for it may be said that primitive tribal justice already had this characteristic. It was accusatorial in the sense that the state did not prosecute, and hence did not question, deviants. In England the administration of justice remained accusatorial because of the development of the grand and petit jury system.

In the 800's, in Western Europe, tribal society was becoming feudal. With the Vikings attacking from the north and the Saracens from the south, kinship ties gave way to the lord-man relationship. The authority of the state waxed; that of the kindred waned. After the Norman conquest feudalism in England became an elaborately organized and symmetrical system due to William the Conqueror's enfeoffment of his captains. As the state's power grew, so too did its jurisdiction over offenses. One of the ways in which the state increased its jurisdiction in this area was by an extension of the king's peace. William the Conqueror announced that his peace included all men, English as well as Norman.

In the 800's, too, the Frankish kings broke through the bounds of the old tribal customs and, where their finances were concerned, abandoned the older modes of proof. The customary moot hill courts with their magical, superstitious procedures were no longer good enough for the Frankish kings when their revenues were involved. They established a new procedure, one unknown to the old Germanic law. This procedure had the name of *inquisitio patriae*, more generally known as the *enquete du pays*, the inquiry of the country or the country-side—the inquiry of neighbors. In 829 an ordinance of Louis I, le Debonnaire, or the Pious (814–840), the third and surviving son of Charlemagne, provided that every inquiry with reference to the royal fisc was to be by the *inquisitio*, the inquiry of neighbors. This kind of *inquisitio* is to be distinguished from the later *inquisitio* of the church, the inquiry by officials. It was the Frankish *inquisitio* which the Normans adopted and developed, and which became our grand and petit jury system.

At first in England the inquiry of neighbors was this: a public official summoned a group of responsible neighbors, put them under oath, and asked them to give him a true answer to some question. It might be a question of fact; it might be a question of law; or it might be what we speak of as a mixed question of fact and law. Who owned certain land? What were the customs in their district? What were the local rights of the king? And the like. Henry II took this institution and step by step extended it, now to disputes like these and now like those, and now to find out whether any crimes had been committed, until in the course of time it became the usual one in the administration of justice.

About 400 years after the Frankish kings started the inquiry of neighbors, Innocent III fashioned inquiry by officials. He developed this procedure in a series of decretals beginning in 1199, possibly 1198, and perfected it in a decretal of the Fourth Lateran Council of 1215–16. Under it an official, by virtue of his office (ex officio), had power to make a person before him take an oath to tell the truth to the full extent of his knowledge as to all things he would be questioned about.

In setting up his new procedure, Innocent, following in the traces of the Roman law, provided for three forms of action: *accusatio*, *denunciatio*, and *inquisitio*. In *accusatio* an accuser formally brought suit and was subject to the *talio* in case of failure. In *denunciatio* a person gave information about an offense to the appropriate official but did not himself become a formal accuser or party to the suit. In *inquisitio* the inquisitor, without any denunciation, cited a suspect, having him imprisoned if necessary. However, under Innocent's decretals, the inquisitor was not supposed to proceed by this third method without some basis, either common report (*"per famam"*) or notorious suspicion (*"per clamosam insinuationem"*). In practice the third form, the *inquisitio*, became the invariable rule. At the same time the safeguards which Innocent III provided were ignored.

Just as the inquiry of neighbors, so the inquiry by officials, was a radical departure from the old modes of proof, including compurgation. In compurgation one swore to a set formula. One's oath helpers swore, for instance, that their principal's oath was clean and unperjured. That was all there was to it. But under the inquisitional oath one swore to tell the truth in response to questions, substantially after the modern manner. It was this system which spread throughout Christendom and to the organs of the state on the mainland of Europe, beginning in France. The point of departure in France was the Ordinance of 1260 of St. Louis. By this ordinance he forbade trial by battle in the king's courts, and substituted for it a procedure which he borrowed from the practice of the ecclesiastical courts: witnesses were to appear before certain delegates of the judge and be questioned. These delegates were to question the witnesses separately and artfully ("subtilement").

The difference between the *inquisitio* of the Frankish and English kings and the *inquisitio* of the church, between the inquiry of neighbors and the secret and artful questioning of witnesses by officials, was subtle yet fundamental. Under the inquiry of neighbors it was the neighbors who sat in judgment; under inquiry by officials, it was some official. The inquiry of neighbors was to help in the development of a fairly independent and relatively more mature citizenry, and a more or less representative form of government; inquiry by officials was not. Of course, the secret and artful questioning of witnesses was more rational than the old modes of proof. Also, the use of secrecy need not necessarily have been an evil. After all, our grand jury proceedings are secret, too. The vice lay in the use of secret questioning, not by a grand jury, but by a professional class, at a time when safeguards for persons who stood accused had not yet been developed. In England those safeguards were developed in connection with the jury system.

The English people resisted the oath ex officio, as the inquisitional procedure came to be designated, precisely because it was inquisitional. Fundamentally, what was involved was a struggle between two different ways of dealing with deviants. Especially to the English and American people there was something improper about putting a person on oath and questioning him. They raised various objections to this procedure: one was entitled to be tried in one's vicinity; to be presented formally with the charges against one; to know one's accusers; one ought not to be questioned about the secret thoughts of one's heart; thought should be free; and, last but not least, one was not bound to be one's own accuser. An important reason for insisting that one should not be made to accuse one's self was to avoid becoming an informer on members of one's family, and on one's friends and associates. The people who made these objections were also the ones who at the same time and in the same struggle developed various protective rights to those who stood accused, such as that to bail, habeas corpus, a public trial, to be confronted with the witnesses against one, to be free from unreasonable searches and seizures, and to be represented by independent counsel of one's own choice. They secured for themselves a number of personal freedoms, such as that of speech and the press, as well as the right peaceably to assemble. They safeguarded from inquiry various confidential communications, between husband and wife, attorney and client, and, in this country, doctor and patient, and priest and penitent. They evolved an individual right of privacy, a right to be let alone. It is relevant further to note that the attorney and client privilege went back to the reign of Elizabeth I, to a time shortly before the final struggle for the successful establishment of the privilege against self-incrimination began. Viewed in this light the struggle against the oath ex officio transcends jurisdictional questions. The privilege against self-incrimination becomes more than just that. It become in truth a right to remain silent. The English and American peoples accorded to the individual not only freedom of speech but also, under certain circumstances, a right of silence.

Some Early Interrogations

Of course, there were some early interrogations of individuals, but usually not before one's neighbors had formally accused one. After this occurred, a defendant now and again had to face questioning. This happened, for instance, to Simon of Shedricks, who tried to put the blame for the death of John of Crewkerne on someone else. "And Simon afterwards testifies that he was present when [John] was slain and that Elias . . . slew him, and that he saw this. And being asked what he did then, he says, Nothing, he did not tell anyone nor raise the hue." He was found guilty and sentenced to be hanged.

A manual of instruction from the 1200's contained this hypothetical case: W. of Multon was arrested for receiving and concealing three stolen cattle. He contended that he bought them at a fair, and offered to do battle. The appropriate official said to him: "And if thou didst buy them with thy money in the fair . . . why didst thou hide them so secretly for so long a time? It seemeth to me that thou didst come by them in some evil manner. . . . there is an evil presumption against thee. . . . thou shouldst put thyself upon the good folk of this vill [i.e., ask for a jury trial].

"Nay, sir, I am not put to that as it seemeth to me, for that I am ready to defend by my body [trial by battle] the aforesaid beasts as my own proper chattel.

"* * * thou didst come by these beasts wrongfully. Therefore answer in some other wise if thou thinkest well to do so.

"Sir, once more I answer thee as before that if there be any man who will sue against me that I came by these beasts wrongfully, ready am I to defend them by my body as my own proper chattel lawfully purchased."

"Sir, will thou say aught else or give other answer?"

"Nay, sir."

*   *   *

"Have him taken to the king's prison."

One must bear in mind however, and it is a significant point, that a person would normally not be questioned until after his neighbors first had formally charged him with a specific offense.

Some Guilty Pleas

Some of course confessed. In 1220 "Alice, wife of William Black, confesses that she was present along with her husband at the slaying of three men and one woman at Barnet. Therefore let her be burned."

Others confessed and became approvers. In 1221 Robert, Patrick's son, confessed himself a horse thief, and turned approver to fight five battles. Approvers were those who betrayed their accomplices, appealed them, and did battle with them and other defendants who were being privately prosecuted. Bracton said that the king could grant life and limb to an approver if he was successful in defeating a given number of defendants. He gave a form of a pardon conditioned on the recipient winning five duels. This may have been taken from Robert's case.

A case from the preceding year reads:

It is testified by the sheriffs of London and other lawful men that Roger Wainer was found seized of a furred cape and a surcoat and a towel which were extracted from the house of Fulk Woader through the window by means of a long stick with a crook at the end, and that Roger confessed that these things were pledged with him by a certain thief who has been hanged. Afterwards he confessed the theft and became an approver. Afterwards he withdrew from his appeal against one of those whom he charged as his receivers, and the other cannot be found. Therefore let him be hanged.

Robin Soaper confessed before the same [sheriffs and others] that he had pledged to the said Roger for threepence halfpenny a counterpane stolen in the said fashion by means of a stick from the house of Hugh Rede. He cannot [be heard to] contradict the king's bailiffs, so let him be hanged. Afterwards he became an approver and confessed all and appealed those whom Roger appealed and one more also.

Peine Forte et Dure

The common law had no difficulty in dealing with one who pleaded one way or the other, either not guilty or guilty, but it ended up at a loss when it had to deal with a defendant who did neither. There were a few early cases in which an accused who refused a jury trial was nevertheless tried and hanged. Three cases from the years 1220–21 may be selected. Agnes appealed Thomas, son of Hubert, for the death of her husband, Robert. "Thomas denies the death but does not wish to put himself upon the country. The 12 jurors say that he is guilty of that death, and 24 knights, chosen for the purpose other than the aforesaid 12, say the same. Therefore let him be hanged."

Thomas of the Heath was indicted for thefts and other crimes. He "does not wish to put himself upon the country. . . . And 24 knights chosen for this say the same as the 12 jurors and that he is a robber of sheep and plough beasts and other things. Therefore let him be hanged."

Thomas of Lyminge was arrested in the company of robbers at St. Albans. "Afterwards it is testified by the steward of the Abbot of St. Albans and by good men [of the Abbot's court] that he confessed himself a robber in that court. Afterwards he declared in the Bench that he knew no one who was so big a thief as Robert of Bermondsey the Archbishop's steward, and afterwards he withdrew this charge. And because there is no one point in his favour and he will not put himself on the country, it is considered that he be hanged."

However, the law developed otherwise. If a defendant stood mute he could not be tried. Accordingly, in 1275 the Statute of Westminster, the First, which also regulated bail, provided: "Notorious felons, and which openly be of evil name, and will not put themselves in Enquests of Felonies, that Men shall charge them with before the Justices at the King's Suit, shall have strong and hard Imprisonment [en la prisone forte & dure], as they which refuse to stand to the common Law of the Land." This was the origin of the so-called peine forte et dure. As the practice developed the usual way of carrying it out was to stretch the prisoner on his back and place stone or iron weights on him until he either pleaded or was pressed to death.

But aside from the peine forte et dure the use of torture was illegal at the common law. In a Year Book case (c. 1300) in which a defendant claimed that his confession had been obtained by duress the justices sent for his jailer and several of his fellow prisoners and took evidence in the prisoner's presence as to the alleged duress. Although they found that his confession had been voluntary, one may draw the inference that they would not have received it against him had they found otherwise. Fortescue, who was successively Lord Chief Justice and Lord Chancellor in the reign of Henry VI, in his *De Landibus Legum Angliae* (c. 1450), referring to the use of torture to obtain a confession, stated: "Verily, such a practice is not to be called a law but is rather a pathway to hell."

Early Pursuits of Heresy

Into this governmental framework, with one group of neighbors presenting formal and specific charges against deviants and another group judging the facts, the Church introduced the inquisitional technique; and soon ran into stiff opposition, which in the long run proved to be insurmountable. The one who introduced the inquisitional procedure into England, or as it came to be designated, the oath ex officio, was Cardinal Otto, a papal legate. He came there in 1237, the year after Henry III married his French wife, Eleanor of Provence. Less than a decade later, when Robert Grosseteste, the crusading Bishop of Lincoln, used it in a general inquisition throughout his extensive diocese the people showed resistance. They complained and Henry III, although regarded as a king who was favorable to the claims of the Church, nevertheless with the advice of his council wrote the sheriff commanding him not to let any laymen of his bailiwick appear before the bishop or his officials to make answer under oath except in causes matrimonial or testamentary ("*nisi in causis matrimonialibus vel testamentariis*"). The bishop questioned the king's motives, which William Prynne described as "an insolent undutiful answer of a furious turbulent willful Prelate," and continued with his visitations. Then the king, the next year, cited the bishop to appear before him and his justices to show cause why he had compelled persons "to appear and take his new devised Oathes." In 1251 the king cited the bishop of Worcester, who had followed Grosseteste's example. The following year he ordered Grosseteste to desist from his inquisitional practices. In his order he recited that the bishop and his officials were still compelling people to "give testimony upon Oath to the private sins of others, whereby many were defamed, and might easily incurre the danger of perjury."

There was no contention in all this that the bishops were exceeding their powers. Rather the objection was to the inquisitional method. Near the end of the same century the *Mirror of Justices* (c. 1290) also contained a criticism of this technique: "It is an abuse that a man is accused of matters touching life or limb *quasi ex officio*, without suit and without indictment."

Thus Professor Wigmore's view that the opposition of the English people to the inquisitional technique represented a jurisdictional struggle would appear to be incorrect. Indeed, it is to be doubted whether their resistance to this technique represented a jurisdictional struggle at all, at least prior to 1606, when Sir Edward Coke went on the bench. Certainly it was not fundamentally this. Fundamentally what was involved was an opposition to the inquisitional procedure itself. To the people of England, who themselves had a hand in the job of governing and where an individual was not questioned until after he had been formally and specifically charged, it seemed wrong to put a person on oath and just generally to question him.

Two legal historians, Professors Frederick Pollock and Frederic W. Maitland, expressed the opinion that because Henry II preceded Innocent III and extended the inquiry of neighbors, England escaped the inquisitional system. This would seem to be what happened. The grand jury system provided a continuity for the accusatorial characteristic of tribal justice: one was not to be proceeded against without being first formally charged. No official took one into custody and questioned one generally. One first had to be presented with specific charges by a jury of one's neighbors. The English people, always having been accustomed to formal and specific charges before being questioned, insisted on them. It was in this way that they began their successful struggle against the inquisitional system. However, their escape from this system, as Pollock and Maitland admitted, was a narrow one.

Insistence on Formal Charges

In England as in France the inquisitional method spread to the organs of the state. It crept into use in the courts of common pleas and king's bench and before the king in council. There was opposition on all fronts. With respect to the church, the *Prohibitio formata de Statuto Articuli Cleri* again prohibited the use of the inquisitional oath except in causes matrimonial and testamentary. Coke assigned this statute to the beginning of the reign of Edward I (1272–1307). Actually it followed the Articuli Cleri of 9 Edward II (1315–16).

As for the use of this oath by the king in council, the Commons protested, and the king promised that it would not be used without reason. A few years later, in 1351–52, a statute, after a reference to the Great Charter, provided that "from henceforth none shall be taken by petition or suggestion made to our lord the King, or to his council, unless it be by indictment or presentment of good and lawful people of the same neighborhood where such deeds be done, in due manner, or by process made by writ original at the common law." This same act also provided that no member of a grand jury which had indicted a suspect was to sit on the petit jury which tried him if the defendant objected. In 1368 another statute, in order "to eschew the mischiefs and damages done to divers of his commons by false accusers" causing them to be brought before the king's council, enacted that "no man be put to answer without presentment before justices, or matter of record, or by due process and writ original, according to the old law of the land." In this century, as in the preceding one, the opposition was to the inquisitional oath itself. The church clearly had jurisdiction over heresy and yet other offenses. The king's council, too, had jurisdiction over the matters it investigated. Yet in all these instances there was opposition, and it was to the inquisitional oath.

The rise of the Lollards caused the prelates to renew their pressure for the use of the oath ex officio against heretics. In 1382 they persuaded Richard II to give them the power they wanted. However, the Commons at their next session asserted that they had never agreed to this enactment and asked that it be declared void. The king consented. But in 1401, under Henry IV, the church got a statute which gave the diocesan power to arrest and imprison heretics and to "determine that same business according to the canonical decrees." So long as this statute remained on the books the church could use the oath ex officio against heretics. A statute of 1414 enlarged the church's power still further by providing that indicted heretics were to be turned over to the ordinary for trial by the church's procedure. However, in an earlier statute in the same year Parliament provided that if one was brought into the spiritual court one was to have a copy of the things complained about, so that one would know whether and how to answer them, or else one was entitled to have a writ of prohibition.

For the rest of the century and into the following one the inquisitional method continued to make headway, with the secular as well as the ecclesiastical authorities. Between 1414 and 1503 a series of a dozen different statutes, and more, empowered justices of the peace and others to question defendants and suspects about various specified offenses. The last in this series of statutes dealt with the offenses of giving liveries and keeping retainers and enacted that "the Justices of the Peace at their opyn Sessyons shall have full Power and auctorite to cause all such persons, as they shall thynke to be suspect" to come before them or two of them and "theym to examen of all such reteynours contrary to this acte, or otherwyse name theymself to be servaunt to any person or of others mysbehavying contrary to this acte by the discrescion of seid Justices." Furthermore, the act provided for informer's suits before "the Chancellor of England or the keper of the Kyng's gret seale in the Sterre Chamber, or before the Kyng in his Benche, or before the Kyng and his Counseill attendying" and gave these officials "power to examen all persons defendauntes and every of theym, as well by oth as oderwyse." Even without suit the "Chauncellor or keper of the gret Seale Justices or Counseill" were empowered to bring persons before them and "the same person or persons to examen by oth or otherwyse by their discressions." The act was to last during the king, Henry VII's, lifetime.

In the next reign opposition to the inquisitional oath renewed itself. Heresy and anticlerical feeling were spreading at this time in England. This caused another bishop of Lincoln, one of Grosseteste's successors, to start after heresy with a plentiful use of the oath ex officio. The people resisted. Their spokesman was Christopher Saint-German, a leading lawyer, and author of *Doctor and Student*. His antagonist was Sir Thomas More. Their controversy took place in 1532–33. In opposing the oath ex officio Saint-German argued: ". . . the partyes haue not knowen who hath accused them, and thereupon they have sometyme bene caused to abiure in causes of heresies; . . . for they have knowen none other accusers and that hath caused moche people in diuers partyes of this realme to thynke great malyce and parcyalyte in the spirituel iudges." Then, referring to the fact that those who named others as well as themselves gained redemption in the eyes of the church, he continued, "This is a daungerous lawe and more lyke to cause untrewe and unlawfulle men to condempne innocentes than to condempne offenders."

More answered that if the church could not use the inquisitional procedure "the stretys were lykely to swarme full of heretykes before that ryght fewe were accused, or peradventure any one eyther." Saint-German responded: "But to put the partie that is complayned on, to answere, and to condempne, if he say contrary to that the witness have seyd, not knowing who be the witnes, ne who be his accusers: it semeth not reasonable to be accepted for a lawe."

The next year Parliament entered the controversy and passed "An Acte for Punyshement of Heresye," which repealed the statute of 1401 and outlawed the *inquisitio* procedure of the church in heresy cases. The preamble, referring to the act of 1401, recited: "And also by cause those wordes canoycall sanctions and suche other lyke conteyned in the seid acte are soo generall, that unneth the most expert and best lerned men of this your Realme diligently lying in wayte uppon hymselff can eschewe and avoyd the penaltie and daunger of the same acte and canonycall sanctions yf he shulde be examyned upon suche capcious interrogatoryes as is and hath byn accustomed to be mynystered by the Ordynaries of this Realme in cases where they wyll suspecte any person or persones of heresye." Section 6 provided that before persons could be proceeded against for heresy they had to be "presented or indicted for hersye or duly accused or detected thereof by two lawfull wytnesses at the leest." Moreover, after they were apprehended, they were to answer "in open Courte and in an open place to their such accusacion and presentmentis."

The same year More was to some extent hoist on his own petard. Henry VIII had him called before some of his councilors to take the oath of supremacy or give his reasons for not doing so. More steadily declined to do either. After all he had committed no overt act: ". . . I nothinge doinge nor nothing sayenge against the statute it were a very harde thinge to compell me to saye either precisely with it againste my conscience to the losse of my soule, or precisely againste it to the destruction of my bodye."

Under the brief reign of Mary the inquisitional technique again made great gains, and it made them with both the lay and clerical authorities. Mary restored the church's jurisdiction as well as its *inquisitio* procedure in heresy cases. Hardly had she concluded her Spanish marriage with Philip than Parliament, in 1554, revived the legislation of 1401 together with that of 1382 and 1414. In the same year justices of the peace, who in 1503 were given inquisitional duties with respect to the offenses of giving liveries and keeping retainers, received an express enlargement of such duties. A statute provided that when any person arrested for manslaughter or felony, or suspicion of manslaughter or felony, who was bailable by law, was brought before two justices, they were to "take the examination of the said prisoner, and information of them that bring him, of the fact and circumstances thereof, and the same, or as much thereof as shall be material to prove the felony shall put in writing before they make the same bailment." The next year another statute extended this procedure to accused persons who were not bailable. It may be that these two statutes did no more than give legal sanction to a practice which had grown up without express statutory authority, especially in the fifty years since the act of 1503. At any rate they now had such power by express grant. However, one must remember that in proceedings before justices of the peace one had the benefit not only of specific charges but also of accusers.

In 1557 Mary took a further inquisitional step in ecclesiastical matters. In order to provide "for a severer way of proceeding against heretics" she appointed a commission of twenty-two persons, and directed them to use the oath ex officio. They were to question persons and in the process compel them "to answer, and swear, upon the holy evangelists, to declare the truth in all such things whereof they or any of them shall be examined." This was one of the successive series of bodies which under Elizabeth I were to be called the court of high commission.

The first piece of legislation under Elizabeth I was the Act of Supremacy (1558). It repealed the legislation of Philip and Mary which authorized the church to use its *inquisitio* procedure, and provided: ". . . That no person or persons shall be hereafter indicted or arraigned for any of the offenses made, ordained revived or adjudged by this act, unless there be two sufficient witnesses or more to testify and declare the said offences whereof he shall be indicted or arraigned: (2) and that the said witnesses or so many of them as shall be living and within this realm at the time of the arraignment of such person so indicted, shall be brought forth in person, face to face before the party so arraigned, and there shall testify and declare what they can say against the party so arraigned, if he require the same." Thus for the offenses covered by that act there had to be both formal charges and confrontation.

Star Chamber

Two tribunals which evolved during the reigns of the Tudors now enter our account: the court of star chamber, and the court of high commission. These two tribunals were separate bodies but they came to work closely together, especially during the seven-year period before the Long Parliament met (1640). This was in the time of the Stuart king, Charles I (1625–49) and his archbishop of Canterbury, William Laud (1633–45). Laud was the head of the high commission as well as a member of the star chamber, and thus used both bodies to carry out the oppressive program of the king and himself. The fact that Laud was a member of both tribunals and used them in a coordinated fashion may have tended to obscure in the minds of some their separate identities.

The star chamber gradually emerged from the king's council in the process of the separation of judicial from executive functions. It was not at first a distinct body. As one writer observed: ". . . while it is necessary to point out that under the Lancastrians the council was also the star chamber, there is equal need to remember that under Henry VII the star chamber was also the council." But by the time the new council register was opened in August 1540, late in the reign of Henry VIII, there was a differentiation between the two bodies, and suitors were not allowed to overlook the fact that the star chamber and the council were distinct. Of this body Sir Thomas Smith wrote in 1565: "In the Terme time . . . everie weeke once at the least . . . the Lord Chauncellor, and the Lordes, and other of the privie Counsell, so manie as will, and other Lords and Barons which be not of the privie Counsell, and be in the towne, and the Judges of England, speciallie the two chiefe Judges, from ix. of the clocke till it be xi. doe sit in a place which is called the Starre chamber, either because it is full of windowes, or because at the first all the roofe thereof was decked with images of starres gilted. There is plaints heard of riots."

Its procedure was largely written and began with an information against the defendant, often by the attorney general, which was drawn up like an old bill in equity. The defendant put in a written answer. Witnesses gave sworn statements. When all was in readiness the case came on for oral argument. The parties appeared by counsel; the information, answer, and depositions were read and commented upon; and finally each member of the court pronounced his opinion and gave his judgment separately.

If one refers to this body as it was after it became distinct from the king's council, in other words the body which the Puritans attacked and before which John Lilburne appeared, one cannot say that it exercised the royal prerogative to inflict torture for the purpose of extracting a confession. Indeed for its *ore tenus* examination, used when a person accused admitted the charge, it had three rules which excluded the use of compulsion:

1. That the private examination should not be on oath.
2. That the confession should not be obtained by compulsion.
3. That when brought into Court, Deft. should openly acknowledge his confession, but if he then denied it, he was to be remanded and proceeded against in a formal manner by witnesses.

Coke explained that in an *ore tenus* proceeding the person involved "again must freely confess in open court," and if he did not do so "then they cannot proceed against him but by bill or information, which is the fairest way."

Both Smith and Coke as well as the antiquary William Lambarde in their time had a high opinion of this tribunal. Smith was one of the most enlightened men in the reign of Elizabeth I. He was a statesman, a philosopher and a lawyer. In his *The Common-wealth of England*, written in 1565 and first published in 1583 under the title *De Republica Auglorum,* he stated that the effect of this court was "to bridle such stout noblemen, or Gentlemen which would offer wrong by force to anie manner men, and cannot be content to demaund or defend the right by order of lawe." Coke declared: "It is the most honourable court (our parliament excepted) that is in the Christian world. . . ." Lambarde extolled it as "this most noble and praiseworthy Court, the beams of whose bright justice do blaze and spread themselves as far as the realm is long or wide."

A few of its cases from the reign of Charles I, prior to Lilburne's case, may be related.

Richard Chambers, a London merchant, was charged with making a seditious speech before the Privy Council. Chambers and other merchants had a dispute with some officials at the Custom House which led to their being summoned before the privy council at Hampton Court. Chambers told the council "that the merchants are in no part of the world so screwed and wrung as in England; that in Turkey they have more encouragement." For this outburst he was fined 2000 pounds and ordered to make a written apology. He refused to make the required apology and was imprisoned in the Fleet, where he stayed for six years.

Three cases, a proceeding against Henry Sherfield and two prosecutions of William Prynne, a Puritan pamphleteer, involved the struggle of Anglican against Puritan. Sherfield was accused of breaking a painted glass window in St. Edmond's church in Salisbury. In his answer he admitted the charge, but sought to justify his conduct:

For this Window that is charged to contain the History of the Creation, he answereth

That it is no true relation or story of the Creation, in that true manner as it is set down in the book of Moses; but there are made and committed by the workmen divers falsities and absurdities in the painting of the same Window, as that he hath put the form of a little old man in a blue and red coat, for God the Father, and hath made seven such pictures; whereas God is but one in Deity. . . .

* * *

. . . he thereupon did with his staff pick out some of the glass in that part of the Window only which represented the Deity . . .

After a long but restrained discussion he "was committed to the Fleet, fined 500£ and ordered to repair to the lord bishop of his diocese, and there make an acknowledgment of his offence and contempt, before such persons as the bishop would call unto him."

The prosecutions against Prynne were for libel. The first one involved a book in which he condemned stage plays and masques. But Charles I had attended plays and his queen had taken part in a masque. The information against him accordingly charged that "he hath presumed to cast aspertion uppon the Kinge, the Queene, and the Common wealth, and indeavored to infuse an opinnyon into the people that itt is lawfull to laye violent handes uppon Princes that are either actors, favourers, or spectatores of stage playes." There were three days of hearings and a fourth day for his condemnation. He was sentenced to be degraded by Oxford, disbarred by Lincoln's Inn, fined 5000 pounds, pilloried, to have his ears cut off, and to be imprisoned for life.

Whether Prynne was released from the Tower is not clear, but in the following years he published more books and an anonymous pamphlet, *Newes from Ipswich*. In the last he attacked the bishop of Norwich, Wren, in particular, and the rest of the bishops in general. He accused them of making innovations in worship and in the ritual; he asserted that their suppression of fasts, preaching and lectures had increased the plague in 1636; and he appealed to Charles to take vengeance on these perfidious prelates. For this pamphlet he was prosecuted along with Henry Burton and John Bastwick. This time he had difficulty in obtaining counsel: they were "backward for fear of offending the court." When he did get them the one who was senior refused to sign Prynne's answer, partly because of some of the things that Prynne wanted to put into it and partly because of fear of the court. Junior counsel finally signed the answer but by this time it was too late to file it. Prynne was sentenced as before. This involved cutting off the stubs of his ears. To these stubs Chief Justice Finch cruelly called attention: "I had thought Mr. Prynne had no ears, but methinks he hath ears . . ."

A different type of prosecution was that against Anthony Roper, knight. He was accused of depopulating "five antient Messuages" and turning 600 arable acres from tilled land to pasture. In the process he tore down three houses, let two more run to ruin, and closed a water corn mill. Many poor people thus lost their houses and employments. He was committed to the Fleet, fined 4000 pounds, required to pay 100 pounds to the prosecutor plus costs, 100 pounds to the minister of the town, a like amount to the poor, condemned to rebuild the buildings within two years, put the land back into tillage, and lease the farms at reasonable rents.

High Commission

The high commission began to evolve in the reign of Henry VIII as a sort of an ecclesiastical privy council. Under Elizabeth I its members held office for sufficiently long periods and developed a sufficiently set procedure to become known as the court of high commission. Actually it was a successive series of bodies, each one created by a separate royal letters patent. As in the case of the star chamber, its proceedings were largely written. Prior to 1600 most of its hearings were probably private, but there is little reason to believe that any attempt was made to conceal the fact that a session was in progress. On the contrary, when important Puritans were involved an interested audience was frequently if not regularly permitted to attend.

Moreover, in proceedings involving Puritans the high commission often came out second best, if the Puritan versions of these proceedings are correct. The first trial of which we have any detailed account is a good example. It involved some "conventiclers" caught in 1567, and was before the Lord Mayor of London, the Bishop of London, the Dean of Westminster, and others. The defendants were brought in by the wardens of the jail and answered to their names. Then the bishop turned to the mayor and asked him to begin. The mayor declined, whereupon the bishop began. During the course of the proceedings, this occurred:

Bishop. What: you mean of our cappes and typettes, which you say come from Rome.

Ireland. It belonged to the Papistes, therefore throwe it to them.

Bishop. I have saide Masse: I am sorie for it.

Ireland. But you goe like one of the Massepriests still.

Bishop. You see mee weare a coape or a surplesse in Pawles. I had rather minister without these things, but for orders sake and obedience to the Prince.

Roper. Maister Crowley sayeth, he could not be perswaded to minister in those conjuring garments of poperie.

Nixon. Your garmentes are accursed as they are used.

Bishop. Where do you find them forbidden in the scriptures?

Nixon. Where is the Masse forbidden in the scriptures?

One other case will suffice, that of Samuel Ward, which arose in the time of Laud and Charles I. Ward was a minister in the busy port of Ipswich who as a result of Laud's measures took his stand with the Puritan faction. In 1633 an informant of the high commission, Henry Dade, advised Laud of two Puritan ships lying in the harbor at Ipswich ready to start for Massachusetts, and added that Ward "by preaching against the Contents of book of Comone prayer & sett prayer and of a fear of altering our religion hath caused (as I am persuaded) this giddiness in our neighbours about Ipswich to desire to goe into newe England." He also mentioned that he had prepared articles against Ward and would have laid them before Laud but for a fear that he would "thereby incurre & endure the hatred of Ward's adherents who are very potent in London & about Ipswich." Laud required him to produce his accusations. The next year Ward was before the star chamber, where "their Lordships, having heard him at large, thought fit to transmit him to the Court of High Commission, to be proceeded with there *ex officio*, both upon the aforesaid complaints and upon anything else that shall be produced against him." The high commission brought forty-three articles against him. They related to various statements he allegedly made, in his sermons and privately, and to his failure to follow different parts of the ritual of the Anglicans. Ward took the oath ex officio and made answer to the many articles against him. As to the statements attributed to him he either denied them or claimed distortion, but as to his failure to follow ritual he made a number of admissions. He was deprived of his ministerial function, suspended and silenced during the king's pleasure, ordered to make submission and recantation both before the high commission and in the church at Ipswich, and to give bond for 200 pounds. He refused to accept the form of submission tendered to him, and offered one of his own, which was rejected, for he did not admit the truth of the statements ascribed to him. After four years in prison he made another submission, which was accepted. In it he said: ". . . I do freely and truly acknowledge, what ever my speeches and meanings were, that as things stand testified and witnessed in court against me, the proceedings of the said court, as also the sentence concluded against me, were just, and I am heartily sorry that my speeches should have given offence. . . ."

Puritan Opposition to the Oath Ex Officio

The Act of Supremacy under Elizabeth I made the crown the head of the church in England, and empowered the queen by letters patent to delegate her authority to commissioners. This she did beginning in 1559. In her first five letters patent, issued before 1583, Elizabeth I said nothing about the oath ex officio. However, her commissioners resorted to it to some extent—after all Mary in 1557 had authorized her commissioners to use it—but the pursuit of heresy was not intensive enough to cause any general resistance. Then in 1583 things changed. Elizabeth I created a new high commission, her sixth, with Archbishop Whitgift at its head, and this time she specifically authorized her commissioners to call suspects before them and "to examine them on their corporeal oaths, for the better trial and opening of the truth." To this end Whitgift drew up a list of twenty-four points, or articles, running the gamut of doctrine, dress and ritual, upon which suspects were to be questioned. The ones who bore the brunt of his attack were the Puritans.

Once again, as on the two previous occasions when there were general investigations into heresy in England—in the time of Grosseteste, shortly after the introduction there of the oath ex officio, and under the reign of Henry VIII—the people strongly opposed the inquisitional oath. This time the Puritans spearheaded the opposition. They and others then out of sympathy with the governing authorities made it plainer than had their predecessors that the objections to the oath ex officio were based not only on the fact that it enabled inquiry into the secret thoughts and knowledge of a person's heart, but also made him into an informer on his family, neighbors and friends.

In 1584, the very next year after Elizabeth I created the Whitgift high commission, Parliament petitioned against the oath ex officio. This step encountered the queen's refusal. One of the Puritan leaders, James Morice, a lawyer and a member of Parliament, wrote a tract against the oath which was published in 1590. In it he explained that by the use of this oath the ecclesiastical judge could require a person "to accuse himselfe even of his most secret and inward thoughtes, or contrarie to christian charitie, yea humanitie it selfe, constrayning him to enforme against his naturall parentes, dearest friends, and nearest neighbors, or to bewray with griefe of heart such matters of secrecie, as otherwise were inconvenient peradventure not honest to be revealed." He went on to tell how in the reign of Henry VIII the "bloudie Bishop" of Lincoln by the oath ex officio "constrayned the children to accuse their parentes, the parentes their naturall children, the wife her husbande, the husbande his wife, one brother and sister another."

In July 1590, when the Puritan minister, John Udall, refused to tell the high commission whether he was the author of a certain book he frankly explained: "My lord, I think the author, for any thing I know, did well, and I know that he is enquired after to be punished; and therefore I think it my duty to hinder the finding of him out, which I cannot do better than thus." When then asked why so, he answered: "Because if every one that is suspected do deny it, the author at length must needs be found out." Later when the oath was urged upon him he offered to take an oath of allegiance to the queen but refused to take the inquisitional oath, saying: ". . . but to swear to accuse myself or others, I think you have no law for it."

Yet another Puritan leader, the preacher, Thomas Cartwright, who was before the high commission in September 1590, was reluctant to take the oath "lest by his answer upon oath in this case others might be prejudiced, who would refuse to answer upon theirs." Daniel Neal in his *History of the Puritans*, in discussing the course of Cartwright and of fifteen more who followed his example, stated: "The rest of

Cartwright's brethren refusing the oath for the same reasons, viz., because they would not accuse themselves, nor bring their friends into trouble . . ." There were of course those who confessed and disclosed who attended their meetings. As to them Neal commented: ". . . but the worst part of their confession was their discovering the names of the brethren that were present, which brought them into trouble." Earlier in his work he related: "When the prisoners were brought to the bar, the court immediately tendered them the oath to answer all questions to the best of their knowledge, by which they were obliged not only to accuse themselves, but frequently to bring their friends and relations into trouble." One will note that in all this, nothing was said of the use of any torture.

At the time Whitgift and his fellow commissioners started on their crusade this much was fairly well established: one was entitled to be accused formally and to know the charges; and one did not have to submit to inquiry about one's secret thoughts and deeds. Also, as a matter of practice one usually knew who one's accusers were and, in a nonpolitical criminal case, was confronted with them. Of course, once one had been formally charged, one could be and was questioned. This was true in lay as well as ecclesiastical proceedings. So far as questioning an accused was concerned, one of the main differences between a lay criminal trial and a case before the high commission was that in a lay criminal trial a defendant was not put under oath. But from a rational point of view, this difference is not a substantial one: questioning is questioning whether one is put under oath or not. As Sir Frederick Pollock rightly remarked, referring to the procedure of the star chamber: "It may perhaps be doubted whether systematic and deliberate interrogations were less fair to a man on his trial than the running fire of cross-examination by the judges restrained by no rules of evidence, which the prisoner had to stand in all ordinary criminal cases down to the Restoration."

Indeed, in a lay criminal trial by the latter part of the 1500's the judge not only questioned a defendant but even badgered him. An illustration is Udall's case, the Puritan minister who was before the high commission. Within the same month as his appearance before that body he was indicted for libelling the queen and the court not only questioned him but also took the then unusual step of offering him an oath: "What say you? Did you make the Book, Udall, yea or no? What say you to it, will you be sworn? Will you take your oath that you made it not? We will offer you that favour which never any indicted of Felony had before; take your oath, and swear you did it not, and it shall suffice." Udall refused. The judge offered to take his unsworn answer: ". . . I will go further with you; Will you but say upon your honesty that you made it not, and you shall see what shall be said unto you?" Udall again refused. Then the judge urged him, "Do not stand in it, but confess it . . ."

But if one had the right to be formally and openly charged and could not be questioned on one's secret thoughts and deeds, and if one as a matter of practice usually knew one's accusers and was confronted with them, the next step followed naturally: one could not be made to accuse one's self. This was the step the English people took to resist the pursuit of heresy which Whitgift and his successors carried on.

In composing their argument against the oath ex officio the Puritans and their lawyers made use of a phrase which they borrowed from an opinion of nine English canonists, one of whom was Richard Cosin, a leading civil lawyer. These canonists about the middle of Elizabeth I's reign prepared a short treatment of the practice in ecclesiastical courts in England and the use of the oath ex officio. They conceded that "no man may be urged to bewray himself in hidden and secret crimes; or simply therein to accuse himself." Then they discussed the *inquisitio* procedure of the church, in the course of which they stated the safeguards which theoretically accompanied it: "Licet nemo tenetur seipsum prodere; tamen proditus per famam, tenetur seipsum ostendere, utrum possit suam innocentiam ostendere, et seipsum purgare [Though no one is bound to become his own accuser, yet when once a man has been accused by general report, he is bound to show whether he can prove his innocence and to vindicate himself by an oath of purgation]." The Puritans and their counsel took the nemo tenetur seipsum prodere and in the course of the next century made it into a household phrase, in the colonies as well as in the mother country. At first they tied it to the nisi in causis matrimonialibus vel testamentariis of the order of 1246 of Henry III to Grosseteste and the Prohibitio formata de Statuto Articuli Cleri of Edward II; but after 1640, the year the Long Parliament convened, a turning-point year in an eventful century for the English people, the phrase was used by itself. On every hand and in every court people simply claimed that no one was bound to be his own accuser.

Even before 1583 there were instances in Elizabeth I's reign in which common law courts on habeas corpus released persons who were in custody for refusal to take the high commission's oath ex officio, but the precise grounds of these decisions are not clear. The three cases most frequently cited later were those of *Skrogges*, involving title of an office, *Hynde*, accused of usury, and *Leigh*, charged with hearing mass at the Spanish ambassador's house. Coke after he got on the bench, cited all three cases for the proposition that no person was bound to accuse himself except in matters matrimonial and testamentary. However, Dyer's report does not support Coke in the cases of *Skrogges* and *Hynde*, and *Leigh's* case is not in any published report. One must further bear in mind that during Elizabeth I's reign the common law courts were not unfavorable to the high commission; they even held it to be a prerogative rather than a statutory court. It was not until after Coke got on the bench in the reign of James I that there were many writs of prohibition against the high commission. Nevertheless, this much may be said: persons were relieved from taking the oath, and, whatever may have been the reasons, the law was also pretty clear that one was entitled to be formally charged and to know what the charges were.

Then came Whitgift and his twenty-four articles. Protest began almost from the start. In 1584 certain ministers who were under attack by Whitgift applied to Lord Burleigh for help. He wrote Whitgift: ". . . But I conclude, according to my simple judgment, this kind of proceeding is too much savouring of the Romish inquisition: and is rather a device to seek for offenders, than to reform any. This is not a charitable way to send them to answer to your common Register upon so many articles at one instant, without any commodity of instruction by your Register, whose office is only to receive their answers. By which the parties are first subject to condemnation, before they be taught their error. . . . I pray your Grace, bear that one (per chance a) fault, that I have willed them not to answer these articles, except their conscience may suffer them. . . ." Whitgift justified his procedure on the ground that it was "the ordinary course in other courts likewise; as in the Star Chamber, the Court of Marches, and other places." Burleigh replied that "he was not satisfied in the point of seeking by examination to have ministers accuse themselves, and then punish them for their own confession."

In 1589 Coke stepped into the picture. He represented one Collier, who was involved before the high commission on a charge of incontinency. Coke sought a writ of prohibition in the common pleas, and argued that no one was bound to accuse himself except in causes matrimonial or testamentary. Wigmore suggested that Coke's argument was newly devised as well as specious. He is wrong on both scores. The use of the phrase neme tenetur seipsum prodere apart from its full context antedated Coke's argument in this case by the number of years. Also, if one will take into account the fact that there was opposition to the inquisitional oath in England in the century and a half after its introduction and under Henry VIII, based on the ground that one was entitled to be formally and openly accused, one will regard a refusal to be the one's own accuser as a logical next step rather than a specious one.

What the outcome was in the *Collier* case is uncertain. According to two reports Coke won, but a third stated that "the court would advise of it." The next year Udall, when he was before the high commission, stressed the older ground: "I pray your lordship, doth not the law say generally, no man shall be put to answer without presentment before justices, or things of record, or by due process, or writ original?" To support his question he cited the statute of 1368! Just before this, when he explained that by law he need not answer, the court responded, in terms reminiscent of the comment in the *Mirror of Justices*, "That is true, if it concerned the loss of your life."

In 1591 in the case of Dr. Jeremiah Hunt the King's Bench held that the high commission could compel him to answer under oath concerning incontinency "where the offence is first presented by two men." The same year the same court gave another favorable decision to the high commission: it held it to be a prerogative court.

Two years later Morice proposed a bill in Parliament for the abolition of the oath ex officio. For this he had to spend some time in the Tower.

At the Threshold of the 1600's

Thus matters stood as the English people entered upon one of their great centuries, the 1600's, a century that witnessed the contest between Edward Coke and James Stuart, the refusal of Edmund Hampden and four others in 1627 to make a forced loan to Charles I, the Petition of Right (1628), the resistance of Edmund Hampden's more famous kinsman John in 1635 and the following years to Charles I's attempts to collect ship money from him, John Lilburne's case before the Star Chamber, which began in 1637, the Long Parliament, which convened in 1640, the abolition of the star chamber and the high commission (1641), John Milton and his *Areopagitica* (1644), James II's flight from England (1688), and the Bill of Rights (1689). It also witnessed the execution of Laud (1645) and of Charles I (1649). Much had already been gained as the century opened; much remained yet to be won. The people would use the rights they had thus far obtained in order to help them perfect these rights and win yet others.

If one looks at the rights of deviants in the year 1600 from the standpoint of today, those rights will seem rather meager. One will see great lacks. For instance, a defendant who was arraigned at the king's suit for a felony was not entitled to counsel. Neither Sir Nicholas Throckmorton nor Sir Walter Raleigh had counsel. But the legal profession was there. In a civil suit one was entitled to make one's answer by a professional pleader. Also, in a criminal case if one was proceeded against by way of the old private appeal rather than by indictment one could have counsel. Curiously enough, one could have counsel, too, in a proceeding before the star chamber and usually in one before the high commission. But the rule was otherwise in case one was indicted for a felony. A somewhat similar rule prevailed in France: only the king and the sovereign lords could sue by procurator. This was the origin of the maxim: "In France no one pleads by procurator save the king." When the justice of such a rule began to be questioned in England in the latter part of the 1500's Edward Coke, who had an advocate's ability for fashioning arguments, had a double explanation: the judge was counsel for the accused; and the prosecutor had the burden of proving his case so clearly that no defense was possible and hence no counsel was necessary. Of course, his own conduct as a prosecutor in Raleigh's trial demonstrated a defendant's need to have counsel, but in a case involving a felony indictment such a right was yet to come.

Another great lack was in the way of witnesses. One's accusers participated in the trial of a felony indictment but not the witnesses for one. Such a right was denied to Throckmorton, for instance. Indeed in criminal cases of a political nature one usually was not even confronted with one's accusers.

A third great shortcoming in the trial of a felony indictment was the absence of adequate independence on the part of the trial jury. True it was that the jurors were the judges of the facts, but if the government did not like the result, jurors could be and were imprisoned or fined or both. Eight of the jurors who acquitted Throckmorton suffered both imprisonment and fine.

But if one compares the position of deviants in the year 1600 with what it was in the times of tribal society, one will see great gains. There was an established judiciary with a bench and bar and a grand and petit jury system, all manifesting some measure of independence and capable of manifesting more. By means of the jury system the people themselves engaged in the business of governing. Bail and habeas corpus existed, although in a limited fashion. One's accusers usually confronted one. One had a chance to plead one's cause, and with one's neighbors. Moreover, the two best characteristics of tribal justice, formal charges and public trials, continued in existence. With these beginnings the English people were able to develop yet further rights for the individual as against the state.

Coke Versus Stuart

Appropriately enough the first major episode in the struggle of the English people against the Stuarts was the contest between Edward

Coke and James Stuart. Just as with Henry II and Innocent III we have here two more individuals who helped shape the course of the treatment to be accorded deviants. It was this James who became James VI of Scotland (1567) and James I of Great Britain and Ireland (1603). He reigned until his death in 1625. Coke and James I were contemporaries. Indeed, Coke was born fourteen years ahead of James, in 1552, and survived him by almost ten, until 1634. Neither of them, certainly not James, had the stature of Henry II or Innocent III. Each had a considerable amount of weakness with his strength. James dissembled to gain his ends. Coke cringed before authority. Yet each had a certain measure of courage and toughness. Each stood by his position. Each had intelligence, learning and a sense of justice. Coke stood for the supremacy of law; James for the divine right of kings.

Coke's career extended from the reign of Elizabeth I into that of Charles I. He was early a success at the bar and his reputation soon became great. At the age of 27 he helped to win a famous piece of litigation known, at least by name, to every lawyer in England and America, *Shelley's Case*, which involved a complicated question of real estate law. In 1592 he became Queen Elizabeth's solicitor general and two years later her attorney general, a position which he retained under James I. As attorney general under James he prosecuted Sir Walter Raleigh in 1603 and the Guy Fawkes Gunpowder Plot conspirators in 1605. The following year James elevated him to the bench, making him Chief Justice of the Court of Common Pleas. It was in this position that there developed, because of his insistence on the supremacy of the common law, his fundamental conflict with James. In 1613, at the suggestion of Francis Bacon and in order to get him out of the way, James promoted him, in the same sense that promotions sometimes occur today, to be Chief Justice of the Court of King's Bench, a position of more dignity but less labor and desirability. However, Coke's conflict with James continued, and in 1616 he was dismissed. But his career was by no means at an end. Among other activities, he was a member of the Parliaments of 1621 and 1624 under James and of the Parliament of 1628 under Charles I. This was during the period when both the king and the House of Commons claimed a mysterious source of liberty and power, which the king called prerogative and the Commons, privilege. Coke became a champion of the privileges of Parliament. As a result of his work in the Parliament of 1621 he went to the Tower for most of nine months from December 1621 to August 1622. In the Parliament of 1628, at the age of 76, he prepared the Petition of Right, one of the important documents, along with the Magna Carta, in English constitutional history. A young member of this Parliament, who silently observed the great struggle for the Petition of Right, was Oliver Cromwell.

Coke was essentially and primarily an advocate, first for private litigants, next the crown, then the common law courts of common pleas and king's bench, and last, Parliament. He was adept, and sometimes devious and specious in devising an argument, and if history stood in the way he ignored it. Some later writers have taken him to task for this characteristic, perhaps too severely, for they do not make sufficient allowance for the fact that he was first, last, always, and foremost, an advocate. A good indication of his importance as a legal authority is this comment of Chief Justice Best in the course of an opinion in a case which was decided on the basis of one of Coke's statements: "The fact is, Lord Coke [on the point in question] had no authority for what he states, but I am afraid we should get rid of a good deal of what is considered law in Westminster Hall, if what Lord Coke says without authority is not law. He was one of the most eminent lawyers that ever presided as a judge in any court of justice . . ." It was as counsel to a private litigant, and later as a judge, that he helped to prepare the way for the establishment of the right to remain silent. It was during his whole career, but especially as judge, that he helped to lay the basis for the establishment of the idea of the supremacy of law. He may not have been as courageous in his opposition to James as he pictures himself in his own accounts, for more than once in a scene with James he grovelled on his knees at a great expense to his dignity, and yet while cringing before the king he nevertheless defied the crown and clung to his position on the supremacy of law.

James received a thorough scholastic training, which gave him a taste for learning and a desire to excel as an author, but he turned out to be a garrulous pedant rather than a scholar. His writings, which embrace poetry as well as prose, tempt one to place him alongside of Alfred, but their quality as literature is mediocre and one remembers the titles of his works rather than their contents. His output included, *The Essayes of a Prentise, in the Divine Art of Poesie* (1585), *Daemonologie* (1597), *The Trew Law of Free Monarchies* (1598), *Basilikon Doron*, or *Kingly Gift* (1599), intended for his elder son, Henry, who died before accession, and *Counterblaste against Tobacco* (1604). One of his early acts as king of Great Britain and Ireland was to cause the leading ecclesiastics in England to be called to a conference at Hampton Court in January 1604 for a three-day discussion of theology. During the course of the conference one of the doctors suggested a new translation of the Bible and James approved. The result was the King James or Authorized Version. In his *Daemonologie* he revealed one of his enormous blind spots: his acceptance of the popular belief in witchcraft, although a few of the better minds of the day were challenging this belief. James argued for it, in question and answer form. One of the questions he put was why more women were witches than men and answered: ". . . for as that sexe is frailer than man is, so is it easier to be entrapped in those gross snares of the Devill, as was ever proved to be true by the Serpent's deceiving Eve at the beginning . . ." He also favored the practice of ducking witches, using the old argument that the water would "refuse to receive them in her bosom that have shaken off the sacred water of baptism." And yet after he became James I he showed skepticism of the evidence produced at a switchcraft trial in Leicester. Sully, Huguenot minister of Henry IV of Navarre, described him as the wisest fool in Christendom.

Events at the time of his marriage may have had something to do with his belief in witches. For a wife he chose Anne, the second daughter of King Frederick II of Denmark. They were married by proxy in August 1589 and Anne prepared to cross the seas to Scotland. But storms drove her back and she landed in Norway. In October, James himself sailed to meet her in Oslo. There in November they were married by a Scotch Presbyterian minister. After the wedding they went south, by a long journey, to Elsinore, and spent the rest of the winter at the court of Copenhagen. Here James visited with the astronomer, Tycho Brahe, and composed a sonnet to him. At the end of April they returned. Not long thereafter Scotland was in the throes of an orgy of hunting people accused of witchcraft. Victims were charged with causing the storm which had prevented Anne from coming to Scotland in 1589 and conspiring to use black magic in order to destroy James. One of the principals was accused of sending a letter which urged the suspects: "Ye sall warne the rest of the sisteris to raise the wind this day, att eleavin houris, to stay the Queen's cuming in Scottland." There were many confessions. The king himself took a hand in the questioning. One of the victims, Geillis Duncane, played on a jews-harp the dance of the witches in his presence. Another, Agnis Sampson, drew the king aside and "declared unto him the verye woordes which passed between the King's Maiestie and his Queene at Upslo in Norway the first night of their marriage, with their answere each to other." Such stories would impress the credulous, and James had almost the credulity of the mass of the people of his time.

Just as Coke treasured the common law, so James treasured the kingship. For a long time he looked forward to the double crown. He finally obtained it. He had ideas of grandeur, but they did not become delusions: his intelligence was too great for that. There dwelt in his mind a vision of himself presiding at a general conference which would bring about universal peace. He and the pope would weld the warring churches into a single church of God, largely on the theological plan of James, and future generations would call him blessed. He had other grandiose plans but they, too, did not come to fruition. In England his absolutist claims for the kingship soon brought him into irreconcilable conflict with Coke and the other judges of the common law courts of common pleas and king's bench, and with Parliament. Under the Tudors, Parliament was still an unproven force; under the Stuarts this force matured and became supreme. James met with his first Parliament in 1604. He expressed his thankfulness to the English for so comfortably receiving him and then explained "the blessings which God in my Person hath bestowed upon you all." He, in his person, had brought them peace—peace with foreign nations, peace between the two parts of the island. "I am the Husband, and all the whole Isle is my lawful Wife; I am the Head, and it is my Body; I am the Shepherd, and it is my Flock; I hope, therefore, no man will be so unreasonable as to think that I, as a Christian King under the Gospel, should be a Polygamist and husband to two wives; that I being the Head, should have a divided and monstrous Body; or that being the Shepherd to so fair a Flock . . . should have my Flock parted in two." But he was not to have his own way, either then or later. When he told the House of Commons in 1621 that he felt himself "very free and able to punish any man's misdemeanors in Parliament, as well during their sitting as after" and should not fail to do so, the Commons responded by declaring free speech to be their "undoubted right and inheritance," and sent a delegation with this message to the king. While the delegation waited on him, he cried out sarcastically: "Bring chairs for the ambassadors." James did not again threaten their freedom of speech but in his second reply to this message wrote that what they called their rights were in fact grants from his predecessors on the throne and they should dutifully have acknowledged it. Coke, in December, moved that they spread on their records a protestation of their rights. The next afternoon by candlelight they protested the inviolable and sovereign nature of their body and of its members, and resolved that the protestation be entered upon the Journals of the House. The next day they were adjourned. On December 27 Coke went to the Tower. Three days later James in Whitehall sent for the Journals and in the presence of his council tore out the page containing the protestation. In the end, however, the English people won; the Stuarts lost.

With James I's accession to the throne the position of the church was probably further strengthened. At the Hampton Court conference a lord objected to the inquisitional procedure of the High Commission: "The proceedings in that Court are like the Spanish Inquisition, wherein men are urged to subscribe more than law requireth, and by the oath *ex officio* forced to accuse themselves . . ." Whitgift answered, not in the positive way in which he had taken care of Lord Burleigh in 1584, but as if the opposition he had encountered had not been without its effect on him, too: "Your lordship is deceived in the manner of proceedings; for, if the article touch the party for life, liberty, or scandal, he may refuse to answer . . ." James gave an exposition in support of the oath ex officio, "the ground thereof, the wisdom of the law therein, the manner of proceeding thereby, and profitable effect from the same."

Later the same year Richard Bancroft succeeded Whitgift as archbishop of Canterbury. He was equally zealous. In the name of the whole clergy he objected to the grant of a writ of prohibition in a case where the high commission sought to question someone before giving him a specification of the charges. The judges answered that parties ought "to have the cause made knowne unto them for which they are called *ex officio*, before they be examined, to the end it may appeare unto them before their examination, whether the cause be of ecclesiastical cognizance, otherwise they ought not to examine them upon oath."

In 1606 Henry Garnet, superior of the Jesuits in England, on trial for high treason as a conspirator in the gunpowder plot, used the phrase about not accusing one's self to describe proceedings before a magistrate: ". . . When one is asked a question before a magistrate, he was not bound to answer before some witnesses be produced against him, 'Quia nemo tenetur prodere seipsum.'" This illustrates how easy it was to proceed from the requirement of a formal accusation to the acknowledgment of a right to remain silent.

It was in that year, also, that James made Coke chief justice of the court of common pleas. Soon thereafter, according to Coke in his *Oath Ex Officio*, the king's council on the motion of the House of Commons asked Popham and him "in what cases the Ordinary may examine any person *ex officio* upon oath." After a study of the law they answered: "1. That the Ordinary cannot constrain any man, ecclesiastical or temporal, to swear generally to answer to such interrogatories as shall be administered unto him; but ought to deliver to him the articles upon which he is to be examined, to the intent that he may know whether he ought by the law to answer them: and so is the course of the Star Chamber and Chancery; the defendant hath the copy of the bill delivered unto him, or otherwise he need not to answer it.

"2. No man ecclesiastical or temporal shall be examined upon secret thoughts of his heart, or of his secret opinion: but something ought to be objected against him what he hath spoken or done. No lay-man may be examined *ex officio,* except in two causes, and that was grounded upon great reason; for lay-men for the most part are not lettered, wherefore they may easily be inveigled and entrapped, and principally in heresy and errors of faith . . ."

After Coke got on the bench the number of writs of prohibition against the high commission increased. In fact there were so many of them that Bancroft complained to the king. On this complaint the king assembled the judges before him one Sunday morning in November 1608. James took the position that he in his own person could decide any cause and therefore he could delegate it to the high commission. Then according to Coke in his *Prohibitions del Roy,* this occurred: "To which it was answered by me, in the presence, and with the clear consent of all the Judges of England, and Barons of the Exchequer, that the King in his own person cannot adjudge any case, . . . but this ought to be determined and adjudged in some Court of Justice, according to the law and custom of England; . . . then the King said, that he thought the law was founded upon reason, and that he and others had reason, as well as the Judges; to which it was answered by me, that true it was, that God had endowed His Majesty with excellent science, and great endownments of nature; but his Majesty was not learned in the laws of his realm of England, and causes which concern the life, or inheritance, or goods, or fortunes of his subjects, are not to be decided by natural reason but by the artificial reason and judgment of law, which law is an act which requires long study and experience, before that a man can attain to the cognizance of it; that the law was the golden met-wand and measure to try the cause of the subjects; and which protected his Majesty in safety and peace: with which the King was greatly offended, and said, that then he should be under the law, which was treason to affirm, as he said; to which I said that Bracton saith, *quod Rex non debet esse sub homine, sed sub Deo et lege* [that the King ought not to be under any man, but under God and the law]."

Coke's account contains his own heavy gloss. James would never have permitted without interruption the long speeches which Coke attributed to himself. From Sir Julius Caesar and various newsletters it appears that at some point James broke in and told Coke he "spoke foolishly." James, himself, was the supreme judge and all the courts were under him. There was nothing to prevent him from sitting on the bench and deciding cases himself if he chose, but nevertheless he would protect the common law.

"The common law protecteth the King," countered Coke.

"A traitorous speech!" erupted James. "The King protecteth the law and not the law the King. The King maketh judges and bishops. If the judges interpret the laws themselves and suffer none else to interpret them, they may easily make, of the law, shipmen's hose." Then rising in his chair and shaking his fist in Coke's face he tongue-lashed him so heatedly that Coke "fell flatt on all fower" before the king and begged his pardon. Robert Cecil interceded for Coke and the king was finally mollified.

But if Coke grovelled before James, what is even more important than his grovelling is the fact that he insisted that the king was under the law.

Not long thereafter Coke made so bold as to assert, in *Dr. Bonham's Case*, that not only the crown but even Parliament itself was subject to the common law: "And it appears in our books, that in many cases, the common law will controul Acts of Parliament, and sometimes adjudge them to be utterly void: For when an Act of Parliament is against common right and reason, or repugnant, or impossible to be performed, the common law will controul it, and adjudge such Act to be void . . ." Coke's idea on this point was not to prevail in England, although it was in our country.

In another case in granting a writ of prohibition Coke said: ". . . the Ecclesiastical Judge cannot examine any man upon his oath, upon the intention and thought of his heart, for *cogitationis poenam nemo emeret* [no man may be punished for his thoughts]. And in cases where a man is to be examined upon his oath, he ought to be examined upon acts and words, and not of the intention or thought of his heart; and if every man should be examined upon his oath, what opinion he holdeth concerning any point of religion, he is not bound to answer the same . . . And so long as a man doth not offend neither in act nor in word any law established, there is no reason that he should be examined upon his thought or cogitation: for as it hath been said in the proverb, *thought is free;* . . ." In his *Second* Institute he wrote: "No person ecclesiasticall or temporall ought in any ecclesiasticall court to be examined upon the cogitation of his heartt or what hee thinketh * * *"

He ruled that the high commission in an *ex officio* proceeding "ought not to examine any man upon his oath, to make him to betray himself, and to incur any penalty pecuniary or corporal." The *ex officio* proceeding here involved was an aftermath of private litigation before the high commission. It was instituted by the king's proctor, and was for the forfeiture of a bond.

The next major piece of litigation involving the high commission's use of the oath *ex officio* occurred after Coke was on the king's bench. It was *Burrowes* case, and arose on applications for, and returns to, writs of habeas corpus on behalf of a group of non-conformists who had been committed by the high commission. Coke proceeded slowly. The court heard argument four separate times in a period of more than a year (1615–16), bailed them after the third argument, but finally remanded them. At the third session Coke after explaining that he did not like sectaries any better than anybody else but that he had to do justice, gave three reasons why the returns to the writs were bad:

I will not by any ways maintain sectaries. But the subject ought to have justice from us in a Court of Justice. For three causes, my conscience and judgment do lead me in this case, that this return here is not good.

First, the statute of 1 Eliz. is a penal law, and so they are not to examine one upon oath upon this law; thereby to make him to accuse himself . . .

A second cause which doth satisfie my conscience, when they demanded the articles, they ought to have had of them a copy . . .

A third reason may be drawn from the liberty of the subject, the which is very great as to the imprisonment of his body, and therefore before commitment, the party ought to be called to make his answer, and if he be committed, yet this ought not be perpetually. . . .

To this Justice Dodderidge added: "If they think they may examine them upon oath, and not to deliver them a copy of the articles, yet shall they still be suffered to lie in prison perpetually; we will not suffer this so to be, but we will bail them until the next term, and in the mean time to conform themselves."

During the pendency of this litigation the king's bench and common pleas in separate cases, involving proceedings between private parties before the high commission, both squarely held that a person was not bound to accuse himself where to do so might subject him to punishment or penalty. In *Spendlow* v. *Smith,* involving a suit before the high commission for dilapidations, the court of common pleas granted a writ prohibiting the high commission from examining the defendant in the suit before it about covin, "for though the original cause belong to their cognizance, yet the covin and fraud is criminal; and the avowing of it to be bona fide is punishable, both in the Star-Chamber, and by the penal law of fraudulent gifts, and therefore not to be extorted out of himself by his oath." The king's bench in *Latters* v. *Sussex,* a comparable case in which there was an allegation of simony, ruled similarly: ". . . none shall be compelled to accuse himself upon his oath; where he is to incurr a temporal punishment, at the common law, or a temporal loss . . . And a prohibition was granted: for by that he is to lose 100£ by the statute. . . ."

Not long after these decisions Coke was dismissed, but the principle that one was not bound to accuse one's self in matters involving punishment or penalty had made headway. That it was to be applied to litigation between private parties before the high commission and to proceedings resulting from such litigation was pretty well established. It had been extended even farther: in the *Burrowes* case it had been one of the grounds for granting bail to a group of non-conformists under attack by the high commission. These circumstances plus the succession of Bancroft, in 1610, by George Abbot, a man of more moderate temperament, led to a lessening for a time of the controversy over the inquisitional oath. But the struggle between the people and the crown continued, and took on greater intensity again under Charles I and Laud, who succeeded Abbot in 1633. Under them the controversy over the oath ex officio resumed in full force with *Lilburne's* case before the star chamber.

John Lilburne

Lilburne in the course of his controversy with the star chamber arrived at the position that no free-born Englishman should take the oath ex officio. This is how he came to be known as "Free-born John." A judge said of him that if the world were emptied of all but him, Lilburne would quarrel with John and John with Lilburne. In December 1637, while John Hampden's case was being argued before the court of exchequer, the star chamber had Lilburne taken into custody on a charge of importing certain seditious books. It is to be noted that without objection he at first answered many questions relating to the charge against him. It was only when the questioning went beyond the charge, specifically when he was asked about other individuals, that he began to object, and started the last phase of the final struggle for the establishment of the right to remain silent. He was in the attorney general's office being questioned by the latter's chief clerk. At first he even answered some questions about other individuals, but as this questioning went afield he refused to continue: ". . . why do you ask me all these questions? these are nothing pertinent to my imprisonment, for I am not imprisoned for knowing and talking with such and such men, but for sending over Books; and therefore I am not willing to answer you to any more of these questions. . . . therefore if you will not ask me about the thing laid to my charge, I shall answer no more: but if you will ask of that, I shall then answer you, and do answer that for the thing for which I am imprisoned, which is for sending over books, I am clear, for I sent none; and of any other matter that you have to accuse me of, I know it is warrantable by the law of God, and I think by the law of the land, that I may stand upon my just defence, and not answer to your interrogatories; and that my accusers ought to be brought face to face, to justify what they accuse me of."

Then began a long effort to get him to be sworn and answer such questions as would be put to him. He was taken to the attorney general, Sir John Bankes, himself, and ten or twelve days later, to the offices of the court of star chamber. He persisted in his refusal to be sworn. The account of what happened, which is by Lilburne, goes on to relate: "So some of the clerks began to reason with me, and told me every one took that oath: and would I be wiser than all other men? I told them, it made no matter to me what other men do . . ." In February 1638 he was taken before the star chamber itself. When the lord keeper asked him why he refused to take the oath he answered: "My honourable Lord, I have answered fully before sir John Banks to all things that belong to me to answer unto: and for other things, which concern other men, I have nothing to do with them." The lord keeper persisted: "But why do you refuse to take the Star-Chamber oath." Lilburne responded: ". . . though I had fully answered all things that belonged to me to answer unto . . . yet that would not satisfy and give content, but other things were put unto me, concerning other men, to insnare me, and get further matter against me . . . And withal I perceived the oath to be an oath of inquiry; and for the lawfulness of which oath, I have no warrant; and upon these grounds I did and do still refuse the oath." The star chamber ordered that he was to be held a close prisoner until Tuesday of the following week, and if in the meantime he did not take the oath he was to be censured and made an example. The following Monday he was again offered the oath, and again he refused, saying, ". . . I am of the same mind I was; and withal I understand, that this Oath is one and the same with the High Commission Oath, which Oath I know to be both against the law of God, and the law of the land . . ." On Tuesday he was again before the star chamber, was once more offered the oath and once more refused to take it. For his continued refusal he was this time fined 500 pounds and sentenced to be whipped and pilloried, a sentence which was executed in April. While he was in the pillory he made a speech against the oath. According to his own account he stated: "Now this oath I refused as a sinful and unlawful oath: it being the High Commission oath. . . . It is an oath against the law of the land. . . . Again, it is absolutely against the law of God; for that law requires no man to accuse himself; but if any thing be laid to his charge, there must be two or three witnesses at least to prove it. It is also against the practice of Christ himself, who, in all his examinations before the high priest, would not accuse himself, but upon their demands, returned this answer, 'Why ask you me? Go to them that heard me.'

"Withal, this Oath is against the very law of nature; for nature is always a preserver of itself and not a destroyer: But if a man takes this wicked oath, he destroys and undoes himself, as daily experience doth witness. Nay, it is worse than the law of the heathen Romans, as we may read, Acts XXV. 16. For when Paul stood before the pagan governors, and the Jews required judgment against him, the governor replied, 'It is not the manner of the Romans to condemn any man, before he and his accusers be brought face to face, to justify their accusation.' But for my part, if I had been proceeded against by a Bill, I would have answered and justified all that they could have proved against me . . ."

He not only made a speech against the oath while at the pillory, but also with acrobatic ingenuity distributed three copies of the offending book, which he had secreted about his person. Finally the star chamber, which was in session, had him gagged.

Long Parliament

On November 3, 1640 the Long Parliament met, and the turning-point in the successful struggle of the people against the crown had arrived. Oliver Cromwell on the opening day presented a petition on behalf of Lilburne, who was still in prison. He was ordered to be released, "being, as I remember, the first prisoner in England set at liberty by them." In May 1641 the House of Commons voted that his sentence was illegal and that he should have reparation. Two months later in two separate acts Parliament abolished both the star chamber and the high commission, and forbade any person exercising ecclesiastical authority to administer "*ex officio*, or at the instance or promotion of any other person whatsoever . . . any corporal oath" where the answers might subject one "to any censure, pain, penalty or punishment whatsoever." The act which abolished the star chamber also extended the writ of habeas corpus to cover any person restrained of his liberty "by the order or decree of any such court of star-chamber, or other court aforesaid, now or at any time hereafter, having or pretending to have the same or like jurisdiction, power or authority to commit or imprison as aforesaid, (2) or by the command or warrant of the King's majesty, his heirs or successors, in their own person, or by the command or warrant of the council-board, or of any of the lords or others of his Majesty's privy council."

The Commons had voted that Lilburne was entitled to reparation, but the Lords had not yet acted. His counsel in arguing before them on his behalf in February 1645 asserted that it was "contrary to the laws of God, nature, and kingdom, for any man to be his own accuser." The Lords agreed, and ordered that his sentence be forever totally vacated "as illegal, and most unjust, against the liberty of the subject, and law of the land, and Magna Charta, and unfit to continue upon record." Finally, in December 1648, Parliament awarded Lilburne 3000 pounds as reparation.

It could be argued that the act which abolished the high commission did not forbid all oaths in criminal matters in ecclesiastical courts but only those in cases in which persons had not been first duly charged. A statute of 1661, passed after the restoration of the Stuarts, disposed of any such argument. This statute made it unlawful for any person exercising ecclesiastical authority "to tender or administer unto any person whatsoever, the oath usually called the oath *ex officio*, or any other oath whereby such person to whom the same is tendered or administered may be charged or compelled to confess or accuse, or to purge him or herself of any criminal matter or thing, whereby he or she may be liable to any censure or punishment."

In this and many other ways the reforms wrought by the Long Parliament endured. Thereafter various rights of the individual, some of which had been growing, established themselves. These included, in addition to the right of silence, the right to bail, habeas corpus, a public trial, to be confronted with the witnesses against one, to produce witnesses in one's favor, to have unhampered juries, to be represented by independent counsel of one's own choosing, and to be free from unreasonable searches and seizures. As David Jardine, a legal scholar, put it: ". . . The law then for the first time became a protection to the subject against the power of the Crown; and so well considered and substantial were the improvements then introduced, that they continued after the Restoration, and through the tumultuous and sanguinary reign which succeeded it. Though the barriers were still insufficient entirely to stop the encroachments of bad princes, encouraged and promoted by unprincipled judges, the administration of the Criminal law, even in the evil days of Charles II, was always better than it had been before the Commonwealth; for the tide of improvement, having once set in, steadily continued to flow, until at length the increase of knowledge, and the power and proper direction of public opinion, led to the final subjection of prerogative to law at the Revolution of 1688."

Final Recognition

After the Lilburne case in the star chamber and the various steps which the Long Parliament took in 1640–41, ordering his release, abolishing the star chamber and high commission, forbidding the use of the oath ex officio by ecclesiastical officials and extending the writ of habeas corpus, people on every hand, no matter what the charge or the proceeding or the court, claimed a right to remain silent; and the courts soon recognized this right. In 1641 in the case of the *Twelve Bishops*, who were charged with high treason before the House of Lords, when they were asked whether a certain document was subscribed by them and in their handwriting, refused to answer because "it was not charged in the impeachment; neither were they bound to accuse themselves." In 1649 in Charles I's trial, when one Holder on being asked to be sworn expressed a desire to be spared from giving evidence against the king, "the Commissioners finding him already a Prisoner, and perceiving that the Questions intended to be asked him, tended to accuse himself, thought fit to waive his examination." In the same year Lilburne, this time on trial under the commonwealth for high treason, insisted on a right of silence. He at first even refused to plead, saying, "Then, Sir, thus, by the Laws of England, not to answer to questions against or concerning myself." Lord Keble responded, "You shall not be compelled." In 1660 in the trial of Adrian Scroop, one of the regicides, Lord Chief Baron Bridgeman said to him: "Did you sit upon the Sentence-day, that is the evidence, which was the 27th of January? You are not bound to answer me, but if you will not, we must prove it."

A striking claim of privilege occurred in 1670 in the trial of William Penn and William Mead, who were indicted for preaching to a tumultuous assembly and disturbing the peace. The Penn in this case was the one who later founded Pennsylvania. Mead in refusing to answer the recorder's question whether he was present at the meeting, stated vividly: "It is a maxim of your own law, 'Nemo tenetur accusare seipsum,' which if it be not true Latin, I am sure it is true English, 'That no man is bound to accuse himself.' And why dost thou offer to insnare me with such a question?" The recorder answered, "Sir, hold your tongue, I did not go about to insnare you." The jurors returned a verdict in which they stated that Penn and Mead were guilty of speaking but refused to find them guilty of what they were charged. The court tried to browbeat the jurors into a verdict of guilty, with the result that they ended up finding both Penn and Mead not guilty.

Another interesting claim of a right of silence took place in 1676 before Charles II and his council. Francis Jenkes was haled before them for presuming to criticize royal policies at a public meeting. He admitted his speech. The king asked: "Who advised you?"

Jenkes replied: "Since I see your majesty and the Lords are angry, though I am sensible that I have not given you any just cause for it;

I must not say I did it without advice, lest you should be more angry; and to name any particular person (if there were such) would be a mean and unworthy thing, therefore I desire to be excused all farther answer to such questions; since the law doth provide, that no man be put to answer to his own prejudice."

Prosecutors as well as judges for a time continued to question defendants, and even urge them to confess. For example, when Lilburne was on trial in 1649, this occurred:

Mr. Attorney. . . . But why will you put us to all this trouble to prove your Books, seeing your hand is to them? My Lord, I had thought that the great champion of England would not be ashamed to own his own hand.

Lilburne. I have answered once for all: I am upon Christ's terms, when Pilate asked him whether he was the Son of God, and adjured him to tell him whether he was or no; he replied, "Thou sayest it:" so say I, Thou Mr. Prideaux sayest it, they are my Books: But prove it; and when that is done, I have a life to lay down to justify whatever can be proved mine.

Judge Jermin. But Christ said afterwards, "I am the Son of God:" Confess, Mr. Lilburne, and give glory to God.

Lilburne. I thank you, Sir, for your good law, but I can teach myself better.

But this practice, too, came to an end. The last judge to use it was Lord Chief Justice Holt, who died in 1710. "To the end of his life," according to Lord Campbell, a later lord chief justice as well as lord chancellor, "he persevered in what we call 'the French system' of interrogating the prisoner." However, during the latter half of the 1600's the right to remain silent firmly established itself, and it extended not only to defendants, but also to witnesses.

A long view establishes that the right of silence grew steadily from the early English opposition to the inquisitional technique. The insistence on being formally presented with charges and on knowing one's accusers, to which was added the practice of confrontation, led naturally and logically to the position that one was not bound to accuse one's self. Thus under our system deviants acquired a right of silence. The four dissenters (Justices Shiras, Gray, White and Field) in *Brown* v. *Walker*, the first federal Supreme Court decision sustaining the government's position under an immunity act, and the two dissenters (Justices Douglas and Black) in *Ullmann* v. *United States*, turn out to have had a better understanding of this right than the majority. A proper regard for the nature of this right should lead one to the position which Justice Douglas took in writing his and Justice Black's dissent in the *Ullmann* case: "My view is that the Framers put it beyond the power of Congress to *compel* anyone to confess his crimes. . . . The critical point is that the Constitution places the right of silence *beyond the reach of government*." Especially should this be true in the area of heresy, the very area in which this right had its growth.

Bushell's Case

The prosecution of William Penn and William Mead provided not only a striking claim of the right of silence but also an aftermath which established the independence of trial juries as judges of the facts. The aftermath is known as *Bushell's Case*, after Edward Bushell, the foreman of the jury which acquitted Penn and Mead. This jury was kept without meat or drink for over two days in order to get them to agree on a verdict satisfactory to the court. When they finally insisted on bringing in a verdict of not guilty the court fined them forty marks apiece and had them committed until their fines were paid. The jurors sought their release before the court of common pleas on a writ of habeas corpus, and won their freedom. The opinion of the court on the request of all the judges was by the chief justice, Sir John Vaughan. He reasoned: ". . . for if it be demanded, What is the fact? the Judge cannot answer it: if it be asked, What is the law in the case, the Jury cannot answer it." It is true that on appeal the judgment was reversed on the ground that the case, being a criminal one, was not cognizable by the court of common pleas. However, Vaughan's opinion was such a sound one that it was thereafter regarded as representing the law. A newsletter account of the opinion stated that it was "business of great concernment and much talked of." Thus trial jurors indeed became the judges of the facts.

John Wilkes

The Anglo-American peoples developed not only a right of silence, but also a cognate right to be free from unreasonable searches and seizures. Still later they added a right to privacy, a general right to be let alone.

What the Puritans and Lilburne did in the 1600s for the right to remain silent, John Wilkes did in the next century for the right to be free from unreasonable searches and seizures. Coke had already said that a man's house was his castle. But it took Wilkes and No. 45 of his paper, the *North Britain*, to give content to the statement.

The practice of issuing search warrants arose in England in the middle of the 1600s. Before that time Coke in his *Fourth Institute* stated that in the absence of an indictment justices of the peace had no power to issue a warrant "to search for a felon, or for stolen goods, for they being created by an act of parliament have no such authority granted unto them by any act of parliament." But after the middle of the century Matthew Hale expressed a contrary opinion: "In case of a complaint and oath of goods stolen, and that he suspects the goods are in such a house, and shews the cause of his suspicion, the justice of peace may grant a warrant to search in those suspected places mentioned in his warrant, and to attach the goods and the party in whose custody they are found, and bring them before him or some justice of peace to give an account how he came by them, and farther to abide such order as to law shall appertain. . . ."

Search warrants were used originally to recover stolen property. With the passage of the 1662 licensing act for publications the crown took to the use of these warrants in a general form to search for writings alleged to be seditious and for their authors, printers and publishers. It was such a warrant which was used against No. 45. This number came out in April 1763 and contained a biting criticism of George III's message to Parliament. The king's ministers regarded it as a seditious libel and Lord Halifax, one of the secretaries of state, issued a general warrant. This warrant was ruled to be illegal, and the various resulting actions against the king's messengers were estimated to have cost the government as much as 100,000 pounds. Wilkes recovered 4000 pounds from Lord Halifax himself.

Not long thereafter Lord Halifax furnished the court with another opportunity to consider general warrants. This time the offending publication was *The Monitor, or British Freeholder*. The warrant differed from that used against Wilkes in that it named the person, John Entinck, whose effects were to be seized, but it put no restrictions upon the officers as to the scope of the search. Entinck sued those who conducted the raid. The jury found a special verdict, stating the facts of the raid but setting up that such warrants had been in common use. Lord Camden, with the unanimous concurrence of the other judges of his court, ruled that general search warrants were illegal. To permit them, he reasoned, "would destroy all the comforts of society, for papers are often the dearest property a man can have." According to another report of the case he stated that to sanction the practice of issuing such warrants "would be subversive of all the comforts of society." Justice Bradley of the United States Supreme Court later stated in his opinion for the Court in *Boyd* v. *United States* that Lord Camden's "great judgment in that occasion is considered as one of the landmarks of English liberty." Thereafter the elder Pitt, Lord Chatham, could declare movingly: "The poorest man may in his cottage bid defiance to all the forces of the crown. It may be frail—its roof may shake—the wind may blow through it—the storm may enter—the rain may enter—but the King of England cannot enter!—all his force dares not cross the threshold of the ruined tenement!"

In the Colonies

The experience in the colonies was not far different from that in the mother country. The colonists insisted on formal charges, on knowing their accusers, on being tried in their own communities, and on a right of silence. When John Wheelwright was summoned before the authorities of Massachusetts Bay Colony in 1637, a half year before Lilburne was taken into custody in England, he demanded to know whether he was sent for as an innocent or a guilty person. He was told as neither, but as a suspect. Then he demanded to know his accusers. It was explained to him that his accuser was one of his sermons and that since he acknowledged it "they might thereupon proceed, *ex officio.*" But "at this word great exception was taken, as if the Court intended the course of the High Commission, &. It was answered that the word *ex officio* was very safe and proper . . . seeing the Court did not examine him by any compulsory meanes, as by oath, imprisonment, or the like . . ." At length, on the persuasion of some of his friends, he agreed to answer questions, but as soon as he was asked about something which did not relate directly to the sermon, he refused to answer, and "hereupon some cried out, that the Court went about to ensnare him, and to make him to accuse himself. . . ."

In November, a month before Lilburne's incarceration in England, Anne Hutchinson, whose views Wheelwright shared, was summoned before Governor Winthrop and the elders. The governor in an opening explanation told her that she was called before them as a disturber of the peace of the commonwealth and the churches. She responded: "I am called here to answer before you, but I hear no things laid to my charge."

In 1642, shortly after Lilburne's victory over the court of star chamber, Deputy Governor Richard Bellingham of Massachusetts Bay Colony wrote to Governor William Bradford of Plymouth Plantation and propounded the following question, among others: "How farr a magistrate may extracte a confession from a delinquente, to acuse him selfe of a capitall crime, seeing Nemo tenetur prodere seipsum." Bradford referred the questions to some of his elders, three of whom replied. All three were opposed to the use of an inquisitional oath. The first said: "That an oath (ex officio) for such a purpose is no due means, hath been abundantly proved by ye godly learned, & is well known." The second answered: ". . . he may not extracte a confession of a capitall crime from a suspected person by any violent means, whether it be by an oath imposed, or by any punishmente inflicted or threatened to be inflicted, for so he may draw forth an acknowledgmente of a crime from a fearfull innocente; if guilty, he shall be compelled to be his owne accuser, when no other can, which is against ye rule of justice." The third responded: "The words of ye question may be understood of extracting a confession from a delinquente either by oath or bodily tormente. If it be mente of extracting by requiring an oath, (ex officio, as some call it,) that in capitall crimes, & fear it is not safe, nor warented by Gods word, to extracte a confession from a delinquente by an oath in matters of life and death." To the Puritan mind, as the answers of these elders show, requiring a suspect to take an inquisitional oath was a form of torture and an even worse one than physical compulsion: the third elder would not have permitted an inquisitional oath although he would have allowed a certain amount of physical compulsion in exceptional circumstances to obtain a confession.

In Virginia, after Bacon's Rebellion in 1677, the house of burgesses in the same year announced: "Upon a motion from Acomac county, sent by their burgesses, *It is answered and declared*, that the law has provided that a person summoned as a witness against another, ought to answer upon oath, but noe law can compell a man to sweare against himselfe in any matter wherein he is lyable to corporall punishment." That the motion which led to this announcement came from Accomac County was no accident, for it was there that Governor Berkeley was at his harshest, both during and after the suppression of the rebellion.

Royal governors in the colonies, patterning themselves after the king in England, exercised what they regarded as their prerogative. They summoned suspects before them and their council and tried to induce confessions. If they were successful such confessions were then used at subsequent trials. The colonists resisted this practice and protested vigorously. In 1689 in Pennsylvania the governor summoned the printer, William Bradford, before him and his council. Bradford had printed the charter of that colony in order to inform the people of their rights. Although the publication was anonymous, he was the only printer there.

Governour: . . . I desire to know from you, whether you did print the Charter or not, and who set you to work?

Bradford: Governour, it is an impracticable thing for any man to accuse himself; thou knows it very well.

Governour: Well, I shall not press you to it, but if you were so ingenious as to confess, it should go the better with you.

Bradford: Governour, I desire to know my accusers; I think it very hard to be put upon accusing myself.

Governour: Can you deny that you printed it? I do know you did print it and by whose directions, and will prove it, and make you smart for it, too, since you are so stubborn.

Bradford: . . . if any thing be laid to my charge, let me know my accusers. I am not bound to accuse myself.

One of the charges against Governor Andros of New England and New York in the New England revolution of 1689, following the flight of James II from England, was that he would too frequently "fetch up persons from very remote Counties before the Governor and Council at Boston (who were the highest, and a constant Court of Record and Judicature) not to receive their tryal but only to be examined there, and so remitted to an Inferior Court to be further proceeded against. The Grievance of which Court was exceeding great. . . . But these Examinations themselves were unreasonably strict, and rigorous and very unduely ensnaring to plain unexperienced men." When some years later, in 1696, the governor of Massachusetts summoned Thomas Maule before him and his council to question him about a book in which Maule criticized both clerical and lay officials and their conduct in the witchcraft prosecutions, he refused to answer any questions and successfully demanded to be tried by a jury of his peers in his own county.

A few years before the Revolution Governor Dunmore of Virginia called before him and his council persons accused of forging paper money. The house of burgesses as a body advised the governor that his mode of proceeding was "different from the usual Mode, it being regular that an examining Court on Criminals should be held, either in the County where the Fact was committed, or the Arrest made." Then followed this explanation: "The duty we owe our Constituents obliges us, My Lord, to be as attentive to the safety of the innocent as we are desirous of punishing the Guilty; and we apprehend, that a doubtful construction and various execution of Criminal Law does greatly endanger the safety of innocent Men."

In the employment of torture to extort confessions the experience in the colonies again was not far different from that in the mother country. There is one recorded instance of the peine forte et dure: in 1692 Giles Corey, who was accused at Salem of witchcraft, was pressed to death for his continued refusal to plead. There is also a recorded instance of a royal governor in the exercise of his prerogative providing for the use of torture to obtain a confession: Governor Berkeley of Virginia as one of his last official acts authorized that a Negro "be racked tortured or Whipt till he confess how this dire misfortune happened."

But aside from these instances the use of torture to extract confessions was probably not much more in use in this country than in England. Two of the three elders of Plymouth Plantation who responded

to the questions which Governor Bradford referred to them were opposed to the use of physical compulsion under any circumstances. The
first stated: "To inflicte some punishmente meerly for this reason, to
extracte a confession of a capitall crime, is contrary to ye nature of
vindictive justice, which always hath respecte to a know crime comitited
by ye person punished; and it will therefore, for any thing which can
before be knowne, be ye provocking and forcing of wrath, compared to
ye wringing of ye nose, Pro: 30.33. which is as well forbiden ye fathers
of ye countrie as of ye family, Ephe. 6.4. as produsing many sad &
dangerous effects." The second answered that a magistrate could not
extract a confession by any violent means whether "by any punishmente
inflicted or threatened to be inflicted." The third would have permitted
the use of torture but only "in matters of higest consequence, such as
doe conceirne ye saftie or ruine of stats or countries, . . . espetially
wher presumptions are strounge; but otherwise by no means." Even
Cotton Mather was against the use of torture. In a communication in
1692 to John Richards, one of the judges in the witchcraft trials at
Salem, in which he recommended the use of "Crosse and Swift Questions" in order to get confessions from suspects, he nevertheless made it
plain that he was "farr from urging the un-English method of torture."

The Body of Liberties of 1641 of Massachusetts Bay Colony did
contain this provision: "Liberty 45. No man shall be forced by Torture
to confesse any Crime against himselfe nor any other unlesse it be in
some Capitall case where he is first fullie convicted by cleare and suf-
fitient evidence to be guilty, After which if the cause be of that nature,
That it is very apparent there be other conspiratours, or confederates
with him, Then he may be tortured, yet not with such Tortures as be
Barbarous and inhumane." However, this exception by its very terms
was limited to a situation where a person had already been convicted.

In the arguments for a federal Bill of Rights at the time of the adoption of the federal Constitution there were a few references to the possibility of the introduction of torture in some form. The one who argued
most vividly on the point was, as usual, Patrick Henry. He declared:
"But Congress may introduce the practice of the civil law, in preference
to that of the common law. They may introduce the practice of France,
Spain, and Germany of torturing, to extort a confession of the crime.
They will say that they might as well draw examples from those countries as from Great Britain, and they will tell you that there is such a
necessity of strengthening the arm of government, that they must have
a criminal equity, and extort confession by torture, in order to punish
with still more relentless severity." But this statement shows the

absence rather than the presence in this country and Great Britain of the practice of the use of torture to obtain confessions.

Just as in the mother country so in the colonies there were objections to general searches. However, in the colonies the resistance was to searches for goods on which duties had not been paid rather than for publications. Parliament at the same session in 1662 in which it enacted a licensing act for publications, passed equally drastic measures for the enforcement of the revenue laws. The chief weapon of enforcement was the writ of assistance. This was a blanket permit issuable to anyone, authorizing him to search any suspected place. The only limitation was that the search had to be in the daytime. Proceedings under this statute appear to have aroused little opposition in England; but in the colonies, where taxation was none too popular irrespective of the methods of collection, the story was otherwise. In the course of time determined opposition arose. In 1761 in Massachusetts the legality of writs of assistance was questioned in *Paxton's Case*. The advocate general for the crown was James Otis and as such it became his duty to argue for their validity. Instead he resigned his office and took the other side of the case. In a masterful address he denounced writs of assistance as "the worst instrument of arbitrary power, the most destructive of English liberty and the fundamental principles of law that ever was found in an English law book." The judges, almost convinced, sent to England for advice; but subsequently in obedience to orders from the ministry, recognized the writs. Although the case was lost, the cause was not. John Adams, who heard Otis's argument, later wrote: "Every man of a crowded audience appeared to me to go away, as I did, ready to take arms against writs of assistance. Then and there was the first scene of the first act of opposition to the arbitrary claims of Great Britain. Then and there the child Independence was born."

Constitutions and Bills of Rights

When the break with the mother country finally came, all the colonies save one, Rhode Island, following habits of thought which had origins going back more than five and a half centuries to the Magna Carta, set forth in written form the structures of their governments and specified various of the rights of the individual as against the state. Rhode Island continued under its charter of 1663. All the rest in the early years of the revolution drafted constitutions. Nine—Connecticut, Delaware, Maryland, New Hampshire, New Jersey, North Carolina, Pennsylvania, South Carolina and Virginia—did so in 1776, the year of the Declaration of Independence; two, Georgia and New York, did so the following year; and one, Massachusetts, did so in 1780. Vermont, which was not one of the original thirteen colonies, drafted a constitution in 1777. Prior to the adoption of the federal Constitution seven states—Maryland, Massachusetts, New Hampshire, North Carolina, Pennsylvania, Vermont and Virginia—either as part of their constitutions or separately, also drafted declarations or bills of rights. In these various documents ten states—Connecticut, Georgia, Maryland, Massachusetts, New Hampshire, North Carolina, Pennsylvania, South Carolina, Vermont and Virginia—made specific provision for bail which would not be excessive; nine—Georgia, Massachusetts, New Hampshire, New Jersey, North Carolina, Pennsylvania, South Carolina, Vermont and Virginia—for trial by jury; eight—Maryland, Massachusetts, New Hampshire, New Jersey, North Carolina, Pennsylvania, Vermont and Virginia—for confrontation and for witnesses in one's favor; an equal number—Georgia, Massachusetts, New Hampshire, North Carolina, Pennsylvania, South Carolina, Vermont, and Virginia—for freedom of speech or of the press or both; seven—Maryland, Massachusetts, New Hampshire, New Jersey, New York, Pennsylvania and Vermont—for counsel; a like number—Maryland, Massachusetts, New Hampshire, North Carolina, Pennsylvania, Vermont and Virginia—for formal charges, a right of silence, and against general warrants; four—Georgia, Massachusetts, New Hampshire and North Carolina—for habeas corpus; two—Pennsylvania and Vermont—for a speedy public trial; and one— New Hampshire—against double jeopardy. Delaware in its charter of 1701 had provisions for counsel and witnesses.

With these efforts as part of their background the framers of the federal Constitution and the first Ten Amendments drafted documents which are as enduring and felicitous as any that human beings have ever produced. A knowledge of the development of the rights of individuals under the Anglo-American legal system makes a reading of the federal Bill of Rights a new and exciting experience.

Further Gains

The embodiment in constitutions and bills of rights of guarantees of various individual rights did not, of course, end the development of those rights. On the contrary, it furthered their development. From time to time court decisions, rules of court, and legislation, both here and in Great Britain, enlarged upon them and established others as well. Especially was such enlargement true of the right of silence.

In this country seven American states—Maryland, Massachusetts. New Hampshire, North Carolina, Pennsylvania, Vermont and Virginia —had put a guarantee of the right of silence in their constitutions or bills of rights before the adoption of the Fifth Amendment. Today, in addition to the Fifth Amendment's protection of this right, all but two states—Iowa and New Jersey—have similar constitutional provisions; and in these two states this right also obtains, in one, Iowa, by judicial decision, and in the other by statute as well as judicial decision. Many states have statutory as well as constitutional provisions.

Moreover, the Fifth Amendment's guarantee of the right of silence is one provision to which the federal courts have nearly always given a liberal interpretation. In 1807 in the *Aaron Burr* case, Chief Justice Marshall sitting as a circuit justice in the federal court for Virginia stated that this right covered not only answers that would in themselves support a conviction but also those which would furnish a link in the chain of evidence needed to prosecute. In *Counselman* v. *Hitchcock* the Court extended this right to a grand jury proceeding, although the Fifth Amendment's guarantee by its terms relates only to a criminal case. The Court through Justice Blatchford pointed out that this provision "must have a broad construction in favor of the right which it was intended to secure." Recent cases, including two in the Supreme Court, *Emspak* v. *United States* and *Quinn* v. *United States*, further extended it to proceedings before congressional committees. The Supreme Court cases involved Thomas Quinn and Julius Emspak, members of the United Electrical Workers. In both cases the Court not only sustained claims of the privilege before a congressional committee, but did so even though they were based only secondarily on the Fifth Amendment. Emspak in refusing to answer certain questions explained: "Because of the hysteria, I think it is my duty to endeavor to protect the rights guaranteed under the Constitution, *primarily the first amendment, supplemented by the fifth.* This Committee will corrupt those rights." Quinn adopted the statement of another, Thomas J. Fitzpatrick, a member of his union. Fitzpatrick commented at one point: "This is a protection of the First Amendment to the Constitution, supplemented by the Fifth Amendment." Another time he said: "I stand on the protection of the Constitution, the First and Fifth Amendments." The opinions in both cases were by Chief Justice Warren. In the *Quinn* case, after pointing out that the guarantees in the federal Constitution were to be accorded a liberal construction he continued: "Such liberal construction is particularly warranted in a prosecution of a witness for a refusal to answer, since the respect normally accorded the privilege is then buttressed by the presumption of innocence accorded a defendant in a criminal trial. To apply the privilege narrowly or begrudgingly—to treat it as an historical relic, at most merely to be tolerated—is to ignore its development and purpose."

In line with this sympathetic application of the Fifth Amendment's right of silence, the Supreme Court recently held in *Slochower* v. *Board of Higher Education* that section 903 of New York City's charter was invalid because it made the claim of a right of silence an automatic basis for the termination of one's employment. The petitioner was Harry Slochower, an associate professor of German at Brooklyn College. The Court ruled: ". . . The privilege against self-incrimination would be reduced to a hollow mockery if its exercise could be taken as equivalent either to a confession of guilt or a conclusive presumption of perjury. . . . There has not been the 'protection of the individual against arbitrary action' which Mr. Justice Cardozo characterized as the very essence of due process."

In yet another recent case, that involving Henry W. (the Dutchman) Grunewald, Max Halperin and Daniel A. Bolich, alleged to be members of a tax-fixing ring, the Court ruled that a trial judge's allowance of the government's cross-examination of a defendant to bring out his prior reliance on his right of silence under the Fifth Amendment when subpoenaed by a grand jury constituted reversible error. The Court in an opinion by Justice Harlan reasoned:

We need not tarry long to reiterate our view that, as the two courts below held, no implication of guilt could be drawn from Halperin's invocation of his Fifth Amendment privilege before the grand jury. Recent re-examination of the history and meaning of the Fifth Amendment has emphasized anew that one of the basic functions of the privilege is to protect *innocent* men. Griswold, The Fifth Amendment Today * * * "Too many, even those who should be better advised, view this privilege as a shelter for wrongdoers. They too readily assume that those who invoke it are either guilty of crime or commit perjury in claiming the privilege." *Ullmann* `v. *United States* * * * See also *Slochower* v. *Board of Higher Education,* * * * when, at the same Term, this Court said * * * : "The privilege serves to protect the innocent who otherwise might be ensnared by ambiguous circumstances."

When we pass to the issue of credibility, we deem it evident that Halperin's claim of the Fifth Amendment privilege before the Brooklyn grand jury in response to questions which he answered at the trial was wholly consistent with innocence. Had he answered the questions put to him before the grand jury in the same way he subsequently answered them at trial, this nevertheless would have provided the Government with incriminating evidence from his own mouth. For example, had he stated to the grand jury that he knew Grunewald, the admission would have constituted a link between him and a criminal conspiracy, and this would be true even though he was entirely innocent and even though his friendship with Grunewald was above reproach.

Justice Black in a concurring opinion in which Chief Justice Warren and Justices Douglas and Brennan joined added:

* * * I agree with the Court that use of this claim of constitutional privilege to reflect upon Halperin's credibility was error, but I do not, like the Court, rest my conclusion on the special circumstances of this case. I can think of no special circumstances that would justify use of a constitutional privilege to discredit or convict a person who asserts it. The value of these constitutional privileges is largely destroyed if persons can be penalized for relying on them. It seems peculiarly incongruous and indefensible for courts which exist and act only under the Constitution to draw inferences of lack of honesty from invocation of a privilege deemed worthy of enshinement in the Constitution. * * *

The federal courts have interpreted the Fifth Amendment's guarantee of a right of silence in the spirit of Justice Bradley's comment in *Boyd* v. *United States*:

. . . And any compulsory discovery by extorting the party's oath, or compelling the production of his private books and papers, to convict him of crime or to forfeit his property, is contrary to the principles of a free government. It is abhorrent to the instincts of an Englishman; it is abhorrent to the instincts of an American. It may suit the purposes of despotic power; but it cannot abide the pure atmosphere of political liberty and personal freedom.

They have interpreted it in the spirit of Justice Rutledge's observation in 1942 while on the Court of Appeals for the District of Columbia Circuit in *Woods* v. *United States*:

. . . With world events running as they have been, there is special reason at this time for not relaxing the old personal freedoms won, as this one was, through centuries of struggle. Men now in concentration camps could speak to the value of such a privilege, if it were or had been theirs. There is in it the wisdom of centuries, if not that of decades.
Large in this is a sense of fairness to the person accused, a respect for his individual integrity, in accusation or even in guilt. But larger still is the sense of the court's own part in justice and its administration. By this we mean the sense of the citizen as well as of the court itself. . . .

In the 1950s alone, the federal courts have sustained a claim of the right of silence in some sixty reported cases, and many more unreported ones. Most of the persons under attack were believed or felt to be communists. A number were persons whom the Kefauver Committee sought to interrogate and who were accused of being racketeers. Yet others were accused of illegal activities in the labor field. In a case involving suspected communists, Judge Delbert E. Metzger in Hawaii declared: "And

I can't see any actual difference, whether the proceeding was before a grand jury or committee of the House of Representatives, and any other inquisitive body . . . the Constitution stands there like the rock of Gibraltar. It has the same force and effect, to my mind, whether a proceeding is before a grand jury or any other body." In a case involving a suspected racketeer, Judge Herbert F. Goodrich, in writing the opinion for the Court of Appeals for the Third Circuit in Philadelphia commented: "If our conclusion permits, in the individual case, a rascal to go unwhipped or a villain unhung, it is because Americans have thought it better policy to lose a conviction now and then than to force a conviction from the defendant's own mouth."

Another recent case involved the secretary-treasurer of one of John Dioguardi (Johnny Dio's) paper locals in the Teamsters Union. The Court of Appeals for the Second Circuit in ruling in his favor reasoned through Circuit Judge Jerome N. Frank: "* * * The purpose of the Bill of Rights was, as Madison declared, 'to oblige the government to control itself.' * * *

"At any such right of privacy [as the right of silence], be it noted, the despotic rulers of totalitarian regimes sneer. They denounce all privacy, since it blocks efficient enforcement of criminal laws. Their position, which logically renders asinine any privilege not to testify, necessarily justifies them logically in subjecting their subjects to constant spying and snooping, for such despotic surveillance plainly aids in the detection of those who violate the law. Our democratic concern with privacy, they call characteristic of our decadent culture. Before we accept their criticism, and sacrifice all our other values to effective law enforcement, we should reflect on the brutal consequences of the totalitarians' alleged efficiency in pursuing suspected criminals. Such reflection should teach us this: An overzealous prosecutor's heaven may be everyone else's hell."

A dramatic recent case was against two of those who participated in the acid blinding of Victor Riesel. They were Gondolfo (Shiekie) Miranti and Domenico (Nick) Bando. They had told their part in the conspiracy to do this to the FBI; and had been indicted and convicted of conspiring to remove the one who allegedly had thrown the acid on Riesel, Abe Telvi, from the state of New York to avoid prosecution for the maiming. At the time of their trial the government announced that it would not proceed against them for conspiring to obstruct justice. Subsequently they were scheduled to be government witnesses in the trial of Johnny Dio, who was charged with masterminding the attack on Riesel. But now they refused to talk, and United States Attorney Paul W. Williams said that their refusal had sabotaged the trial.

It was then that they were taken before the grand jury which had returned the original indictments and which was reconvened to investigate the alleged intimidation of witnesses. (Telvi was killed, probably murdered.) They were asked to acknowledge their previous statements to the FBI, but they still refused to talk, relying instead on the Fifth Amendment's provision for a right of silence. Federal District Judge William B. Herlands held them guilty of contempt, declaring: "The Court's conclusion, therefore, is that this is not a case of constitutional silence. It is a case of underworld lockjaw." But the Court of Appeals for the Second Circuit reversed, saying through Chief Judge Charles E. Clark: "We are thus faced with the novel question whether or not a witness can invoke his privilege against self-incrimination where practically there is only a slight possibility of prosecution. * * * We find no justification for limiting the historic protections of the Fifth Amendment by creating an exception to the general rule which would nullify the privilege whenever it appears that the government would not undertake to prosecute. * * *

"We appreciate the government's frustration in this case and we honor the trial's justifiable anger over the defendants' recalcitrance. But the Constitution is for the despicable as well as for the admirable."

Not only have constitutional provisions, legislation, and judicial decisions protected the right of silence itself, but also governing authorities, both here and in Great Britain, have surrounded this right with yet additional safeguards. In this country statutory provisions and rules of court have required arresting officers to take arrested persons promptly before a committing authority. The Federal Rules of Criminal Procedure, which were transmitted to Congress in 1945 and which went into effect the following year, made the general requirement in Rule 5(a) that federal arresting authorities take their prisoners "without unnecessary delay before the nearest available commissioner." Nearly all the states have enacted a comparable provision. The purpose of such a requirement was to check resort by officers to "secret interrogation of persons accused of crime." Rule 5(b) added these requirements:

The commissioner shall inform the defendant of the complaint against him, of his right to retain counsel and of his right to have a preliminary examination. He shall also inform the defendant that he is not required to make a statement and that any statement made by him may be used against him. The commissioner shall allow the defendant reasonable time and opportunity to consult counsel and shall admit the defendant to bail as provided in these rules.

Great Britain similarly has given the right of silence further protection by both legislation and rules of court. In 1848 Parliament passed a statute, known as Sir John Jervis' Act, which specifically required a justice of the peace to advise an accused person before him in a preliminary proceeding of his right to remain silent at such an examination. The act provided that he "shall say to him these Words, or Words to the like Effect: 'Having heard the Evidence, do you wish to say anything in answer to the Charge?—you are not obliged to say anything unless you desire to do so, but whatever you say will be taken down in Writing, and may be given in Evidence against you at your Trial'. . . ."

In 1912 the judges at the request of the Home Secretary drew up some rules as guides for police officers. These rules provided in part:

2. Whenever a police officer has made up his mind to charge a person with a crime he should first caution such person before asking any questions or any further questions as the case may be.

3. Persons in custody should not be questioned without the usual caution being first administered.

4. If the prisoner wishes to volunteer any statement, the usual caution should be administered. . . .

These rules are known as the Judges' Rules. Subsequently, the judges issued some more. The first sentence of Rule 7 specified: "A prisoner making a voluntary statement must not be cross-examined, and no questions should be put to him about it except for the purpose of removing ambiguity in what he has actually said."

In 1929 a Royal Commission on Police Powers and Procedures, which had been appointed the preceding year, made a report in which it recommended, among other things:

Questioning of Persons in Custody. (xlviii) a rigid instruction should be issued to the Police that no questioning of a prisoner, or a "person in custody," about any crime or offence with which he is, or may be, charged, should be permitted. This does not exclude questions to remove elementary and obvious ambiguities in voluntary statements, under No. (7) of the Judges' Rules, but the prohibition should cover all persons who, although not in custody, have been charged and are out on bail while awaiting trial.

A case and an anecdote will illustrate the English approach to deviants. A woman was on trial with another for the murder of her husband. She had stated at the time of her arrest that she had done it and that the murder weapon had been a mallet. The arresting officer had not followed up these statements with any question. Defense counsel asked him why not, and this colloquy took place:

Mr. Justice Humphreys: Do you really suggest, Mr. O'Connor, if after a woman has said—believe it or not—that she was a party to a crime like this, the police officer would be justified in cross-examining her at all?

Mr. O'Connor: I accept your lordship's suggestion at once, and apologise for the question.

The anecdote is about a British constable on the witness stand who was asked whether it was not true that the accused had made a statement. He answered: "No: he was beginning to do so; but I knew my duty better, and I prevented him."

No General Searches

The Fourth Amendment by its provisions against unreasonable searches and seizures extended yet further the area about the individual which was free from intrusion by governmental authorities. To these provisions, as well as to most of the others of the federal Bill of Rights, the Supreme Court has usually given a sympathetic application. In two leading cases, *Gouled* v. *United States* and *United States* v. *Lefkowitz*, the Court held that search warrants could not be issued solely to search for evidence. In the *Gouled* case the Court ruled that search warrants "may not be used as a means of gaining access to a man's house or office and papers solely for the purpose of making search to secure evidence to be used against him in a criminal or penal proceeding, but that they may be resorted to only when a primary right to such search and seizure may be found in the interest which the public or the complainant may have in the property to be seized, or in the right to the possession of it, or when a valid exercise of the police power renders possession of the property by the accused unlawful, and provides that it may be taken." In the *Lefkowitz* case the Court held:

Respondents' papers were wanted by the officers solely for use as evidence of crime of which respondents were accused or suspected. They could not lawfully be searched for and taken even under a search warrant issued upon ample evidence and precisely describing such things and disclosing exactly where they were.

These holdings were embodied in the Federal Rules of Criminal Procedure. Rule 41(b) limited search warrants to such items as stolen or embezzled goods, contraband, or articles used or to be used in the commission of a crime. Now it might well be, and often was the case, that material obtained as a result of a lawful search and seizure was used as evidence, but a search warrant could not be issued solely for this purpose.

Furthermore, the Court held recently in *Kremen* v. *United States* that even a lawful search could not be too general. The case involved two of the eight defendants in the first two Foley Square Smith Act prosecutions, Thompson and Steinberg, and two others. Steinberg and the two others were charged with harboring Thompson. The FBI had warrants for the arrest of Thompson and Steinberg. When they took the four into custody they also seized the contents of the cabin where they were staying. Steinberg and his two codefendants were convicted, but the Court reversed, saying per curiam: ". . . While the evidence seized from the persons of the petitioners might have been legally admissible, the introduction against each of petitioners of some items seized in the house in the manner aforesaid rendered the guilty verdicts illegal. * * *"

At the following term the Court voided convictions in two more cases because of illegal searches. In the one the Court reasoned through Justice Brennan: "From earliest days, the common law drastically limited the authority of law officers to break the door of a house to effect an arrest. Such action invades the precious interest of privacy summed up in the ancient adage that a man's house in his castle. * * *" In this opinion Justice Brennan quoted the elder Pitt's eloquent statement.

In the other case the Court said through Justice Harlan: "It is settled doctrine that probable cause for belief that certain articles subject to seizure are in a dwelling cannot of itself justify a search without a warrant. *Agnello* v. *United States,* * * * *Taylor* v. *United States,* * * * The decisions of this Court have time and again underscored the essential purpose of the Fourth Amendment to shield the citizen from unwarranted intrusions into his privavy. * * *"

In a recent state case the court went even beyond some earlier federal Supreme Court cases and rendered a decision in accordance with the approach in the recent *Kremen* case. The Kentucky Court of Appeals held that a warrant of arrest and its execution in a man's home did not justify an unlimited search there. The arresting officers could search his person. "However, it is a totally different thing to search a man's pockets, and use against him what they contain, from ransacking his house for everything which may incriminate him, once a peace officer has gained lawful entry." The Kentucky constitution, in forbidding unreasonable searches and seizures, did not "mean to substitute the good intentions of the police for judicial authorization except in narrowly confined situations." History, both before and after the adoption of the Fourth Amendment, had shown that police intentions were inadequate safeguards for the fundamental rights of individuals.

The question of the extent of a valid search even when connected with a lawful arrest is currently before the federal Supreme Court in the case of the Soviet spy, Rudolph Ivanovich Abel. The arrest was under an administrative warrant of the Immigration and Naturalization Service.

The federal Supreme Court and various state courts have additionally strengthened provisions against unreasonable searches and seizures by holding material obtained as a result of them to be inadmissible in evidence. The leading federal case is *Weeks* v. *United States*. There the Court upset a conviction because of the admission into evidence of material illegally seized by a federal official. Recently the Court of Appeals for the District of Columbia Circuit reached the same result even though the illegal seizure was by state officials who acted independently: "In cumulative effect these several pronouncements by so many Justices of the present Court support the rational argument that the Weeks and Wolf decisions, considered together, make all evidence obtained by unconstitutional search and seizure unacceptable in federal courts. * * *"

Protection of Confidential Relationships

Our regard for human dignity was such that we not only accorded deviants a right of silence, and individuals generally a right to express their views whenever in an appropriate manner they so saw fit; we also gave a measure of protection to certain confidential relationships. We safeguarded from inquiry various confidential communications, between attorney and client, husband and wife, and in this country, priest and penitent, doctor and patient, and, more recently, a news reporter and his source of information. Suitably enough, the protection of the confidential communications between attorney and client went back to the reign of Elizabeth I. Similar protection to the confidential communications between husband and wife may be traced back to a case as early as 1684. Those between priest and penitent received actual protection, but in England not a formal legal one. After the Fourth Lateran Council of 1215–16 priests insisted on keeping confidential the confessions of penitents. The case of Robert Devon in 1220 furnishes an example. He was arrested in London for ill fame and confessed to his jailers "that if a certain chaplain of Dartford, who came to the gaol to inquire after some clothes and other things he had lost, would get him out of prison, he would show him where his clothes were and deliver them to him. And the chaplain came and confessed that his things had been stolen and that he went to the gaol as aforesaid, but he will not say more, because he is a priest." However, the courts in England, although usually respecting such a refusal, did not legally sanction it. In this country on the other hand more than half of the states protected such communications by statute. In a similar fashion three-fourths of the states protected the confidential communications between patients and physicians. Recently the Court of Appeals for the District of Columbia

Circuit not only recognized the priest and penitent privilege without a statute but also extended it to a confession to a Lutheran minister made in preparation of receiving communion. The court thought it highly probable that the priest and penitent privilege was part of the common law of England in the centuries preceding the Reformation, and stated through Judge Charles Fahy: "It thus appears that nonrecognition of the privilege at certain periods in the development of the common law was inconsistent with the basic principles of the common law itself. It would be no service to the common law to perpetuate in its name a rule of evidence which is inconsistent with the foregoing fundamental guides furnished by that law. * * * In our own time, with its climate of religious freedom, there remains no barrier to adoption by the federal courts of a rule of evidence on this subject dictated by sound policy."

Twelve states by legislation also protected from disclosure a news reporter's source of information. However, the protection of such or other confidential informants would seem to be of dubious worth. If an individual's liberty or status or reputation or property is at stake, it would seem that confidential informants ought not to be allowed to assume the role of anonymous talebearers. They should be made to confront the accused face to face, and the Court of Appeals for the Second Circuit so held in the Marie Torre case. Miss Torre, a television columnist for the *New York Herald Tribune*, told a tale (ascribed to an unnamed executive of the Columbia Broadcasting System) about Judy Garland. Miss Garland sued C.B.S. for breach of contract and libel, and Miss Torre was asked to reveal her source of information. When she refused she was found guilty of contempt. The Court of Appeals affirmed her conviction, saying through Judge Potter Stewart, now a Supreme Court Justice: "* * * * Freedom of the press, hard-won over the centuries by men of courage, is basic to a free society. But basic too are courts of justice, armed with the power to discover truth. The concept that it is the duty of a witness to testify in a court of law has roots fully as deep in our history as does the guarantee of a free press." Freedom of the press had to "give place under the Constitution to a paramount public interest in the fair administration of justice."

To the protection of various confidential relationships we have added a recognition of a general right of privacy, a right to be let alone. Over half of the states as well as the District of Columbia have recognized such a right.

Doctrine of Waiver

However, there is one area, apart from cases dealing with immunity acts and legislation requiring certain records to be kept, in which the

Supreme Court has failed to give a wholly sympathetic treatment to the right of silence, and that area may be designated as the doctrine of waiver. The two leading federal cases are *Rogers* v. *United States* and *Brown* v. *United States*. The former case involved Mrs. Jane Rogers, who was treasurer of the Communist party of Denver until 1948. She told about herself, but refused to identify the person to whom she had given the party's books, saying, "I don't feel that I should subject a person or persons to the same thing that I am going through." Subsequently she based her refusal on her right of silence. The Court in an opinion by Chief Justice Vinson told her she had waived it.

The other case involved a denaturalization suit against Stephana Brown. At the trial the government called her as an adverse witness and she refused to answer certain questions on the ground of her right of silence. When it came to her case she took the stand as a witness in her own behalf. On cross-examination the government asked her the same questions it had before and she again claimed her privilege, but this time the district court, the Court of Appeals for the Sixth Circuit and the Supreme Court all held that she had waived it. There were four dissenters: Chief Justice Warren and Justices Black, Douglas and Brennan.

The Court of Appeals for the Second Circuit extended the waiver doctrine to the testimony of sureties for defendants in federal criminal cases. These rulings involved Frederick V. Field, W. Alphaeus Hunton and Dashiell Hammett, trustees of the bail fund of the Civil Rights Congress. The bail of the defendants in the Foley Square Smith Act prosecutions came from this bail fund. When eight of the defendants from the two conspiracy indictments there decamped en masse, the court held not only that Field could be required to produce the records of the bail fund as well as to answer questions about their location but also that the trustees had to answer questions about the fugitives.

However, in a later case involving the secretary-treasurer of one of Johnny Dio's paper locals, the Supreme Court not only characterized the statement in one of the *Field* cases about the propriety of the questions relating to the records of bail fund as dictum but also commented that the cases which the court cited did not support its dictum. In the later case the Court held that the "petitioner's personal privilege against self-incrimination attaches to questions relating to the whereabouts of the union books and records which he did not produce pursuant to subpoena."

The result in the *Rogers* case was facilitated by a misplaced emphasis on an erroneous idea and an exaggerated emphasis on an incidental one.

The erroneous idea is that one cannot remain silent in order to protect another: in the *Rogers* case Chief Justice Vinson said for the Court: "Petitioner expressly placed her original declination to answer on an untenable ground, since a refusal to answer cannot be justified by a desire to protect others from punishment * * *." But the Puritans, who led the final and successful struggle for a right of silence, insisted on this right in order to avoid naming associates.

The incidental idea is that the right of silence is also for the protection of innocent persons caught in the toils of compromising circumstances: in the *Slochower* case the Court stated: "The privilege serves to protect the innocent who otherwise might be ensnared by ambiguous circumstances. See Griswold, *The Fifth Amendment Today* (1955)." Even Dean Griswold stressed this point. But the undue emphasis of this point is misleading: it obscures the more important reason why the Puritans insisted on remaining silent, namely, to avoid disclosing their associates. The waiver doctrine is an aberration. No one should be compelled to betray one's confederates.

Treatment of Confessions

Our accusatorial method in the treatment of deviants, the right of silence and trial by jury help to explain why our trials did not abound in confessions the way those in communist countries do. In our litigated cases we rarely had confessions. They rarely have litigated cases. Alexis de Tocqueville in his *Democracy in America* correctly saw trial by jury as raising the people "to the bench of judges" and investing them "with the direction of society."

Moreover, even the confessions which were offered in our trials were often rejected by the courts. In England a confession which was obtained from a person in custody without advising him of his right to remain silent was usually excluded. In the United States two complementary lines of authorities reached a comparable result. A confession which was obtained as a result of persistent questioning plus a violation of a statutory provision or a rule of court requiring a prisoner to be taken without unnecessary delay before a committing authority was excluded. The leading case is *McNabb* v. *United States*. Without reference to any statutory provision or rule of court, a confession in a state court proceeding which was obtained as a result of persistent questioning plus a failure to take a prisoner before a committing authority within a reasonable period of time was excluded as violating the due process clause of the Fourteenth Amendment. A leading case is *Chambers* v. *Florida*. Periods of five, seven, thirty, thirty-three, and thirty-six hours were held to constitute undue delay. There has also been a recent decision in each line of authorities: *Mallory* v. *United States* in the *McNabb* line; and *Fikes* v. *Alabama* in the Chambers line.

A series of examples will illustrate the English treatment of confessions. In 1793, over a half century before the statute requiring that an accused be advised of his right to remain silent, the court excluded an examination before a magistrate where the accused had refused to sign it. The judge reasoned that the accused had a right "to retract what he had said, and to say that it was false." In 1817, still before the statute requiring a caution, Chief Baron Richards excluded an examination before a magistrate where the accused had not been cautioned, saying: "An examination of itself imposes an obligation to speak the truth. If a prisoner will confess, let him do so voluntarily."

In a similar ruling in 1850, after the statute but without reference to it, Chief Justice Wilde, in rejecting such an examination, declared: ". . . I reject it upon the general ground that magistrates have no right to put questions to a prisoner with reference to any matters having a bearing upon the charge upon which he is brought before them. The law is so extremely cautious in guarding against anything like torture, that it extends a similar principle to every case where a man is not a free agent in meeting an inquiry . . ."

In further similar rulings, attributable to the statute, the courts successively stated: (1885) "When a prisoner is in custody, the police have no right to ask him questions . . . A prisoner's mouth is closed after he is once given in charge, and he ought not to be asked anything"; (1893) ". . . the prisoner should be previously cautioned. . . ."; (1898) ". . . when a prisoner is once taken into custody, a policeman should ask no questions at all without administering previously the usual caution"; (1905) "When he [police officer] has taken anyone into custody, and also before doing so when he has already decided to make the charge, he ought not to question the prisoner. . . . I am not aware of any distinct rule of evidence that if such improper questions are asked the answers to them are inadmissible, but there is clear authority for saying that the judge at the trial may in his discretion refuse to allow the answer to be given in evidence, and in my opinion that is the right course to pursue."

In 1918 in *Rex* v. *Voisin* the Court of Criminal Appeal announced with reference to the Judges' Rules that "statements obtained from prisoners, contrary to the spirit of these rules, may be rejected as evidence by the judge presiding at the trial." Three years later the same court in reversing a conviction said through Lord Chief Justice Lawrence: ". . . The police had no right to examine Grayson. . . . This sort of proceeding—it was in fact an informal preliminary trial in private by the police—is not fair to prisoners and, as this Court has already observed, is not in accordance with principles of English justice." The rulings of English judges have by no means all been consistent, but the trend has certainly been in the direction here indicated.

In the United States, although the route was a little different, the general direction was the same. In the *McNabb* case Justice Frankfurter speaking for the court, after listing the various statutory provisions of the various states and of the District of Columbia requiring arrested persons to be taken promptly before a committing authority, explained that these provisions were due to our regard for the dignity of human beings and our desire to avoid the dangers inherent in a secret inquisitional process. He wrote:

The purpose of this impressively pervasive requirement of criminal procedure is plain. A democratic society, in which respect for the dignity of all men is central, naturally guards against the misuse of the law enforcement process. . . . Legislation such as this, requiring that the police must with reasonable promptness show legal cause for detaining arrested persons, constitutes an important safeguard—not only in assuring protection for the innocent but also in securing conviction of the guilty by methods that commend themselves to a progressive and self-confident society. For this procedural requirement checks resort to those reprehensible practices known as the "third degree" which, though universally rejected as indefensible, still find their way into use. It aims to avoid all the evil implications of secret interrogation of persons accused of crime. It reflects not a sentimental but a sturdy view of law enforcement. It outlaws easy but self-defeating ways in which brutality is substituted for brains as an instrument of crime detection . . .

In *Chambers* v. *Florida* Justice Black for a unanimous court elaborated eloquently on the dangers of a secret inquisitional method. He said: "The determination to preserve an accused's right to procedural due process sprang in large part from the knowledge of the historical truth that the rights and liberties of people accused of crime could not be safely entrusted to secret inquisitional processes. The testimony of centuries, in governments of varying kinds over populations of different races and beliefs, stood as proof that physical and mental torture and coercion had brought about the tragically unjust sacrifices of some who were the noblest and most useful of their generations. The rack, the thumbscrew, the wheel, solitary confinement, protracted questioning and cross questioning, and other ingenious forms of entrapment of the helpless or unpopular had left their wake of mutilated bodies and shattered minds along the way to the cross, the guillotine, the stake and the hangman's noose . . ."

The *McNabb* decision (1943) once again found the writer in general disagreement with prosecutors. The previous occasion was in 1940 when he questioned the validity of the advocacy provisions of the Smith Act at a meeting in the Department of Justice of states' attorneys general. The second occasion was again at a meeting at the Department of Justice, but this time the prosecutors were federal district attorneys. They were condemning the *McNabb* decision vehemently and without measure: to listen to their complaints one would gather that this decision made it very difficult if not virtually impossible for them to get convictions. The writer was not in sympathy with these complaints. Although he had not been a prosecutor as long as most of the district attorneys present, he had obtained convictions in every case he had tried in Louisiana, and he had never sought confessions. He had simply used a grand jury in the traditional way of Anglo-American peoples: when reports of wrongdoing came to his attention he subpoenaed people to appear before this body. Nearly all told their stories.

In the recent *Fikes* case Justice Frankfurter, in a concurring opinion in which Justice Brennan joined, stated:

* * * For myself, I cannot see the difference, with respect to the "voluntariness" of a confession, between the subversion of freedom of the will through physical punishment and the sapping of the will appropriately to be inferred from the circumstances of this case—detention of the accused virtually incommunicado for a long period; failure to arraign him in that period; horse-shedding of the accused at the intermittent pleasure of the police until confession was forthcoming. * * *

In yet another case Justice Frankfurter in a concurring opinion wrote:

An impressive series of cases in this and other courts admonishes of the temptations to abuse of police endeavors to secure confessions from suspects, through protracted questioning carried on in secrecy, with the inevitable disquietude and fears police interrogations naturally engender in individuals questioned while held incommunicado, without the aid of counsel and unprotected by the safeguards of a judicial inquiry . . . Legislation throughout the country reflects a similar belief that detention for purposes of eliciting confessions through secret, persistent, long-continued interrogation violates sentiments deeply embedded in the feelings of our people. . . .

The high point in the exclusion of confessions probably came in June 1949, the last month that Justices Murphy and Rutledge sat. This was the month that the Supreme Court in three different cases from three different states held confessions inadmissible. In one of them Justice Frankfurter explained the difference in approach between the accusatorial and inquisitional methods: "Ours is the accusatorial as opposed to the inquisitional system. Such has been the characteristic of Anglo-American criminal justice since it freed itself from practices borrowed by the Star Chamber from the Continent whereby an accused was interrogated in secret for hours on end . . . Under our system society carries the burden of proving its charge against the accused not out of his own mouth. It must establish its case, not by interrogation of the accused even under judicial safeguards, but by evidence independently secured through skillful investigation."

But just as there was somewhat of a retreat in the early 1950's in the protection of various individual rights, especially of political deviants, so there were fewer judicial rulings excluding confessions. In June 1953 in three different cases from two different states and in a fourth case involving courts-martial trials the Supreme Court permitted them. In the last case confessions were allowed even though there were two-day detentions before arraignment. In one of the state cases, known as the *Reader's Digest* case because the murder there involved was committed in the course of a robbery of some *Reader's Digest* mail, the trial judge held that the delay in arraignment was unreasonable as a matter of law and a violation of the statutes of New York but nevertheless admitted the confessions. The Supreme Court affirmed the convictions. This case had four defendants, three of whom gave confessions. At the trial two of these repudiated their confessions. The third became state's evidence. The confessions were admitted in evidence not only against those who gave them but also against the one who did not. The courts-martial case involved two confessants, one of whom was held incommunicado for a period of five days and questioned repeatedly. At the preceding term in two more cases, one from Nebraska and the other from Alaska, the Supreme Court approved confessions which were obtained during prolonged detentions. In one of these the Supreme Court did vote for the reversal of a conviction, but on other grounds than the illegality of the confession.

In the *Reader's Digest* case the petitioners argued that the confessions were obtained as a result of psychological coercion. The petitioner who did not confess, further argued that he was not confronted with the witnesses against him: the two defendants who repudiated their confessions did not take the stand. Justice Jackson wrote the opinion of the Court. In answer to the claim of psychological coercion he said: "Interrogation is not inherently coercive, as is physical violence." He was entirely unaware of the compulsion to confess in human beings.

Justices Black, Frankfurter and Douglas, dissented. Justice Black wrote: "More constitutional safeguards go here—one, the right of a person to be free from arbitrary seizure, secret confinement and police bludgeoning to make him testify against himself in absence of relative, friend or counsel; another, the right of an accused to confront and cross-examine witnesses who swear he is guilty of crime. Tyrannies have always subjected life and liberty to such secret inquisitorial and oppressive practices." Mr. Justice Frankfurter commented: "It is painful to be compelled to say that the Court is taking a retrogressive step in the administration of criminal justice. I can only hope that it is a temporary, perhaps an *ad hoc*, deviation from a long course of decisions."

To Justice Douglas it seemed "clear that these confessions would be condemned if the constitutional school of thought which prevailed when" the three cases of June 1949 and a case from the term which preceded them "were decided still was the dominant one."

There were dissents in the other cases too. In the case from Nebraska Justice Black wrote magnificently: "Americans justly complain when their fellow citizens in certain European countries are pounced upon at will by state police, held in jail incommunicado, and later convicted of crime on confessions obtained during such incarceration. Yet in part upon just such a confession, this Court today affirms Nebraska's conviction of a citizen of Mexico who can neither read nor understand English. . . .

"There are countries where arbitrary arrests like this, followed by secret imprisonment and systematic questioning until confessions are obtained, are still recognized and permissible legal procedures. See 'The Trap Closes' by Robert A. Vogeler with Leigh White . . . My own belief is that only by departure from the Constitution as properly interpreted can America tolerate such practices."

The case from Alaska involved a confession on one charge while the defendant was in custody on another. Justice Douglas in a concurring opinion (for the conviction was reversed, although not on the confession point) wrote:

* * * We should make illegal such a perversion of a "legal" detention.

The rule I propose would, of course, reduce the "efficiency" of the police. But so do the requirements for arraignment, the prohibition against coerced confessions, the right to bail, the jury trial, and most of our other procedural safeguards. We in this country, however, early made the choice —that the dignity and privacy of the individual were worth more to society than an all-powerful police.

In England too during the cold war confessions seemed to have a readier admissibility.

One could hope, as Justice Frankfurter did with respect to the Supreme Court's decision in the *Reader's Digest* case, that the retrogressive steps which the Court took in the first part of the 1950's were but temporary deviations. It is safe to say that this hope has been realized since the appointment of Chief Justice Warren in October, 1953. Since then the Court has thrown out confessions in four important cases: *Leyra* v. *Denno; Fikes* v. *Alabama;* and *Mallory* v. *United States;* and *Spano* v. *New York.* In the *Mallory* case the Court upset a conviction based on a confession obtained after less than two hours of questioning. This decision has led to criticism in Congress and demands for legislation to change the law as announced by the Supreme Court. In the *Leyra* case the Court excluded a confession to a police officer which followed a confession induced by a psychiatrist.

The latest case in which the Court voided a confession involved a state court proceeding. The confession was that of Vincent Joseph Spano, who was under sentence of death in New York. He gave his confession after eight hours of questioning. Moreover, he gave it because a buddy of his, who was a fledgling police officer, begged him to do so. This officer told him that if he did not give the confession the officer would be in trouble with his superiors. Chief Justice Warren in the Court's opinion explained that our abhorence to such confessions involved "the deep-rooted feeling that the police must obey the law while enforcing the law; that in the end life and liberty can be as much endangered from illegal methods used to convict those thought to be criminals as from the actual criminals themselves."

Federal courts of appeals likewise became more exacting in determining the admissibility of confessions. In one recent case the Court of Appeals for the Second Circuit held that a state prisoner was entitled to a writ of habeas corpus because his conviction in a state court proceeding was on confessions that the court deemed inadmissible. Judge Jerome N. Frank writing for the court said:

. . . It has no significance that in this case we must assume there was no physical brutality. For psychological torture may be far more cruel, far more symptomatic of sadism. Many a man who can endure beatings will yield to fatigue. To keep a man awake beyond the point of exhaustion, while constantly pummelling him with questions is to degrade him, to strip him of human dignity, to deprive him of the will to resist, to make him a pitiable creature mastered by the single desire—at all costs to be free of torment. Any member of this or any other court, to escape such anguish would admit to almost any crime. Indeed, the infliction of such psychological punishment is more reprehensible than a physical attack: It leaves no discernible marks on the victim. Because it is thus concealed, it has, under the brutalitarian regimes, become the favorite weapon of the secret police, bent on procuring confessions as a means of convicting the innocent.

The English and American treatment of confessions has come in for much criticism, and not only from prosecutors. Professor Wigmore, too, was critical of some of the decisions excluding confessions, and failed to perceive all that was involved in these lines of authorities. He reasoned that the basis for excluding a confession was its untrustworthiness under certain conditions, and felt that in a number of cases courts excluded confessions which under the circumstances Wigmore deemed reliable. But more is involved than the truth or falsity of confessions. More is involved than their voluntariness or involuntariness. More is involved than a "sporting instinct" or "playing the game." English and American courts in a number of the authorities cited have thrown out confessions irrespective of their truth or falsity and irrespective of their voluntariness or involuntariness in order to provide an additional safeguard against a resort by investigating authorities to the inquisitional method. As Justice Frankfurter put it in the *McNabb* case: "Plainly, a conviction resting on evidence secured through such a flagrant disregard of the procedure which Congress has commanded cannot be allowed to stand without making the courts themselves accomplices in wilful disobedience of law. Congress has not explicitly forbidden the use of evidence so procured. But to permit such evidence to be made the basis of a conviction in the Federal courts would stultify the policy which Congress has enacted into law." Or again in the *Watts* case: "In holding that the Due Process Clause bars police procedure which violates the basic notions of our accusatorial mode of prosecuting crime and vitiates a conviction based on the fruits of such procedure, we apply the Due Process Clause to its historic function of assuring appropriate procedure before liberty is curtailed or life is taken." In the same case Justice Douglas in a concurring opinion stated: "We should unequivocally condemn the procedure and stand ready to outlaw, as we did in *Malinski* . . . and *Haley* . . . any confession obtained during the period of the unlawful detention." In the *Haley* case Justice Douglas wrote the opinion of the Court and Justice Frankfurter a concurring one. Said the former: "Neither man nor child can be allowed to stand condemned by methods which flout constitutional requirements of due process of law." Wrote the latter: "To remove the inducement to resort to such methods this Court had repeatedly denied use of the fruits of illicit methods." Judges in this area may turn out to have been wiser than lawyers and legal writers, and even they themselves, have realized.

CHAPTER XI

COMPULSORY TESTIMONY ACTS

History of Immunity Acts

But human beings rarely follow with complete consistency even the most constructive of courses. So it was with the right of silence. We permitted exceptions. The earliest, and one which arose in England, was the grant of a pardon to an offender in order to obtain his testimony. The most general was an act which gave the offender immunity from prosecution but compelled his testimony under the pain of punishment for contempt if he insisted on refusing to talk. We called such acts either compulsory testimony or immunity acts.

Perhaps the earliest such act dates from 1697 in the colony of Connecticut. This act related to witnesses: they were called upon to give testimony under oath "always provided that no person required to give testimonie as aforesaid shall be punished for what he doth confesse against himselfe when under oath." This was but a short time after the right to remain silent had been extended to witnesses as distinguished from defendants.

The first compulsory testimony provision that attained any general vogue was in an act against gaming. The initial act was passed in England in 1710, the same year that marked the death of Lord Holt, the last English judge to persist in the practice of questioning a defendant. According to this act the loser could sue the winner to recover his losses, and the winner had to answer under oath, but when he had answered and returned what he had won he was to "be acquitted, indemnified, and discharged from any further or other punishment, forfeiture, or penalty." Similar statutes were enacted in various of the colonies, and even without such enactment the act of 1710 was declared to be in force in this country.

Thereafter from time to time the people became concerned about certain conduct, passed an act regulating it, and often put in a compulsory testimony provision. In addition to further acts against gaming, there were acts against lotteries, usury, bribery of public officials, duelling, frauds on creditors, and for the regulation of the sale of spirituous liquors which included compulsory testimony provisions.

Federal District Judge Peter S. Grosscup of Illinois had the feel of most of these statutes when he wrote concerning the decisions sustaining their validity: ". . . It is interesting to note, however, that all of these cases related to offenses, the wisdom of which were then somewhat debated questions, and the prosecution of which was, to some extent, the triumph or defeat of the prevailing popular opinion . . . Some of these cases naturally aroused the indignation of the community in which the court sat. All of them were cases, doubtless, where the immunity claimed by the witness aroused no just sympathy. They each presented a situation where the fifth amendment, if construed broadly, seemed to offer an obstacle to a just administration of the criminal law. . . ."

In comparing our accusatorial with the inquisitional system he commented: "In the one, grew up a criminal procedure that was almost purely inquisitorial, and whose history now appalls the enlightened conscience; in the other, grew up a system purely accusatory, where the offending individual could lawfully stand in silence, and demand proof from sources other than himself. In the one, the power of the sovereign pervaded every nook and corner of the individual; in the other, the power of the sovereign came only to the outward person of the subject, and there stopped. This jealousy against any touch, until the right of individual liberty was shown forfeited, proved the corner stone of popular liberty." In the next paragraph Judge Grosscup called the privilege the "right of silence." The dissent in the *Ullmann* case relied heavily on Judge Grosscup's opinion and referred to the privilege variously as the "privilege of silence," "federally protected right of silence," "this right of silence" and simply "right of silence."

The first federal act was in 1857. The circumstance which led to its enactment was the refusal of a correspondent of *The New York Times*, James W. Simonton, to disclose to a select committee of the House of Representatives the names of the members of the House who had indicated to him that their votes were for sale with reference to certain measures then pending before Congress. Simonton had written a letter to *The Times* on the subject of congressional corruption, which *The Times* had published over his initials. *The Times* had also commented on the subject editorially. These items had led to the appointment of the special committee which had sought Simonton's testimony. The result of his refusal to divulge names was the act of 1857. It provided, among other things, that a person had to testify, but he was not to "be held to answer criminally in any court of justice, or subject to any penalty or forfeiture for any fact or act touching which he shall be required to testify," and his statements were not to "be competent testimony in any criminal proceeding against such witness in any court of justice."

This act was soon abused. Deviants, including at least two who had already been indicted, arranged to give testimony before a congressional investigating committee, and in this way obtained immunity. The two who were indicted had the indictment against them dismissed. The indictment was for the embezzlement of some $2,000,000 of Indian trust bonds from the Interior Department.

Congress accordingly amended the act of 1857 in 1862 by eliminating the prohibition against prosecution but leaving that against the subsequent use of testimony given. As amended, the immunity provision of the act of 1857 became in turn Rev. Stat. §859 (1875), 28 U.S.C. (1940) §634, and 18 U.S.C. (1952) §3486. It was this immunity provision which was again amended in August 1954 to become the new federal immunity act of that year.

In 1868 Congress adopted companion legislation to the act of 1857 as amended. The occasion this time was the decision by Vice Chancellor Sir William Page Wood in *United States* v. *McRae*, affirmed on this point on appeal in an opinion by Lord Chancellor Chelmsford, that the United States in a suit in equity in England against a Confederate agent could not compel him to make discovery because this might expose him to a forfeiture in this country. It was this case which the government did not cite and everyone else overlooked in *United States* v. *Murdock*. The decision on appeal in the *McRae* case was in December 1867. The next month a bill was introduced in Congress, and passed in February, which provided that "no discovery, or evidence obtained by means of any judicial proceeding from any party or witness in this or any foreign country, shall be given in evidence, or in any manner used against such party a witness. . . ." This provision became Rev. Stat. §860.

At first there was no activity under Rev. Stat. §859, and very little under Rev. Stat. §860. Several federal courts of first instance held that the latter section took away one's right of silence, but the question did not reach the Supreme Court until the case of *Counselman* v. *Hitchcock*, decided almost a quarter of a century after the passage of the act of 1868. In the meantime there had occurred the expansion of the railroads, their unfair and discriminatory rates and practices, and the passage by Congress, in 1887, of the Interstate Commerce Act. This act contained two limited immunity provisions, but the *Counselman* case did not arise under these immunity provisions; it arose under Rev. Stat. §860. A grand jury in Illinois was inquiring whether certain shipments of grain had been carried for less than the published and legal tariff rate. The defendant claimed his right of silence, and the Supreme Court sustained him on the ground that the immunity provided by Rev. Stat. §860 was not broad enough: it did not include immunity from prosecution. The next year Congress amended the Interstate Commerce Act by providing that a person subpoenaed under the provisions of that act had to testify but was not to "be prosecuted or subjected to any penalty or forfeiture for or on account of any transaction, matter or thing, concerning which he may testify. . . ." Three years later the Supreme Court sustained the constitutionality of this act in *Brown* v. *Walker*.

This act became known as the Compulsory Testimony Act of 1893, and was sometimes specifically referred to in future immunity provisions. The case of *Brown* v. *Walker*, with some exceptions, became the basis for such provisions. The exceptions included the Bankruptcy Act of 1898, an act of 1917 prohibiting the manufacture or sale of liquor in Alaska, the Federal Food, Drug, and Cosmetic Act, the Federal Insecticide, Fungicide, and Rodenticide Act, and the Internal Security Act of 1950. These acts for some reason used the old form of immunity provision, and forbade only the subsequent use of the testimony or statement obtained. The provision in the Bankruptcy Act of 1898 came before the Supreme Court and was of course held not to take away an individual's right of silence. Nevertheless, the provision was not only retained but even further restricted, in 1938, to "except such testimony as may be given" by the bankrupt "in the hearing upon objections to his discharge."

In February 1903, as part of a legislative program for the correction of corporate abuses, Congress put immunity provisions in three different statutes: the act establishing the Department of Commerce and Labor, which conferred upon a commissioner of corporations investigatory powers similar to those possessed by the Interstate Commerce Commission; the Elkins Amendment to the Interstate Commerce Act; and an act making large appropriations for the enforcement of the Interstate Commerce Act, the Sherman Law and other enactments. Three years later District Judge Humphrey, in a case involving an indictment in Illinois against the members of the "beef trust" for alleged violations of the Sherman Act, sustained pleas in bar of the individual defendants, although not of the corporate defendants, on the ground that the individual defendants had obtained immunity by making available to the federal commissioner of corporations at his demand, certain books and records. However, these defendants had not been subpoenaed and they had not been put under oath. There was sharp criticism of this decision. President Theodore Roosevelt declared that it came "measurably near to making the law a farce," and asked Congress to "pass a declaratory act stating its real intention." Congress thereupon enacted that the immunity granted by the act of 1893 and the three acts of February 1903 was to "extend only to a natural person who, in obedience to a subpoena, gives testimony under oath or produces evidence, documentary or otherwise, under oath."

During all this period both Rev. Stat. §§859 and 860 continued on the books. In 1910 Congress repealed section 860 on the ground that after the *Counselman* decision it had "become a shield to the criminal and an obstruction to justice." But for some reason Congress overlooked section 859; it remained in force to become, as we have seen, the new federal immunity act.

Later in 1910 Congress passed the Mann Act and in 1914 the first Federal Trade Commission Act, and included in both a broad immunity provision. The one in the latter act was similar to the one in the act of 1893 as amended in 1906. Between this time and the enactment of the Securities Act of 1933 Congress passed seven more acts which contained similar immunity provisions: the Shipping Act of 1916; an act creating a tariff commission; the National Prohibition Act of 1919; the Packers and Stockyards Act; the Grain Futures Act; the Perishable Agricultural Commodities Act, 1930; and the Tariff Act of 1930.

With the Securities Act of 1933 came a new refinement. The careful drafters of that act provided that in order to get immunity a person first had to claim his privilege. Since then Congress has enacted thirty regulatory measures which contained immunity provisions. Twenty-five of these measures contained the refined form of immunity provision in the Securities Act of 1933. Of the remainder, three used the older style of the 1893 act as amended in 1906; and three simply forbade the subsequent use of any evidence or statement obtained. The drafters of the Securities Act of 1933 proved to be foresighted on behalf of the government, for in *United States* v. *Monia* the Supreme Court held that under the older form, in that case one of the acts of February 1903 as amended in 1906, a witness got immunity even though he had not made any claim to his right of silence.

A history of immunity acts thus shows three things. Such acts began almost as soon as the right of silence established itself. However, they were almost never of general application but always limited to a particular area. For instance, although Congress has passed at least fifty acts containing immunity provisions, all but two, Rev. Stat. §§859 and 860, have been restricted to specific types of violations. Most important of all, immunity acts generally have not applied to deviations from prevalent beliefs, thoughts, opinions, associations, and utterances—the fields also protected by the guarantees of the First Amendment. On the contrary, nearly all federal immunity provisions have been in statutes providing for some form of economic regulation.

The fact that until the present period federal immunity provisions have not been directed at the field of heresy increases in significance when we remember that the right of silence had its growth in this very field and that it made its greatest gains during the time of the Puritan opposition to then constituted authorities. The right to be free from unreasonable searches and seizures grew up in the same field.

Although the Supreme Court held in the *Rogers* case that one could not claim one's right of silence in order to protect a confederate, District Judge Grosscup nevertheless correctly understood the history and circumstances of its growth when in the course of his opinion holding the Immunity Act of 1893 to be unconstitutional he expressed the fear that with such an act "the government could probe the secrets of every conversation, or society, by extending compulsory pardon to one of its participants, and thus turn him into an involuntary informer." Those who submitted the Minority Report in the House on S. 16, which became the new federal immunity act of 1954, shared this view. They said: "By this device to compel testimony, we turn men of conscience into informers. This is nasty business."

Furthermore, the successful resistance of the English people to the inquisitional system was part of a yet larger picture, one which included additional individual rights such as those to bail, habeas corpus, a public trial, and to be confronted with the witnesses against one, as well as the successful struggle of the English people against the Stuarts and of the American colonists against George III, the rise of the idea of the supremacy of law, and the final supremacy of law over royal prerogative. The larger picture was also to contain the protection of various confidential relationships, such as that between attorney and client, and husband and wife, and the recognition of a general right of privacy. Important instrumentalities in the development of individual rights were a rather independent bench and bar, and a court and jury system. When Bentham, and Wigmore after him, explained the right of silence on the ground that the English people were so aroused over the abuses of power by the high commission and the court of star chamber that they got rid not only of these courts but of their inquisitional methods as well, they did not take a comprehensive enough view of history.

If one were to give a brief characterization of the English and American approach to deviants, and to people generally one would say that it tended to be equalitarian. We have a regard for human dignity. We treat people as adults rather than as children. This is one of the basic differences between us and the East. Our approach is a more mature one. The result is a comparatively independent citizenry, and a more or less representative form of government.

The holding in *Brown* v. *Walker*, based as it is on an insufficient appreciation of the history and nature of the right of silence, should not have been extended beyond the field of economic regulation. Chief Judge Clark of the Second Circuit said in concurring reluctantly in the affirmance of the *Ullmann* case: "I concur, but regretfully. For the steady and now precipitate erosion of the Fifth Amendment seems to me to have gone far beyond anything within the conception of those justices of the Supreme Court who by the narrowest of margins first gave support to the trend in the 1890's. And serious commentators have found this new statute peculiarly disturbing in policy and in law. . . . It undermines and so far forth nullifies one of the basic differences between our justice and that of systems we contemn, namely the principle that the individual shall not be forced to condemn himself."

Specifically, the holding in *Brown* v. *Walker* should not have been extended to the field of beliefs. If that means a different result in cases involving economic regulation than in those involving beliefs, that will not be out of character for us either. Contrary to what the communists would have the world believe, we place as high a value on the worth of the individual as any group on earth. We give considerably more latitude to the individual in the expression of his opinions than in the conduct of his business affairs. A judge who spoke for us most ably on this point was Justice Holmes, and of his opinions Justice Frankfurter wrote: "Accordingly, Mr. Justice Holmes was far more ready to find legislative invasion where free inquiry was involved than in the debatable area of economics."

Those who submitted the Minority Report in the House on S. 16 drew substantially the distinction we have suggested. After referring to the powers of various special agencies of the executive branch of government to grant immunity, they said: "Furthermore, the functions of these agencies are generally related to the field of economic regulation where the inquiries touch more upon the rights of corporations, to which no privilege against incrimination attaches, than to the rights of individuals." Near the end of their report they added: "We are dealing here with elements of the First as well as the Fifth amendment of the Constitution."

Dean Griswold of the Harvard Law School drew the distinction we are urging when he wrote:

Where matter of a man's belief or opinions or political views are essential elements of the charge, it may be most difficult to get evidence from sources other than the suspected or accused person himself. Hence, the significance of the privilege over the years has perhaps been greatest in connection with resistance to prosecution for such offenses as heresy or political crimes. In these areas the privilege against self-incrimination has been a protection for freedom of thought and a hindrance to any government which might wish to prosecute for thoughts and opinions alone.

In discussing the inferences to be drawn from a claim of a right of silence, he stressed the same distinction:

. . . The question whether a bank teller stole funds entrusted to him is one sort of question. But the closer the questions asked get to the area of opinion and political belief, the less significant, I suggest to you, is the refusal to answer questions. Or, to put this another way, the more the interrogation gets into what might be called the free-speech area of the First Amendment, the more difficult it is to come up surely with a sound inference from the refusal to answer a question.

If supporters of the new federal act point out that it applies to treason, sabotage and espionage as well as sedition, the answer is that charges of treason as well as sedition were the traditional way in which monarchs compelled conformity in politics and religion. Such charges were a favorite weapon of Henry VIII.

If some of the supporters of the new federal act were to suggest that if the English people had been more harsh with the Puritans, the latter might never have come to power, the answer is that probably the very leniency of the English people kept their civil war from being worse than it was and made possible the bloodless revolution of 1688 and the bill of rights of 1689. One can point to a country where the authorities used methods with dissenters that left little to be desired in the way of harshness—Russia—and with fearful results. The czars sent a steady trek of political exiles to Siberia. Ironically enough, in the decade when this trek was reaching its height, from 1875–85, Friedrich Engels was adding to Marxism the idea of the withering away of the state. The destructive concepts of Marxism flourished in the minds of the repressed nihilists, and the result was a ruthless as well as a bloody revolution.

The new federal immunity act of 1954 is a further step in the direction of an inquisitional system, and one which we ought not to have taken. However, we did take it.

Developments During the Cold War

What propelled us on that course was the aggressive and proselytizing character of international communism. One of the many resulting committees investigating subversion was the House of Representative's Special Committee on Un-American Activities, which was created in 1938 and was continued from time to time until 1945, when it became the Committee on Un-American Activities, and a standing committee. Thereafter it was sometimes known by the name of one of its subsequent chairmen, John S. Wood of Georgia, J. Parnell Thomas of New Jersey, Harold H. Velde of Illinois or Francis E. Walter of Pennsylvania.

The peak in congressional investigations of communists and communist sympathizers or those thought to be such occurred in the years 1953 and 1954. During this period Congress had not one but a number of bodies engaged in such investigations. The three most active ones were: Permanent Subcommittee on Investigations of the Committee on Government Operations, chaired by Senator McCarthy; Subcommittee on Internal Security of the Committee on the Judiciary, headed by Senator William E. Jenner of Indiana; and the House Committee on Un-American Activities, headed by Representative Velde. These three committees were often known from their respective chairmen as the McCarthy, Jenner, and Velde Committees. The Senate Internal Security Subcommittee in turn created a task force under the chairmanship of Senator John M. Butler of Maryland to investigate communist infiltration into labor unions. The House also had a Special Committee to Investigate Foundations, chaired by B. Carroll Reece of Tennessee.

The longest-lived of these committees, and consequently the one that had the most to do with alleged subversives, was the House Committee on Un-American Activities. At first those who refused to testify or produce requested documents before this body raised the objection that the resolution authorizing the committee's investigations was unconstitutional on the ground, among others, that it trespassed on First Amendment freedoms. However, the lower federal courts sustained the validity of the resolution, and the Supreme Court denied review.

Meanwhile the Department of Justice began presenting evidence to a grand jury in the Southern District of New York, and in July 1948 obtained an indictment against William Z. Foster, national chairman, Eugene Dennis, general secretary, and ten other top leaders of the American Communist Party, charging them with a conspiracy to organize the Communist Party of the United States as a group to teach and advocate the overthrow of our government by force and violence in violation of the Smith Act, passed in 1940. This case sent to trial in 1949 as to all but Foster, who was severed from it because of ill health, and after nine months resulted in a verdict of guilty as to all remaining eleven defendants. The Court of Appeals for the Second Circuit affirmed a judgment of conviction in July 1950.

With these events witnesses before grand juries and congressional committees began to claim their Fifth Amendment privilege against self-incrimination. One such witness was Patricia Blau, before a federal grand jury in Denver. The Supreme Court sustained her claim in December 1950. That this claim was also available to a witness before a congressional committee was generally recognized, and later cases repeatedly so held. Then the following June the Supreme Court affirmed the *Dennis* case.

The stage was now set for numerous claims of privilege, and they were forthcoming. They took various forms. Some of the early claimants of this right before the House Committee on Un-American Activities offered to waive it and tell everything about themselves if the Committee would excuse them from naming their associates. For instance, Miss Lillian Hellman wrote to the chairman of the Committee: "I am prepared to waive the privilege against self-incrimination and to tell you everything you wish to know about my views or actions if your committee will agree to refrain from asking me to name other people." The Committee would not agree and Miss Hellman claimed her privilege.

It became evident that the issue was one of identifying one's associates. It did not satisfy the various committees investigating subversion to beat one's breast and confess the sins of one's youth. In addition one had to be an informer. These committees made this plain time and again. Senator McCarthy in his questioning of Mr. James A. Wechsler, the editor of the *New York Post*, furnished another illustration. He showed clearly that for him a good ex-communist was one who named names:

THE CHAIRMAN. I may say, Mr. Wechsler, there is a big difference between the ex-Communist on our committee and your ex-communism, either real or alleged. Mr. Rushmore has testified before a very sizable number of committees. He has cooperated with the FBI. He has given all the information, complete information, on the Communists that he has worked with on the *Daily Worker*. There is no doubt about his anti-communism and his being a real ex-communist. He does not spend his time, you see, trying to smear and tear down the people who are really fighting communism.
MR. WECHSLER. Senator, let's face it. You are saying that an ex-Communist who is for McCarthy is a good one and an ex-Communist who is against McCarthy is suspect. I will stand on that distinction.
THE CHAIRMAN. No; that is incorrect. I will say you can judge whether a man is really an ex-Communist quite well by a number of things. No. 1, if you find that he cooperates with the Government agencies which are digging out the Communists, with the committees, gives all the information, not a matter of perhaps giving six names, not knowing whether he

gave the names or not—a real ex-Communist does not take it upon himself to fight and smear every real ex-Communist who decides to expose his former fellow Communists. There is a big difference, you see, a huge difference.

*   *   *

THE CHAIRMAN. * * * Was there any overt act that would convince anybody reading your books, looking for something to put in the Voice of America, to show that you had changed?

MR. WECHSLER. I suggest that my articles on the Hiss case, which I intend to introduce as exhibits, would answer that question. * * *

THE CHAIRMAN. It is easy to write anti-Communist articles. The easiest thing in the world to get up and say "communism is bad." That hard thing is to do a thing like Budenz: get up and testify against your former comrades to see that they are deported or sent to jail. * * *

Moreover, witnesses who told about themselves and then refused to divulge names ran into a legal problem: the courts would hold that they had waived their right of silence. This is what the Supreme Court held in the *Rogers* case. Interrogators now worsened the plight of political deviants by asking them if they had engaged in espionage. If they answered this question in the negative and then sought to claim their privilege as to questions about Communist party membership and about associates, interrogators told them they had waived their privilege. Some ex-communist witnesses took what they called a qualified Fifth: they denied espionage, testified about the period after their membership ceased, but otherwise claimed their privilege.

However, most of the persons whom the authorities interrogated either made a straight claim of privilege or gave names. Probably more persons gave names privately to such investigative agencies as the F.B.I. than publicly before committees investigating subversion, but the committees obtained their share: a multitude of names poured in from many persons. Some witnesses, such as Larry Parks, gave names in an abject way, begging to be spared the distasteful course of becoming an informer on old associates. Parks pleaded with the House Committee on Un-American Activities not to make him "crawl through mud" by informing. Later he did give a list of names, telling the Committee that since his first appearance his anti-communist beliefs had "deepened and strengthened." Others gave names with somewhat more dignity, if one can ever be said to be an informer with any dignity at all. Dr. William Lee Mahaney, Jr., for instance, at first politely refused to give this body names. Later he was persuaded to change his mind. He ascribed his original position to a false sense of loyalty and bad advice, and ended up by giving the Committee sixteen names. Even Mr. Wechsler gave names.

Despite the multitude of names which the authorities procured, they were still not satisfied. What they, and many among us, now wanted was one grand confession of faith on our side. They wanted this just as did Henry VIII and Elizabeth I and as the communists do today. All deviants had to make a public confession of their sins—and name their associates. Because all deviants did not take this course, there came a mounting demand that witnesses talk, and for an immunity act, which would confront them with the alternative either of doing so or going to jail for contempt. Benjamin F. Wright, the president of Smith College, wrote: "The central issue may be divided into two parts: Should one who is called before such a committee testify about his present and past memberships and activities in the Communist Party? Should a witness give the names of persons whom he knew to be engaged in such activity? In my opinion the answer to both of these questions is 'yes'. . . ." A former magistrate in New York, Morris Ploscowe, in discussing the Fifth Amendment's privilege against self-incrimination, stated: "In the course of this article, I am going to tell you how, by using a very simple, ingenious legal device, we can effectively deal with the gangsters and Communists who are trying to destroy our society while hiding behind this shield which has been furnished them by the Constitution itself." His remedy was of course an immunity statute. In October 1953, Attorney General Herbert Brownell, Jr., in an address before the National Press Club, Washington, D.C., declared, "Subversives and criminals have not been slow to rely upon this provision which was written into our Constitution to protect law-abiding citizens against tyranny and despotism"; and followed by asking, "Can we afford to permit these wrongdoers to destroy the institutions of freedom by hiding behind the shield of this constitutional privilege?" He concluded his address with the announcement that the Department of Justice would seek an immunity statute at the forthcoming session of Congress. President Eisenhower in his State-of-the-Union message in January 1954 referred to the Attorney General's proposed immunity bill.

Federal Act of 1954

After the Supreme Court's decision in the *Blau* case various immunity bills were introduced in Congress. The first one was by Senator Pat McCarren of Nevada, in May 1951, S. 1570, 82d Congress. It authorized a congressional committee by a two-thirds vote, including at least one member of the minority party, to grant immunity to a witness. In the same session the Special Committee to Investigate Organized Crime in Interstate Commerce, frequently known as the Kefauver Committee, after its chairman, Senator Estes Kefauver of Tennessee, proposed a bill, S. 1747, to vest immunity powers in the attorney general in any proceeding before a federal court or grand jury, and endorsed not only its own bill but also that of Senator McCarran. So too did the American Bar Association Commission on Organized Crime. Neither bill passed, but new bills were introduced in 1953. Senator McCarran's bill was S. 16, 83d Congress, and the Kefauver Committee's bill was S. 565. The Department of Justice, because it was charged with the prosecution of offenses, and aware of the fact that under the law as it then stood all grants of immunity from prosecution rested solely with agents of the executive branch of government, objected to S. 16 on the ground that it gave no participation to the attorney general. Deputy, later Attorney General, William P. Rogers wrote to Senator William Langer, then Chairman of the Senate Committee on the Judiciary: "This Department is disturbed, however, by the failure of the bill to provide that the Attorney General shall participate in the granting of any immunity to a witness before a congressional committee or before either House of Congress. The Attorney General is the chief legal officer of the Government of the United States. . . . Not only must this responsibility be coupled with an authority adequate to permit its discharge, but in addition it would seem inadvisable for others to be cloaked with an authority capable of preventing the Attorney General from fully performing his duty." Nevertheless S. 16 passed the Senate in 1953, but not the House.

In January 1954 Representative Kenneth B. Keating of New York introduced an immunity bill, H.R. 6899, which had the endorsement of the attorney general. This bill applied not only to witnesses before congressional committees or before either House, but also before federal courts or grand juries. The ultimate decision to grant immunity rested in all instances with the attorney general. Yet other immunity bills were introduced in the House, both in 1953 and 1954. Senator McCarran objected to H.R. 6899 on the ground that "any such grant of a veto power to the Attorney General . . . would be a violation of the separation of powers." Both of Senator McCarran's bills, S. 1570, 82d Congress and S. 16, 83d Congress, which related only to witnesses before congressional committees, provided for a grant of immunity without the approval of any outside agency. After a long tug of war between Senator McCarran and Attorney General Brownell a compromise was finally arrived at pursuant to which S. 16 was revised to provide for three participants in grants of immunity. Two of the participants were to be the attorney general and a federal district court. In the case of congressional witnesses the third hand was to be Congress or one of its committees; and in the case of other witnesses, a federal district attorney. The court was to be the final arbiter in all instances. This revision occurred in the House.

On August 4, 1954 the House passed this revision of S. 16 by a vote of 294 to 55. A week later the Senate concurred in the House amendments with but a single dissenting voice, that of Senator Herbert H. Lehman of New York, and even his opposition to the passage of the measure was limited "to the manner in which it has been brought up." On August 20, 1954 the President approved it.

The same day Congressman Keating declared: "This is the most important and effective piece of legislation dealing with the Communist conspiracy that has been enacted at this session. It will loosen the tongues of some reluctant witnesses and prevent higher-ups from escaping punishment for lack of evidence. Armed with this weapon, our law enforcement officials should be greatly fortified in their continuing war against our internal enemies."

A few days later President Eisenhower explained: "Last week I signed a bill granting immunity from prosecution to certain suspected persons in order to aid in obtaining the conviction of subversives. Investigation and prosecution of crimes involving national security have been seriously hampered by witnesses who have invoked the constitutional privilege against self-incrimination embodied in the Fifth Amendment. This act provides a new means of breaking through the secrecy which is characteristic of traitors, spies and saboteurs."

As finally passed the new federal immunity act applies to witnesses before either House of Congress, congressional committees, and federal courts and grand juries, and to investigations into treason, sabotage, espionage, sedition, seditious conspiracy and the overthrow of the government by force or violence. Court approval must be secured in every instance. For an offer of immunity to a congressional witness there must be an affirmative vote of a majority of the members present if the witness is before either House, and of two-thirds of the members of the full committee if he is before a committee. The attorney general must be notified when either House or any congressional committee proposes to grant immunity, and also of any application for court approval of the proposed grant. The immunity granted is freedom from prosecution for or subjection to "any penalty or forfeiture for or on account of any transaction, matter, or thing concerning which he is so compelled, after having claimed his privilege against self-incrimination, to testify or produce evidence," except prosecution for "perjury or contempt while giving testimony or producing evidence."

In form, the new immunity act is an amendment of the first federal immunity statute, passed in 1857, and amended in 1862. In fact it was almost a complete substitution.

As originally proposed the new act applied to all types of crime. As finally passed it sought to compel the testimony of communists and other political deviants. Representative, now Senator, Keating, who sponsored S. 16 in the House, in explaining the final form of this measure stated: "Mr. Speaker, this bill is a very important piece of legislation to further the struggle against the Communist conspiracy on all fronts, in the activities of investigating committees representing the legislative arm of Government and in the prosecutive functions carried on through the executive branch. . . . This bill as now worded and now before us exclusively applies only to investigations dealing with or prosecutions for the crime of treason, sabotage, espionage, sedition, seditious conspiracy, and violations of certain specific statutes, all of which deal with the Communist conspiracy."

Attorney General Herbert Brownell, Jr., shortly after the passage of the act, in an address at Plymouth, Massachusetts to the twentieth general congress of the General Society of Mayflower Descendants, commented: "Another new law is the so-called Immunity Law. This was requested by the Administration in order to prevent persons from making a sham of the Fifth Amendment privilege against self-incrimination. Those persons—subversives, their sympathizers or misguided persons— have been using the Fifth Amendment in order to shield persons they knew to be part and parcel of the communist conspiracy."

In the same speech he urged remorseful communists who wanted to "rejoin decent society" to take advantage of this act and inform on their leaders. This reminds one of the story which later came out of communist China about the informer who got an A. Wu Teh-yuan, a handicraftsman, in a period of five years denounced, so the story went, 281 "counter-revolutionaries, and criminals." For this he was given the title in Peiping of "Grade A Anti-Counter-Revolutionary Security Model." The government was encouraging competition in informing. Then there was the story about the two brothers Li who were proclaimed "model" members of the Young Communist League because they reported their sister as a spy. One can hope that Matusow at least did not get an A.

The Department of Justice soon selected the first person on whom to test the efficacy and validity of the new federal act. He was William L. Ullmann, a former Treasury Department official whom Elizabeth Bentley linked with an espionage ring which Nathan Gregory Silvermaster, another Treasury Department official, assertedly headed. The government took him before a federal grand jury in New York City under paragraph (c) of the new act. He claimed his right of silence. His case went all the way to the federal Supreme Court. All three courts sustained the validity of this paragraph. The Court of Appeals affirmed reluctantly and with regret on the basis of the district court's opinion. In the Supreme Court Justice Douglas wrote a dissenting opinion in which Justice Black concurred. He was emphatic: ". . . I would overrule the five-to-four decision of *Brown* v. *Walker* . . . and adopt the view of the minority in that case that the right of silence created by the Fifth Amendment is beyond the reach of Congress. . . . My view is that the Framers put it beyond the power of Congress to *compel* anyone to confess his crime. The evil to be guarded against was partly self-accusation under legal compulsion. But that was only part of the evil. The conscience and dignity of man were also involved. So too was his right to freedom of expression guaranteed by the First Amendment. The Framers, therefore, created the federally protected right of silence and decreed that the law could not be used to pry open one's lips and make him a witness against himself. * * * The Fifth Amendment protects the conscience and the dignity of the individual, as well as his safety and security, against the compulsion of government. . . . The critical point is that the Constitution places the right of silence *beyond the reach of government*. . . ." Justice Douglas quoted with approval from Dean Griswold's *The Fifth Amendment Today*. But a majority of seven reaffirmed *Brown* v. *Walker*.

The new act consists of but two sections, and of these, one deals with the title. The act thus reduces itself to a single section, divided into paragraphs. Paragraphs (a) and (b) relate to congressional witnesses and paragraph (c) relates to witnesses before federal courts and grand juries. Pertinent portions of these paragraphs provide:

(a) * * * Such an order [requiring a witness to testify or produce records] may be issued by a United States district court judge upon application by a duly authorized representative of the Congress or of the committee concerned. * * *

(b) Neither House nor any committee thereof nor any joint committee of the two Houses of Congress shall grant immunity to any witness without first having notified the Attorney General of the United States of such action and thereafter having secured the approval of the United States district court for the district wherein such inquiry is being held. * * *

(c) * * * he [United States attorney], upon the approval of the Attorney General, shall make application to the [district] court that the witness shall be instructed to testify or produce evidence * * *.

The Court in sustaining the validity of paragraph (c) expressly left open the question of the constitutionality of paragraphs (a) and (b):

"We are concerned here only with §(c) and therefore need not pass on this question [function of the federal district court] with respect to §§(a) and (b) of the Act."

In reaching this result the Court assumed, as had District Judge Weinfeld, that paragraphs (a) and (b) were separable from paragraph (c) without discussing the question. But there would seem to be great doubt about this, for Congress would not have passed one part without the other.

The new act not only reduces itself to a single section, but also contains no separability clause. Furthermore, in view of the history of the new act and the long struggle between Congress and the attorney general over its form, it is clear that Congress would not have been satisfied with paragraph (c), which the attorney general wanted, if this paragraph had not been accompanied by paragraphs (a) and (b), which Congress wanted.

Whether the invalid parts of an act are separable from the valid ones is a question of legislative intent. Because of the fact that many modern statutes contain a separability clause, the absence of such a clause results in the strict application today of a presumption of indivisibility. The leading federal case on separability and separability clauses is *Carter* v. *Carter Coal Co.* That case involved a separability clause which read: "If any provision of this Act, or the application thereof to any person or circumstances, is held invalid, the remainder of the Act and the application of such provisions to other persons or circumstances shall not be affected thereby." After quoting it the Court said: "In the absence of such a provision, the presumption is that the legislature intends an act to be effective as an entirety—that is to say, the rule is against the mutilation of a statute; and if any provision be unconstitutional, the presumption is that the remaining provisions fall with it."

A modern statute without a separability clause is not necessarily indivisible. However, the absence of such a clause requires the proponents of divisibility to overcome a strong presumption against them. Even without the benefit of any presumption one can suggest that in the case of the new federal act it affirmatively appears that Congress would not have passed paragraph (c) without paragraphs (a) and (b). All three paragraphs should stand or fall together.

It is the writer's position that the whole act should fall. In addition to being an immunity act in the field of heresy, it imposes on federal courts a nonjudicial function contrary to our requirements for the separation of governmental powers and in violation of the Constitution.

The new act calls upon federal courts to participate in the determination of the advisability of proposed grants of immunity. Clearly this is the case in the instance of such a proposed grant to a witness before one of the Houses of Congress or a congressional committee, for here paragraph (b) of the act specifically calls for the "approval" of a federal district court. Congress intended no difference in result between this paragraph and the following paragraph (c), relating to a witness before a federal court or grand jury, despite the fact that the latter paragraph refers only to an "order" of a federal district court.

Originally neither Congressman Keating's bill, H.R. 6899, nor Senator McCarran's bill, S.16, contained any provision for court approval. Then S.16 was revised in the House to provide for court approval in all instances, or at least so Congress thought. The House Report on S.16 in its revised form, after summarizing paragraphs (a)-(c), specifically states: "In all cases where the bill authorizes a grant of immunity after privilege has been claimed, there are at least two other independent but interested parties who must concur in the grant of immunity in order to meet the requirements of the bill." District Judge Weinfeld tried to escape from the effect of this language by suggesting that the phrase "independent but interested parties" referred, in the case of paragraph (c), to a district attorney and the attorney general. But the language is not "two independent but interested parties"; it is "two other independent but interested parties." The words "two other" can refer only, in the case of paragraph (c), to a district judge as well as the attorney general.

Moreover, Congressman Keating, a member of the Judiciary Committee of the House, and the measure's leading sponsor in that body, specifically took the position that so far as court approval was concerned there was no difference between paragraphs (b) and (c). In debate on the measure he stated:

. . . it does not leave the final determination as to the granting of immunity in either the hands of the investigating committee, or the Attorney General, but rather the court. . . .

As to (a), proceedings before a congressional committee, it provides that if a congressional committee or either House of Congress itself concludes that it is desirable to grant immunity to some witness in order to obtain evidence regarding some higher up or someone else, then the congressional committee shall give notice to the Attorney General of an application to a court and the court shall be the final arbiter as to whether or not immunity should be granted. The Attorney General can appear in court and say: "I agree with the committee," or he can appear there and say, "I disagree with the committee. This is a case where immunity should not be granted," and the court will have the final word in the matter.

Section (c) deals with proceedings before a court or grand jury. In that case it says that if the United States attorney in a particular area has a prosecution before him and feels that immunity should be granted to some prospective witness, he shall first get the approval of the Attorney General to the granting of that immunity and then shall appeal to the court and the court will pass on the question, and if convinced of the propriety, issue the order for immunity.

After explaining that a grant of immunity was "really a sort of bargaining process," and pointing out that a prosecutor or a congressional committee might sometimes get out-traded, Congressman Keating went on to make plain that courts were to be a part of this process in every instance of a proposed grant of immunity under the new act:

The feature of the bill before us which I especially commend to your favorable attention—is intended to take care of this problem of blind bargaining. It requires, in the case of congressional investigations, virtual agreement between all three branches of the Government—legislative, executive, and judicial—before an effective grant of immunity is conferred. In court proceedings it requires approval of both the prosecutor and the court.

Senator McCarran, who introduced S.16, and was the bill's leading sponsor in the Senate, took the same position in debate there that Congressman Keating had taken in the House.

Before the *Ullmann* case arose, the Attorney General, too, took the same position as Congressman Keating. In his speech at Plymouth, Massachusetts he said that immunity "will be granted by a Federal District Judge, after advice from the Attorney General, upon petition of a United States Attorney or a representative of Congress."

Judge Weinfeld, after questioning the weight to be given to remarks made in general debate by individual members of a reporting committee in determining congressional intent, referred to a statement by Congressman Francis E. Walter of Pennsylvania, who was also a member of the House Judiciary Committee, and commented that he "took a quite different view" from Congressman Keating. Congressman Walter did say at one point that "before a person can be granted immunity the court is to act on the question of the materiality and the germaneness of the matter under inquiry"; but a few moments later, in response to Representative Jacob K. Javits of New York, who remarked, ". . . The court would not I believe inquire into the advisability or lack of it in giving an immunity bath," stated: "After all, when it comes to the question of the wisdom, I just think that is a question of materiality." Either he did not distinguish between the question of the wisdom of a proposed grant of immunity and questions of materiality and pertinency, or he equated all of them. Then this interchange took place:

MR. JAVITS. The Congress will have decided that [materiality] and the court will just rely upon the decision made by the committee or the House?

MR. WALTER. I do not think so. I think this goes much further than that.

Thus he ended up taking the same position as Congressman Keating on the role of the courts: district judges had to pass upon the advisability of proposed grants of immunity. In taking this position he did not distinguish between congressional witnesses and witnesses before federal courts or grand juries.

But the determination of the advisability of proposed grants of immunity is not a judicial function. Rather such determinations properly belong to the investigative agencies of the executive branch of the government. In deciding whether to offer a grant of immunity the questions to be answered are investigative and policy ones: Is it expedient to make the offer? Is it timely to do so? Which suspect in the commission of the offense under investigation is the most appropriate one to whom to make the offer? Was he a minor participant? Will he talk? Will what he has to tell help to make out a case against the major participants? The expression of one's view on the correctness of the answers given to such questions does not even rise to the status of an advisory opinion. Such a task is investigative, not judicial, in nature.

Moreover, a court proceeding under paragraphs (a) and (b) will not be adversary in character in so far as the witness to whom it is proposed to grant immunity is concerned. To begin with, it is not clear under the act whether witnesses have any standing in court at all. In the first case under these paragraphs federal District Judge David A. Pine in the District of Columbia held that they did not, "on the ground that the statute 'does not provide for adversary proceedings * * *.'" This case involved: Robert McElrath, a broadcaster; Wilfred M. Oka, a columnist for *The Honolulu Record*; Myer C. Symonds, a lawyer; and Harold Glasser, a former Treasury Department economist. The Court of Appeals for the District of Columbia Circuit reversed Judge Pine, but the point did not reach the Supreme Court.

Even if a witness does have a standing in court, his position cannot by its very nature be adversary. Let us suppose that a congressional committee and the Attorney General are in disagreement as to a proposed grant of immunity. Committee counsel argues to the court that the testimony of the proposed grantee is necessary for the legislative purposes of Congress. A representative of the Attorney General counters that the proposed grantee is one who ought to be prosecuted. Committee counsel responds that the proposed grantee was but a minor participant in the offense which the department of justice is investigating.

What will the proposed grantee be able to argue—that he was a major participant! The approval of a proposed grant of immunity is in no way a part of the judicial function. If there is to be an immunity act the granting of immunity should rest with investigative agencies.

The approach suggested here is by no means novel. Mr. John M. Kernochan, author of the American Bar Association's Model State Witness Immunity Act, wrote in support of a similar position:

[T]he agency best qualified to make the determination [of whether or not to grant immunity] will be one thoroughly and currently conversant with both the general and the detailed situations regarding enforcement of the criminal laws. To make a wise decision, that agency should be informed with respect to the particular witness involved, his offense, and his importance to the proceeding. It should be equipped to weigh this proceeding against others pending or planned, not merely locally but on a wider basis. These considerations seem to point clearly to the enforcement authorities as the proper agency to exercise the principal control over grants of immunity. Such a solution conforms to the essential nature of immunity legislation as an instrument in aid of law enforcement.

Furthermore, if the federal courts assume the burdens sought to be imposed upon them by paragraphs (a) and (b) and pass upon the investigative and policy questions involved in proposed grants of immunity, they will take a step away from our accusatorial method in dealing with deviants and in the direction of the inquisitional technique; federal judges will undertake a duty which will remind one of the role of the French *juge d'instruction.*

Congress to date has passed at least fifty acts containing immunity provisions but, with the exception of the 1954 act and the Narcotic Control Act of 1956, none of these provisions require court approval of a proposed grant of immunity. The earliest act which related to a witness before a federal court or grand jury simply provided that "no discovery, or evidence obtained by means of any judicial proceeding from any party or witness in this or any foreign country, shall be given in evidence, or in any manner used against such party or witness." It was this act which was involved in the well known case of *Counselman* v. *Hitchcock.* There the Supreme Court held that despite the immunity act the defendant was still entitled to claim his right of silence under the fifth amendment because the immunity granted was not broad enough—it did not include immunity from prosecution. Subsequently Congress repealed the act on the ground that this decision made it "a shield to the criminal and an obstruction to justice." After that the department of justice was without a general immunity act of its own. Various specialized agencies such as the Interstate Commerce Commission, the Federal Trade Commission, the Securities and Exchange Commission, and the National Labor Relations Board had such acts, but not the Justice Department. A promise by a federal district attorney of immunity in return for testimony, except in certain very narrow areas, was unenforceable. As Mr. Justice Frankfurter stated in his dissenting opinion in *United States* v. *Monia*: "Indeed, so sensitive has Congress been against immunizing crime that it has not entrusted prosecutors generally with the power to relieve witnesses from prosecution in exchange for incriminating evidence against others."

Until the new federal act the role of a federal court with respect to a witness who claimed a right of silence was purely a judicial one. In the case of a witness before a court or a grand jury the court determined whether the claim was a valid one. If the court decided that it was, that ended the matter. If the court decided that it was not, it ordered the witness to answer. If the witness still refused, the court then ruled upon the question of contempt. In the case of a witness before an administrative body the court, whenever a statute provided for it, gave its aid to enforce the subpoena of such a body, for administrative agencies did not have the power to enforce their own subpoenas. In no case did the court pass upon the advisability of a grant of immunity. In the case of a witness before an administrative body the court also did not pass upon the question whether a subpoena *ought* to issue. Moreover, any proceedings that took place in court were truly adversary in character. In the leading case on the judicial enforcement of subpoenas issued by administrative bodies, *Interstate Commerce Comm'n* v. *Brimson*, Justice Harlan, writing for the Court, said: "Is it not clear that there are here parties on each side of a dispute involving grave questions of legal rights, that their respective positions are defined by pleadings, and that the customary forms of judicial procedure have been pursued?"

But the new federal act in paragraph (b) requires the "approval" of a federal district court to a proposed grant of immunity to a congressional witness, while in paragraph (c) such a court's "order" is required in case of a proposed grant of immunity to a witness before it or a federal grand jury. In the *Ullmann* case the Supreme Court and District Judge Weinfeld equated the procedure in paragraph (c) with that involved in the *Brimson* case. One can suggest that if the provision of this paragraph requiring the district attorney to "make application to the court that the witness shall be instructed to testify or produce evidence subject to the provisions of this section, and upon order of the court such witness shall not be excused from testifying or from producing books, papers, or other evidence" means no more than the Court said it did, then it becomes wholly unnecessary. It requires courts to do no more or other than they have always done without it. Courts would have continued to do precisely this. Such a strained construction reduces the quoted portion of paragraph (c) to an embellishment which served no other purpose than that of deceiving Congress. Nevertheless that is what the Court ruled.

Had Congress put in unescapable language in paragraph (c) its intent to have federal district courts pass on the advisability of proposed grants of immunity, the federal courts would probably have had little difficulty in holding this paragraph unconstitutional because it imposed on them nonjudicial functions. Indeed, in a recent case where a federal district judge offered immunity to a silent witness before him and, when the witness continued in his refusal to answer, found him guilty of contempt, the Court of Appeals for the Eighth Circuit reversed, saying:

> The [federal] court declared that it would grant immunity from prosecution if appellant would answer the interrogatories and it is argued that in these circumstances the appellant could not rely upon the Constitutional privilege of refusing to answer. The short answer to this contention is that the court was without authority to grant immunity from prosecution. The attempt to grant such an immunity was not within the judicial power but was an attempted exercise of executive or legislative power. *United States* v. *Ford* * * * *McCarthy* v. *Arndstein* * * * *Ullmann* v. *United States* * * *

But Congress did not make its intent unmistakably clear and the Court interpreted the language in paragraph (c) requiring a court order into surplussage.

Since then the Department of Justice has proceeded against a second individual under this paragraph. He was Edward J. Fitzgerald, a former government economist and researcher whom Elizabeth Bentley named as a member of an alleged Victor Perlo espionage group. He, like Ullmann, remained silent and, like him, appealed. The first reviewing court was again the Court of Appeals for the Second Circuit and it of course again upheld the validity of paragraph (c). The Supreme Court denied review.

In addition, the provisions of this paragraph have been followed in the Narcotic Control Act of 1956. Here too these provisions have been sustained. Also, in a recent case, *Brown* v. *United States*, involving the very immunity provision in the Compulsory Testimony Act of 1893 which the Supreme Court first sustained in *Brown* v. *Walker*, the Court reaffirmed its holding in that case as well as in the *Ullmann* case. The petitioner in this recent ruling was a manufacturer who shipped his dresses with a trucking company that the government said was owned by Johnny Dio. The Court through Justice Stewart commented, referring to the ruling in *Brown* v. *Walker:* "* * * The context in which the doctrine originated and the history of its reaffirmance through the years have been so recently re-examined by this Court in *Ullmann* v. *United States* * * * as to make it a needless exercise to retrace that ground here. Suffice it to repeat that *Brown* v. *Walker* has become 'part of our Constitutional fabric.' * * *" Chief Justice Warren, in an opinion in which Justices Black, Douglas and Brennan joined, dissented on a procedural point.

However, the downgrading of paragraph (c) of the 1954 act in the *Ullmann* case in order to save it, will not help the supporters of paragraphs (a) and (b) of this act, for paragraph (b) specifically requires court "approval" of a proposed grant of immunity, and this is exactly what Congress intended. Although the Court in the *Ullmann* case left open the question whether these paragraphs attempt to confer on federal courts a nonjudicial function, Judge Weinfeld went further. After quoting these words, "Such an order may be issued by a United States district court judge," from paragraph (a), and these words, "without first having notified the Attorney General of the United States of such action and thereafter having secured the approval of the United States district court for the district wherein such inquiry is being held," from paragraph (b), and italicizing the words "may" and "approval," he continued: "The language in these sections of the act purports to vest discretion in the court and specifically requires its approval of any grant of immunity." Thus he at least intimated a real doubt as to the validity of these paragraphs.

Nor can supporters of these paragraphs find any help in the *ex parte* issuance of search warrants, or the like issuance of warrants to wiretap. Insofar as search warrants are concerned, they are issued, not in order to procure evidence, but to obtain property which another person or the state claims is wrongfully held or used. As for warrants to wiretap, there is no federal provision for them; and any such provision which sought to impose on federal courts the duty to approve their issuance would be unconstitutional for the same reason that it is submitted paragraphs (a) and (b) are unconstitutional, namely, the imposition on federal courts of a nonjudicial function.

Justice Jackson in his posthumously published book, *The Supreme Court in the American System of Government*, described the judicial function, and indicated his doubts as to the validity of legislation of the type which paragraphs (a) and (b) contain:

But perhaps the most significant and least comprehended limitation upon the judicial power is that this power extends only to cases and controversies. We know that this restriction was deliberate, for it was proposed in the Convention that the Supreme Court be made a part of a Council of Revision with a kind of veto power, and this was rejected.

The result of the limitation is that the Court's only power is to decide lawsuits between adversary litigants with real interests at stake, and its only method of proceeding is by the conventional judicial, as distinguished from legislative or administrative, process. This precludes the rendering of advisory opinions even at the request of the nation's President and every form of pronouncement on abstract, contingent, or hypothetical issues. It prevents acceptance for judicial settlement of issues in which the interests and questions involved are political in character. It also precludes imposition on federal constitutional courts of nonjudicial duties. Recent trends to empower judges to grant or deny wiretapping rights to a prosecutor or to approve a waiver of prosecution in order to force a witness to give self-incriminating testimony raise interesting and dubious questions. A federal court can perform but one function—that of deciding litigations—and can proceed in no manner except by the judicial process.

A consideration of our governmental practice of the separation of powers, and of the nature of judging, will demonstrate the validity of Justice Jackson's doubts.

Separation of Powers

Our practice of separating governmental functions had some of its origins almost eight centuries ago. As early as 1166 Henry II assembled the archbishops, bishops, abbots, earls and barons of all England and legislated: the result was the Assize of Clarendon. Here he separated legislative from executive functions. A decade later he organized the eyre system on a continuing basis, and in 1178 he reorganized it into a permanent court of professional judges: ". . . on the advice of the wise men of his realm he chose five only, namely two clerks and three laymen, all members of his private household. These five he commanded to hear all the complaints of the realm and to do right judgment, and that they should not depart from the king's court, but should remain there for the purpose of hearing the complaints of the people, so that if any case should come before them which they could not bring to a decision, it should be presented to the king, and determined as it might seem good to him and the wise men of the realm." Some six centuries later the framers of our Constitution provided in Art. III, §1: "The judicial Power of the United States, shall be vested in one supreme Court, and in such inferior Courts as the Congress may from time to time ordain and establish."

The English governmental system became Montesquieu's model, and Montesquieu became the guide of the Constitution's framers. They were acutely aware of the danger of vesting too much power in fallible human beings. Accordingly they constructed our federal Constitution along the lines of their understanding of Montesquieu's classic triple division of governmental functions into legislative, executive, and judicial branches, and their own ideas and those of Montesquieu, John Locke and James Harrington of checks and balances between the different agencies which exercise governmental power. Montesquieu based his three-fold division on Locke, who in his *Second Treatise on Civil Government*, licensed for printing in 1689, the year after James II was forced to flee from England, had a chapter entitled, "Of the Legislative, Executive and Federative Power of the Commonwealth." The Federative part was that relating to foreign affairs. In this chapter he commented that "it may be too great temptation to human frailty, apt to grasp at power, for the same persons who have the power of making laws to have also in their hands the power to execute them." In a later chapter he observed that legislative and executive power were in distinct hands "in all moderate monarchies and well-framed governments."

Yet earlier James Harrington in *The Commonwealth of Oceana*, published in 1656, also made a threefold division of governmental powers. He dedicated it to Oliver Cromwell: "To his highness the Lord Protector of the Commonwealth of England, Scotland, and Ireland." Harrington put the query: "But seeing they that make the laws in commonwealths are but men, the main question seems to be, how a commonwealth comes to be an empire of laws, and not of men?" He in effect answered by saying, separation of powers. He began with the illustration of two girls dividing a cake. One said to the other, "Divide and I will choose; or let me divide and you shall choose." His threefold division consisted of a council or senate, made up of the wiser heads, an assembly, representing the whole body of the people, and a magistracy. The council or senate debated and proposed but it did not choose, for this would be like one of the two girls both dividing the cake and choosing which part she wanted. The assembly was the one which chose. The magistracy was the one which executed the laws. Moreover, the magistracy was not to stay in office too long, for this would destroy the life of the commonwealth: rather it was to be rotated regularly by the ballot of the people. Thus Harrington arrived at his formula "of the senate debating and proposing, of the people resolving, and of the magistracy executing."

But it was Montesquieu who in his *L'Esprit des Lois* (1748) arrived at the three-fold division of legislative, executive, and judicial. He had dealt with the subject in an earlier piece, *The Grandeur and the Fall of the Romans* (1734), an anticipation in title of Gibbon's work. Montesquieu was the one who had the greatest influence on our founding fathers. Of him James Madison wrote: "The oracle who is always consulted and cited on this subject is the celebrated Montesquieu." Montesquieu began with Locke's triple division: "In every government there are three sorts of power: the legislative; the executive in respect to things dependent on the law of nations; and the executive in regard to matters that depend on the civil law. . . . The latter we shall call the judiciary power, and the other simply the executive power of the state." Because he built on Locke it has been asserted that our founding fathers misunderstood him, for Locke's triple division, as did Harrington's, really reduced itself to two, legislative and executive. And Montesquieu did in one place minimize the importance of the judicial branch: "Of the three powers above mentioned, the judiciary is in some measure next to nothing: there remain, therefore, only two." However, he did insist on the independence of the judiciary as necessary to liberty: "Again, there is no liberty, if the judiciary power be not separated from the legislative and executive." And of course he made the same point as to the separation of legislative and executive powers: "When the legislative and executive powers are united in the same person, or in the same body of magistrates, there can be no liberty." The three branches, legislative, executive, and judicial, were to function in the interest of liberty by balancing and checking each other: ". . . it is necessary from the very nature of things that power should be a check to power."

The founding fathers sought to put the ideas of Montesquieu, and of Locke and Harrington, into operation. The framers of our federal Constitution agreed that the concentration of governmental powers spelled tyranny. Washington, Madison, Jefferson and Adams all explicitly said so. Washington in his *Farewell Address* cautioned: ". . . The spirit of encroachment tends to consolidate the powers of all departments in one, and thus to create, whatever the form of government, a real despotism." Madison wrote: "The accumulation of all powers, legislative, executive, and judiciary, in the same hands, whether of one, a few, or many, and whether hereditary, self-appointed, or elective, may justly be pronounced the very definition of tyranny."

Our framers not only divided governmental powers into three branches, but they also carried their ideas of checks and balances so far as to apply them even as between the Senate and the House of Representatives. In this respect they were adapting Harrington.

By way of contrast the Russian Communists asserted that the Soviet Union repudiated the idea of the separation of powers. Andrei Y. Vyshinsky, at one time chief authority on Soviet law and formerly attorney-general of the Soviet Union, in commenting on the 1936 Constitution declared: "We do not have the separation of powers but the distribution of functions . . . This has nothing in common with the Montesquieu doctrine." A textbook on constitutional law published in 1938 under his editorship and published a decade later in this country under the title, *The Law of the Soviet State*, asserted: "From top to bottom the Soviet Social Order is penetrated by the single general spirit of the oneness of the authority of the toilers. The program of the All-Union Communist Party (of Bolsheviks) rejects the bourgeois principle of separation of powers."

We separated not only governmental powers; we also separated state and church. Again there is a contrast between the West and the East. Byzantine Christianity resulted in the absence of an effective separation between church and state, with the consequent growth of a greater secular absolutism in Russia than in the West. Clerical leaders in Russia never became strong and independent enough to act as an effective check on lay rulers. It is true that in 1568 Philip, the Metropolitan of Moscow, at a church service condemned Ivan IV to his face for his execesses in persecuting the old nobility: "Most merciful Czar and Grand Duke, how long wilt thou shed the innocent blood of thy faithful people and Christians? How long shall unrighteousness last in this Russian empire? The Tatars and the heathen and the whole world knows that all other peoples have law and justice, only in Russia is there none . . ." But Philip was arrested and murdered by the czar's henchmen. And when Adrian, the patriarch of Moscow went to Peter I in 1598 and begged him to be merciful to the condemned streltzi (marksmen), Peter told him to go back to his church and mind his own business.

On the other hand, in the West great popes such as Gregory VII (Hildebrand) (1073–85) and Innocent III, and outstanding archbishops of Canterbury such as Anselm and Becket, not only restrained lay rulers but occasionally even humbled them. Gregory VII it was who made Henry IV, the German Holy Roman Emperor, yield at Canossa. Innocent III had a series of triumphs. He made King John of England subordinate that country and Ireland to the status of fiefs of the Holy See. He compelled Philip Augustus of France to give up Agnes of Merau and take back his Danish wife Ingebord, whom he had divorced, Peter of Aragon to forego his intended marriage with Bianca of Navarre, and Alphonso IX of Leon to put away his wife Berengaria of Castile, who was related to him within the prohibited degrees. Peter also had to reduce his kingdom to the status of a fief of the Holy See. Anselm rebuked William Rufus (1087–1100). Although Becket was murdered, it was difficult for a time to say who had won, he or Henry II.

A recent working illustration of our separation of governmental powers was President Harry S. Truman's refusal even after he was out of office to honor a subpoena of the House Committee on Un-American Activities. The then chairman of this committee, Congressman Velde, issued the subpoena in order to question Mr. Truman about Harry Dexter White. Mr. Truman replied: ". . . if the doctrine [of the separation of powers] is to have any validity at all, it must be equally applicable to a President after his term . . . has expired . . . The doctrine would be shattered, and the President . . . would become a mere arm of the Legislative Branch . . . if he would feel during his term of office that his every act might be subject to . . . possible distortion for political purposes."

There have been times when this system of checks and balances has seemed too cumbersome and unworkable to many of us. For instance, in the days of the New Deal under President Franklin D. Roosevelt, many became impatient with the Supreme Court for holding unconstitutional certain of the legislation which the president had proposed and Congress had passed. Some made references in derogatory fashion to the judges on the Court as "the nine old men." The president proposed packing the Court by enlarging its membership. Fortunately his proposal was defeated. The experiences of the world in the twentieth century with authoritarian governments should give us a greater appreciation of the wisdom in Lord Acton's dictum: "Power tends to corrupt, and absolute power corrupts absolutely."

If we apply our concept of the separation of power to the treatment of deviants we arrive at these conclusions: the Congress passes the laws which define offenses and prescribe the penalties; the executive branch investigates offenses and prosecutes offenders; the courts interpret the laws, pass upon their constitutionality, determine whether accused persons are innocent or guilty, and if guilty impose the appropriate penalties. On the basis of this division, if there are to be immunity acts, the power to grant immunity, with one possible exception, should rest with the investigative agencies of the executive branch of government. The possible exception is for the House of Representatives when in the exercise of its power of impeachment. Beyond that, neither House should have any power to grant immunity from prosecution. The primary business of Congress is to legislate, not to investigate offenses. For this purpose, as the Minority Report in the House on S.16 made plain, there is no need of any power to grant immunity. In order to legislate, Congress has always been able to get enough information without any such power, and will continue to be able to do so. Thus Attorney General Brownell, Jr., in his tug of war with Senator McCarran over the attorney general's request to participate in a grant of immunity to a congressional witness, had the better of the argument: if there is to be an immunity act the power to grant immunity should rest with the executive branch of the government.

The Nature of Judging

In any event the determination of the desirability of a grant of immunity is not a judicial function. A consideration of the nature of the business of judging will demonstrate this.

The business of judging involves the resolution of disputes about legal rights between adverse claimants. A classic example of the exercise of the judicial function was that of King Solomon hearing the adverse contentions of two women who each claimed to be the mother of the same child, making a determination in favor of one of them, and awarding the child to her. For the judicial function to come into operation there must first be a real, substantial and concrete controversy about valuable legal rights. This controversy must be between actual antagonists, each of whom presents his side to the court. In the third place this controversy must admit of an immediate and definitive determination of the legal rights of the parties by a decree of a conclusive character. Only if there are adverse litigants will the various aspects of disputed questions be fully presented, and only under such circumstances can the courts do their work well.

In accord with the nature of the judicial process the Constitution provides in Art. III, §2 that the "judicial Power shall extend to all Cases, in Law and Equity, arising under this Constitution, the Laws of the United States, and Treaties made, or which shall be made, under their Authority"; and to various additional kinds of "cases" and "controversies." The word "controversies," according to Justice Field in *In re Pacific Ry. Comm'n*, whose opinion on this point the federal Supreme Court quoted with approval in the leading cases of *Muskrat* v. *United States* and *Aetna Life Ins. Co.* v. *Haworth*, "if distinguishable at all from 'cases,' is so in that it is less comprehensive than the latter, and includes only suits of a civil nature."

Because of the nature of the judicial function and the necessity of an adversary proceeding for its exercise, the federal courts, and courts generally, have refused to give advisory opinions. The federal Supreme Court has presented us with a consistent line of authorities to this effect. The earliest ones were *Hayburn's Case* and *United States* v. *Yale Todd*, both of which arose under a veterans' pension act of 1792. This act gave circuit courts of the United States the duty of examining into the claims to pensions as invalids of members of our armed forces during the Revolutionary War and certifying their opinion to the secretary of war.

The different circuit courts, consisting of Chief Justice Jay, Justice Cushing and District Judge Duane in New York, Justices Wilson and Blair and District Judge Peters in Pennsylvania, and Justice Iredell and District Judge Sitgreaves in North Carolina, were of the opinion that the duties assigned by this act were not of a judicial nature. The circuit court for the district of New York stated: "That by the constitution of the United States, the government thereof is divided into *three* distinct and independent branches, and it is the duty of each to abstain from, and to oppose, encroachments on either. That neither the legislative nor the executive branches, can constitutionally assign to the judicial any duties, but such as are properly judicial, and to be performed in a judicial manner." However, the circuit court for the district of New York, in an effort to cooperate, gave its members the option of acting as commissioners, but not as judges, in carrying out the provisions of the act. But the circuit court for the district of Pennsylvania respectfully refused to act at all. Accordingly the attorney general made a motion ex officio in the Supreme Court for a writ of mandamus to compel the circuit court for the district of Pennsylvania to act in the case of one Hayburn. The court denied the motion. The attorney general then changed his ground and stated that he was in court on behalf of Hayburn. This caused the court to take the motion under advisement until the next term. In the meantime Congress repealed the act of 1792, but put in a saving clause for the determination of the validity of the action taken by those judges who accommodatingly acted as commissioners. It was under this saving clause that *United States* v. *Yale Todd* arose.

In the interim President Washington had his secretary of state, Thomas Jefferson, write to Chief Justice Jay and his associate justices and ask them whether their advice would be available to the executive branch on various important legal questions. They answered in the negative, "especially as the power given by the Constitution to the President, of calling on the heads of departments for opinions, seems to have been *purposely* as well as expressly united to the *executive* departments."

The next year (1794) the Court decided the *Yale Todd* case in favor of the United States on the ground that the act of 1792 in violation of the Constitution sought to impose nonjudicial functions on federal circuit courts. In the words of Chief Justice Taney the Court decided:

1. That the power proposed to be conferred on the circuit courts of the United States by the act of 1792 was not judicial power within the meaning of the constitution, and was, therefore, unconstitutional, and could not lawfully be exercised by the courts.

2. That as the act of Congress intended to confer the power on the courts as a judicial function, it could not be construed as an authority to the judges composing the court to exercise the power out of court in the character of commissioners.

The leading case is *Muskrat v. United States*. There the plaintiffs sought to have determined the validity of certain legislation which undertook to increase the number of persons entitled to share in the final distribution of the lands and funds of the Cherokees by permitting the enrollment of children living on a designated date. Although the United States was the defendant the proceedings were not really adversary in character. The Supreme Court ordered the suits dismissed saying: ". . . That judicial power, as we have seen, is the right to determine actual controversies arising between adverse litigants, duly instituted in courts of proper jurisdiction. . . .

". . . If such actions as are here attempted, to determine the validity of legislation, are sustained, the result will be that this court, instead of keeping within the limits of judicial power, and deciding cases or controversies between opposing parties, as the Constitution intended it should, will be required to give opinions in the nature of advice concerning legislative action, a function never conferred upon it by the Constitution, and against the exercise of which this court has steadily set its face from the beginning."

The necessity of adversary proceedings in order to obtain the best results from the judicial process has compelled courts to refuse to decide friendly or collusive suits. For example, in *United States v. Johnson,* the Supreme Court ordered dismissed a case brought by a tenant against a landlord at the landlord's instigation in order to test the validity of certain provisions of the Emergency Price Control Act of 1942, saying: "Such a suit is collusive because it is not in any real sense adversary. It does not assume the 'honest and actual antagonistic assertion of rights' to be adjudicated—a safeguard essential to the integrity of the judicial process, and one which we have held to be indispensable to adjudication of constitutional questions by this court."

In an earlier case in an opinion by Chief Justice Taney the Court held even more forcefully:

It is the office of courts of justice to decide the rights of persons and of property, when the persons interested cannot adjust them by agreement between themselves—and to do this upon the full hearing of both parties. And any attempt, by a mere colorable dispute, to obtain the opinion of the court upon a question of law which a party desires to know for his own interest or his own purposes, where there is no real or substantial controversy between those who appear as adverse parties to the suit, is an abuse which courts of justice have always reprehended, and treated as a punishable contempt of court.

Accordingly, where during the course of a litigation the control of the corporate opponents passed into the hands of the same persons the litigation was no longer a controversy for it had "ceased to be between adverse parties."

Nor will the courts pass on abstract, hypothetical, contingent or remote questions. In a recent case the Supreme Court ordered the dismissal of a complaint seeking to enjoin the district director of the Immigration and Naturalization Service from construing the Immigration and Nationality Act of 1952 so as to treat aliens domiciled in the continental United States returning from temporary work in Alaska as if they were aliens entering the United States.for the first time, saying: "Determination of the scope and constitutionality of legislation in advance of its immediate adverse effect in the context of a concrete case involves too remote and abstract an inquiry for the proper exercise of the judicial function." For the same reason the Court in *United Public Workers* v. *Mitchell*, a suit by certain federal employees, refused to pass on the validity of a provision of the Hatch Act which forbade federal employees from engaging in specified political activities, and in *Alabama State Federation of Labor* v. *McAdory*, a suit by various labor organizations, declined to pass on the constitutionality of certain sections of an Alabama statute for the regulation of labor unions. In the former case the Court explained:

. . . For adjudication of constitutional issues "concrete legal issues, presented in actual cases, not abstractions," are requisite. . . .
The Constitution allots the nation's judicial power to the federal courts. Unless these courts respect the limits of that unique authority, they intrude upon powers vested in the legislative or executive branches. Judicial adherence to the doctrine of the separation of powers preserves the courts for the decision of issues, between litigants, capable of effective determination. Judicial exposition upon political proposals is permissible only when necessary to decide definite issues between litigants. When the courts act continually within these constitutionally imposed boundaries of their power, their ability to perform their function as a balance for the people's protection against abuse of power by other branches of government remains unimpaired. Should the courts seek to expand their power so as to bring under their jurisdiction ill-defined controversies over constitutional issues, they would become the organs of political theories. Such abuse of judicial power would properly meet rebuke and restriction from other branches. By these mutual checks and balances by and between the branches of government, democracy undertakes to preserve the liberties of the people from excessive concentrations of authority.

In the latter case Chief Justice Stone speaking for the Court stated that it had long been the Court's "considered practice not to decide abstract, hypothetical or contingent questions."

Nor will courts consider academic or moot problems. In *St. Pierre* v. *United States* the Supreme Court dismissed a writ of certiorari to review a contempt sentence of imprisonment which had been served, ruling: "A federal court is without power to decide moot questions or to give advisory opinions which cannot affect the rights of litigants in the case before it."

In 1959 the Court disposed of one of the three cases before it arising out of the security hearings of employees on the ground of mootness: in *Taylor* v. *McElroy* it ordered the complaint dismissed as moot after the Defense Department notified all interested parties that Taylor had been granted clearance.

Indeed the courts in this country were so sparing and self-disciplined in their exercise of the judicial function that remedial legislation providing for declaratory judgments became necessary. Professor Edson R. Sunderland in the first American article on declaratory judgments commented: "We have canonized the ancient tradition of a cause of action, in all its original crudeness, and have made it the condition and the measure of judicial action." In order to remedy the situation various of the states and federal government passed legislation providing for declaratory judgments. The federal act was passed in 1934, and held constitutional in *Aetna Life Insurance Co.* v. *Haworth.*

In addition, a few states in their constitutions provided for advisory opinions. However, such provisions have been largely limited to constitutional questions. Moreover, they have not been adopted generally: those who have studied advisory opinions have been divided in their estimates of them. This was Justice Frankfurter's estimate: "However much provision may be made on paper for adequate arguments (and experience justifies little reliance) advisory opinions are bound to move in an unreal atmosphere. . . . They are ghosts that slay."

Some critics of judicial self-restraint were more caustic in their comments than Professor Sunderland. For instance, Professor Robert J. Harris suggested that " 'cases and controversies,' 'adverse parties,' 'substantial interests,' and 'real questions,' are no more than trees behind which judges hide when they wish either to throw stones at Congress or the President or to escape from those who are urging them to do so." But the business of judging involves the peaceful resolution of concrete controversies between actual litigants who insist on a determination of the issues involved between them. If the courts undertake to accomplish more than this they may be bargaining for trouble. While there have been cases which support the argument that the federal Supreme Court has avoided issues, for example, during the cold war the cases involving the constitutionality of the House Committee on Un-American Activities, by and large the Court has not refrained from deciding controversial questions. In the recent past the Court has passed upon such difficult problems as those relating to segregation, to claims of the Fifth Amendment's privilege against self-incrimination, to a contention that a state sedition law was invalid, to the assertion that the government's security program was illegal in its application to employees in nonsensitive positions, and yet others. Indeed, the Court has decided so many controversial issues that it has itself been accused, and by no less a body than the National Conference of Chief Justices, of lacking the judicial self-restraint which Professor Harris criticizes it for exercising. Professor Harris overstated his case.

With the growth of administrative regulation the courts have distinguished not only between judicial, legislative and executive functions, but also between judicial and administrative processes. In line with this distinction the federal courts have determined that rate making, the approval of increases in the capital stock of public utilities, the granting or renewal of a radio broadcasting station license, the granting of a patent, of a trademark registration, the issuance, renewal, denial or revocation of a liquor license, and the approval of an annexation to a municipality involved legislative or administrative functions and not a judicial one. The radio license case arose under the Radio Act of 1927, which gave an appeal from the Federal Radio Commission to the Court of Appeals of the District of Columbia, and then provided that the court "shall hear, review and determine the appeal upon said record and evidence, and may alter or revise the decision appealed from and enter such judgment as to it may seem just." The Court of Appeals reversed an order of the commission which had cut down the hours of service of a broadcasting station at Schenectady, New York, which the General Electric Company owned and operated. Conceding the power of Congress to vest the courts of the District of Columbia with nonjudicial functions, the Supreme Court denied review on the ground "that the powers confided to the commission respecting the granting and renewal of station licenses are purely administrative and that the provision for appeals to the court of appeals does no more than make that court a superior and revising agency in the same field." Congress promptly revised the act to provide that "review by the court shall be limited to questions of law and that findings of fact by the commission, if supported by substantial evidence, shall be conclusive unless it shall clearly appear that the findings of the commission are arbitrary or capricious."

After this change the Supreme Court, in a case involving the commission's termination of two licenses in order to extend the time of a station in Gary, Indiana, which specialized in foreign language programs and broadcast to an area where the population was 60% foreign born, granted review; and in an opinion by Chief Justice Hughes explained the proper but limited scope of judicial review over administrative action: "Whether the Commission applies the legislative standards validly set up, whether its proceedings satisfy the pertinent demands of due process, whether, in short, there is compliance with the legal requirements which fix the province of the Commission and govern its action, are appropriate questions for judicial decision. . . . And an inquiry into the facts before the Commission, in order to ascertain whether its findings are thus vitiated, belongs to the judicial province and does not trench upon, or involve the exercise of administrative authority. Such an examination is not concerned with the weight of evidence or with the wisdom or expediency of the administrative action."

In a liquor license case the Court of Appeals for the Ninth Circuit held that the territorial legislature of Alaska in burdening the district court of Alaska and its judges with the responsibility in the first instance of granting, refusing or revoking a liquor license violated the letter of Alaska's Organic Act and the clear intent of Congress, saying: ". . . The discretion exercised in granting or revoking a license to sell intoxicating liquor is not a function of the judiciary but an exercise of ultimate police power. The province of a court or judge is not to exercise such power in the first instance, but to hear and determine in a case or controversy between adverse parties constitutional or legal questions as to the grant or refusal of such a privilege to a designated person."

Further experience with administrative action after the radio license cases enabled the Supreme Court in a recent case, *United States* v. *Morton Salt Co.*, in an opinion by Justice Jackson to describe with greater definiteness the nature of such action and to point out that it involved investigative and prosecutive elements not appropriate to the judicial function. In that case the Court ruled that the Federal Trade Commission had power to require corporations to file with it reports showing how they had complied with a court decree enforcing one of its cease and desist orders. Justice Jackson with his usual clarity wrote:

The Trade Commission Act is one of several in which Congress, to make its policy effective has relied upon the initiative of administrative officials and the flexibility of the administrative process. Its agencies are provided with staffs to institute proceedings and to follow up decrees and police their obedience. While that process at times is adversary, it also at times is inquisitorial. These agencies are expected to ascertain when and against whom proeedings should be set in motion and to take the lead in following through to effective results. It is expected that this combination of duty and power always will result in eager action but it is feared that it may sometimes result in harsh and overzealous action.

To protect against mistaken or arbitrary orders, judicial review is provided. Its function is dispassionate and disinterested adjudication, unmixed with any concern as to the success of either prosecution or defense. Courts are not expected to start wheels moving or to follow up judgments. Courts neither have, nor need, sleuths to dig up evidence, staffs to analyze reports, or personnel to prepare prosecutions for contempts. Indeed, while some situations force the judge to pass on contempt issues which he himself raises, it is to be regretted whenever a court in any sense must become prosecutor. Those occasions should not be needlessly multiplied by denying investigative and prosecutive powers to other lawful agencies.

As the work of administrative bodies grew, the self-restraint of courts again came in for criticism. This time the critics asserted that the courts were abdicating their responsibilities to administrative agencies. Although the courts may at times have been oversold on expertise, and even overawed by it, one wonders whether the objections of such critics could not better be met by adopting the recommendation of the Hoover Commission for the creation of "a court of special jurisdiction, to be known as the Administrative Court of the United States," to which would be transferred the judicial functions of administrative agencies.

State cases have held unconstitutional as conferring upon courts nonjudicial functions statutes which empowered courts to approve the issuance of liquor licenses, to issue licenses permitting betting and bookmaking, to try de novo the issuance by a commission, of licenses to construct dams, to approve sales made under deeds of trust, to revoke licenses granted for the sale of nonintoxicating beer, to supervise the sale of forfeited and delinquent lands, to approve the annexation of specified areas to municipal corporations, on their severance from them, or the alteration of the territory of school districts, to fix the salaries of other state officers, to supplement such salaries, to appoint any other than court officials, to appoint an administrator for an insolvent municipal corporation with authority to control its fiscal affairs, to approve the enactments of county boards of supervisors, to pass on the propriety of the discharge of municipal officials, to determine whether drainage districts should be organized and what lands should be included in them, to determine whether proposed drainage ditches would be conducive to the public health, convenience or welfare, and whether their proposed routes were practicable, to approve the organization of conservation districts, of electric light, heat and power districts, to fix reasonable rates for common carriers, for title insurance, for ginning cotton, to confirm the apportionment of the expenses of a county among its municipalities, to determine the amounts of property assessments for taxes, to approve the accounts of certain officials, to approve the location and layout of street railways, and yet others.

The last case cited, *Norwalk Street Ry. Co.'s Appeal*, is a leading state case. In it the court reasoned: ". . . One controlling consideration in deciding whether a particular act oversteps the limits of judicial power is the necessary inconsistency of such acts with the independence of the judicial department, and the preservation of its sphere of action distinct from that of the legislative and executive departments. . . ."

One recent state case involved a statutory provision making justices of the peace members of township boards. The court struck it down. Another dealt with an act which required one who contemplated filing an action for divorce, separate maintenance or annulment of marriage, to file preliminarily with the clerk of the court a written statement announcing an intention to file the complaint. The clerk was to take this statement to the judge, and the judge was authorized to invite the prospective parties and their counsel to confer with him in chambers. Attendance was to be voluntary. The court invalidated the act on the ground that the function to be performed by the judge "cannot fairly be described as judicial."

Courts have demonstrated the self-restraint and self-discipline which are characteristic of the judicial process at its best by other restrictions which they have applied to themselves. They have refused, for instance, to pass upon questions which they have deemed to be political. A precise description of such questions is difficult. The best that one can do is to enumerate some of them. They have arisen in disputes which the courts for one reason or another have felt they could not effectively or adequately resolve. Courts have thus refused to rule on which government was to be recognized as representing a foreign state, the policy which was to govern recognition, the policy toward aliens and foreign policy generally, the wisdom of an arrangement for the waiver by the United States of jurisdiction over offenses committed in Japan by members of our armed forces, whether a foreign state was in a position to perform its treaty obligations, which governments were the established ones in our 48 states, whether these governments were republican in form, the way in which our states geographically distributed their electoral strength among their political subdivisions, how many members in the House of Representatives our various states were to have, the way in which our states divided themselves into congressional districts, the terms on which a new political party was to go on the ballot, whether a certified amendment to the federal Constitution was properly adopted, whether a legislative act was passed in the form in which it was authenticated, the duration of a state of war, the extent to which the power to prosecute violations of the laws of war were to be exercised before peace was declared, the control and dominion over the three-mile marginal ocean belt adjoining our shores, and yet others. Justice Jackson in his *The Supreme Court in the American System of Government* took pains to list various of the questions of a political nature which the Court passed by:

The Court has also observed a number of other self-limitations which are intended to keep it out of active participation in the political processes. It has refused to inquire whether a state government complies with the guarantee of a republican form of government or has properly ratified a proposed constitutional amendment. It has given finality to the certification by the other branches of government that a federal statute is as signed, as against a claim of variance with the language actually adopted. The duration of a state of war, the abrogation of treaties, the recognition or non-recognition of foreign governments, and matters of foreign policy generally, have been held to be political questions.

Even more controversial has been the effort to use the Supreme Court to control the districting of states for the elections of members of Congress, to fix the terms on which a new political party may go on the state ballot, to abolish the "county unit" system used in some states. Of course, it would be nice if there were some authority to make everybody do the things we ought to have done and leave undone the things we ought not to have done. But are the courts the appropriate catch-all into which every such problem should be tossed? One can answer "Yes" if some immediate political purpose overshadows concern for the judicial institution. But in most such cases interference by the Court would take it into matters in which it lacks special competence, let alone machinery of implementation.

The judicial self-restraint which courts practice probably has made it easier for them than for the other branches of government to stay within the bounds of their prescribed functions. In three recent cases the federal courts refused to interfere with the activities of Senator McCarthy and the Permanent Subcommittee on Investigations of the Senate Committee on Government Operations. In one the court reasoned:

Were a court empowered to limit in advance this subject matter of Congressional investigations, violence would be done to the principle of separation of powers upon which our entire political system is based. Justice Brandeis warned of the danger of encroachment by one department of the government upon another, when he spoke of the dangers of "[U]surpation, proceeding by gradual encroachment rather than by violent acts; subtle and

often long-concealed concentration of distinct functions, which are beneficent when separately administered and dangerous only when combined in
the same persons. . . . The makers of our Constitution had in mind like
dangers to our political liberty when they provided so carefully for the
separation of governmental powers."

In another recent case a three-judge district court in the District of
Columbia refused to enjoin the members of the Senate Internal Security
Subcommittee and the public printer from disseminating 75,000 copies
of a handbook on the communist party, which described the plaintiff
as a communist front. Judge Edgerton pointed out "that nothing authorizes anyone to prevent Congress from publishing any statement"
and "that a judgment for the plaintiff would invade the constitutional
separation of powers." In yet another, the Court of Appeals for the
District of Columbia Circuit held that the courts would not enjoin the
Senate Select Committee on Improper Activities in the Field of Management and Labor from turning over records which it had obtained
from a labor union to a county district attorney in Pennsylvania for inspection and copying.

In a recent state case in New York the Court of Appeals in a comparable fashion held that Joseph (Socks) Lanza could not enjoin the
New York State Joint Legislative Committee on Government Operations from using a wiretapped conversation between him and his lawyer,
saying: "* * * To claim inherent power here is nothing more than an
assumption of power on the part of one branch of the government as
against a co-ordinate branch. This we decline to do. * * *"

Not only have courts confined themselves to disputed issues within
their competence to resolve; they have also prevented grand juries,
which are arms of the courts, from making charges against named persons unless those charges could be controverted. A recent example is
Application of United Electrical, Radio & Machine Workers. There
the court ordered a "presentment" expunged from the court records because those whom it named did not have "the right to defend themselves and to have their day in a Court of Justice—their absolute right
had the Grand Jury returned an indictment." To allow the document to
stand would "defeat that fundamental fairness which must mark all
judicial proceedings." A state court said of such a document: "A presentment is a foul blow. It wins the importance of a judicial document; yet
it lacks its principal attributes—the right to answer and to appeal. It
accuses, but furnishes no forum for a denial."

General Sessions Judge Mitchell D. Schweitzer of New York was
thus right in his recent ruling impounding a grand jury presentment on
television quiz programs. One of the quiz shows involved was *Twenty-*

One, whose originators were Jack Barry and Dan Enright. Of course, what Congress may do is another matter: the House Special Subcommittee on Legislative Oversight headed by Representative Oren Harris of Arkansas has begun its own investigation into charges of deception in TV programs.

Because of the desire that the judiciary have the confidence and respect of the people in the highest degree many judges, although not legally required to do so, have declined offers of political nominations and appointments to other offices. Chief Justice Warren removed himself from political life. Chief Justice Stone refused the chairmanship of the Atomic Energy Commission and membership on the United States Ballot Commission. Cardozo, while chief judge of the New York Court of Appeals, refused an appointment to the Permanent Court of Arbitration at The Hague. He wrote Secretary of State Charles Evans Hughes: "After many inward struggles I have come to the conclusion that a Judge of the Court of Appeals best serves the people of the State by refusing to assume an obligation that in indeterminate, if improbable, contingencies might take precedence of the obligations attached to his judicial office." Federal Judge Thomas F. Murphy, after consulting with his judicial brethren, turned down President Truman's proposal that he conduct an investigation of corruption in the executive branch. Recently, retired Justice Stanley F. Reed, after first accepting, withdrew as chairman of the new federal Civil Rights Commission. He wrote President Eisenhower that for him "to accept such an investigatory and advisory office in the Executive Department" seemed to him incompatible with his "obligations as a judge." To serve on this Commission might possibly result in a "lowering of respect for the impartiality of the Federal judiciary."

Just as the courts will not give advisory opinions, or entertain amicable or collusive suits, or rule on abstract, hypothetical, remote, contingent, academic or moot questions, or exercise legislative, administrative or executive functions, or consider problems which they regard as political, so also the courts will not exercise general investigative powers. The case of *Webster Eisenlohr, Inc.* v. *Kalodner* furnishes a good illustration. A preferred stockholder brought a class action to have the court adjudge that the preferred stockholders had the exclusive voting power in the corporation. During the course of the litigation the corporation sent its annual report to stockholders and thereafter wrote to its preferred stockholders offering to purchase their interests. The plaintiff and other preferred stockholders whom he represented availed themselves of this offer. Judge Kalodner was advised of this development and felt that the letter and the annual report were misleading. Accordingly he appointed a special master to investigate the acts and assets of the corporation. The court of appeals disagreed with his action, saying:

The fundamental proposition which probably no one would dispute is that a court's power is judicial only, not administrative nor investigative. . . .

We do not think this view imposes unduly restrictive limitations upon courts. . . . No doubt a great deal goes on in the world which ought not to go on. If courts had general investigatory powers, they might discover some of these things and possibly right them. Whether they would do as well in this respect as officers or bodies expressly set up for that purpose may be doubted, but until the concept of judicial power is widened to something quite different from what it now is courts will better serve their public function in limiting themselves to the controversies presented by parties in litigation.

Another illustrative case is *Bestel* v. *Bestel*, involving a divorce proceeding and the question of the custody of a child. The judge, who had jurisdiction over the department of domestic relations, ordered his staff to make an investigation of the child and its parents and the parents' relatives. After obtaining information in this manner the judge entered a decree. The Supreme Court of Oregon reversed, saying: "Such a course of procedure is unknown to our law. It is contrary to the very essence of the administration of law in any judicial proceeding."

Judges are judges and not mediators, arbitrators, administrators or investigators. Accordingly, the federal courts should challenge the imposition on them of a function that would involve them in the business of investigating offenses rather than judging deviants, a function which, when in the hands of the judiciary, involves the importation of a feature of the inquisitional system. The new federal immunity act of 1954, seeking as it does to burden federal courts with a nonjudicial function of an essentially inquisitional nature, should have been declared unconstitutional.

Attacks on the Court

Moreover the determination of the cases and controversies which the Constitution assigns to the federal courts is enough of a work load for them. In order to do this job effectively they should not add duties to the business of judging which do not properly belong to it. Even if the federal courts restrict themselves to their assigned task they will at times come in for criticism by those who feel aggrieved by their decisions. Professor Harris asserted that the Court indulged in too much judicial self-restraint. Many others made just the opposite accusation. In the past few years the Court has encountered an unparalleled volume of harsh attacks because of its necessary rulings in sensitive areas, such as segregation, passports, congressional committees, security programs, state measures dealing with subversion, and cases generally involving Communists or Communist sympathizers or persons thought to be such. There have been loud protests, both in and out of Congress, against a score and more of the Court's recent necessary decisions: for instance, *Brown* v. *Board of Education*, outlawing segregation in the public schools; *Pennsylvania* v. *Nelson*, invalidating Pennsylvania's sedition law and casting doubt on such laws of other states; *Cole* v. *Young*, ruling that the government's security program, set up in President Eisenhower's Executive Order 10450, could not legally be applied to an employee in a nonsensitive position; *Jencks* v. *United States*, requiring the government in a criminal case to produce for inspection by the defendant statements made to it by witnesses testifying for it; *Watkins* v. *United States*, reversing a contempt conviction of a labor union organizer who admitted Communist associations but refused to name names before a subcommittee of the House Committee on Un-American Activities; *Yates* v. *United States*, reversing a judgment of conviction against fourteen American Communists in the Los Angeles Smith Act conspiracy prosecution; *Mallory* v. *United States*, invalidating a confession of a defendant who was not promptly arraigned but which was obtained after less than two hours of questioning; and *Kent* v. *Dulles*, upsetting the State Department's passport regulations.

Two weeks after the Nelson decision, Representative Noah M. Mason of Illinois, after referring to it as well as the segregation decision and that in the *Slochower* case, demanded to know in the House: "Mr. Speaker, where is the usurpation of States' rights by the United States Supreme Court going to end?" Congressman James C. Davis of Georgia charged "that the Supreme Court is driving this country closer to a complete judicial dictatorship." Representative L. Mendel Rivers of the same state asserted: "Mr. Speaker, something has got to stop that Supreme Court. They are a greater threat to this Union than the entire confines of Soviet Russia. If some way is not found to stop them, God help us." Two days after *Cole* v. *Young*, Congressman Walter inserted in the *Congressional Record* an article by David Lawrence which declared that the Court's decision had "stricken down the most effective weapon against subversive activity available to the government."

Since then, there has been a crescendo of criticism of the Court. Senator Strom Thurmond of South Carolina on a television program called for the impeachment of Supreme Court justices. He described the Court as a "great menace to this country" and said its recent decisions on individual rights had jeopardized the nation's security to a greater extent than "any other branch of the Government in the history of the country." Senator James O. Eastland of Mississippi in a speech read for him at a luncheon at the Waldorf-Astoria Hotel in New York City denounced the Court as "the greatest single threat to the Constitution." The National Conference of Chief Justices told the Court to exercise to the full its power of judicial self-restraint. Chief Judge Hutcheson of the Court of Appeals for the Fifth Circuit thought that Congress ought to come in every now and then and limit the Court's jurisdiction. Even Dean Griswold of Harvard, with the best interests of the Court at heart, suggested that it hew to the narrow line.

In February 1959 came the report of the American Bar Association's special committee on Communist tactics, strategy and objectives, and its recommendations calling on Congress for legislation to alter the law as announced in Supreme Court decisions dealing with internal security and communism. The special committee was headed by Peter Campbell Brown, former New York City corporation counsel and a former member of the federal Subversive Activities Control Board. The report had appended to it a description of twenty-four Supreme Court decisions of the past few years which were suggested to be "illustrative of how our security has been weakened." It charged generally:

Many cases have been decided in such a manner as to encourage an increase in Communist activities in the United States, although these cases might easily have been disposed of without so broadly limiting national and state security efforts.

Our internal security has been weakened by technicalities raised in judicial decisions which too frequently in the public mind have had the effect of putting on trial the machinery of the judicial process and freeing the subversive to go forth and further undermine our nation.

The special committee in a series of recommendations asked for legislation which would: let the states have their own sedition laws; give the Secretary of State broad power to withhold passports from alleged subversives; extend the Smith Act; apply the federal security program for employees to non-sensitive as well as sensitive jobs; and tighten immigration laws for the deportation of Communists. The Association's Board of Governors supported these broad recommendations, and its House of Delegates with minor changes adopted them. As finally adopted they read:

Be it further resolved that wherever there are reasonable grounds to believe that as a result of court decisions internal security is weakened, remedial legislation be enacted by the Congress of the United States, including a specific pronouncement of Congressional intentions that state statutes proscribing sedition against the United States shall have concurrent enforceability. * * *

*   *   *

Whereas, recent decisions of the United States Supreme Court, in cases involving national and state security and with particular reference to Communist activities, have been severely criticized and deemed unsound by many responsible authorities; and

Whereas the problems of safeguarding national and state security have been exposed or created thereby which this association feels would be best solved by the careful study of each decision, and the prompt enactment of sound amendments to existing laws within the Constitutional powers of the Congress;

Now, therefore, be it resolved that this association recommend to the Congress the prompt and careful consideration and study of recent decisions of the United States Supreme Court and the preparation and passage of separate amendments to the laws involved so as to remove any doubt as to the intent of the Congress, and to remedy any defect in the existing law revealed by the decisions.

Be it further resolved that legislation be promptly enacted to eliminate obstacles to the preservation of our internal security in the following areas:

(a) Amend the Smith Act to define the word "organize" to include the recruitment of new party members, the formation of new party units, and the regrouping, expansion or other activities of an organizational nature performed by members of existing clubs, cells, classes and other units so as to insure the applicability of this section of the act to Communist actionists, agents, organizers, columnists or members currently performing organizational work.

(b) Amend the Smith Act to make it a crime intentionally to advocate the violent overthrow of the Government of the United States or to teach the necessity, desirability, or duty of seeking to bring about such overthrow; in order that (1) this nation might take protective steps to prevent acts which, if not prevented, could result in bloodshed and treachery; and (2) this nation need not be forced to delay the invoking of the judicial process until such time as the resulting damage has already been wrought. (See *Yates v. United States*).

(c) Establish the right of each branch of Government to require as a condition of employment that each employee thereof shall not refuse to answer a query before a duly constituted committee of the Congress or before duly authorized officers of either the Executive or judicial branches of the Government with respect to Communists, Communist-front or other subversive activities or any other matter bearing upon his loyalty to the United States, as the Government has a right to know his record.

(d) Invest the Executive branch of the Government with the right to protect our internal security against the activities of aliens who were Communists at the time of their entry into the United States, or subsequent thereto, by providing for their deportation without any deprivation of due process; and the right to make and enforce reasonable restrictions on aliens awaiting deportation to prohibit them from engaging in any activities identical or similar to those upon which the alien's deportation order was based, with the further rights fully to interrogate aliens awaiting deportation concerning their subversive associates or activities.

(e) Insure the effectiveness of the Foreign Agents Registration Act of 1948 by a requirement that political propaganda by agents or foreign principals be labeled for what it is where such agents are situated outside the limits of the United States, but nevertheless directly or indirectly disseminate such propaganda within the United States.

The principal change did no more than eliminate the phrase "or wherever technicalities are invoked against the protection of our nation" after the word "weakened" in the first of the quoted paragraphs. During the debate in the House of Delegates on the recommendations, Loyd Wright of Los Angeles, a former president of the Association, contended: "Isn't it time that we tell the Court to read and interpret the law and to quit writing ideological opinions and that we tell the American people that we are against subversion."

Despite the recommendations, the Association's president, Ross L. Malone of New Mexico, has been at pains in a series of speeches which he has made to assure us that the criticism of a large body of the Court's recent decisions is not at all a criticism of the Court itself.

Pursuant to the recommendations, Senator Eastland offered a series of seven bills to curb the "disastrous trend" of recent Supreme Court decisions. In doing so he quoted extensively from the report of the Bar Association's special committee, especially its section on the perils of not recognizing the aims of international communism. He declared: "The court is taking to itself powers, and exercising those powers, without any justification in statute or Constitution, without any reliance on recognized principles of law, without any basis whatever except its own naked thirst for power." Later in the year he added that the Court had transformed itself into a "super legislature."

Senator John L. McClellan of Arkansas in a speech before the Economic Club of New York at the Astor Hotel accused the Court of an instability that threatened "the very foundations of our republic." He charged that the Court in a dozen or more of its recent decisions had usurped the legislative powers of Congress, favored Communist and criminal elements, and set aside precedents and decisions "established at a time when the court was composed of justices learned in the law and schooled in the rudiments of American jurisprudence." The inevitable consequences of such decisions were "frightening" for him to contemplate.

In August 1959 the National Conference of Chief Justices adopted a resolution requesting an advisory role for itself in future revisions of federal court jurisdiction.

During the course of the attacks on the Court some members of the bench and bar resigned from the American Bar Association. These included Chief Justice Warren, Justice Eugene F. Black of the Michigan Supreme Court, and Warren Olney 3d, director of the Administrative Office of the United States Courts.

One measure, purportedly to alter the law as laid down in Supreme Court opinions, has already passed. This was in 1957. The opinion involved was that in the *Jencks* case. This measure provided for the production of statements of government witnesses but only "[a]fter a witness called by the United States has testified on direct examination." But this was all that the Court held in the *Jencks* case. The Department of Justice was unhappy not only about this decision but also about a holding of the Court of Appeals for the District of Columbia Circuit in *Fryer* v. *United States*, a capital case. In a capital case the government has to furnish the defendant with a list of its witnesses three days before trial. To this the Court of Appeals for the District of Columbia Circuit added the requirement under Rule 17(c) of the Federal Rules of Criminal Procedure of furnishing as well for the defendant's pre-trial inspection the statements of the government's witnesses. By complaining about the Court's opinion in the *Jencks* case the Department of Justice was able to get legislation rushed through Congress which took care of the *Fryer* holding too.

In 1958 measures to modify the law as laid down in the Court's opinion in the *Mallory* case, invalidating a confession, passed both branches of Congress, Senate-House conferees ironed out differences in the respective measures, and the House agreed to the Conference Report, but it lost out in the Senate on a point of order on the day of adjournment. Also, Congressman Smith's H.R. 3 to change the law in the *Nelson* case passed the House and almost passed the Senate.

Moreover, a new Congress is in session and during its first two months no less than forty bills were introduced to change the law as the Supreme Court announced it in its recent opinions. In the same two months there were an additional score of bills affecting the Court and its jurisdiction, or an aggregate of sixty bills. Some of the latter group sought to limit the appellate jurisdiction of the Court. Others dealt with the qualifications of persons appointed to be justices. One bill even undertook to direct the Court how to conduct the cases before it. In view of the chorus of criticism of the Court's opinions, led by the recommendations of the American Bar Association, some of these bills will probably become law. Indeed, four measures directed at Supreme Court decisions have already passed the House: Congressman Smith's biennially introduced H.R. 3, aimed at the *Nelson* opinion; Congressman Walter's H.R. 2369, extending the Smith Act by defining the word "organize" to include continuing communist activities, aimed at the *Yates* case; H.R. 4957, providing that confessions are not to be inadmissible solely because of a delay in taking an accused person before a committing magistrate, aimed at the *Mallory* decision; and H.R. 9069, relating to passports, aimed at the *Kent* and *Briehl* rulings. Of course the Court's limitation of its Nelson opinion in its 1959 *Uphaus* holding has removed some of the pressure for the passage of H.R. 3. H.R. 2369 follows part of one of the recommendations of the American Bar Association for changing the law in the *Yates* case. The House passed the measure unanimously and without debate—thus reminding one of the way in which legislative bodies in Communist countries take action. A few minutes later, again unanimously and without debate, the House voted to expand the espionage law to permit the prosecution of Americans for spying anywhere in the world.

The attacks on the Court resulting from the performance of its constitutional duties emphasize the invalidity of the federal immunity act of 1954 in seeking to impose on federal courts the nonjudicial function of approving proposed grants of immunity. Ironically enough, one of Senator Keating's current bills, a wiretap measure which would upset the law in *Benanti* v. *United States*, provides for court approval of warrants to wiretap. If such a measure becomes law it should be declared unconstitutional on the same ground that the federal immunity act of 1954 should have been so declared, namely, the imposition on federal courts of an investigative rather than a judicial function.

Immunity Acts Under Our Federal System

Another question which the federal immunity act of 1954, and federal immunity acts generally, present is whether they should protect against the danger of state prosecution. A proper regard for the right of silence as embodied in the Fifth Amendment requires an affirmative answer to this question whenever the danger of a state prosecution is a substantial one.

Under *Counselman* v. *Hitchcock*, an immunity act, to be valid, must give a protection that is coextensive with the privilege accorded by the Fifth Amendment. This would seem to mean, under our close-knit federal system, that a federal immunity act to be constitutional would have to protect against prosecution under state laws wherever the danger of such prosecution is of the same substantiality as prosecution under federal laws. Our federal and state governments are but parts of one integrated governmental system. Taken together they form the government of one federal state. It would therefore seem that a federal immunity act would have to protect against the danger of state prosecution to the same extent that it protects against the danger of federal prosecution.

A good illustration of the measure of protection that is necessary against federal prosecution may be found in *Heike* v. *United States*. There the defendant pleaded in bar to an indictment for frauds on the revenue the immunity provision in an act aimed at the correction of certain corporate abuses. He had previously testified in a grand jury investigation into possible violations of the Sherman anti-trust act. During the course of this testimony he had produced a table showing how many pounds of sugar his company had melted during a certain period of time. Some of this sugar was also involved in the fraud case. But the Court held that the immunity provision did not protect him, saying through Justice Holmes:

. . . We see no reason for supposing that the act offered a gratuity to crime. It should be construed, so far as its words fairly allow the construction, as coterminous with what otherwise would have been the privilege of the person concerned. . . .

. . . When the statute speaks of testimony concerning a matter it means concerning it in a substantial way, just as the constitutional protection is confined to real danger, and does not extend to remote possibilities out of the ordinary course of law. . . .

It would thus seem that a federal immunity provision should extend this measure of protection against the danger not only of federal but also state prosecution. Indeed, such a formulation will reconcile the results in all the Supreme Court cases as well as most of the various statements in the opinions.

In two of the first cases dealing with the danger of state prosecution the Supreme Court held that such a danger did provide the basis for a claim of privilege. In one case, *United States* v. *Saline Bank*, the opinion was by Chief Justice Marshall, and in the other, *Ballmann* v. *Fagin*, by Justice Holmes. The former case involved a creditors' bill for discovery and other relief and a plea that the discovery would subject the defendants to penalties under a Virginia statute which prohibited unincorporated banks. The Court sustained the plea: "The rule clearly is, that a party is not bound to make any discovery which would expose him to penalties, and this case falls within it." In the latter case a claim of privilege included reliance on an Ohio statute which made it a crime to operate a "bucket shop." The Court ruled for the accused: "According to *United States* v. *Saline Bank* . . . he was exonerated from disclosures which would have exposed him to the penalties of the state law."

In the same term as *Ballmann* v. *Fagin* there were two decisions which have been taken as pointing in an opposite direction to that case. However, Justice Holmes, who wrote the opinion in *Ballmann* v. *Fagin*, sat in both of those cases and dissented in neither. One of them, *Hale* v. *Henkel*, did not involve the problem at all: it held that an agent or officer of a corporation may not claim the right of silence on its behalf.

The other, *Jack* v. *Kansas*, involving an immunity provision of an antitrust act of the state of Kansas, may be explained on the ground of the remoteness of the danger of federal prosecution. The state court, after pointing out that the inquiries in that case were limited to intrastate transactions, and discussing *Brown* v. *Walker*, concluded that the possibility that the defendant's answers might disclose violations of the federal anti-trust law "was not a real and probable danger." The United States Supreme Court agreed.

A little earlier, in *Brown* v. *Walker*, the first federal Supreme Court decision sustaining the constitutionality of an immunity act, the Court, in answer to an objection that the federal act there involved did not grant immunity from state prosecution stated:

But even granting that there were still a bare possibility that by his disclosure he might be subjected to the criminal laws of some other sovereignty, that, as Chief Justice Cockburn said in *Queen* v. *Boyes*, 1 B. & S. 311, in reply to the argument that the witness was not protected by his pardon against an impeachment by the House of Commons, is not a real and probable danger, with reference to the ordinary operations of the law in the ordinary courts, but "a danger of an imaginary and unsubstantial character, having reference to some extraordinary and barely possible contingency, so improbable that no reasonable man would suffer it to influence his conduct." Such dangers it was never the object of the provision to obviate.

Thus the law stood until *United States* v. *Murdock*, a case which has been regarded as establishing the proposition that a federal immunity act need not protect against state prosecution. But that case, too, may be explained upon the ground that there was no real danger of state prosecution. The defendant in each of two federal income tax returns had deducted $12,000 which he claimed to have paid to others. A revenue agent wanted him to name the recipients. He declined and claimed his privilege. That there was no real danger of state prosecution is indicated in this language of the Court: "The plea does not rest upon any claim that the inquiries were being made to discover evidence of crime against state law. Nothing of state concern was involved. The investigation was under federal law in respect of federal matters. The information sought was appropriate to enable the Bureau to ascertain whether appellee had in fact made deductible payments in each year as stated in his return, and also to determine the tax liability of the recipients."

However, the Court did say, among other things: "The English rule of evidence against compulsory self-incrimination, on which historically that contained in the Fifth Amendment rests, does not protect witnesses against disclosing offenses in violation of the laws of another country. . . ."

But in neither of the two English cases which the Court cited for this proposition was there any real danger of prosecution by any country. One of the cases, *Queen* v. *Boyes*, did not involve another jurisdiction at all. There the defendant took the position that a pardon from the Crown did not take away the recipient's right of silence for the reason that it was not pleadable to an impeachment by the House of Commons. The court held against the defendant on the ground that the danger of such an impeachment was imaginary and unsubstantial.

In the other case, *King of the Two Sicilies* v. *Willcox*, agents of a revolutionary government in Sicily bought a vessel in England and registered her in the name of two English subjects. The king of the Two Sicilies brought a bill for discovery. The defendants, none of whom was in Sicily, pleaded that their production of the requested documents would expose them to criminal prosection in Sicily. Again there was no real danger of prosecution, and the court ruled against the defendants.

Today, for instance, if a witness in this country were to claim a right of silence on the ground that his answer might incriminate him in Russia, no court would pay any attention to it. But if a witness before a congressional committee or a federal court or grand jury were to claim his privilege on the ground of substantial danger of state prosecution, why should his claim not be respected?

In the later English case of *United States* v. *McRae* involving a bill for discovery by the United States against a confederate agent, both the lower court and the Court of Appeals in Chancery ruled for the defendant on the ground that to compel him to make discovery might expose him to a forfeiture in the United States, another international state. Both courts distinguished *King of the Two Sicilies* v. *Willcox*, and restricted any language in the opinion in that case to the actual holding. Referring to that case, Lord Chancellor Chelmsford in the *McRae* case said: "There it was not shewn that the Defendants had rendered themselves liable to criminal prosecution. . . . There it was doubtful whether the Defendants would ever be within the reach of a prosecution. . . ." Indeed, it was the decision in the *McRae* case which produced the second federal immunity act, the act of 1868, later Rev. Stat., section 860. The English law thus goes further than the position we are urging, for it extends the protection of the privilege to cover the danger of a prosecution or infliction of a penalty by a foreign state, whereas we are asking no more than the privilege cover the danger, and a substantial one, of a prosecution by another governmental unit of the same federal state.

After citing *King of the Two Sicilies* v. *Willcox* and *Queen* v. *Boyes,* the Court in the *Murdock* case went on to say that immunity from state prosecution was not essential for the validity of a federal immunity act and a lack of state power to protect against federal prosecution did not defeat a state immunity statute. For these propositions the Court cited *Counselman* v. *Hitchcock, Brown* v. *Walker, Jack* v. *Kansas,* and *Hale* v. *Henkel.* As we have already seen, in only two of these cases, *Brown* v. *Walker* and *Jack* v. *Kansas,* was the problem involved; and in both of these cases the danger of prosecution by another jurisdiction was so remote that it was not entitled to serious consideration.

None of the counsel or the Court in the *Murdock* case as much as cited the *McRae* case. The quoted language in the *Murdock* case was accordingly based on an inadequate presentation by counsel on both sides, and a misunderstanding of the English law by the court.

After the *Murdock* case there were several Supreme Court decisions which did not show the regard for the right of silence that one could wish, but in none is the holding inconsistent with the proposition that a federal immunity act, to be valid, must give protection against the danger of state prosecution wherever that danger is substantial. Indeed, this proposition will reconcile the result in the *Murdock* case with the results and opinions in the earlier Supreme Court cases.

The time has come for a reexamination of the opinion in the *Murdock* case, and two federal courts, the Court of Appeals for the Fifth Circuit and the District Court for the Northern District of Ohio, in recent cases have done just this. Both cases involved claims of privilege before a subcommittee of the Kefauver Committee. In both the real danger was not federal but state prosecution. In both the court sustained the claim. In both it reached for this result, in the one by going out of its way to find a danger of federal prosecution and in the other by stressing the fact that the investigation was into violations of state law. In both the court relied on *United States* v. *Saline Bank* and *Ballman* v. *Fagin,* and refused to apply the *Murdock* case. In one of these two recent cases, *Marcello* v. *United States,* the defendant was asked whether he knew one Vitalli, who was supposed to be connected with a murder. The trial judge considered the murder a state offense and ruled against the defendant's claim of privilege. The court of appeals reversed, pointing out that the defendant might be confronted with a charge of causing Vitalli to travel in interstate or foreign commerce with intent to avoid prosecution. In the course of its opinion the court said:

. . . With much inconsistency, we may indulge the hope that more state courts will follow the lead of the Supreme Court of Michigan in the view that,

"It seems like a travesty on verity to say that one is not subjected to self-incrimination when compelled to give testimony in a State judicial proceeding which testimony may forthwith be used against him in a Federal criminal prosecution."

In the other recent case, *United States* v. *DiCarlo*, the court after discussing *United States* v. *Saline Bank*, with a quotation of the opinion in extenso, and *Ballmann* v. *Fagin*, with a pertinent quotation, continued:

Thus, in cases decided before *United States* v. *Murdock*, supra, two of the most illustrious jurists ever to sit upon the Supreme Court, speaking for the court, recognized the privilege of the witness and of parties in a federal proceeding, to immunity against disclosures that would expose them to the danger of state prosecutions; and in the only Supreme Court decision relied upon by the government the court made special note of the absence of any matter of "state concern."

Law review comment generally has been favorable to the *DiCarlo* decision.

On the measure of protection to be given under our federal system by immunity acts, recent state court opinions have been in advance of those of the federal Supreme Court. Excellent opinions have come from the highest courts of Michigan and Kentucky. In a leading case, *In re Watson*, the Michigan Supreme Court, after a careful consideration of the authorities, rejected the opinion in the *Murdock* case and stated:

We believe that this ancient privilege should be maintained against limitations that we conceive tend to make it ineffectual, futile, and subversive of the spirit and letter of the Bill of Rights. Under our Federal system of government, with co-extensive jurisdiction of State and national government, a person subject to the laws of a State is, at the same time, subject to the laws of the Federal government. A citizen of a State is a citizen of the United States. . . . After a review of the authorities and consideration of the constitutional provisions and the principles involved, we are of the opinion that the privilege against self-incrimination exonerates from disclosure whenever there is a probability of prosecution in State or Federal jurisdictions. . . .

To overcome the privilege, the extent of the immunity would have to be of such a nature that it would protect, not only against State prosecution, but also against any reasonably probable Federal prosecution. The claim of the privilege in the face of a State immunity statute cannot be used as a subterfuge or pretense to refuse to answer in proceedings to detect or suppress crime. But neither can the grant be used to compel answers that will lead straight to Federal prosecution. Whenever the danger of prosecution for a Federal offense is substantial and imminent as a result of disclosures to be made under a grant of immunity by the State, such immunity is insufficient to overcome the privilege against self-incrimination.

In a yet more recent case, *People* v. *Den Uhl*, that court termed the restriction of the privilege accorded by a state to exclude federal prosecutions "a travesty on verity":

. . . It seems like a travesty on verity to say that one is not subjected to self-incrimination when compelled to give testimony in a State judicial proceeding which testimony may forthwith be used against him in a Federal criminal prosecution. * * *

The court in *Marcello* v. *United States* quoted this language with approval.

The Kentucky Court of Appeals, in ruling similarly in *Commonwealth* v. *Rhine*, reasoned:

. . . We believe that to render effective the quoted Constitutional provision against self-incrimination, it is essential that it apply to prosecutions by the United States as well as to those by the Commonwealth. To hold otherwise would be to ignore the fact that our citizens are in the very real sense, as well as in a technical one, citizens of both the State of Kentucky and of the United States. The jurisdiction of both governments is coextensive. * * *

The court then quoted from the opinion of the Michigan Supreme Court in the *Den Uhl* case.

In another decision on the point, *Putnik Travel and Tourist Agency* v. *Goldberg*, a state court in Pennsylvania held and said:

There is, however, some authority in support of the view that the constitutional privilege against self-incrimination extends to protect a witness as to matters which may subject him to prosecution in another jurisdiction, particularly where the danger of prosecution in such other jurisdiction is impending rather than remote: *Ballman* v. *Fagin* * * *

The court after a study of all the aforesaid cases feels that the proper view is the holding in the case of *Ballman* v. *Fagin*, supra.

Moreover, many, if not most, of the state cases which have denied a claim of privilege where it was based on the asserted danger of a prosecution by another jurisdiction can be explained on the ground that the danger of such prosecution was too remote to be given serious consideration. For example, in *Matter of Doyle*, a case arising out of an investigation by a joint committee of the legislature into bribery of public officials in the city of New York, the New York Court of Appeals, in an opinion by Chief Judge Cardozo, "put aside as remote and unsubstantial the supposed peril of exposure to prosecution for the making of false tax returns to State or Federal officers." Or again, in the recent case of *Knapp* v. *Schweitzer*, the New York Appellate division concluded its opinion with the statement that there was no "real and substantial danger that the testimony compelled by the State will be used in a subsequent Federal prosecution."

However, the United States Supreme Court in affirming the *Knapp* case said: ". . . This [compelling testimony] cannot be denied on the claim that such state law of immunity may expose the potential witness to prosecution under federal law. See *Jack* v. *Kansas* * * *." Thereafter the New York Appellate Division in two cases, one involving Frank Costello and the other, seven individuals whom the authorities wished to question about an alleged gangland meeting at the Apalachin, New York, home of the late Joseph Barbara, Sr., held that a state immunity statute did not have to protect against the danger of federal prosecution.

It is also true that since the *Murdock* case a body of holdings and dicta have arisen to the effect that an immunity act does not have to protect against the danger of prosecution by another jurisdiction. In the *Ullmann* case District Judge Weinfeld, although of the view that the federal act of 1954 did and could protect against the danger of state prosecution, nevertheless stated, relying on the *Murdock* opinion, that it did not have to do so. The Supreme Court did not reach the question. The writer submits that such holdings and dicta represent not only an unsympathetic approach to the right of silence but also constitute too narrow a view of our federal system. The ill-considered dictum in the *Murdock* case should be repudiated.

However, in March 1959 the New York Court of Appeals affirmed as to the seven Apalachin individuals; in April as to Costello; and in June the federal Supreme Court applied its *Knapp* holding in *Mills* v. *Louisiana*. Chief Justice Warren wrote a dissenting opinion in which Justices Black and Douglas joined, and Justice Douglas wrote a dissenting opinion in which Chief Justice Warren and Justice Black concurred. Justice Douglas in his dissenting opinion quoted from the *Den Uhl* case in Michigan. We thus have what may be called the narrow federal and New York rule and by way of contrast the liberal Michigan and Kentucky rule. It is still to be hoped that the liberal Michigan and Kentucky view will ultimately prevail.

Nevertheless, constitutionally we have reached the point that a state immunity act is valid without affording protection against the danger of prosecution by another jurisdiction. Yet it does not follow that a comparable federal statute is likewise valid: the applicable constitutional provisions are different. A state immunity statute need only satisfy the requirements of the Fourteenth Amendment's due process clause; a federal statute must comply with the Fifth Amendment's right of silence.

Three interesting situations can and have arisen: testimony obtained from an individual by state officials under a state immunity statute is sought to be introduced against him by federal officials in a federal criminal proceeding (1) where there has not been collaboration between federal and state officials; (2) where there has been such collaboration; and (3) where there has been no specifically arranged collaboration but federal and state officials contemporaneously investigate the same individual. The first situation was presented in *Feldman* v. *United States*, and the Court held such testimony admissible in the federal proceeding. However, the decision was by a four to three vote with two justices not participating. Moreover, in the *Knapp* case the four dissenters, Chief Justice Warren and Justices Black, Douglas and Brennan, cast doubt on *Feldman*. In the more recent *Mills* case Justice Brennan, although concurring, did so with the statement: "He also reiterates his belief that nothing in this decision forecloses reconsideration of the *Feldman* holding in a case presenting the issue presented by *Feldman*."

The existence of the second situation, collaboration between federal and state officials, is claimed in a case arising out of a federal indictment in New York City against twenty-three of the individuals in attendance at the Apalachin meeting. The indictment charges them with conspiring to obstruct justice. Those at this meeting, and yet others, have been contemporaneously investigated by federal grand juries, a Congressional committee, and the New York Commission of Investigation. Moreover, the act creating the state Commission of Investigation expressly provides: "The Commission shall cooperate with departments and officers of the United States government in the investigation of violations of the federal laws within this state." It is difficult to believe that there was not cooperation between state and federal officials in this case. Judge Kaufman assumed there was, but ruled that testimony obtained by the state Commission of Investigation was federally admissible: "Certainly, cooperation, ipso facto, between law-enforcement agencies, state and federal, is not per se a derogation of constitutional rights. Indeed, such cooperation is desirable and necessary particularly in these days of mounting crime statistics."

At least the third, if not the second, situation exists in the Apalachin investigations, for there have been publicized contemporaneous investigations by federal agencies as well as one by the state; and the act creating the state Commission of Investigation specifically calls for cooperation with federal officials. Two of the seven Apalachin individuals, Paul Castellano and Rosario Mancuso, are relying on this provision in appeals to the federal Supreme Court. Since they are in a state court proceeding, this point will not prevail. In the *Mills* case the parties stipulated that there had been and was "cooperation and collaboration" between state and federal officials, and yet the individuals lost.

But suppose that testimony so obtained from an individual by state officials is then sought to be introduced against him by federal officials in a federal criminal proceeding. It should not be admitted. It is all well and good to have the cooperation between state and federal officials of which Judge Kaufman speaks, but this should not be permitted to destroy an individual's right of silence. The same result should follow where federal and state officials know they are simultaneously investigating the same individuals, as they certainly did in the Apalachin case, and there is at least an unspoken cooperation between them.

Now suppose that testimony obtained by state officials under a state immunity statute where there has been cooperation between state and federal officials results in a federal case which federal officials can prove without the use of such testimony. Should they be permitted to do so? Under the *Counselman* case a federal immunity statute to be valid must protect not only against the use of the testimony sought to be compelled but also against future prosecution. It was to this situation that Chief Justice Warren addressed himself in his dissent in the *Mills* case: "I come then to the question left open in the *Knapp* case: whether, where, as here, a State is used as an instrument of federal investigation, witnesses can successfully assert their federal privilege against self-incrimination in state proceedings. *Knapp* v. *Schweitzer, supra,* suggests that where testimony is compelled in such circumstances, the testimony would be inadmissible in a subsequent federal prosecution. * * * But this is only partial protection. To compel testimony in a federal investigation, a witness must be assured at the outset complete immunity from any prosecution which might result from his compelled disclosures. *Counselman* v. *Hitchcock* * * * There is no indication that such protection obtains here—that petitioners are protected from federal prosecutions which might result from their testimony even though that testimony is not admissible in the subsequent proceeding. * * *"

We are left with a Hobson's choice. The law is settled that a state immunity act is constitutionally valid even though it does not protect against the danger of federal prosecution. If the Court were now to rule that proceedings under such an act resulted in immunity from federal prosecution in cases of cooperation between state and federal officials, it might place in the hands of state officials the power to grant immunity from federal prosecutions. Federal officials could not abide such a result. Besides, such a rule might lead to the kind of unfortunate experiences that occurred under the first federal immunity act, which gave Congress the power to grant immunity from federal prosecution.

The best that one can hope for is that state-compelled testimony will be ruled federally inadmissible, but it is fair to hope for this much. It is safe to predict that the next time the *Feldman* situation comes before the Supreme Court, and it probably will in the case in which Judge Kaufman recently ruled, the *Feldman* case will be overruled. Judge Kaufman's ruling will be reversed.

Such a result will not be entirely perfect in the eyes of Chief Justice Warren and Justices Black and Douglas; but few if any things in life are. We will be able to live with the result. State compelled testimony under a state immunity act and a resulting federal indictment that is proved by other evidence than the compelled testimony will rarely occur. In that rare situation the individual will lose. A state immunity statute, even if used to aid federal prosecutors, need not meet the requirements of the *Counselman* case, although a federal act must do so.

If and when the *Feldman* case is overruled, it is further to be hoped that in the next appropriate case the Court will reconsider the Murdock dictum, overrule it, and hold that federal immunity acts to be valid must protect against the danger of state prosecution whenever that danger is substantial.

Danger of State Prosecution

If a federal immunity act, to be valid, is to protect against the danger of state prosecution whenever that danger is a substantial one, then a question arises as to whether in the area covered by the federal act of 1954, namely, treason, sedition, subversion and sabotage, there is such a danger. If so, does and can the federal act protect against it?

In this area, despite the Supreme Court's decision in *Pennsylvania* v. *Nelson*, invalidating a state sedition law, the danger of state prosecution is certainly great. To begin with, there is a mass of state and local legislation. During the past fifty years the states have had more legislation in this area than the federal government; and likewise, until the Smith Act cases, which only began in 1948, more prosecutions.

Today all of the states either in their constitutions or statutes, and often in both, have provisions defining treason. Thirty-three states prohibit misprison of treason. Nineteen states and Hawaii have criminal anarchy statutes; of these states four also make it a crime knowingly to attend an assemblage of persons defined as criminal anarchists, or to permit an assemblage of such persons on one's premises. Twenty jurisdictions, including Alaska and Hawaii, have statutes on criminal syndicalism; of which statutes fourteen also forbid participation in meetings and permitting such meetings on one's premises. Thirty-five states have laws prohibiting the display of certain types of flags and other emblems. Thirty-three jurisdictions, including Alaska and Hawaii, have sedition statutes. Twenty-eight states have provisions against insurrection and rebellion. Thirty-two jurisdictions, including Alaska and Hawaii, have some form of statute dealing with sabotage. Fifteen jurisdictions, including Hawaii, have on their books, often with some variations or modifications, the Model Sabotage Prevention Act, which was drafted in 1941 after the Federal-State Conference on Law Enforcement Problems of National Defense, held under the auspices of the Department of Justice, the Interstate Commission on Crime, the National Association of Attorneys General, the Governors' Conference, and the Council of State Governments. In addition, various of the states have registration statutes, provisions for loyalty oaths, teachers' loyalty statutes, and laws excluding communists and subversives from elective office, from public office, and from state employment.

In 1949 Maryland enacted a comprehensive and drastic statute against subversion, the Ober Law, formally designated as the Subversive Activities Act of 1949, and New York passed an act for further insuring the loyalty of its teachers, the Feinberg Law, which provided for the preparation of a black list of organizations. During the next few years eight states—Florida, Georgia, Louisiana, Mississippi, New Hampshire, Ohio, Pennsylvania and Washington—followed Maryland's lead and put on their statute books acts modeled in substantial parts on the Ober Law. Ten states—Alabama, Arkansas, California, Delaware, Louisiana, Michigan, Montana, New Mexico, South Carolina and Texas—passed registration acts or elaborated existing ones. The acts of Alabama, Arkansas, Delaware, Louisiana, Michigan, New Mexico and Texas referred specifically to the Communist Party. The Delaware statute requires every communist or front member who resides in or passes through the state to register. Four states—Indiana, Massachusetts, Pennsylvania and Texas—passed laws which outlawed the Communist Party by name.

Beginning in 1950 a hundred or more cities and counties across the country adopted measures against subversion. The list included: Bessemer and Birmingham, Alabama; Los Angeles, Oakland and Redondo Beach, California; Jacksonville and Miami, Florida; Atlanta and Macon, Georgia; Indianapolis and Terre Haute, Indiana; Cumberland, Maryland; Detroit and Saginaw, Michigan; Minneapolis, Minnesota; Omaha, Nebraska; Jersey City, New Jersey; New Rochelle, New York; Cincinnati, Columbus and Lorain, Ohio; Erie, Lancaster, McKeesport and York, Pennsylvania; Knoxville, Tennessee; and Tacoma and Seattle, Washington. Los Angeles, California and New Rochelle, New York by ordinance required registration with the police of any member of a "communist organization" who "resides in, is employed in, has a regular place of business in, or who regularly enters or travels through any part" of the city. Birmingham, Alabama by ordinance imposed a fine and imprisonment for each day that a known communist remained in the city. A Jacksonville, Florida ordinance made it unlawful for any Communist Party member to be within the city limits during the period of hostilities in Korea. A Seattle, Washington ordinance made it unlawful for any subversive organization to rent or use the Civic Auditorium. Various ordinances of other cities prohibited advocacy, required the registration of communists and subversives, forbade the use of certain types of flags, and provided for loyalty oaths. Many cities prescribed loyalty oaths for their employees. Los Angeles and Detroit set up administrative procedures for determining the loyalty of their employees.

Various of the states—Arizona, California, Florida, Illinois, Montana, Massachusetts, New Hampshire, New Jersey, New York, Ohio, Washington and Hawaii—have set up committees or commissions to investigate un-American activities. Of these bodies the most active have been the Tenney Committee in California; the Broyles Commission in Illinois; the Lusk (1919–20) and Rapp-Coudert Committees in New York; and the Canwell Committee in the state of Washington.

Not only have the states had all manner of measures in the area covered by the new federal act, but they have also brought many prosecutions under various of the statutes to which reference has been made. Most of these prosecutions of course did not go to reviewing courts. Of the few that did, a still smaller number reached the United States Supreme Court. There, although a number of these statutes were invalidated, a number of others were sustained. While it is true that in *Pennsylvania* v. *Nelson* the Court ruled against the validity of a Pennsylvania sedition law, and cast doubt on such laws of other states, on the ground that the federal Smith Act preempted the field, the Court was careful to confine its ruling. The prosecution in that case was for sedition, not against Pennsylvania, but against the United States. Chief Justice Warren writing for the Court took pains to point out the boundaries of the opinion: ". . . Neither does it limit the right of the state to protect itself at any time against sabotage or attempted violence of all kinds. Nor does it prevent the state from prosecuting where the same act constitutes both a Federal offense and a state offense under the police power. . . ."

In earlier cases the Court sustained the validity of various state statutes dealing with subversion. It upheld the constitutionality of three of New York's statutes, two of them in prosecutions: the criminal anarchy act of 1902 in *Gitlow* v. *New York;* its registration act in *New York ex rel. Bryant* v. *Zimmerman;* and the Feinberg Law in *Adler* v. *Board of Education.* The Court upheld a Minnesota sedition act in a criminal prosecution in *Gilbert* v. *Minnesota;* and the California criminal syndicalism act in criminal prosecutions in *Whitney* v. *California* and *Burns* v. *United States.* The Court, in *Garner* v. *Board of Public Works,* sustained the validity of the oath requirements which Los Angeles prescribed by ordinance for its office holders and employees; and, in *Gerende* v. *Board of Supervisors,* on a restricted interpretation of what the law required, held valid an oath provision of Maryland's Ober Law.

Then in June 1959 in *Uphaus* v. *Wyman* the Supreme Court sustained a civil contempt finding against the petitioner under the New Hampshire Subversive Activities Act of 1951 and a joint resolution of the New Hampshire legislature constituting that state's attorney general a one-man legislative investigating committee; and in *Raley* v. *Ohio* a criminal contempt conviction for refusing to answer questions before the Ohio Un-American Activities Commission. It was in the *Uphaus* case that the Court made clear that its *Nelson* ruling was confined to a state sedition law which sought to deal with sedition against the federal government rather than that of the state.

Not only do the states have a multitude of measures against subversion and not only have there been many prosecutions under these provisions, but also the states are going to insist on what they deem their rights and powers to proceed with further such prosecutions. Indeed, of late, state officials have increasingly urged that the states play an even greater role than heretofore in the fight against subversion. Moreover, Attorneys General Brownell and Rogers have encouraged state action in this field.

In *Pennsylvania* v. *Nelson,* when Pennsylvania petitioned the federal

Supreme Court for certiorari, four states—Illinois, Massachusetts, New Hampshire and Texas—filed briefs as amici curiae supporting the petitioner; and the attorneys general of twenty-four states, including Massachusetts, joined in the brief of the state of New Hampshire. The United States too, after the Court's invitation to the solicitor general for the views of the federal government, filed a brief amicus curiae in which it supported the validity of Pennsylvania's sedition law. In this brief the United States, after pointing out that;

. . . Forty-two states plus Alaska and Hawaii have statutes which prohibit advocacy of the violent overthrow of established government. Most of these statutes have been in existence for many years. . . .
. . . Every state has made provisions for treason either in its constitution or statutes, often in both. . . .
. . . As of January 1955, some 30 states plus Alaska and Hawaii had sedition laws on their statute books, and 12 others had either criminal syndicalism or criminal anarchy statutes or both, making a total of 42 states plus Alaska and Hawaii which had criminal legislation in this general field. . . .

took the position:

. . . Moreover the problem of subversion, as we think Congress recognized, is of such magnitude as to invite federal-state cooperation in the enforcement of their respective sedition laws. Thus the Attorney General of the United States recently informed the attorneys general of the several states in this connection that a full measure of federal-state cooperation would be in the public interest.

The role of the states in the fight against subversion was also one of the main topics of discussion at the 1954 and 1955 conferences of the National Association of Attorneys General, an association comprised of the attorneys general of all the states and territories. At the 1954 conference Attorney General Louis C. Wyman of New Hampshire asserted that the states had a place in the fight against subversion alongside the federal government. He said that a state investigation, properly conducted, would supplement the work of the F.B.I. and other federal agencies engaged in the enforcement of security statutes. He described the procedures under New Hampshire's legislation against subversion, and referred to various New Hampshire cases which, in his opinion, supported the view that this legislation did not conflict with federal statutes. A committee headed by the attorney general of Massachusetts presented a report recommending that the association in its fight against subversion set up a standing committee to interchange information and ideas with the legislative and executive branches of the federal government.

At the 1955 conference Mr. Wyman declared that it was "sheerest nonsense" to say that the federal government had the exclusive right to investigate subversive activities within the states. He was apprehensive of the possible influence "of the smiles and blandishments of Communist diplomats." If this resulted in "further curbing of the Federal security program," the attorneys general of the states were to see to it that state security programs were "not so susceptible to seduction."

The association's committee on subversive activities recommended that each state set up a permanent division of subversive activities in its state police system to cooperate with the local police and the Federal Bureau of Investigation. The association approved a resolution urging its members to take such action as they deemed compatible with the interests of their own states in the promotion of national security.

Indeed, the attorneys general were not satisfied that the states should have simply a share in the struggle against subversion: they wanted an immunity act which would protect witnesses in state cases against the danger of federal prosecution. State prosecutors had complained that their investigations had been hampered by the fact that witnesses who might have given valuable information under grant of state immunity were reluctant to do so because of fears of federal prosecution. The attorneys general after a sharp debate approved by a vote of 23 to 14 a resolution for the enactment of a law that would grant immunity from federal prosecution to witnesses who would receive immunity in state cases involving subversion.

It was at this conference that Attorney General Brownell assured the attorneys general of the states that the department of justice did not regard the country's internal security as the exclusive prerogative of the federal government. He advised them that the government would take this position in its amicus curiae brief in *Pennsylvania* v. *Nelson,* and added, "We believe that state sedition laws should be enforced and that a full measure of Federal-state cooperation will be in the public interest." The following month the government filed its brief, in which it took this position.

Despite the Supreme Court's decision in *Pennsylvania* v. *Nelson* and its denial of a petition for rehearing, the controversy which this decision raised has by no means come to an end. The attorneys general of thirty-four states and the territory of Alaska joined Pennsylvania in its petition for rehearing. Even before the Supreme Court's decision, indeed, on the first day of the session of Congress which met the year before that decision, Congressman Smith of Virginia introduced his H.R. 3 to let the states have their own sedition laws. He has had such a bill, always numbered H.R. 3, before every session of Congress since then.

In 1956 the National Association of Attorneys General by a vote of 31 to 10 approved a resolution in favor of the "enactment of Federal legislation authorizing the enforcement of state statutes prescribing criminal penalties for subversive activities involving state or national governments or either of them"; and the Conference of Governors at its 48th annual meeting by what was described as an almost unanimous vote adopted a resolution which "recommended to the Congress that Federal laws should be so framed that they will not be construed to pre-empt any field against state action unless this intent is stated. . . ." Then in 1959 came the American Bar Association's recommendations, the first one of which favored letting the states have their own sedition laws. This year Congressman Smith's H.R. 3 again passed the House.

The danger of state prosecution against subversion is thus substantial. Can and does the federal immunity act of 1954 protect against it? The Court in the *Ullmann* case, and Judge Weinfeld, answered these two questions in the affirmative.

In doing so, it would seem that no one gave sufficient consideration to several factors. For one thing, no one paid sufficient attention to the mass of state and local legislation in this area.

For another, no one noted that the federal criminal code, of which the federal act of 1954 became a part in the form of an amendment of one of the code's sections, in another section expressly provides: "Nothing in this title shall be held to take away or impair the jurisdiction of the courts of the several States under the laws thereof." This provision, as the dissent in *Pennsylvania v. Nelson*, decided a week after the *Ullmann* case, pointed out, is but a recognition of the fact that under our federal system the prosecution of offenses is committed primarily to the states: "It recognizes the fact that maintenance of order and fairness rests primarily with the States." If the federal act of 1954 protects against state prosecutions, then the jurisdiction of state courts will be impaired.

Moreover, the area covered by the new federal immunity act is so large that it involves the police power of the states to a great extent, and the Supreme Court has ruled repeatedly that the "intention of Congress to exclude States from exercising their police power must be clearly manifested." If Congress intended the new federal act to protect against the danger of state prosecution, it should have put that intent into express language. It did not do so.

If one considers the state legislation in the area covered by the federal

immunity act of 1954, the prosecutions which have taken place under
this legislation, and the mounting determination on the part of the
states to be included in the struggle against subversion, one cannot dismiss as lightly as either the Court or the district judge did the point that
if the federal act contains a prohibition against state prosecutions it
may then violate the Tenth Amendment. One can certainly make a
strong argument that subversion covers such a large area that some
of it is bound to be within the scope of reserved powers beyond the
reach of Congress. Indeed, in *Pennsylvania* v. *Nelson*, the Court specifically excluded from the scope of its opinion sabotage, attempted
violence of all kinds, and offenses under the police power of the states.
In *Burns* v. *United States* the Court indicated that the punishment of
those who intentionally destroyed or damaged the property of others was
within the province of the states. Such destruction or damage is involved
in either sabotage or insurrection. In an early case, the Court, after
adverting hypothetically to a local insurrection, stated: "In such cases
the State has inherently the right to use all the means necessary to put
down the resistance to its authority, and restore peace, order, and
obedience to law." The states would likewise seem to have the power
to punish those who swore falsely under a state statute requiring loyalty
oaths of state employees or office holders, or a municipal ordinance with
a similar requirement.

The Tenth Amendment point gains further support from the fact that
the prosecution of offenses is primarily the concern of the states.

Attorney General Wyman of New Hampshire in that state's amicus
curiae brief in *Pennsylvania* v. *Nelson*, joined by the attorneys general
of twenty-four other states, made the Tenth Amendment his basis for
asserting: "Congress lacks constitutional power to supersede either expressly or by implication the States' reserved right to make criminal
within their border acts seeking overthrow of their own government by
force and violence." At the 1955 conference of the National Association
of Attorneys General he enlarged his position, and challenged the power
of Congress, under the Tenth Amendment, "to take from the states
their reserve power to seek to find out who within their borders con-
spires to overthrow" either a state or the federal government.

With the states contending vigorously for their part in the struggle
against subversion, and with subversion covering a territory so extensive
that it includes such diverse items as injury to property on the one hand
and false loyalty oaths on the other, it is difficult to see how the entire
area constitutionally can be held to be within the scope of a federal
immunity act which prohibits state prosecutions. In any event, since
Congress deliberately left the prohibition against prosecution ambigu-

ous, the Court should not have increased the prohibition to include state prosecution.

Utility of Immunity Acts

One question remains, and that is as to the utility of immunity acts. A study of confessions indicates that the results expected from such statutes may be largely illusory. A majority of deviants will confess without them. On the other hand, confirmed rebels will not confess even with them. For example, in the *Rosenberg* case, involving espionage, Harry Gold and David Greenglass confessed without any immunity statute, but Julius and Ethel Rosenberg did not confess and would not have done so even if there had been an immunity statute with a death penalty attached to it.

For the purpose of detecting the authors of forbidden acts immunity statutes are not necessary, because human beings whether innocent or guilty of the acts in question have a compulsion to confess to something in any event. Confessions have an appeal to those that give them and an interest for the rest of us. Why did the Catholic church progress? One of the reasons was the practice of auricular confession, another of the tremendous changes of Innocent III, who also devised the inquisitional technique. Why did Parson Weems' fictional story about the boy George Washington chopping down his father's cherry tree become universally popular in this country? Because it involved a confession. Why have a majority of the guilty as well as many of the innocent confessed to the commission of offenses? Because of the compulsion to confess. How have the communists obtained such a multitude of confessions, many of which they are now confessing to be false? In part it is because of this same compulsion. No human characteristic is more general than the compulsion to confess. There are confessions in court and out of court, in church and out of church, in life and in literature, and yet a multitude of others. There are those which are consciously given and those which are unconsciously supplied. Even the common human failing of talking too much involves the same compulsion. Confessions without immunity acts are so numerous and varied that the writer has devoted a volume to them, *Why Men Confess* (1959).

Because of the compulsion to confess, many communists and ex-communists have confessed: communists in communist countries and ex-communists here. We are not aware of most of the ex-communist confessants in this country, for we do not hear about them. They usually acquire a status of confidential informants and secret witnesses—there are many types of determinations today, such as those relating to loyalty and security questions, the status of aliens, draft classifications, and the blacklisting of organizations in which one has not to date been held entitled to face one's accusers.

Ex-communist confessants and other informants have in all likelihood already told the government most of the story of the communist conspiracy which can be obtained from persons in this country. Indeed of the confessions of ex-communists at this point we would seem to have enough and to spare. What part of the small balance of the story that remains to be told can be obtained from those who have not yet talked is problematical, and so is its worth. The ones who have so far refused to talk are largely confirmed rebels. A number of them, like Julius and Ethel Rosenberg, would not talk under any circumstances. An immunity act may make a few talk who otherwise would not. If we had an inquisitional system such as the communists do we could get still more confessions, but would we want them? Certainly we should want no additional confessions such as those of Harvey Matusow. Even more surely we should want no confessions like those of Laszlo Rajk, formerly minister of the interior and then minister of foreign affairs of Hungary, and numerous others which the communists are now admitting to be false.

The futility of the new federal act so far as congressional witnesses are concerned was ably described in the Minority Report in the House on S. 16:

> What legislative lack does section (a) and (b) of the reported bill fill? . . . It is not the function of Congress to relieve the executive branch of the Government of its constitutional responsibility of law enforcement. When a committee of Congress investigates, it does so to gather evidence for its own purposes, that of legislating wisely and adequately. The investigations of Pearl Harbor, Teapot Dome, the work of the Truman Defense Committee and the LaFollette Civil Liberties Committee did not suffer for lack of congressional power to immunize witnesses. In the areas of treason, sabotage, espionage, . . . the Communist conspiracy, etc., the Congress has not heretofore hesitated to legislate, though lacking the power of immunization, session after session in its history.
>
> The sought-after evidence of the recalcitrant witness can now give us— what? More of the same thing? The facts of the evil and danger of the international Communist conspiracy have been spread before the Congress by a march of voluntary witnesses, ranging from employees of the Federal Bureau of Investigation to the ubiquitous ex-Communists. Beyond that lie only the exposure and prosecution of guilt, which is the business of the executive.

The experience of the Department of Justice to date under the new act would seem to bear out the views in the Minority Report on the act's worth. When the decision in the *Ullmann* case became final the defendant advised the district court that he wanted to purge his contempt by appearing before the grand jury and answering the questions previously put to him. Ullmann was a former Treasury Department official whom Elizabeth Bentley had linked with an espionage ring which Nathan Gregory Silvermaster, another Treasury Department official, assertedly headed. Another alleged member of this ring was Harry Dexter White. Ullmann, after his purging grand jury appearance, issued this statement to the press:

. . . As I have done in the past, I have again denied participating in espionage and have denied knowing anyone who has. I have denied ever being a member of the Communist party and have denied knowledge of Communist party activities on the part of others.

I have specifically denied knowledge of the things which my former superior, the late Harry Dexter White, has been charged with—and believe, in fact, that he was a great and faithful public servant.

Now that the authorities had his answers they were not happy with them. The grand jury wanted his contempt sentence held over his head until he gave more satisfactory ones. However, Judge Weinfeld told them that if they felt Ullmann had committed perjury they could take appropriate action.

Nor did the department make much headway with its second reported case under the new act, that of Edward J. Fitzgerald.

Another illuminating illustration of the futility of immunity acts came from a state level. It involved the seven individuals whom the New York State Investigation Commission wanted to question about the alleged gangland Apalachin meeting. When the seven had spent seven months in jail, two of them, the Valenti brothers, indicated through their lawyer that they were desirous of answering the Commission's questions as soon as possible. After the first one testified, Jacob Grumet, State Investigation Commissioner, denounced his story as "inherently incredible," and termed his testimony "unequivocally unworthy of belief" and "a sham designed to impede the commission's investigation." Mr. Grumet was equally irritated with the other brother's story. The Commissioner finally asked him why he went to see Barbara in the first place. Valenti explained that he went because Barbara was ill, and that seeing sick people was "a nice thing to do." In response to a similar question the other brother had answered that he had gone along to please his brother, just for the ride as it were.

A further striking demonstration of the futility of immunity acts is the growing obsolescence of the very act of 1954. In the first big espionage prosecution after the Ullmann and Fitzgerald cases, that involving Jack Soble, the Department carefully refrained from using the immunity act. Furthermore, the Department obtained confessions, beginning with a full one from Soble himself.

The Senate Internal Security Subcommittee is even more dissatisfied with the act of 1954 than the Department of Justice. In the Subcommittee's first cases, those of McElrath, Oka, Symonds and Glasser, it requested immunity orders before the witnesses' appearances. The Court of Appeals for the District of Columbia Circuit held the requests premature. The Subcommittee in its annual report for 1957 characterized the resulting procedure "so unwieldy as to be for all practical purposes unworkable" and recommended that the act of 1954 be amended "so as to provide a clean-cut method, not involving judicial intervention, for granting immunity from prosecution to witnesses before congressional committees, with respect to matters and things about which they are forced to testify." So we end up with neither the Department of Justice nor the Senate Internal Security Subcommittee using the act of 1954, and the Subcommittee wanting it amended.

With or without an immunity act, some deviants will remain wholly uncooperative, as were the Rosenbergs, others will be insufficiently cooperative in the eyes of the authorities, as were Ullmann and Fitzgerald, and yet others will be overly cooperative, and overly submissive, as were Matusow, Crouch and too many more. The new act may even worsen this situation. It has been highly overrated.

Moreover, in order to try to reach the illusion of the additional information which such acts hold out to us we take a step in the direction of the inquisitional technique, and degrade individuals by giving them the choice either of confessing their sins and naming their associates or going to jail. We give up part of our birthright for less than a mess of pottage. Our accusatorial method has helped us to develop a more independent and mature citizenry than will be found in eastern countries. With us an individual does not have to be submissive when the state points an accusing finger at him: he has a right to remain silent, along with a right to counsel, to a formal accusation, to bail in nearly all cases, to a public trial, to be confronted with his accusers, and to be proved guilty beyond a reasonable doubt. We should not let any of these rights atrophy, least of all the right of silence. The compulsory confession of one's sins and the naming of one's associates may be standard operating procedure in authoritarian regimes, but it is unbecoming a free people.

Also, immunity acts are a mirage. We think we are going to get much additional information by the use of them, when the truth of the matter is that in all probability we shall get most of the information we want without them. We shall get this information because human beings have a compulsion to confess to something. Immunity acts are thus unnecessary. The government has most of the story of the communist conspiracy in this country. An immunity act will add little, if anything, to our store of knowledge in this field. By passing an immunity act in order to obtain this possible additional mite we give up part of our heritage. The cost is too great.

Nevertheless, new immunity acts and demands for them have continued to be forthcoming. Congress put an immunity provision in the Narcotic Control Act of 1956. Demands for such a provision occur whenever numbers of individuals have refused to answer the inquiries of governmental authorities. In May 1959 Attorney General Rogers told Congress that there was an urgent need for immunity statutes which would compel testimony from witnesses in labor racketeering and extortion cases. Congress put an immunity provision in the Labor-Management and Disclosure Act of 1959.

Required Records Doctrine

Legislation has helped to produce another exception to the right of silence, the required records doctrine. Under this doctrine, if the law requires one to keep certain records, they are not protected from production by one's right of silence. This exception the Supreme Court enunciated in *Shapiro* v. *United States*. Chief Justice Vinson delivered the opinion, as he did in the later *Rogers* case. The records in question were only the customary ones of the defendant but OPA regulations required them to be kept. The Court reasoned that they thus became public documents and did not fall within the scope of the right of silence.

The Internal Security Act of 1950 takes us into this exception, and even beyond it, for under the Supreme Court's ruling in the *Dennis* case the leaders of the American Communist party were engaged in a conspiracy, whereas the defendant in the *Shapiro* case was conducting a lawful business. Nevertheless, the Court of Appeals for the District of Columbia Circuit sustained the act's validity. It would seem however that the dissenting judge, David L. Bazelon, had the better of the argument: "Suppose an Act of Congress required bands of bank robbers to file with the Attorney General statements of their memberships and activities, and imposed criminal penalties upon their leaders and members for failure to do so. Such an Act would compel individuals to disclose their connection with a criminal conspiracy. No argument could reconcile such an Act with the Fifth Amendment's command. . . ." The Supreme Court granted review but did not reach the constitutional issue. Rather it sent the case back to the Subversive Activities Control Board for reconsideration because of the alleged false testimony of three government witnesses: Harvey Matusow, Paul Crouch, and Manning Johnson.

Our Better Angels

With all the criticism to which the Supreme Court and its decisions have been subjected in recent years, the writer is reluctant to say that the Court should have gone even further than it did in its protection of the correlative rights of freedom of utterance and to silence, and yet that is his view. He will express it, confident that in the long course of time, if human beings survive, the attacks on the Court will have as little effect as the comparable attacks on Washington and Jefferson, and on Lincoln and Franklin D. Roosevelt.

In only one major area would the writer fail to go beyond the Court, and that is in the area of states' rights. The writer believes that states and local communities must learn to govern themselves and that we must, within certain limits, permit them to do so, indeed, even encourage them to do so. More particularly, the writer feels that under the First and Tenth Amendments sedition and obscenity are the business of the states and not that of the federal government.

With reference to the rights of freedom of utterance and to silence the writer takes a position in advance even of that of the Warren Court. He feels that both rights should be nearly absolute. Under the First Amendment the right to freedom of utterance, at least so far as Congress is concerned, is absolute unless connected with criminal conduct other than advocacy. The writer cannot take quite the same position with reference to Fifth Amendment's right of silence for historically immunity acts in some form are older than the Fifth Amendment.

Nevertheless, the writer feels that rather than limit we should extend the right of silence. An individual, as to any accusation which may tend to incriminate him, should have an absolute right to remain silent. Furthermore, any confession which has been obtained from an accused who has not been taken promptly upon arrest before a committing authority, and any confession which an accused repudiates in court, should not be admissible in evidence.

As to an accused who has been taken into custody one can accept this recommendation by Wigmore: "Let every accused person be required to be taken before a magistrate, or the district attorney, promptly upon arrest, for private examination; let the magistrate warn him of his right to remain silent; and then let his statement be taken in the presence of an official stenographer, if he is willing to make one . . . This meets a real need, both psychologic and detective." Later, Wigmore proposed that the interview between an accused and the examining magistrate should be recorded on a sound film. His earlier recommendation amounts in substance to the English practice, which is preferable to our own.

The suggested procedure is in the best interests of the state as well as the individual. If an accused is guilty and has a strong compulsion to confess upon detection, the state will get the benefit of it. If he is innocent he has an immediate chance, if he wants it, to tell his story. In order to ensure that the investigating authorities will not resort to the inquisitional method, all challenged confessions should be excluded from evidence.

Lawyers, legal writers and courts have differed considerably in their estimates of the right to remain silent and the inquisitional technique. Bentham, writing in 1824, in his *Rationale of Judicial Evidence*, attacked the right to remain silent. He saw no reason why an accused should not be compelled under pain of contempt to speak. If one was innocent one had nothing to hide and if one was guilty such a course was not unjust. Here was the way he answered some of the arguments he attributed to those who favored this right:

2. The old woman's reason. The essence of this reason is contained in the word *hard*: 'tis hard upon a man to be obliged to criminate himself. Hard it is upon a man, it must be confessed, to be obliged to do anything that he does not like . . . What is no less hard upon him, is, that he should be punished: but did it ever yet occur to a man to propose a general abolition of all punishment, with this hardship for a reason for it? . . .
3. The fox-hunter's reason. This consists in introducing upon the carpet of legal procedure the idea of *fairness*, in the sense in which the word is used by sportsmen . . . 4. Confounding interrogation with torture; with the application of physical suffering, till some act is done; in the present instance, till testimony is given to a particular effect required. On this occasion it is necessary to observe, that the act of putting a question to a person whose station is that of defendant in a cause, is no more an act of torture than the putting the same question to him would be, if, instead of being a defendant, he were an extraneous witness . . . 5. Reference to unpopular institutions [Courts of Star Chamber and High Commission] Whatever Titius did was wrong; but this is among the things that Titius did; therefore this is wrong; such is the logic from which this sophism is deduced.

Wigmore answered Bentham by arguing that the inquisitional technique lent itself to bullying and the use of physical torture:

The real objection is that *any system of administration which permits the prosecution to trust habitually to compulsory self-disclosure as a source of proof must itself suffer morally thereby.* The inclination develops to rely mainly upon such evidence, and to be satisfied with an incomplete investigation of the other sources. The exercise of the power to extract answers begets a forgetfulness of the just limitations of that power. The simple and peaceful process of questioning breeds a readiness to resort to bullying and to physical force and torture. If there is a right to an answer, there soon seems to be a right to the expected answer,—that is, to a confession of guilt. Thus the legitimate use grows into the unjust abuse; ultimately, the innocent are jeopardized by the encroachments of a bad system. Such seems to have been the course of experience in those legal systems where the privilege was not recognized.

Sir James Stephen, an English lawyer and judge, who drafted the Indian Code of Civil Procedure, in his *History of the Criminal Law of England* earlier made the same point as Wigmore: "During the discussion which took place on the Indian Code of Civil Procedure in 1872, some observations were made on the reasons which occasionally lead native police officers to apply torture to prisoners. An experienced civil officer observed, 'there is a great deal of laziness in it. It is far pleasanter to sit comfortably in the shade, rubbing red pepper into a poor devil's eyes than to go about in the sun digging up evidence.'"

However, Wigmore disagreed with Bentham only up to a point: he agreed with him in his condemnation of the equation of the inquisitional process with torture. If physical force was not in fact used, Wigmore did not condemn confessions obtained as a result of the inquisitional technique. When a court wrote: "So the inquisition of torture is restored, only without the rack and thumbscrew"; Wigmore commented: "This attitude of maudlin sentimentality, repeating the misnomer of 'torture', has not disappeared ever since Bentham's day . . .'" But Bentham and Wigmore wrote before we were as aware as we are today of the fact that the mind is divided against itself. Also Bentham did not know, and neither really did Wigmore, the devastating use which the communists would make of the inquisitional technique. In the light of our present knowledge the world should have done away not only with this technique but also with the confessions it produces.

The Supreme Court should reconsider its decisions in *Ullmann* v. *United States* (federal compulsory testimony act of 1954), *Brown* v. *Walker* (federal) compulsory testimony act of 1893), *Brown* v. *United States* (ibid.), *Rogers* v. *United States* (doctrine of waiver), and *Shapiro* v. *United States* (required records doctrine) and adopt the views of the dissenters. An accused should have an absolute right to remain silent as to any incriminating situation involving him. The government could still require the keeping of records in appropriate situations. A taxpaper, for instance, could be required to keep records for the determination of the amount of his tax liability. Or again, a shopkeeper could be required to keep records to be used to determine ceiling prices. But the only result that should flow from a failure to keep such records, or a refusal to produce them if kept, in situations incriminating to the individual, would be a pecuniary loss to him, and furthermore such pecuniary loss should bear some relation to the object for which the government required the records to be kept. If a taxpayer failed to keep appropriate records, his gross income might be increased or claimed deductions might be disallowed. If a shopkeeper failed to keep appropriate records his ceiling prices (in the days when we had them) might be lowered. However, in neither case should the individual's right to remain silent including his right to refuse to produce records as to any incriminating situation be infringed.

On a related question, that of compelling one to be an informer in order to keep one's job, surely in the long range of time the position of New York State Education Commissioner, James E. Allen, Jr., who refused to impose such a requirement on teachers, will be remembered with respect and admiration, rather than that of the many who acted in a contrary fashion. The New York City Board of Education in March 1955 adopted, with one dissenting vote, a resolution authorizing the superintendent of schools to require teachers to reveal the names of any of their associates who had been members of the Communist party. Under this resolution the Board of Education suspended a principal, three teachers and a clerk for refusing to name others teachers who were or had been Communist party members. The principal was Samuel S. Cohen; the teachers were Harry Adler, Julius Nash and Irving Mauer; and the clerk was Miss Minerva T. Feinstein. Commissioner Allen reversed the suspensions. As to the teachers and the clerk, he said: ". . . I am convinced in the overall administration of the public school system that the institution of the policy under consideration here would do more harm than good and that this type of inquisition has no place in the school system. . . ." As to the principal he understandably ruled somewhat differently: ". . . He has subordinates under him for whom he is responsible. The principles heretofore enumerated are not applicable to him in so far as they relate to those teachers under his jurisdiction in the school. A board would clearly be justified in expecting him, even without a request, to report to it the name of any person in his school whom he knows or believes to be a Communist or otherwise unfit to be an employee of his school. . . ."

Peter Campbell Brown, then New York City's corporation counsel, declared: "The ruling radically affects the conduct of the entire anti-subversive program of the Board of Education and the Board of Higher Education, and involves interpretation of the fundamental rights and obligations of teachers. This is a problem of such importance that I feel compelled, in the public interest, to obtain a definitive declaration from the courts." He did take Mr. Allen to court. The courts sustained Mr. Allen.

Mr. Allen's stand shows, as does the right of silence itself, a regard for the worth and dignity of individual human beings that will in the long run aid us all.

CHAPTER XII

UNENUMERATED RIGHTS

Ninth Amendment

Claims to silence and to freedom of utterance are based on rights which are well-known as well as protected by specific constitutional guarantees. Other claims are not as fortunate. Indeed, many arose after the adoption of the federal Bill of Rights. How are they to obtain recognition? One can suggest that existing constitutional provisions should be construed to cover them. This has happened in various instances. One can suggest a constitutional amendment to provide for them. This takes too long. One can also consider the provisions of the Ninth Amendment.

With reference to this amendment Justice Robert H. Jackson in his posthumously published *The Supreme Court in the American System of Government* commented: ". . . But the Ninth Amendment rights which are not to be disturbed by the Federal Government are still a mystery to me. * * *' Mr. Patterson's book, *The Forgotten Ninth Amendment* was published in the same year.

Little use has been made of this amendment. However, it is possible to ascertain what its framers meant by it. In doing so we shall also discover why it has fallen into disuse. We shall learn why lawyers who represented clients with unenumerated rights came to rely on the due process clauses of the Fifth and Fourteenth Amendments rather than on the provisions of the Ninth Amendment.

When various of the states in their conventions on the adoption of the Constitution suggested provisions for a federal Bill of Rights as well as other amendments to the Constitution, they then had to guard against the danger that lay in the possible contention that an enumeration of the rights of the individual was exhaustive. Madison's state, Virginia, the tenth one to ratify the Constitution, accordingly suggested as one of its proposed amendments:

17th. That those clauses which declare that Congress shall not exercise certain powers, be not interpreted, in any manner whatsoever, to extend the powers of Congress; but that they be construed as either making exceptions to the specified powers where this shall be the case, or otherwise, as inserted merely for greater caution.

Hamilton's state, New York, in ratifying declared:

. . . that those clauses in the said Constitution, which declare that Congress shall not have or exercise certain powers, do not imply that Congress is entitled to any powers not given by the said Constitution; but such clauses are to be construed either as exceptions to certain specified powers, or as inserted merely for greater caution.

North Carolina, although it neither ratified nor rejected the Constitution in 1788, convened a convention in that year which adopted a set of suggestions patterned after those of Viriginia.

Madison in his own set of amendments, in order to meet the danger in the contention that an enumeration of individual rights was exhaustive, proposed:

The exceptions here or elsewhere in the Constitution, made in favor of particular rights shall not be so construed as to diminish the just importance of other rights retained by the people, or as to enlarge the powers delegated by the Constitution; but either as actual limitations of such powers, or as inserted merely for greater caution.

The special committee to which the House sent Madison's proposals revised this proposal to read: "The enumeration in this Constitution of certain rights, shall not be construed to deny or disparage others retained by the people." With the change of "this" to "the" and the addition of a comma, this became the Ninth Amendment.

Suppose a conflict were to arise between an unenumerated right and the exercise of a power under Article I, section 8, clause 18 empowering the Congress: "To make all Laws which shall be necessary and proper for carrying into Execution the foregoing Powers, and all other Powers vested by this Constitution in the Government of the United States, or in any Department of Officer thereof." Which would prevail? Although the debates in the House of the first Congress did not pair off an unenumerated right against an implied power, a study of these debates will permit one safely to say that the implied power would prevail. In 1789 the framers of the first Ten Amendments were concerned that there be no weakening of the newly established federal government.

Madison, before he offered the House his proposals, took note of the demands for a bill of rights and, in the course of doing so, commented:

. . . And if there are amendments desired of such a nature as will not injure the Constitution, and they can be ingrafted so as to give satisfaction to the doubting part of our fellow-citizens, the friends of the Federal Government will evince that spirit of deference and concession for which they have hitherto been distinguished.

Then he referred to the "two States" which had not yet ratified the Constitution and continued:

. . . I have no doubt, if we proceed to take those steps which would be prudent and requisite at this juncture, that in a short time we should see that disposition prevailing in those States which have not come in, that we have seen prevailing in those States which have embraced the Constitution.

But I will candidly acknowledge, that, over and above all these considerations, I do conceive that the Constitution may be amended; that is to say, if all power is subject to abuse, that then it is possible the abuse of the powers of the General Government may be guarded against in a more secure manner than is now done, while no one advantage arising from the exercise of that power shall be damaged or endangered by it. We have in this way something to gain, and, if we proceed with caution, nothing to lose. And in this case it is necessary to proceed with caution; for while we feel all these inducements to go into a revisal of the Constitution, we must feel for the Constitution itself, and make that revisal a moderate one. I should be unwilling to see a door opened for a reconsideration of the whole structure of the Government—for a reconsideration of the principles and the substance of the powers given; because I doubt, if such a door were opened, we should be very likely to stop at that point which would be safe to the Government itself. But I do wish to see a door opened to consider, so far as to incorporate those provisions for the security of rights, against which I believe no serious objection has been made by any class of our constituents; such as would be likely to meet with the concurrence of two-thirds of both Houses, and the approbation of three-fourths of the State Legislatures. . . .

With specific reference to his proposal which became the Ninth Amendment, Madison explained:

It has been objected also against a bill of rights, that, by enumerating particular exceptions to the grant of power, it would disparage those rights which were not placed in that enumeration; and it might follow, by implication, that those rights which were not singled out, were intended to be assigned into the hands of the General Government, and were consequently insecure. This is one of the most plausible arguments I have ever heard urged against the admission of a bill of rights into this system; but, I conceive, that it may be guarded against. I have attempted it, as gentlemen may see. . . .

During the course of his presentation he commented:

In our Government it is, perhaps, less necessary to guard against the abuse in the Executive Department than any other; because it is not the stronger branch of the system, but the weaker. It therefore must be levelled against the Legislative, for it is the most powerful, and most likely to be abused, because it is under the least control. Hence, so far as a declaration of rights can tend to prevent the exercise of undue power, it cannot be doubted but such declaration is proper. But I confess that I do conceive, that in a Government modified like this of the United States, the great danger lies rather in the abuse of the community than in the Legislative body.

He concluded his explanation of his amendments with the observation:

. . . if we can make the Constitution better in the opinion of those who are opposed to it, without weakening its frame, or abridging its usefulness, in the judgment of those who are attached to it, we act the part of wise and liberal men to make such alterations as shall produce that effect.

One may thus summarize Madison's thinking to the extent that it has a bearing on a conflict between an unenumerated right and an implied power. The federal government was one of delegated and limited powers. Hence a bill of rights was not really necessary. Nevertheless, he was agreeable to having a declaration of individual rights in order to make assurance doubly sure that in various areas the federal government was not to act at all, and in certain other areas was to act only in a particular manner. For example, in the areas of speech, press and religion, the federal government was not to act at all. Or, to take a case in the other field, although the federal government was to collect its taxes, it was not to do so by means of general warrants.

But in the matter of amendments Madison had one important proviso, and he emphasized it: any revisions of the Constitution were not to weaken the federal government. Nor is there any indication in Madison's thinking that he regarded properly implied congressional powers as of a lesser standing than express powers. On the contrary, his position on the Tenth Amendment indicates that he equated the two. So far as Madison was concerned, implied powers were necessary and they were as good as express powers.

Madison in his comments, neither then nor later, juxtaposed implied powers against unenumerated rights. On the contrary, he indicated that he thought a line could be drawn between them.

Edmund Randolph of Virginia was thus substantially correct when, in his opposition to the Ninth Amendment, he characterized it as an opiate. In the Virginia legislature he objected to this amendment on the ground that "there was no criterion by which it could be determined whether any other particular right [than those specified in the other amendments] was retained or not." In a letter of December 6, 1789 to

George Washington he wrote that this amendment "is exceptionable to me, in giving a handle to say, that Congress have endeavored to administer an opiate, by an alteration which is merely plausible." Madison in a letter of December 5, 1789 to Washington answered Randolph's position in the Virginia legislature with the observation that if a line could not be drawn between implied powers and unenumerated rights, then the declaration in the Ninth Amendment would be a futile one: "If a line can be drawn between the powers granted and the rights retained, it would seem to be the same thing, whether the latter be secured by declaring that they shall not be abridged, or that the former shall not be extended. If no such line can be drawn, a declaration in either form would amount to nothing."

The most that can thus be said is that the framers of the Ninth Amendment intended it as a declaration, should the need for it arise, that the people had other rights than those enumerated in the first eight amendments; and the federal judiciary and the state legislatures could so use it if they had to do so in order to pass judgment on the validity of an act of Congress. The Ninth Amendment was not so used. Even Madison did not so use it.

Implied Powers

One can further suggest that the Ninth Amendment's declaration of the existence of unenumerated rights could also be used as an added weight in the balance to support a restrictive interpretation of the necessary and proper clause. It was not so used either. Again Madison himself, although he was soon to become concerned about the growing power of the federal government and the claims of additional powers for it by the rising Federalists, did not so use the Ninth Amendment.

Originally Madison had expressed himself in favor of a broad interpretation of the necessary and proper clause. Early in 1788 he had written in The Federalist, No. 44: "No axiom is more clearly established in law, or in reason, than that wherever the end is required, the means are authorized; wherever a general power to do a thing is given, every particular power necessary for doing it is included." The following year he carried this approach forward in his drafts of the Ninth and Tenth Amendments.

But within three years thereafter he was to change his emphasis and be on his way to a stricter construction of the Constitution with reference to implied powers. The change began in 1791. It came in the controversy over the national bank bill. Hamilton, in December 1790, had presented to Congress his plan for the establishment of a national bank. The Senate, in January 1791, passed the bank bill without a roll call. In the House Madison argued against its constitutionality on the ground, among others, that no power to charter a bank could be found in the necessary and proper clause: "If implications, thus remote and thus multiplied, can be linked together, a chain may be formed that will reach every object of legislation, every object within the whole compass of political economy." The House nevertheless passed the bill.

Washington, doubtful of the constitutionality of the measure, asked his cabinet officers for opinions on the point. Jefferson and Hamilton were of course of different views. Jefferson was in favor of a narrow interpretation of the necessary and proper clause; Hamilton a broad one. Jefferson argued: ". . . the Constitution restrained them to the *necessary* means, that is to say, to those means without which the grant of the power would be nugatory."

Late the same year Hamilton submitted to the House his famous *Report on Manufactures*. In it he contended that Congress had express authority to provide for the general walfare. The objects to which money could be devoted were not narrower than the general welfare itself, and Congress could say that those objects were. The next month Madison wrote to Henry Lee, referring to the Constitution: "If not only the *means*, but the objects are *unlimited*, the parchment had better be thrown into the fire at once."

Six years later in his opposition to the Sedition Act of 1798 Madison again stated his views on the proper interpretation of the necessary and proper clause. It was in his *Report* on the Virginia Resolutions of 1798. He was in the process of answering the contention that under the express power of Congress to "suppress Insurrections" one could "imply the power to *prevent* insurrections, by punishing whatever may lead or tend to them." His answer was that if libels tended to insurrections, then the thing to do was to pass and execute laws for the suppression of insurrections, but not for the punishment of libels. He quoted the necessary and proper clause and argued: "It is not a grant of new powers to Congress, but merely a declaration, for the removal of all uncertainty, that means of carrying into execution those otherwise granted are included in the grant."

*　　*　　*

Madison in his *Report* and Jefferson in his opinon on the constitutionality of the national bank bill quoted the Tenth Amendment. But they did not rely on the Ninth.

A little over two decades later came the Supreme Court's guiding decision in *McCulloch* v. *Maryland*. In language reminiscent of that of Madison in *The Federalist*, No. 44, Chief Justice John Marshall speaking for the Court gave the classic statement on the interpretation of the necessary and proper clause: ". . . Let the end be legitimate, let it be within the scope of the constitution, and all means which are appropriate, which are plainly adapted to that end, which are not prohibited, but consist with the letter and spirit of the constitution, are constitutional."

Madison was critical of the court's opinion. In a letter of September 2, 1819 to Judge Spencer Roane of Virginia he referred to "their latitudinary mode of expounding the Constitution," and commented:

But what is of most importance is the high sanction given to a latitude in expounding the Constitution which seems to break down the landmarks intended by a specification of the Powers of Congress, and to substitute for a definite connection between means and ends, a Legislative discretion as to the former to which no practical limit can be assigned. * * *

* * *

* * * There is certainly a reasonable medium between expounding the Constitution with the strictness of a penal law, or other ordinary statute, and expounding it with a laxity which may vary its essential character, and encroach on the local sovereignties with wch. it was meant to be reconcilable.

Toward the end of his life Madison suggested a moderate construction of the Constitution with respect to implied powers. In a letter of January 6, 1831 to Reynolds Chapman, after commenting that in interpreting the Constitution, "where a language technically appropriate may be deficient, the wonder wd. be far greater if different rules of exposition were not applied to the text by different commentators," he continued:

Thus it is found that in the case of the Legislative department particularly, where a division & definition of the powers according to their specific objects is most difficult, the Instrument is read by some as if it were a Constitution for a single Govt. with powers co-extensive with the general welfare, and by others interpreted as if it were an ordinary statute, and with the strictness almost of a penal one.

Between these adverse constructions an intermediate course must be the true one, and it is hoped that it will finally if not otherwise settled be prescribed by an amendment of the Constitution. * * *

Yet not even here, nor in his letter to Judge Roane, did Madison cite the Ninth Amendment.

The Supreme Court carried forward its approach in *McCulloch* v. *Maryland* in the *Legal Tender Cases*. There it reasoned that an implied power did not have to be directly traceable to a particular express power: "Its existence may be deduced fairly from more than one of the substan-

tive powers expressly defined, or from them all combined. * * *
Congress has often exercised, without question, powers that are not
expressly given nor ancillary to any single enumerated power. Powers
thus exercised are what are called by Judge Story in his Commentaries
on the Constitution, resulting powers, arising from the aggregate powers
of government."

Recent decisions of the Court have further held that the federal government in its conduct of this country's foreign affairs has certain inherent powers. For example, in *Perez* v. *Brownell* the Court sustained
the validity of an act of Congress which deprived a native-born American citizen of his nationality for voting in a political election in a foreign state, despite the first sentence of the first section of the Fourteenth
Amendment, which expressly provides: "All persons born or naturalized
in the United States, and subject to the jurisdiction thereof, are citizens
of the United States and of the State wherein they reside." The Court,
speaking through Justice Frankfurter, ruled: "Although there is in the
Constitution no specific grant to Congress of power to enact legislation
for the effective regulation of foreign affairs, there can be no doubt of
the existence of this power in the law-making organ of the Nation."

A combination of various circumstances contributed to the lack of
vitality of the Ninth Amendment. To begin with, it was never more
than a declaration that the people had unenumerated rights. Even its
framers forgot about it. For another thing, the first Ten Amendments
were applicable only to the federal government and not to state governments, and the Supreme Court so held. In the third place, early constitutional questions involved either individual rights under the first eight
amendments or disputes primarily between the federal government and
one of the states or state officials. For instance, Madison and Jefferson
and their supporters rested their opposition to the Sedition Act of 1798
on the First and Tenth Amendments. Under these amendments they
contended that the federal government had no power over advocacy
unless connected with criminal conduct other than advocacy. Fourthly,
the unenumerated rights which come to mind today, such as the right of
privacy, to engage in political activity, of freedom of movement across
national boundaries, to knowledge, to confrontation in other than criminal cases, a jury trial in contempt cases, the use of the mails, and to
engage in peaceful picketing, did not receive their development until
after, and in most instances much after, the adoption of the first Ten
Amendments; and in the interim two other clauses of the Constitution
have been applied to safeguard to the individual those rights which
"have been found to be implicit in the concept of ordered liberty:" the
due process clause of the Fifth Amendment as against federal action,

and of the Fourteenth Amendment as against state action, principally the latter clause.

Recent advocates on behalf of unenumerated rights have occasionally relied on the Ninth Amendment, usually in connection with the Tenth, but such efforts have not been successful. Sometimes such advocates have relied on yet other constitutional provisions than the due process clauses. For example, in *Olmstead* v. *United States*, a prohibition case, counsel objected to the use in evidence of wiretapped conversations on the grounds of a violation of the Fourth Amendment's prohibition against unreasonable searches and seizures, and the Fifth Amendment's guarantee of the privilege against self-incrimination. Or again, in *United Public Workers* v. *Mitchell*, involving a challenge to the constitutionality of a portion of Section 9(a) of the Hatch Act, counsel rested the right to engage in political activity on the First, Ninth and Tenth Amendments as well as the due process clause of the Fifth Amendment. More and more, however, counsel who urged the recognition of unenumerated rights relied on the due process clauses of the Fifth and Fourteenth Amendments.

In the *Olmstead* and *United Public Workers* cases the individual lost. On the other hand, the response of the Court has been such to claims under the due process clauses that in two passport cases at the last term, those of Rockwell Kent, an artist, and Dr. Walter Briehl, a Los Angeles psychiatrist, the government conceded that under the due process clause of the Fifth Amendment individuals had a constitutional right to travel. A consideration of some unenumerated rights will help to fill in the picture.

Privacy

During the current century we developed a general right to privacy, a right to be let alone. The starting point for this development was an article by Justice Brandeis, before he reached the bench, and Samuel D. Warren in the December 1890 issue of the *Harvard Law Review*. Later Justice Brandeis, in his dissenting opinion in *Olmstead* v. *United States*, described the right to be let alone as "the most comprehensive of rights and the right most valued by civilized men." Not quite fifteen years after the Brandeis and Warren article the Supreme Court of Georgia recognized a right of privacy. Since then twenty-three more states and the District of Columbia recognized such a right judicially and three others provided for it to a modified extent by statute. Only four states denied it, and one of these, New York, was one of the three which provided for it in modified form by legislation. It did so almost immediately after the decision denying the right.

But during the current century we also developed a practice which invaded one's right of privacy—wiretapping. In recent years many public officials have taken the position that wiretapping is necessary in certain cases in order to protect this country's national security. For instance, in May 1953 Attorney General Herbert Brownell, Jr., announced that he had submitted to Congress a bill to legalize the use of evidence obtained by wiretapping in federal criminal cases involving national security; and asserted that legislation such as he proposed was "vital for the adequate safeguarding of our country and its way of life." Before and since that time various members of Congress introduced many such bills, but so far they have failed of passage.

The reason for legislation is that it may fairly be contended that Congress sought to outlaw wiretapping in Section 605 of the Federal Communications Act of 1934: ". . . and no person not being authorized by the sendor shall intercept any communication and divulge or publish the existence, contents, substance, purport, effect, or meaning of such intercepted communication to any person. . . ." However, this measure is only part of wiretapping's brief but interesting history.

In 1924 Stone as attorney general forbade wiretapping by the FBI as "unethical tactics." But in 1928 in *Olmstead* v. *United States* the Supreme Court in a five to four split allowed the use of wiretap evidence. Chief Justice Taft wrote the majority opinion. The four dissenters were Justices Holmes, Brandeis, Butler and Stone. It was in this case that Justice Holmes in his dissent characterized wiretapping as dirty business: ". . . We have to choose, and for my part I think it a less evil that some criminals should escape than that the government should play an ignoble part. . . . If the existing code does not permit district attorneys to have a hand in such dirty business it does not permit the judge to allow such iniquities to succeed."

Three years later Attorney General Mitchell announced that the Department of Justice would approve wiretapping when requested by the director of the bureau concerned. Despite the enactment of Section 605, the Department of Justice continued to countenance wiretapping in criminal cases of "extreme importance," although not "in minor cases, nor on Members of Congress, or officials, or any citizen except where charge of a grave crime had been lodged against him."

Two states under certain circumstances sanctioned wiretapping. Massachusetts by statute permitted it "when authorized by written permission of the attorney general of the commonwealth, or of the district attorney for the district." New York after an intense and prolonged debate in its constitutional convention of 1938 adopted a provision authorizing ex parte warrants to wiretap. A few years later a statute implemented this provision.

But the federal Supreme Court in three cases between 1937–39 broadly enforced the prohibition in Section 605. It refused to permit the use in a federal court of evidence so obtained, as well as leads from such evidence, and extended its rulings to wiretaps of intrastate communications. The next year Attorney General Jackson announced a return to the Stone policy of 1924. He concluded that wiretapping could not be done unless Congress saw fit to modify the existing statutes. However, a year later he changed his mind about the proper interpretation of Section 605. In March 1941 in a letter to the House Judiciary Committee urging the adoption of pending wiretap legislation he stated: ". . . The only offense under the present law is to intercept any communication and divulge or publish the same. Any person, with no risk of penalty, may tap telephone wires . . . and act upon what he hears or make any use of it that does not involve divulging or publication." In the following years wiretapping grew apace. Public officials, national, state and municipal, as well as private persons engaged in it, so much so that one writer concluded:

. . . For despite the statutes and judicial decisions which purport to regulate wire tapping, today this practice flourishes as a wide-open operation at the federal, state, municipal, and private levels.

A wealth of collected information discloses that the conversations of public officials in every sort of government agency, bureau, and political subdivision have been tapped. Reports are legion that private citizens have had their conversations recorded. All kinds of business organization and social, professional, and political groups have been listed as victims. There are charges that wire tapping may be an essential part of the Federal Bureau of Investigation's population-wide "loyalty" probe. And recently complaints have been made that telephones of United Nations delegates and employees are under surveillance, as well as the telephones of foreign embassies, legations, and missions in the United States.

*   *   *

In short, although wire tapping is a crime in almost every state, and although there is a federal law prohibiting the interception and divulging of the contents of telephone communications, wire tapping is carried on virtually unimpeded in the United States today.

Moreover, during the time of Chief Justice Vinson the judiciary weakened somewhat in its stand against the use of wiretap evidence in court proceedings. In *Schwartz* v. *Texas* the Supreme Court sustained the use of such evidence in a state court proceeding even though the state, Texas, had a statutory provision which rendered inadmissible in criminal trials evidence obtained in violation of the constitution or laws of the state or the Constitution of the United States. Only Justice Douglas dissented: ". . . It is true that the prior decisions of the Court point to affirmance. But those decisions reflect constructions of the Constitution which I think are erroneous. They impinge severely on the liberty of the individual and give the police the right to intrude into the privacy of any life. The practices they sanction have today acquired a momentum that is so ominous I cannot remain silent and bow to the precedents that sanction them." Three years later the federal Court of Military Appeals in three cases held that Section 605 did not bar the use of wiretap evidence in court-martial proceedings where it was obtained under these circumstances: (1) by interception of messages initiated and received on facilities operated by the Army independently of commercial telephone systems; (2) by interception of telephone messages initiated and received in foreign countries; and (3) by listening on an extension telephone, with an informer's consent, to a conversation which the informer initiated with an accused person. The next year in *Sugden* v. *United States* the Supreme Court held that the government could tap radio communications broadcast over a licensed farm radio station by unlicensed operators.

Of course, private individuals who violated section 605 were indicted, convicted and sentenced. A similar thing has happened to individuals in state prosecutions in Massachusetts and New York. The individual in New York was John G. (Steve) Broady, who was a lawyer. After his as in the case of capital punishment, where society permits itself conduct conviction he was also disbarred. This is but another of the instances, which it denies to the individual.

Although the *Sugden* case was decided during the time of Chief Justice Earl Warren, the stand of the Court against the use of wiretap evidence has again become strong. Recently in *Benanti* v. *United States* the Court, speaking through Chief Justice Warren, held that wiretap evidence, even though procured by New York officials in accordance with that state's constitutional and statutory provisions and without participation by federal authorities, was nevertheless inadmissible in a federal criminal prosecution because of Section 605.

But suppose Congress were now to make a law that in any instance where the attorney general approved it, wiretapping was permissible in investigations relating to our national security. On what constitutional grounds would counsel for the individual attack it? In view of the eloquent dissenting opinions in *Olmstead* v. *United States* his first ground would be the Fourth Amendment. He would quote, as Justice Brandeis did, Chief Justice Marshall's language to the effect that it is a constitution, the Constitution, which the Court is expounding and that the Court is to construe it in such a way as to make it as nearly immortal as human institutions can ever be, and that under such an approach wiretapping violates the Fourth Amendment's prohibition against unreasonable searches. His second ground would be the due process clause of the Fifth Amendment. If he relied on the Ninth Amendment at all, it would only be at best as an added last ground.

Political Activity

One of the oldest of the unenumerated rights is probably that to engage in political activity. At the time of the framing and adoption of the first Ten Amendments political parties were still in the process of forming. There were federalists and antifederalists. There were antirepublicans and republicans. But there were as yet no political parties. Indeed, Washington frowned upon their growth. He regarded them as both factional and sectional. When he was conferring with Madison in May 1792 about his wish to retire at the end of his first term and about the manner of his announcement to do so, he complained about the "spirit of party" that was growing in the government and was dividing the Secretaries of State and the Treasury (Jefferson and Hamilton). Madison responded that the new spirit of party was an argument for Washington's remaining.

Washington asked Madison to prepare for him a draft of a farewell address. Madison did so, but in his draft he did not condemn political parties. However, when Washington and Hamilton finished with Madison's draft four years later it did contain such a condemnation. Washington in his Farewell Address, published in September 1796, warned "in the most solemn manner against the baneful effects of the Spirit of Party."

Madison could not have condemned political parties, for he favored their development. Indeed, he may be said to have been the first to have given a name as such to a political party in this country. In an article entitled A Candid State of Parties, published in September 1792, he said, referring to the party of Jefferson and himself: "The republican party, as it may be termed. . . ." Before that the name, as Irving Brant pointed out, "was simply the expression of a state of mind."

Thus political parties and the right to engage in political activity, although not contemporaneous with the framing and adoption of the federal Bill of Rights, go back almost that far. And in a recent case, Sweezy v. New Hampshire, involving a contempt conviction of a socialist who lectured at the University of New Hampshire and who refused to answer the inquiries of the attorney general of New Hampshire about his lecture and about the activities of his wife and others in the formation of the Progressive Party in that state, Mr. Justice Frankfurter in a concurring opinion in which Mr. Justice Harlan joined, recognized not only a right to engage in political activity but also a right of political privacy: "* * * But the inviolability of privacy belonging to a citizen's political loyalties has so overwhelming an importance to the well-being of our kind of society that it cannot be constitutionally encroached upon on the basis of so meagre a countervailing interest of the State as may be argumentatively found in the remote, shadowy threat to the security of New Hampshire allegedly presented in the origins and contributing elements of the Progressive Party and in petitioner's relations to these."

But Section 9(a) of the Hatch Act, as amended, now provides in its second sentence: "No officer or employee in the executive branch of the Federal Government, or any agency or department thereof, shall take any active part in political management or in political campaigns." Is such a provision constitutional? The Court in *United Public Workers* v. *Mitchell* held that it was, saying: ". . . when objection is made that the exercise of a federal power infringes upon rights reserved by the Ninth and Tenth Amendments, the inquiry must be directed toward the granted power under which the action of the Union was taken. If granted power is found, necessarily the objection of invasion of those rights, reserved by the Ninth and Tenth Amendments must fail. * * *" This language was quoted with approval in the recent *Roth* case. The Court, although it did not distinguish between express and implied powers, was dealing with an implied power. Specifically the Court ruled: ". . . for regulation of employees it is not necessary that the act regulated be anything more than an act reasonably deemed by Congress to interfere with efficiency of the public service. * * *" In the case of a conflict between an implied power and an unenumerated right, the power will prevail. Madison would have assumed as much, for he felt that the best check to power was a rival power.

Freedom of Movement

The unenumerated right which the government conceded was that to travel. King John of England more than seven centuries earlier made a comparable concession in clause forty-two of the Magna Carta: "It shall be lawful in future for any one (excepting always those imprisoned or outlawed in accordance with the law of the kingdom * * *) to leave our kingdom and to return, safe and secure by land and water, except for a short period in time of war, on grounds of public policy—reserving always the allegiance due to us." Our government gave its concession in its brief in the *Kent* and *Briehl* cases.

In view of the insistence in this country, almost from colonial times, on the freedom to cross state lines as one of the privileges of citizenship, it could be contended that egress and ingress across national boundaries was an implied constitutional privilege of federal citizens. But if one were to rest one's argument on this ground, it would benefit only those who are citizens. It would not help those who have a resident status here but who are not citizens. In view of this and in view of the government's concession in the *Kent* and *Briehl* cases and the Court's statement in those cases that the Fifth Amendment's due process clause protected an individual's freedom of movement, one will base one's support of this right on that clause.

Infringements on the right of freedom of movement have arisen in various ways. For one thing, the State Department has refused to validate or to issue passports for travel to certain countries. For instance, in 1956 the State Department announced that it would refuse to validate United States passports for American newsmen to travel to Communist China. Three newsmen nevertheless went. One of these was William D. Worthy of The Baltimore Afro-American. He had his passport revoked. In 1957 the State Department refused to validate Mrs. Franklin D. Roosevelt's passport for travel to Communist China. She wanted to make a newsgathering journey there and hoped to interview some of the members of the Communist regime. Or again the following year the State Department took similar action with reference to Waldo Frank, an author, who had been invited to lecture at the University of Peiping on the works of Walt Whitman. The State Department also refused a passport to Mr. Worthy. In the second place, the State Department has denied passports to those Americans whom it regarded as members, or followers, or supporters of the international Communist movement. This list is a long one. In addition to Rockwell Kent, Dr. Walter Briehl and Weldon Bruce Dayton, it includes: Paul Robeson, the singer; Martin D. Kamen of St. Louis, an atomic scientist; Leonard B. Boudin, a New York lawyer; Dr. Otto Nathan, Albert Einstein's executor; engineer Henry Willcox and his wife; screen writer Carl N. Foreman; and playwrights Edward Chodorov and Donald Ogden Stewart. It includes many others that we do not know about. In the third place, the State Department has often denied passports on the basis of confidential information.

A few of those to whom the State Department denied passports went to court, and recently the Supreme Court in the *Kent* and *Briehl* and *Dayton* cases held that the Secretary of State in denying passports to the petitioners acted without authority. However, in the instances of Messrs. Worthy and Frank the courts have so far sustained the State Department. On September 30, 1959 both asked the Supreme Court to review their cases. Representative Charles O. Porter of Oregon also asked the State Department for a passport for travel to communist China, was turned down and went to court. He felt that it was "the duty and prerogative of a Congressman to see the world about which he legislates." Federal District Judge Matthew F. McGuire granted the government's motion for a summary judgment. In addition, many passport restrictions still remain.

Furthermore, and despite the Supreme Court's opinions in the *Kent* and *Briehl* and *Dayton* cases, the President and the Secretary of State urgently requested legislation to authorize the latter to do what he sought to do in those and other cases. Just three weeks after the Court's decisions in those cases President Eisenhower sent a message to Congress in which he said: ". . . It is essential that the Government today have power to deny passports where their possession would seriously impair the conduct of the foreign relations of the United States or would be inimical to the security of the United States. * * *

"The Secretary of State will submit to the Congress a proposed draft of legislation to carry out these recommendations.

"I wish to emphasize the urgency of the legislation I have recommended. * * *"

The next day Secretary of State John Foster Dulles sent to Congress the administration's proposed bill. The same day Senator Theodore F. Green of Rhode Island introduced it in the Senate and Representative, now Senator, Kenneth B. Keating of New York in the House. This bill contained many restrictive provisions. It proposed the denial of a passport wherever to grant it would be inimical to the security of the United States. An applicant had to state whether at any time within the past ten years he had been a supporter of the international Communist movement. The bill sought to create a Passport Hearing Board, consisting of three officers of the State Department, which could consider oral or documentary evidence without making such evidence part of the open record. Both before and after the introduction of the administration's bill various members of Congress introduced many similar bills. Some of these were even more restrictive of an individual's right to freedom of movement than was the administration's bill. None of these measures passed, but another Congress is in session.

Such a measure will impair at least three unenumerated rights: freedom of movement; to knowledge; and to be confronted with the witnesses against one. As for the right to freedom of movement, counsel's reliance will be on the due process clause of the Fifth Amendment. He will probably not even cite the Ninth Amendment.

Knowledge

One of the newest of the unenumerated rights is that to knowledge. Our attention was focused on this right not only by the restrictive policy of the State Department in the issuance of passports and the granting of visas, but also by the studies of the Special Subcommittee on Government Information into official secrecy. This Subcommittee is under the chairmanship of Representative John E. Moss of California. It prepared a report in which it concluded:

Slowly, almost imperceptibly, a paper curtain has descended over the Federal Government. Behind this curtain lies an attitude novel to democratic government—an attitude which says that we, the officials, not you, the people, will determine how much you are to be told about your own Government.

The paper curtain, now many layers thick, is not the fault of any one administration or any one party. It has developed over a 30-year period. And it began with the very "bigness" of Federal Government that is accepted today by the leadership of both political parties.

*   *   *

Unfortunately, there has existed and still does exist in high governmental and military circles a strange psychosis that the Government's business is not the people's business. . . . This psychosis persists to the point where some Government officials decide what is good for the public to know.

The Subcommittee noted as one of "the most ominous developments" an effort to extend government control over non-security information which was not eligible for classification. It further found that the informational policies and practices of the Defense Department were "the most restrictive—and at the same time the most confused—of any major branch of the Federal Government. . . . The Defense Department and its component branches are classifying documents at such a rate that the Pentagon may some day become no more than a huge storage bin protected by triple-combination safes and a few security guards."

During the course of the hearings which the subcommittee conducted, Trevor Gardner, former Assistant Secretary of the Air Force for research and development, related an incident which epitomized what has happened. He told of the case of a scientist of international reputation who had his clearance withdrawn, but who had such inventive ability that he kept coming up with secret and top secret ideas. The Air Force solved the problem by giving him an unclassified contract. However, as soon as he produced interesting results, they classified the result and he no longer had access to them.

The problem of official secrecy reached such proportions that two leading newspapermen published books on it in 1956: Kent Cooper, *The Right to Know*; and James Russell Wiggins, *Freedom or Secrecy?* Cooper was formerly executive director of the Associated Press, and Wiggins was executive editor of the *Washington Post* and *Times-Herald*. Cooper had written his book some years earlier. In a newly written foreword he said:

Practically all of this book was written five years ago. At that time and earlier a trend in the withholding of news was discernible. I decided to defer publication for a few years to see if within that time the government of this free country would reverse the trend.

It has not done so. Instead, in its treatment of news it is in some respect slowly pressing toward the totalitarian pattern. It is doing so, in my opinion, with no intention of contravening a canon of liberty and without realizing that it was the antithesis of this practice that helped to make this nation great. * * *

Wiggins had earlier criticized the "ominous" secrecy prevalent in the Defense Department and the National Security Council. Under one of Secretary Wilson's directives, advising defense project contractors to release no information that might be of "possible value to a potential enemy," the military can encourage management to suppress the release even of certain unclassified economic information.

The Federal Bar Association devoted the January 1959 issue of its Journal to the subject, *Executive Privilege: Public's Right to Know and Public Interest*, with an introduction by Congressman Moss and articles by Mr. Wiggins and Senator Thomas C. Hennings, Jr., of Missouri, among others. Senator Hennings' article was also inserted in the Congressional Record, on the request of Senator Lyndon B. Johnson of Texas, the Senate leader. Yet more recently Senator Clinton P. Anderson of New Mexico, chairman of the Joint Committee on Atomic Energy had an article in the *New York Times Magazine* entitled *"Top Secret"—But Should It Be?*

In opposition to this trend toward official secrecy has come some ameliatory legislation, beginning on a state level. In 1955 Ohio enacted a law which requires all meetings of local government boards, commissions and agencies to be open to the public. Some of Ohio's local governing bodies had found the federal government's practice of official secrecy too tempting to resist. In 1957 California, Connecticut, Illinois and Pennsylvania adopted similar legislation. California enacted a total of sixty-six separate statutes providing for open meetings of various governing bodies. Such laws came to be known as right-to-know laws. Then the following year, as a result of the labors of Congressman Moss and his Subcommittee, the federal government itself adopted a so-called anti-secrecy law. This act was in the form of a one-sentence addition to 5 U.S.C. §22, which was formerly Rev. Stat. §161, and which in turn derived from a number of acts, including a series of four enacted in 1789. The four acts of 1789 simply gave the Secretaries of State, War, and the Treasury custody of the records of their departments. Section 22, among other things, simply authorized the heads of departments "to prescribe regulations, not inconsistent with law, for * * * the custody, use, and preservation of" records. The one-sentence addition provides: "This section does not authorize withholding information from the public or limiting the availability of records to the public." With reference to the passage of this measure Congressman Moss wrote: "Each of the ten Cabinet departments opposed this amendment. The reasons ranged from the attitude that the law had been on the books for 168 years and therefore should not be changed, to the contention that the amendment was unclear.

"Passage of the amendment is merely a first, timid step toward eradicating unnecessary Government secrecy. The new legislation merely eliminates one glaring violation of the right to know."

As Congressman Moss indicated, despite this legislation most of the current restrictions on an individual's right to knowledge remain. Moreover, the government and various of its officials are seeking yet additional such restrictions. The administration is seeking them with reference to the issuance of passports. As another illustration, the government's Commission on Government Security made a report in 1957 in which it recommended that Congress make it a crime for one to publish information classified as "top secret" or "secret" if one knew or had reason to believe that such information was so classified.

Suppose this Commission's proposed legislation were to pass and suppose that the Atomic Energy Commission in conformity with an appropriate executive order were to classify information about hydrogen bomb tests and the fallout of radioactive strontium-90 as secret. Or suppose that newspapers were to send reporters to Communist China in violation of passport restrictions. The newspapers' position in both instances would be that in this country the people decide issues and that they are not in a position intelligently to do so unless they first have the facts. If the government were to proceed punitively against such newspapers, what would the constitutional defense of counsel representing them be? In the case of violations of passport restrictions, since such

restrictions also involve an impairment of the right of freedom of movement, counsel will rely on the due process clause of the Fifth Amendment. To the extent that the right to knowledge is involved, since this
right has not yet been recognized under the due process clauses, counsel
will rely on the First and Ninth Amendments as well as the due
process clause of the Fifth Amendment. In the other suppositious case,
involving as it does the right to knowledge, counsel will again urge the
First, Fifth and Ninth Amendments. Counsel will argue that freedom
of the press, guaranteed by the First Amendment, includes not only the
publication but also the gathering of news, and that the freedom of
speech guarantee of this amendment includes the right to knowledge in
order that one may speak intelligently.

Confrontation

Our State Department's restrictions on the issuance of passports
impair a third unenumerated right, that to be confronted with the
witnesses against one. Of course, this right is secured in criminal cases
by various constitutional and statutory provisions. In federal criminal
cases it is protected by the Sixth Amendment's provision that "the
accused shall enjoy the right * * * to be confronted with the witnesses
against him." Forty-three states have similar constitutional provisions.
Four more have statutory provisions to this effect. Some have both. Only
one of the forty-eight states, Idaho, apparently has no provision for
confrontation.

However, these provisions relate to criminal proceedings. In other
types of proceedings the right to confrontation has not established itself.
On the contrary, there have been increasing instances in which an individual's rights and status have been determined on the basis of the
statements of secret informers. Included among them are the State
Department's determinations with reference to the denial or issuance of
passports. The State Department still claims that it can make such
determinations without confrontation, and the courts have not yet
finally ruled against it. The federal district judges have divided on the
question. Federal Judge Luther W. Youngdahl in *Boudin* v. *Dulles*
ruled for confrontation. But Federal Judge Joseph C. McGarraghy in
Dayton v. *Dulles* reached a contrary conclusion and sustained a passport
denial which was based in part on confidential information. The Court
of Appeals for the District of Columbia Circuit did not find it necessary
at this point to reach the question. When the *Dayton* case came before
Judge McGarraghy a second time, he again ruled against confrontation.
This time the Court of Appeals did reach the issue and ruled similarly:
"* * * the problem is whether disclosure would adversely affect our

internal security or the conduct of our foreign affairs. The cases and common sense hold that the courts cannot compel the Secretary to disclose information garnered by him in confidence in this area. If he need not disclose the information he has, the only other course is for the courts to accept his assertion that disclosure would be detrimental in fields of highest importance entrusted to his exclusive care. We think we must follow that course." But this time the Supreme Court did not find it necessary to reach the question.

Yet other types of proceedings in which an individual's rights and status have been determined without confrontation have been: loyalty and security investigations and hearings of federal, often state, and even a multitude of employees of private employers who have had defense or research contracts with the federal government, and of members and former members of our armed forces; determinations involving aliens; and selective service hearings to determine whether an individual was a conscientious objector. In one recent instance the Military Sea Transportation Service, a Navy branch, ordered a marine engineer and two seamen off an American President Lines ship for security reasons. All three seamen had Coast Guard clearance. The Navy branch took this step without notice or charges. According to this governmental agency, even to disclose the reasons would "endanger the security of the United States." The government has also denied cash benefits due more than 250 former Korean war prisoners because of secret Army charges of collaboration. Various cases arising in such types of proceedings have reached the Supreme Court, and three of them were there at the last term, but so far the Court has not spoken out against the practice of using secret informers. On the contrary, the Court has sustained it. The Court did so in the first two such cases to come before it, *Bailey* v. *Richardson*, and *Washington* v. *McGrath*, but by an evenly divided court. These cases arose out of federal loyalty investigations and hearings. In a third such case, that of Dr. John P. Peters of Yale University, the Court ducked the issue. In *United States* v. *Nugent* the Court sustained the practice of using secret informers in Selective Service hearings, and in *Jay* v. *Boyd* in suspension of deportation proceedings.

The three recent cases which involved the issue of confrontation were: *Vitarelli* v. *Seaton; Greene* v. *McElroy;* and *Taylor* v. *McElroy.* In all three cases the lower courts ruled against confrontation. The Supreme Court reversed, but in two of the cases did not reach the issue, and in the third said that it did not.

The right of confrontation, as Chief Justice Warren indicated in the Court's opinion in the *Greene* case, should exist in any proceeding which involves a determination as to one's future status. We have no less a

protagonist for the position than President Eisenhower himself. In an
address to the B'nai B'rith Anti-Defamation League in Washington
D.C., in which he described Wild Bill Hickock's code in Abilene,
Kansas, he said:

I was raised in a little town of which most of you have never heard. But
in the West it is a famous place. It is called Abilene, Kansas. We had as
our Marshal for a long time a man named Wild Bill Hickock. If you don't
know anything about him, read your Westerns more. Now that town had a
code, and I was raised as a boy to prize that code.

It was: meet anyone face to face with whom you disagree. You could
not sneak up on him from behind, or do any damage to him, without suffering the penalty of an outraged citizenry. If you met him face to face and
took the same risks he did, you could get away with almost anything, as
long as the bullet was in the front.

And today, although none of you has the great fortune, I think, of being
from Abilene, Kansas, you live after all by the same code, in your ideals and
in the respect you give to certain qualities. In this country, if someone dis-
likes you, or accuses you, he must come up in front. He cannot hide behind
the shadow. He cannot assassinate you or your character from behind, without suffering the penalties an outraged citizenry will impose.

And his advice was not entirely lost. Justices Frankfurter and Douglas
in *Jay* v. *Boyd* both quoted from this speech—in dissenting opinions.
Mr. Justice Frankfurter said: "President Eisenhower has explained what
is fundamental in any American code. A code devised by the Attorney
General for determining human rights cannot be less than Wild Bill
Hickock's code in Abilene, Kansas: * * *" Justice Douglas added: "The
statement that President Eisenhower made in 1953 on the American
code of fair play is more than interesting Americana. As my Brother
Frankfurter says, it is Americana that is highly relevant to our present
problem."

So far there has been but one strong decision in favor of confrontation
in cases arising out of loyalty—security programs, that of *Parker* v.
Lester. In that case the Court of Appeals for the Ninth Circuit invalidated the Coast Guard's security procedure because it failed to provide for this. Judge Walter L. Pope of Montana in the court's opinion
wrote: "But surely it is better that these agencies suffer some handicap
than that the citizens of a freedom loving country shall be denied that
which has always been considered their birthright. Indeed, it may well
be that in the long run nothing but beneficial results will come from a
lessening of such talebearing. . . . The objective of perpetuating a
doubtful system of secret informers likely to bear upon the innocent as
well as upon the guilty and carrying so high a degree of unfairness to

the merchant seaman involved cannot justify an abandonment here of the ancient standards of due process. . . . the time has not come when we have to abandon a system of liberty for one modeled on that of the Communists. . . ."

With reference to the right of confrontation in other than criminal cases, there is no doubt as to the constitutional ground on which counsel contending for the right will rest their cases: it will be on the due process clauses. It has been on the due process clause of the Fifth Amendment that such cases have already been considered. It was on this clause that the court rested its decision in *Parker* v. *Lester*. It was on this ground, to take another instance, that Justice Douglas rested his concurring opinion in the *Peters* case, saying: "Confrontation and cross-examination under oath are essential, if the American ideal of due process is to remain a vital force in our public life. * * * If the sources of information need protection, they should be kept secret. But once they are used to destroy a man's reputation and deprive him of his 'liberty,' they must be put to the test of due process of law. * * *" To the extent that the right to confrontation in other than criminal cases will be recognized without specific constitutional or statutory provisions, it will be under due process clauses. It will not be under the Ninth Amendment.

Jury Trial in Contempt Cases

Another right which, like confrontation, some have urged be extended beyond its traditional bounds, at least in cases of a punitive nature, is that to a jury trial. A recent controversy and several recent cases produced an insistence that the right to a jury trial be extended to criminal contempt of court cases, particularly if an individual's liberty was involved. The recent controversy involved the power to be given to federal judges to punish alleged contempts, and arose during the deliberations on the Civil Rights Act of 1957. After long and, at times, heated debates in Congress, the compromise which became law contained this third proviso: "*Provided further, however,* That in the event such proceeding for criminal contempt be tried before a judge without a jury and the sentence of the court upon conviction is a fine in excess of the sum of $300 or imprisonment in excess of forty-five days, the accused in said proceeding, upon demand therefor, shall be entitled to a trial de novo before a jury, which shall conform as near as may be to the practice in other criminal cases." Very recently under this section a federal district judge in Alabama ordered a state circuit judge to appear before him to show cause why he should not be held in criminal contempt for refusing the federal Civil Rights Commission access to voter registration records.

The federal judge later cleared the state judge: he found that the latter had in fact aided the federal Commission, although feigning to defy it.

The recent cases involved the power of federal judges to impose criminal contempt of court sentences on Gus Hall, Robert Thompson, Gilbert Green and Henry Winston, four of the defendants in the *Dennis* case, the first Foley Square Smith Act conspiracy prosecution of leaders of the American Communist party. After the Supreme Court's affirmance of the judgments of conviction in that case, these four defendants, together with four of the defendants in the *Flynn* case, the second Foley Square Smith Act conspiracy indictment, staged a mass flight. Hall was former Ohio chairman and acting national chairman of the American Communist party; Thompson, New York State chairman; Green, Illinois chairman; and Winston, national organization secretary. All four, who had already been convicted and sentenced on their conspiracy indictment, also drew sentences for criminal contempt of court for willful disobedience of a surrender order. Green, Winston and Hall each drew three years, and Thompson four. All sentences were affirmed on appeal. The Supreme Court granted certiorari in the case of Green and Winston but denied it in those of Hall and Thompson. However, the Supreme Court, as did the Court of Appeals for the Second Circuit, affirmed the contempt sentences. Four members of the Court dissented, Chief Justice Warren and Justices Black, Douglas and Brennan. Justice Black wrote a vigorous dissent in which Chief Justice Warren and Justice Douglas joined. He argued:

The power of a judge to inflict punishment for criminal contempt by means of a summary proceeding stands as an anomaly in the law. In my judgment the time has come for a fundamental and searching reconsideration of the validity of this power which has aptly been characterized by a State Supreme Court as, "perhaps, nearest akin to despotic power of any power existing under our form of government." * * * I would hold that the defendants here were entitled to be tried by a jury after indictment by a grand jury and in full accordance with all the procedural safeguards required by the Constitution for "all criminal proceedings." * * *

The right to a jury trial in criminal contempt of court cases, like confrontation, cannot depend for its recognition on the Ninth Amendment. Rather it will have to rely either on new statutory or constitutional provisions, or on new constructions of existing constitutional requirements for jury trials in criminal cases, for example, that part of the federal Constitution's Sixth Amendment which states: "In all criminal prosecutions, the accused shall enjoy the right to a speedy and public trial, by an impartial jury * * *".

Use of the Mails

The Post Office Department long contended that the use of the mails was a privilege which Congress could regulate at will. This contention is obsolete, so much so, that Justice Harlan in his dissenting opinion in the recent case of *Roth* v. *United States* characterized it as a "hoary dogma." Today the use of the mails is a right, and an important one. As Justice Holmes expressively put it in *Milwaukee Publishing Co.* v. *Burleson:* "* * * The United States may give up the Post Office when it sees fit, but while it carries it on the use of the mails is almost as much a part of free speech as the right to use our tongues * * *." He said this in a dissenting opinion, but today it represents the law.

Today the mails are so much a part of our daily lives that an order barring one from the use of them, as the Court remarked in *Reilly* v. *Pinkus,* "could wholly destroy a business." Or as the Court of Appeals for the District of Columbia Circuit observed in *Pike* v. *Walker:* "Whatever may have been the voluntary nature of the postal system in the period of its establishment, it is now the main artery through which the business, social and personal affairs of the people are conducted and upon which depends in a greater degree than upon any other activity of government the promotion of the general welfare. * * *"

Today if the government were to act in an arbitrary, or unfair, or exclusionary way with reference to one's use of the mails, one would have a constitutional objection. However, one would rest one's objection either on the First Amendment or on the due process clause of the Fifth, or both; but not on the Ninth Amendment. For instance, in the *Pike* case the court further said: ". . . It would be going a long way, therefore, to say that in the managment of the Post Office the people have no definite rights reserved by the First and Fifth Amendments of the Constitution * * *."

Peaceful Picketing

Because of the Supreme Court's identification of peaceful picketing with freedom of speech, relief in this field against governmental action will depend on the First Amendment as to federal action and on the due process clause of the Fourteenth Amendment as to state action. Once again it will not rest on the Ninth Amendment.

Construing a Constitution

The Ninth Amendment thus ends up with a small role. Nor will the fact that we have before us a constitutional provision augment that role appreciably.

It may help a little, for in construing a constitution one is engaged in an effort to make the document as timeless as possible. As Chief Justice Marshall emphasized in *McCulloch* v. *Maryland*: "* * * we must never forget that it is a *constitution* we are expounding. * * * a constitution, intended to endure for ages to come, and consequently, to be adapted to the various *crises* of human affairs. * * *" Or as he added in the Court's opinion in *Cohens* v. *Virginia*: "* * * a constitution is framed for ages to come, and is designed to approach immortality, as nearly as human institutions can approach it. * * *" Or as the Court elaborated in *Weems* v. *United States*:

Legislation, both statutory and constitutional, is enacted, it is true, from an experience of evils but its general language should not therefore be necessarily confined to the form that evil had theretofore taken. Time works changes, brings into existence new conditions and purposes. Therefore a principle, to be vital, must be capable of wider application than the mischief which gave it birth. This is peculiarly true of constitutions. They are not ephemeral enactments, designed to meet passing occasions. They are, to use the words of Chief Justice Marshall, "designed to approach immortality as nearly as human institutions can approach it." The future is their care, and provision for events of good and bad tendencies of which no prophecy can be made. In the application of a constitution, therefore, our contemplation cannot be only of what has been, but of what may be. Under any other rule a constitution would indeed be as easy of application as it would be deficient in efficacy and power. Its general principles would have little value, and be converted by precedent into impotent and lifeless formulas. Rights declared in words might be lost in reality. * * *

But even if one takes this approach, and even if one accepts the fact that the Court as final arbiter has a molding as well as a judicial function, one should not carry this approach as far as Justice Black does. He would hold, for instance, that the privileges and immunities and due process clauses of the Fourteenth Amendment make the first eight amendments applicable to the states. Or again, he would construe the Sixth Amendment's provision for a jury trial to be applicable to criminal contempt of court cases. One should stop somewhat short of his position or one will no longer be engaged in construing the Constitution by applying it to new situations; one will be engaged in amending it.

If one takes the approach of a broad but not amendatory construction of the Constitution, this estimate of Professor Leslie W. Dunbar will prove to be substantially correct as to the role of the Ninth Amendment: "Neither the Court's progress in filling the privileges and immunities clauses of the Constitution with content, nor its efforts to keep manageable and contained all the matter read into 'due process' gives encouragement to the idea that the ninth amendment provides another fertile garden for cultivation." One will occasionally cite the Ninth Amendment in the case of an unenumerated right not yet established under the due process clauses, such as that to knowledge; but even here one will rely on the due process clauses as well. Moreover, one will usually rely on these clauses for the protection of established unenumerated rights without a further reference to the Ninth Amendment; and these clauses, by virtue of their historic roots and historical role, will in most instances satisfactorily meet the demands on them.

CHAPTER I

P. 4, 1. 26, 343 U.S. 250, 288; p. 4, 1. 28, 332 U.S. 46, 71–72; p. 4, 1. 37, 338 U.S. 25, 39–40 (A federal conviction based upon such evidence, at least if seized by a federal official, would have been reversed. Weeks v. United States 232 U.S. 383. In a recent case the court reached the same result even though such evidence was illegally seized by a state official. Hanna v. United States, 260 F.2d 723. Cf. Benanti v. United States, 355 U.S. 96); p. 5, 1. 30, 302 U.S. 319, 325; p. 8, 1. 17, A woman claiming to be one of the daughters, Anastasia, says that she escaped; p. 8, 1. 38, Gitlow v. New York, 268 U.S. 652; p. 9, 1. 5, People v. Lloyd, 304 Ill. 23; p. 9, 1. 28, 32 STAT. 1214; p. 10, 1. 4, 249 U.S. 47; 268 U.S. 652; p. 11, 1. 7, 250 U.S. 616, 631.

CHAPTER II

P. 12, 1. 21, 2 FARRAND, RECORDS OF THE FEDERAL CONVENTION 144 (A report written by James Wilson of Pennsylvania and edited by Rutledge contained a similar provision. 2 id. at 173); p. 12 1. 31, 2 id. at 617–18; 5 ELLIOT, DEBATES ON THE FEDERAL CONSTITUTION 545 (rev. ed.); p. 13, 1. 10, PAMPHLETS ON THE CONSTITUTION 156 (Ford ed.); p. 13, 1. 27, 2 ELLIOT, DEBATES ON THE FEDERAL CONSTITUTION 436–37 (2d ed.); p. 14, 1. 23, 12 THE PAPERS OF THOMAS JEFFERSON 440 (Boyd ed.) (Article II of the Articles of Confederation 1777 provided: "Each State retains its sovereignty, freedom, and independence, and every power, jurisdiction, and right, which is not by this confederation, expressly delegated to the United States in Congress assembled."); p. 14, 1. 30, 3 ELLIOT, DEBATES ON THE FEDERAL CONSTITUTION 620, 626–27 (2d ed.); p. 15, 1. 19, 5 THE WRITINGS OF JAMES MADISON 271–72 (Hunt ed.); p. 15, 1. 34, 14 THE PAPERS OF THOMAS JEFFERSON 659–60 (Boyd ed.) (Wythe, Blair and Pendleton were celebrated judges who constituted Virginia's High Court of Chancery. The quotation is from HORACE, ODES, bk. III, ode iii.) (All of Jefferson's private letters came by diplomatic pouch, so that his letter of March 15, 1789 probably reached Madison before the latter presented his proposed amendments to the House of Representatives of the First Congress on June 8, 1789); p. 16, 1. 39, 1 ANNALS OF CONG. 436–38, 738, 439 (Gales comp.); p. 17, 1. 25, BRANT, JAMES MADISON FATHER OF THE CONSTITUTION 267; p. 17, 1. 32, CHAFEE, FREE SPEECH IN THE UNITED STATES 22; p. 17, 1. 36, 6 THE HISTORY OF ENGLAND 360–73, 7 id. at 168–69 (new ed.) (In the colonies licensing came to an end by 1725. See DUNIWAY, THE DEVELOPMENT OF FREEDOM OF THE PRESS IN MASSACHUSETTS 89, n.2); p. 17, 1. 41, Edward's Case, 13 Co. Rep. 9, 10; p. 18, 1. 11, 13 & 14 Chas. 2, c. 33; p. 18, 1. 42, Vol. 4 at *151–52, *150–51 (Coke in De Libellis Famosis, 5 Co. Rep. 125a, explained: "Every libel . . . is made either against a private man, or against a magistrate or public person. *If it be against a private man it deserves a severe punishment,* for although the libel be made against

307

one, yet it incites all those of the same family, kindred, or society to revenge, and so tends *per consequens* to quarrels and breach of the peace, and may be the cause of shedding of blood and of great inconvenience: *if it be against a magistrate, or other public person, it is a greater offence;* for it concerns not only the breach of the peace, but also the scandal of Government; for what greater scandal of Government can there be than to have corrupt or wicked magistrates to be appointed and constituted by the King to govern his subjects under him? . . .''); p. 19, l. 39, ANNALS OF CONG., 3d Cong., 2d Sess. 934. (See also, e.g., the Virginia Declaration of Rights (1776), written by George Mason, which provided in the second paragraph: "That all power is vested in, and consequently derived from, the people; that magistrates are their trustees and servants, and at all times amenable to them." When the Federal Convention of 1787 took up the manner of choosing the chief executive, Mason made this point in converse fashion: ". . . Having for his primary object, for the pole star of his political conduct, the preservation of the rights of the people, he held it as an essential point, as the very palladium of Civil liberty, that the great officers of State, and particularly the Executive should at fixed periods return to that mass from which they were at first taken, in order that they may feel & respect those rights & interests, Which are again to be personally valuable to them. . . ." 2 FARRAND, RECORDS OF THE FEDERAL CONVENTION 119–20. Madison in the proposed amendments which he put before the first Congress borrowed from the second paragraph of the Virginia Declaration of Rights. In his first amendment he proposed: "That there be prefixed to the Constitution a declaration, that all power is originally vested in, and consequently derived from, the people." 1 ANNALS OF CONG. 433); p. 20, l. 6, Vol. 2, at 300; p. 20, l. 29, 2 AMERICAN STATE PAPERS, FOREIGN RELATIONS 191, 196; p. 20, l. 32, 341 U.S. 494, 503; p. 20, l. 39, 1 STAT. 596; p. 20, l. 42, CONG. GLOBE, 24th Cong., 1st Sess. 10; p. 21, l. 2, Letters of September 30, 1805 to Benjamin Rush. OLD FAMILY LETTERS: COPIED FROM THE ORIGINALS FOR ALEXANDER BIDDLE, Series A, 78, 84; p. 21, l. 8, 32 Geo. 3, c. 60 (". . . on every such trial, the jury sworn to try the issue may give a general verdict of guilty or not guilty upon the whole matter put in issue . . . and shall not be required or directed, by the court or judge . . . to find the defendant . . . guilty, merely on the proof of the publication by such defendant . . . of the paper charged to be a libel, and of the sense ascribed to the same in such indictment or information."); p. 21, l. 16, 4 ELLIOT, DEBATES ON THE FEDERAL CONSTITUTION 541, 542–43, 545 (2d ed.); p. 22, l. 4, 6 THE WRITINGS OF JAMES MADISON 339 (Hunt ed.) (A little over a decade after Madison in his *Report* cut the ground from under the argument that Congress had power to punish crime under the common law of England, the Supreme Court so ruled in a case which involved an indictment for a libel on the President and the Congress. United States *v.* Hudson, 7 Cranch (11 U.S.) 31, 32. The Court specifically stated: "Although this question is brought up now, for the first time, to be decided by this Court, we consider it as having been long since settled in public opinion. In no other case, for many years, has this jurisdiction been asserted; and the general acquiescence of legal men shows the prevalence of opinion in favor of the negative of the proposition."); p. 22, l. 11, U.S. CONST. art I, §8, cl. 15; p. 22, l. 28, 6 THE WRITINGS OF JAMES MADISON, 383–84, 386–90, 392–93 (Hunt ed.); 4 ELLIOT, DEBATES ON THE FEDERAL CONSTITUTION 568, 569–73 (2d ed.); p. 24, l. 39, 3 ANNALS OF CONG. 3004–5; p. 25, l. 9, AN INQUIRY INTO THE PRINCIPLES AND POLICY OF THE GOVERNMENT OF THE UNITED STATES 437 (1950); p. 25, l. 31, 1 MESSAGES AND PAPERS OF THE PRESIDENTS 322 (Richardson ed.); p. 25, l. 42, 250 U.S. 616, 630 (Justice Jackson in his dissenting opinion in Beauharnais *v.* Illinois, 343 U.S. 250, 289, commented: ". . . I think today's better opinion regards the enactment as a breach of the First Amendment and certainly Mr. Justice Holmes and Mr. Justice Brandeis thought so."); p. 26, l. 2, 6 A HISTORY OF THE AMERICAN PEOPLE 39 (documentary ed.); p. 27, l. 15, S.Rep. 118, 24th Cong., 1st Sess. 1–5; (The committee's observation that the struggle over the Sedition Act of 1798 caused a great political revolution which brought the Republican, now Democratic, party into power is an overstatement. Schachner in his THE FOUNDING FATHERS 549 pointed out: "Geographical divisions—the South against the North, with the Middle States wavering uneasily in between—were far more potent influences; and had not changed since the preceding election or even the beginning of the nation. These were the same divisions that were to culminate in the great Civil War, and were bottomed on the same essential conflicts. Nor did the Alien and Sedition Acts contribute appreciably to the result—another common claim that must be dismissed. There is no evidence that any votes were shifted from one party to another because of them. Those who opposed the Acts had been Republicans before, and continued to be so. Jefferson had failed of election four years before by a hairsbreadth without their aid and benefit."); p. 27, l. 23, CONG. GLOBE APP., 24th Cong., 1st Sess. 437, 443; p. 27, l. 28, CONG. GLOBE, 24th Cong., 1st Sess. 299 (During the course of the debates Calhoun pointed out that "if they once acknowledge the power of Congress to suppress the transmission of these incendiary papers directly, and to say what was incendiary, it would be conceding to it to decide what was not incendiary, as they were in their nature correlative rights. . . ." Id. at 298); p. 27, l. 33, CONG. GLOBE APP., 24th Cong., 1st Sess. 439, 437, 440; p. 28, l. 22, 5 Stat. 87; p. 28, l. 28, Esquire v. Hannegan, 151 F.2d 49, 55, aff'd, 327 U.S. 146; p. 28, l. 34, 96 U.S. 727, 734; p. 29, l. 9, 49 NILES' WEEKLY REGISTER 236 (Of course the Southern states by local measures tried to prevent the distribution of abolitionist literature. Nye in his FETTERED FREEDOM 65–66, 68–69, wrote: "Failure to control the distribution of abolitionist literature by federal legislation did not mean, however, that the mails were thrown open at once to the antislavery presses. Southern States which did not already have laws governing the publication and circulation of 'incendiary' matter quickly passed them, and other states strengthened existing legislation. South Carolina depended upon its law of 1820, and Kentucky upon laws passed in 1799 and 1831. North Carolina had passed similar legislation in 1830, Louisiana and Mississippi in 1831, and Alabama in 1832 and 1835. Maryland's law of 1835 sufficed for a time; Missouri enacted legislation of the usual type in 1837; and Georgia relied upon local legislation. Virginia, in 1836, passed a law requiring postmasters to notify justices of the peace whenever they received 'incendiary' publications in their offices; that officer would then judge their offensiveness, burn them publicly if they violated the law, and arrest the addressee if he had subscribed to them with the aim of assisting an abolition society. Throughout the years to 1861 the Southern states reaffirmed and strengthened their laws adding new interpretations and closing loopholes. . . .

"In general the Southern interpretation of the federal mails law of 1836 held that state laws, governing the reception and distribution of 'incendiary' matter through the post office, were supreme. Virginia's Attorney General Tucker summarized the Southern view, stating that the federal power over the mails ceased when the mails reached their destination; 'At that point, the power of the State becomes exclusive. Whether the citizens shall receive the mail matter, is a question exclusively for her determination.' Since most Southern states had statutes requiring inspection of the mails by the postmaster or local authorities, the federal law was effectively nullified. In the Yazoo case of 1857 United States Attorney General Cushing gave this interpretation official sanction when he ruled that a Mississippi statute forbidding delivery of 'incendiary' matter was not in conflict with the federal law of 1836, and that no postmaster was required to deliver materials 'the design and tendency of which are to promote insurrections.' Similarly, Postmaster General Holt in 1859 ruled that the Virginia statute of 1836 did not conflict with federal law. To the postmaster at Falls Church, Virginia, he wrote that any postmaster might, after inspection of the mails, withhold delivery of any matter of 'incendiary character.' 'The people of Virginia,' he said, 'may not only forbid the introduction and dissemination of such documents within their borders, but, if brought there in the mails, they may, by appropriate legal proceedings have them destroyed.' ");

p. 29, 1. 10, 249 U.S. 47; p. 29, 1. 35, 2 THE PAPERS OF THOMAS JEFFERSON 546 (Boyd ed.) (In a letter of July 3, 1801 to Elijah Boardman, Jefferson wrote: "But we have nothing to fear from the demoralizing reasonings of some, if others are left free to demonstrate their errors. And especially when the law stands ready to punish the first criminal *act* produced by the false reasoning. These are safer correctives than the conscience of a judge."); p. 30, 1. 17, LETTERS OF THE HONOURABLE MR. JUSTICE BLACKSTONE 53-55; p. 30, 1. 18, Of him Madison in THE FEDERALIST, no. 47, wrote, in discussing the idea of the separation of powers: "The oracle who is always consulted and cited on this subject is the celebrated Montesquieu."; p. 30, 1. 29, Bk. 12, c. 12; p. 30, 1. 38, At 95 (Harrison ed.); p. 31, 1. 3, 268 U.S. 652, 673; p. 31, 1. 11, 354 U.S. 298, 326, 350, reversing 225 F.2d 146; p. 31, 1. 22, 54 Stat. 670-71, as amended, 18 U.S.C. §2385 (Supp. IV, 1956); p. 31, 1. 30, 341 U.S. at 512; p. 32, 1. 2, 354 U.S. at 314-15, 318, 350 (Subsequently the district court, on the motion of the government, dismissed the indictment as to the nine, and, on its own motion, added a tenth who was not tried with the others because of illness.); p. 32, 1. 20, 354 U.S. at 340; p. 32, 1. 22, 341 U.S. at 590; p. 32, 1. 25, 357 U.S. 468; 357 U.S. 399, 415; p. 32, 1. 35, 357 U.S. 545; 357 U.S. 513, 536-37; p. 33, 1. 3, 354 U.S. 476, 514, affirming 237 F.2d 796, and 138 Cal. App. 2d Supp. 909; p. 33, 1. 10, 354 U.S. 284, 297; p. 33, 1. 23, 354 U.S. at 495; p. 33, 1. 24, 354 U.S. 436, 446; p. 34, 1. 8, The Supreme Court has not yet passed on the validity of the membership clause of the Smith Act. But the Courts of Appeals for the Second, Fourth and Seventh Circuits have sustained it. United States v. Noto, 262 F.2d 501; Scales v. United States, 227 F.2d 581, rev'd, 355 U.S. 1, and 260 F.2d 21, cert. granted, 358 U.S. 917; Lightfoot v. United States, 228 F.2d 861, rev'd, 355 U.S. 1.

CHAPTER III

P. 35, 1. 25, Commonwealth v. Sharpless, 2 S. & R. (Pa.) '91 (1815). As late as 1795 Leach in his edition of 2 HAWKINS, PLEAS OF THE CROWN 130, said: "And it seems, that a writing full of obscene ribaldry, without any kind of reflection upon any one, is not punishable at all by any prosecution at common law, as I have heard agreed in the court of king's bench." In Reg. v. Read, 11 Mod. 142 (1708), the court so held, stating that obscenity was punishable only in the spiritual court. Later this case was overruled. Rex v. Curl, 2 Str. 788 (1727).

But the Court in Roth v. United States, 354 U.S. 476, 483, stated: "At the time of the adoption of the First Amendment, obscenity law was not as fully developed as libel law, but there is sufficiently contemporaneous evidence to show that obscenity, too, was outside the protection intended for speech and press." In support of this statement the Court cited the Sharpless case, and Knowles v. State, 3 Day (Conn.) 103, and Commonwealth v. Holmes, 17 Mass. 336, as well as a statute of Connecticut of 1821 and one of New Jersey of 1798, among others. Knowles was charged with exhibiting an indecent and unseemly picture "representing a horrid and unnatural *monster*," but on appeal his conviction was reversed. Also, the New Jersey statute to which the Court referred is not in point. It prohibited stage performances but did not deal with obscenity. New Jersey Laws 331-32 (Paterson, 1800). It would thus seem that the Court's statement is somewhat too broad.

However, an act of 1711 of the colony of Massachusetts Bay made it an offense to write, print or publish "any Filthy Obscene or Prophane Song, Pamphlet, Libel or Mock-Sermon, in Imitation or in Mimicking of Preaching, or any other part of Divine Worship. . . ." Acts and Laws of Massachusetts Bay 219, 222 (1714). On the basis of this act the Court, in the Roth case, concluded: "Thus, profanity and obscenity were related offenses." One will have to concede the validity of this conclusion. The attitude which excluded blasphemy from free speech guarantees would deal similarly with obscenity when that offense developed; p. 35, 1. 29, 1

ANNALS OF CONG. 435, 441, 755; p. 36, l. 23, 5 DOCUMENTARY HISTORY OF THE CON-
STITUTION 193, 197 (Dept. of State); p. 36, l. 37 ANNALS OF CONG., 5th Cong.,
2d Sess. 2142, 2152, 2153; St. George Tucker in his Appendix to his 1803 edition
of 1 BLACKSTONE, COMMENTARIES 299 wrote: ". . . the judicial courts of the
respective states are open to all persons alike, for the redress of injuries of this
nature [libel] . . . But the genius of our government will not permit the federal
legislature to interfere with the subject; and the federal courts are, I presume,
equally restrained by the principles of the constitution, and the amendments which
have since been adopted."; p. 37, l. 10, 6 THE WRITINGS OF JAMES MADISON 334
(Hunt ed.); p. 37, l. 12, Id. at 393; 4 ELLIOT, DEBATES ON THE FEDERAL CONSTITU-
TION 573 (2d ed.); p. 37, l. 24, Letter of Sept. 11, 1804. 10 THE WORKS OF
THOMAS JEFFERSON 89–90 n. (Fed. ed. by Ford). A decade and a half earlier he
had written Madison from Paris: ". . . A declaration that the federal government
will never restrain the presses from printing any thing they please, will not take
away the liability of the printers for false facts printed. . . ." 13 THE PAPERS OF
THOMAS JEFFERSON 440, 442 (Boyd ed.); p. 37, l. 35, 10 THE WORKS OF THOMAS
JEFFERSON 133–34 (Fed. ed. by Ford); p. 37, l. 40, CONG. GLOBE APP., 24th Cong.,
1st Sess., 439; p. 38, l. 4, 1 ANNALS OF CONG. 436, 761, 767; p. 38, l. 19, 32 U.S. (7
Pet.) 243, 250; p. 38, l. 26, 32 U.S. (7 Pet.) 469, 552–53; p. 38, l. 31, Knapp v.
Schweitzer, 357 U.S. 371; Ohio ex rel. Lloyd v. Dollison, 194 U.S. 445; Bolln
v. Nebraska, 176 U.S. 83; Brown v. New Jersey, 175 U.S. 172; Thorington v.
Alabama, 147 U.S. 490; McElvaine v. Brush, 142 U.S. 155; Eilenbecker v. Plymouth
County, 134 U.S. 31; Spies v. Illinois, 123 U.S. 131; Edwards v. Elliott, 88 U.S.
(21 Wall.) 532; Twitchell v. Pennsylvania, 74 U.S. (7 Wall.) 321; Pervear v.
Massachusetts, 72 U.S. (5 Wall.) 475; Withers v. Buckley, 61 U.S. (20 How.)
84; Fox v. Ohio, 46 U.S. (5 How.) 410; see Miller v. Texas, 153 U.S. 535, 538;
In re Sawyer, 124 U.S. 200, 219; United States v. Cruikshank, 92 U.S. 542; The
Justices v. Murray, 76 U.S. (9 Wall.) 274; p. 39, l. 33, At *163, 164; p. 40, l. 4,
see, e.g., District Judge Grosscup in United States v. James 60 Fed. 257, 263; and
Justice Douglas in a dissenting opinion in which Justice Black concurred in Ullmann
v. United States, 350 U.S. 422, 440, 446, 449. Judge Grosscup and Justice Douglas
also referred to this right as a "privilege of silence." 60 Fed. at 264; 350 U.S.
at 445; p. 40, l. 8, Rex v. Watkinson, 2 Strange 1122. The attorney and client
privilege goes back to the reign of Elizabeth I. Berd v. Lovelace, Cary 62; Kelway v.
Kelway, Cary 89; Dennis v. Codringham, Cary 100. In United States v. Burr, In Re
Willie, 25 Fed. Cas. 38, 39–40, Chief Justice Marshall referred to "the principle
by which every witness is privileged not to accuse himself."; p. 40, l. 29, ANNALS
OF CONG., 16th Cong., 2d Sess. 1129; p. 40, l. 33, 5 ELLIOT, DEBATES ON THE
FEDERAL CONSTITUTION 487 (rev. ed.); 2 FARRAND, RECORDS OF THE FEDERAL
CONVENTION 443; p. 40, l. 38, 2 ROWLAND, LIFE OF GEORGE MASON 384; p. 41, l. 6,
3 Stat. 545 (the other measure was a Joint Resolution of March 2, 1821, No. 1,
3 Stat. 645); p. 41, l. 10, MO. CONST., art. III, §26 (1820); p. 41, l. 18, ANNALS
OF CONG., 16th Cong., 2d Sess. 1129, 1134, 1135. Subsequently on the motion of
Henry Clay of Kentucky, the House referred the problem to a committee of 23—the
number of states in the Union at that time. Id. at 1219–20. On the report of
this committee the House and the Senate resolved that Missouri was to be admitted
"upon the fundamental condition, that the fourth clause of the twenty-sixth section
of the third article of the constitution . . . shall never be construed to authorize
the passage of any law, and that no law shall be passed in conformity thereto, by
which any citizen, of either of the states in this Union, shall be excluded from
the enjoyment of any of the privileges and immunities to which such citizen is
entitled under the constitution of the United States. . . ." Joint Resolution of
March 2, 1821, No. 1, 3 Stat. 645. This measure further provided that when the
Missouri legislature made a declaration of assent to this fundamental condition and
furnished a copy to the president, he should by proclamation declare the new state
to be admitted. The Missouri legislature at a special session in June 1821 made

the required declaration and on August 10, 1821 President Monroe proclaimed Missouri a state. 3 Stat. 797, App. II; p. 41, l. 40, 6 Fed. Cas. 546, 551–52. Two early state cases deserve mention: Campbell v. Morris, 3 Md. 535, 554 (general court); Abbot v. Bayley, 23 Mass. (6 Pick.) 89, 91. In Campbell v. Morris, Judge Samuel Chase for himself and Justice Gabriel Duvall wrote: "It seems agreed, from the manner of expounding, or defining the words immunities and privileges, by the counsel on both sides, that a particular and limited operation is to be given to these words, and not a full and comprehensive one. It is agreed it does not mean the right of election, the right of holding offices, the right of being elected. The courts are of opinion it means that the citizens of the states shall have the peculiar advantage of acquiring and holding real as well as personal property, and that such property shall be protected and secured by the laws of the state, in the same manner as the property of the citizens of the state is protected. It means, such property shall not be liable to any taxes or burdens which the property of the citizens is not subject to. It may also mean, that as creditors, they shall be on the same footing with the state creditor, in the payment of the debts of a deceased debtor. It secures and protects personal rights." In Abbot v. Bayley, Chief Justice Parker for the court reasoned: "* * * The privileges and immunities secured to the people of each State in every other State, can be applied only in case of re-moval from one State into another. By such removal they become citizens of the adopted State without naturalization, and have a right to sue and be sued as citizens; and yet this privilege is qualified and not absolute, for they cannot enjoy the right of suffrage or of eligibility to office, without such term of residence as shall be prescribed by the constitution and laws of the State into which they shall remove. They shall have the privileges and immunities of citizens, that is, they shall not be deemed aliens, but may take and hold real estate, and may, according to the laws of such State, eventually enjoy the full rights of citizenship without the necessity of being naturalized. * * *"; p. 42, l. 29, Vol. 3 at 674–75 (1833). Similarly Justice Field speaking for a unanimous court in Paul v. Virginia, 75 U.S. (8 Wall.) 168, 180 said: "It was undoubtedly the object of the clause in question to place the citizens of each State upon the same footing with citizens of other States, so far as the advantages resulting from citizenship in those States are con-cerned. It relieves them from the disabilities of alienage in other States; it inhibits discriminating legislation against them by other States; it gives them the right of free ingress into other States, and egress from them; it insures to them in other States the same freedom possessed by the citizens of those States in the acquisition and enjoyment of property and in the pursuit of happiness; and it secures to them in other States the equal protection of their laws. It has been justly said that no provision in the Constitution has tended so strongly to constitute the citizens of the United States one people as this.

"Indeed, without some provision of the kind removing from the citizens of each state the disabilities of alienage in the other States, and giving them equality of privilege with citizens of those States, the Republic would have constituted little more than a league of States; it would not have constituted the Union which now exists."

P. 42, l. 35, 332 U.S. 46, 74; p. 43, l. 5, S. DOC. No. 711, 63d Cong., 3d Sess. 17 (KENDRICK, JOURNAL OF THE JOINT COMMITTEE OF FIFTEEN ON RECON-STRUCTION 61); p. 43, l. 10, CONG. GLOBE, 39th Cong., 1st Sess. 1034, 1088, 1089. Bingham's emphasis on the due process clause reflected the use anti-slavery people made of it; p. 43, l. 40, S. DOC. No. 711, 63d Cong., 3d Sess. 30 (KENDRICK, JOURNAL OF THE JOINT COMMITTEE OF FIFTEEN ON RECONSTRUCTION 87). One of Bingham's colleagues on the Joint Committee, Congressman George S. Boutwell of Massachusetts, later wrote of him: "The part relating to 'privileges and im-munities' came from Mr. Bingham of Ohio. Its euphony and indefiniteness of meaning were a charm to him." 2 REMINISCENCES OF SIXTY YEARS IN PUBLIC AFFAIRS 41–42. The Senate added the definition of citizenship on the motion of

Senator Jacob M. Howard of Michigan. CONG. GLOBE, 39th Cong., 1st Sess. 2869, 2890, 2897; p. 44, l. 20, CONG. GLOBE, 39th Cong., 1st Sess. 2542; p. 44, l. 34, CINCINNATI COMMERCIAL, Aug. 27, 1866, p. 1, cols. 2–3; p. 44, l. 37, 17 Stat. 13; p. 44, l. 39, 106 U.S. 629; p. 45, l. 2, CONG. GLOBE APP., 42d Cong., 1st Sess. 84; p. 45, l. 37, CONG. GLOBE, 39th Cong., 1st Sess. 2459; p. 45, l. 41, CONG. GLOBE APP. 42d Cong., 1st Sess. 151; p. 47, l. 4, CONG. GLOBE, 39th Cong., 1st Sess. 2765; p. 47, l. 17, Laws of 1859, No. 138, §§1, 7, at 391, 393; 2 MICH. COMP. LAWS ch. 261, §§7939, 7943 (1871); p. 47, l. 26, 32 U.S. (7 Pet.) 243; p. 47, l. 27, 30 Mich. 201, 208; p. 48, l. 12, CONG. GLOBE, 39th Cong., 1st Sess. 2766; p. 48, l. 23, 20 Mich. 525, 530; p. 48, l. 30, Fairman, *Does the Fourteenth Amendment Incorporate the Bill of Rights? The Original Understanding*, 2 STAN. L. REV. 5, 139; p. 48, l. 32, 83 U.S. (16 Wall.) 36, 79–80. The quoted language of Chief Justice Taney is from his dissenting opinion in the Passenger Cases, 48 U.S. (7 How.) 283, 492, where the Court invalidated certain Massachusetts and New York statutes which Taney regarded as imposing a tax exclusively upon arriving alien passengers. Taney, although dissenting, toward the close of his opinion made plain that what he had said did not apply to a tax on American citizens: ". . . Living as we do under a common government, charged with the great concerns of the whole Union, every citizen of the United States, from the most remote States or Territories, is entitled to free access, not only to the principal departments established at Washington, but also to its judicial tribunals and public offices in every State and Territory of the Union . . . For all the great purposes for which the Federal government was formed we are one people, with one common country. We are all citizens of the United States; and as members of the same community, must have the right to pass and repass through every part of it without interruption, as freely as in our own States. . . ."; p. 49, l. 23, In Williams v. Fears, 179 U.S. 270, 274, the Court through Chief Justice Fuller said: "Undoubtedly the right of locomotion, the right to remove from one place to another according to inclination, is an attribute of personal liberty, and the right, ordinarily, of free transit from or through the territory of any State is a right secured by the Fourteenth Amendment and by other provisions of the Constitution." In Twining v. New Jersey, 211 U.S. 78, 97, the Court through Justice Moody gave this summary: "Thus among the rights and privileges of national citizenship recognized by this court are the right to pass freely from State to State. . . ; the right to petition Congress for a redress of grievances. . . ; the right to vote for National officers, . . . ; the right to enter the public land, . . . ; the right to be protected against violence while in the lawful custody of a United States marshal, . . . ; and the right to inform the United States authorities of violation of its laws, . . ."; p. 49, l. 24, 332 U.S. 46, 61–62; p. 49, l. 34, 314 U.S. 160; p. 49, l. 39, 307 U.S. 496. In addition to the Slaughter-House Cases, Justice Roberts relied on United States v. Cruikshank, 92 U.S. 542, 552, where the Court, again by way of dictum, said: "The right of the people peaceably to assemble for the purpose of petitioning Congress for a redress of grievances, or for anything else connected with the powers or the duties of the national government, is an attribute of national citizenship, and, as such, under the protection of, and guaranteed by, the United States. . . ." Justice, later Chief Justice, Stone rested his opinion, in which Justice Reed joined, on the due process clause of the Fourteenth Amendment: "No more grave and important issue can be brought to this Court than that of freedom of speech and assembly, which the due process clause guarantees to all persons regardless of their citizenship, but which the privileges and immunities clause secures only to citizens, and then only to the limited extent that their relationship to the national government is affected. I am unable to rest decision here on the assertion, which I think the record fails to support, that respondents must depend upon their limited privileges as citizens of the United States. . . . It is enough that petitioners have prevented respondents from holding meetings and disseminating information whether for the organization of labor unions or for any other lawful purpose." At 524, 525;

p. 50, l. 4, 73 U.S. (6 Wall.) 35, 49. In Traux v. Raich, 239 U.S. 33, 39, Justice, later Chief Justice, Hughes speaking for the Court said with reference to an alien duly admitted into the United States: ". . . He was thus admitted with the privilege of entering and abiding in the United States, and hence of entering and abiding in any State in the Union. . . ."; p. 50, l. 14, 296 U.S. 404, 444; p. 50, l. 15, 279 U.S. 245, 251; p. 50, l. 18, 314 U.S. 160, 180; p. 50, l. 22, Kent v. Dulles, 357 U.S. 116, reversing 248 F.2d 600 and 248 F.2d 561; p. 50, l. 24, Dayton v. Dulles, 357 U.S. 144, reversing 254 F.2d 71; p. 50, l. 36, Brief for respondent, p. 26; p. 50, l. 40, 357 U.S. at 125. In its concluding paragraph the Court added: "To repeat, we deal here with a constitutional right of the citizen, a right which we must assume Congress will be faithful to respect." At 130. The actual holding was that Congress had not authorized the Secretary of State to deny a passport to one because of a refusal to swear whether one was or ever had been a Communist.

In Schachtman v. Dulles, 225 F.2d 938, Circuit Judge Charles Fahy in the court's opinion characterized the freedom to go from place to place as "a natural right." At 941. Chief Judge Henry W. Edgerton in a concurring opinion stated: "Freedom to leave a country or a hemisphere is as much a part of liberty as freedom to leave a State." At 944. The government in its brief in the Kent and Briehl cases adopted both concepts. Justice Douglas for the Court regarded freedom of movement as a constitutional rather than a natural right. P. 51, l. 17, 268 U.S. 652; p. 51, l. 21, See, e.g., Poulos v. New Hampshire, 345 U.S. 395, 396–97; Zorack v. Clauson, 343 U.S. 306, 309; McCollum v. Board of Education, 333 U.S. 203, 210; Everson v. Board of Education, 330 U.S. 1, 8; Pennekamp v. Florida, 328 U.S. 331, 335; West Virginia Board of Education v. Barnette, 319 U.S. 624, 639; Murdock v. Pennsylvania, 319 U.S. 105, 108; Bridges v. California, 314 U.S. 252, 263 n. 6; Minersville School District v. Gobitis, 310 U.S. 586, 593; Cantwell v. Connecticut, 310 U.S. 296, 303; Schneider v. State, 308 U.S. 147, 160; United States v. Carolene Products Co., 304 U.S. 144, 152 n. 4. See also Kunz v. New York, 340 U.S. 290, 293; p. 51, l. 23, 343 U.S. 250, 268. In his dissenting opinion in Adamson v. California, 332 U.S. 46, 85 he said: "And the Court has now through the Four- teenth Amendment literally and emphatically applied the First Amendment to the states in its very terms."; p. 51, l. 34, 268 U.S. at 666, 672; p. 52, l. 7, 249 U.S. 47, 52; p. 52, l. 16, 343 U.S. 250, 288, 291; p. 52, l. 32, 357 U.S. 449, 460. In his concurring and dissenting opinion in Alberts v. California and Roth v. United States, 354 U.S. 476, 501, 503, Justice Harlan took note of Justice Jackson's dissent in the Beauharnais case. He said: ". . . We can inquire only whether the state action so subverts the fundamental liberties implicit in the Due Process Clause that it cannot be sustained as a rational exercise of power. See Jackson, J., dissent- ing in Beauharnais v. Illinois . . . The States' power to make printed words criminal is, of course, confined by the Fourteenth Amendment, but only insofar as such power is inconsistent with our concepts of 'ordered liberty.' Palko v. Connecti- cut. . . . I agree with Mr. Justice Jackson that the historical evidence does not bear out the claim that the Fourteenth Amendment 'incorporates' the First in any literal sense." Justice Brennan in the Court's opinion in this case showed the im- pact of Justice Harlan's argument, for after stating "that obscenity is not expression protected by the First Amendment," he added in a footnote: "For the same reason. we reject, in this case, the argument that there is greater latitude for state actior. under the word 'liberty' under the Fourteenth Amendment than is allowed to Congress by the language of the First Amendment." At 492 n. 31.

But earlier in the term the Court said in Staub v. City of Baxley, 355 U.S. 313, 321: "The First Amendment of the Constitution provides: 'Congress shall make no law * * * abridging the freedom of speech * * *.' This freedom is among the fundamental personal rights and liberties which are protected by the Fourteenth Amendment from invasion by state action * * *." See in addition the concurring opinion of Justice Black, in which Justice Douglas joined, in Speiser v. Randall,

357 U.S. 513, 530, and First Unitarian Church v. Los Angeles 357 U.S. 545; the concurring opinion of Justice Douglas with which Justice Black agreed, in Speiser v. Randall, supra at 535; and his dissenting opinion, again with Justice Black's concurrence, in Lerner v. Casey, 357 U.S. 468, and Beilan v. Board of Public Education, 357 U.S. 399, 412. These opinions were delivered the same day as the Court's unanimous opinion in the NAACP case.

Chief Justice Hughes was consistently careful not to say that the due process clause of the Fourteenth Amendment made the First applicable to the states, but his discriminating language apparently went generally unnoted. See, e.g., his opinions for the Court in Stromberg v. California, 283 U.S. 359, 368 ("It has been determined that the conception of liberty under the due process clause of the Fourteenth Amendment embraces the right of free speech."); Near v. Minnesota, 283 U.S. 697, 707 ("It is no longer open to doubt that the liberty of the press, and of speech, is within the liberty safeguarded by the due process clause of the Fourteenth Amendment from invasion by state action."); De Jonge v. Oregon, 299 U.S. 353, 364 ("Freedom of speech and of the press are fundamental rights which are safeguarded by the due process clause of the Fourteenth Amendment of the Federal Constitution. * * * The right of peaceable assembly is a right cognate to those of free speech and free press and is equally fundamental. * * * The First Amendment of the Federal Constitution expressly guarantees that right against abridgment by Congress. But explicit mention there does not argue exclusion elsewhere. For the right is one that cannot be denied without violating those fundamental principles of liberty and justice which lie at the base of all civil and political institutions—principles which the Fourteenth Amendment embodies in the general terms of its due process clause.").

Justice Cardozo was equally careful in the Court's opinion in Palko v. Connecticut, 302 U.S. 319, 324 ("On the other hand, the due process clause of the Fourteenth Amendment may make it unlawful for a state to abridge by its statutes the freedom of speech which the First Amendment safeguards against encroachment by the Congress, * * *."). So was Justice Sutherland in the Court's opinion in Grosjean v. American Press Co., 297 U.S. 233, 243 ("The First Amendment to the federal constitution provides * * *. While this provision is not a restraint upon the powers of the states, the states are precluded from abridging the freedom of speech or of the press by force of the due process clause of the Fourteenth Amendment.")

CHAPTER IV

P. 54, l. 1, Palko v. Connecticut, 302 U.S. 319, 325 (Justice Cardozo). In the recent case of Bartkus v. Illinois, 359 U.S. 121, 127, where the Court in a five to four decision sustained a state prosecution based on the same facts on which the defendant had been acquitted in a federal prosecution, Justice Frankfurter quoted the sentence from which the chapter heading comes, and introduced the quoted sentence with the observation: "* * * The statement by Mr. Justice Cardozo in Palko v. Connecticut * * * has especially commended itself and been frequently cited in later opinions. * * *"; p. 54, l. 33, N.Y. Laws 1948, chs. 553–557, pp. 993–1000; p. 54, l. 34, N.Y. Laws 1949, ch. 388, p. 1056; p. 55, l. 18, PUBLIC PAPERS OF GOVERNOR THOMAS E. DEWEY 225–26 (1948); NEW YORK STATE LEGISLATIVE ANNUAL 210–11 (1948); p. 55, l. 25, 1 N.Y. 2d 1952, 163; p. 56, l. 8, Record, pp. 35–37, 32–36, 35, 38, People v. Codarre, 285 App. Div. 1087, 140 N.Y.S. 2d 289; p. 58, l. 19, Id. at 44–46, quoted with the exception of the last paragraph, in People v. Codarre, 8 Misc. 2d 145, 146–48, 167 N.Y.S. 2d 443, 445–46; p. 58, l. 21, Record at 40–43; p. 59, l. 13, People v. Codarre, 5 A.D. 2d 1016, 174 N.Y.S. 2d 123, pet. for leave to appeal to the Court of Appeals denied, affirming 8 Misc. 2d 145, 167 N.Y.S. 2d 443 (Dutchess County Ct. 1957); People v. Codarre, 285 App. Div. 1087, 140 N.Y.S. 2d 289, affirming 206 Misc. 950, 138 N.Y.S. 2d 18;

p. 59, l. 25, Chicago, M. & St. P. Ry. Co. v. Minnesota, 134 U.S. 418. In Federal
Power Comm'n v. Natural Gas Pipeline Co., 315 U.S. 575, Justices Black, Douglas
and Murphy in a concurring opinion and Justice Frankfurter in a separate concurring
opinion gave historical expositions on the point; p. 59, l. 29, 94 U.S. 113; p. 59,
l. 31, 94 U.S. 164; p. 59, l. 35, 205 U.S. 454, 462; p. 59, l. 41, 259 U.S. 530, 543;
p. 60, l. 5, 268 U.S. 652; p. 60, l. 8, 343 U.S. 250, 291; p. 60, l. 17, 261
U.S. 86; p. 60, l. 18, 273 U.S. 510; p. 60, l. 19, 287 U.S. 45; p. 60, l. 21, 297 U.S.
278; p. 60, l. 28, 345 U.S. 206, 222, 224; p. 61, l. 20, 315 U.S. 575, 600 n. 4,
600–1. Justice Holmes in his dissenting opinion in Baldwin v. Missouri, 281 U.S.
586, 595, said ". . . I have not yet expressed the more than anxiety that I feel at
the ever increasing scope given to the Fourteenth Amendment in cutting down
what I believe to be the constitutional rights of the States. As the decisions now
stand, I see hardly any limit but the sky to the invalidating of those rights if they
happen to strike a majority of this Court as for any reason undesirable." In his
dissenting opinion in an earlier case, Lochner v. New York, 198 U.S. 45, 75, he
made his famous statement: "The Fourteenth Amendment does not enact Mr.
Herbert Spencer's Social Statics." In that case the Court, under the due process
clause of the Fourteenth Amendment, invalidated a New York statute regulating
the hours of labor in bakeries and confectionery establishments. Dean Roscoe
Pound in an article dealing with due process cases invalidating early labor legislation concluded with this comment: "The evil of those cases will live after them
in impaired authority of the courts long after the decisions themselves are forgotten." Liberty of Contract, 18 YALE L. J. 454, 487; p. 62, l. 5, 348 U.S. 483,
488; p. 62, l. 15, 309 U.S. 227, 236; p. 62, l. 27, Mendelson, A Missing Link in
the Evolution of Due Process, 10 VAND. L. REV. 125, 126; p. 62, l. 39, 28 Edw.
III, c. 3 (1354); p. 62, l. 42, 2 INST. *46. See also 2 id. at *50; p. 63, l. 2, See, e.g.,
DEL. CONST. art. I, §7 (1792), ILL. CONST., art. VIII, §8 (1818); MD. Declaration
of Rights, art. 21 (1776); N.H. CONST. part I, art. 15 (1784) (". . . but by the
judgment of his peers or the law of the land."); p. 63, l. 3, Dartmouth College v.
Woodward, 17 U.S. (4 Wheat.) 518, 561, 581; p. 63, l. 13, 59 U.S. (18 How.)
272, 276. In Twining v. New Jersey, 211 U.S. 78, 100, the Court through Justice
Moody explained: ". . . There are certain general principles, well settled, however,
which narrow the field of discussion and may serve as helps to correct conclusions.
These principles grow out of the proposition universally accepted by American
courts on the authority of Coke, that the words 'due process of law' are equivalent
in meaning to the words 'law of the land,' contained in that chapter of Magna
Charta which provides . . .". In a yet later case, Hebert v. Louisiana, 272 U.S.
312, 316–17, the Court said: ". . . What it [due process clause] does require is
that state action, whether through one agency or another, shall be consistent with
the fundamental principles of liberty and justice which lie at the base of all our civil
and political institutions and not infrequently are designated as 'law of the
land.' . . ."; p. 63, l. 26, In attempting to distinguish between substance and form
one is reminded of Sir Henry Maine's statement in his EARLY LAW AND CUSTOM
389 about substantive law having "at first the look of being gradually secreted in
the interstices of procedure." Justice Brandeis in his dissenting opinion in Burdeau v.
McDowell, 256 U.S. 465, 477 wrote: "And in the development of our liberty insistence upon procedural regularity has been a large factor." In a leading case
invalidating confessions, McNabb v. United States, 318 U.S. 332, 347, Justice
Frankfurter said in the Court's opinion: "The history of liberty has largely been the
history of observance of procedural safeguards."

The related ideas of the due process of law and the supremacy of law we have
often embodied in the sentence, we are a government of laws and not of men.
James Harrington, in his COMMON-WEALTH OF OCEANA 27 (Morley ed.), first
published in 1656, after the execution of Charles I of England, and dedicated to
Oliver Cromwell, wanted "an empire of laws, and not of men." John Adams in
his The Report of A Constitution, or form of Government, for the Commonwealth

of Massachusetts proposed: "In the government of the Commonwealth of Massachusetts, the legislative, executive, and judicial power shall be placed in separate departments, to the end that it might be a government of laws, and not of men." 4 CHARLES FRANCIS ADAMS, THE WORKS OF JOHN ADAMS 230. In United States *v.* Mine Workers 330 U.S. 258, 307-8, Justice Frankfurter began his concurring opinion with these words: "The historic phrase 'a government of laws and not of men' epitomizes the distinguishing character of our political society. When John Adams put that phrase into the Massachusetts Declaration of Rights he was not indulging in a rhetorical flourish. He was expressing the aim of those who, with him, framed the Declaration of Independence and founded the Republic." He quoted this in his concurring opinion in Cooper *v.* Aaron, 358 U.S. 1, 23, arising out of the resistance of Arkansas under the leadership of Governor Orval E. Faubus to desegregation in the public schools as required by the Court's decision in Brown *v.* Board of Education, 347 U.S. 483. Justice Douglas in his concurring opinion in Joint Anti-Fascist Refugee Committee *v.* McGrath, 341 U.S. 123, 177, said with emphasis: "This is a government of *laws*, not of *men*."; p. 63, l. 30, Dred Scott *v.* Sandford, 60 U.S. (19 How.) 393, 450; p. 63, l. 42, The more radical theorists, such as Alvan Stewart, found in the federal due process clause a source of congressional power to abolish slavery even in the states; p. 64, l. 15, 343 U.S. 250, 269; p. 64, l. 17, 319 U.S. 624, 639; p. 64, l. 32, 347 U.S. 128, 138-39; p. 65, l. 15, In his dissenting opinion in Irvine *v.* California, 347 U.S. 128, 141-42, in which Justice Douglas joined, he said: "Though not essential to disposition of this case, it seems appropriate to add that I think the Fourteenth Amendment makes the Fifth Amendment applicable to states and that state courts like federal courts are therefore barred from convicting a person for crime on testimony which either state or federal officers have compelled him to give against himself. The construction I give to the Fifth and Fourteenth Amendments make it possible for me to adhere to what we said in Ashcraft *v.* Tennessee, . . . that 'The Constitution of the United States stands as a bar against the conviction of an individual in an American court by means of a coerced commission.' "; p. 65, l. 16, 342 U.S. 165, 175, 177. In his dissenting opinion in Adamson *v.* California, 332 U.S. 46, 69, 70, he said: "This decision reasserts a constitutional theory spelled out in Twining *v.* New Jersey, . . . that this Court is endowed by the Constitution with boundless power under 'natural law' periodically to expand and contract constitutional standards to conform to the Court's conception of what at a particular time constitutes 'civilized decency' and 'fundamental liberty and justice.' * * * "* * * But I would not reaffirm the Twining decision. I think that decision and the 'natural law' theory of the Constitution upon which it relies degrade the constitutional safeguards of the Bill of Rights and simultaneously appropriate for this Court a broad power which we are not authorized by the Constitution to exercise. * * *"; p. 65, l. 37, See, *e.g.*, his dissenting opinion in Beauharnais *v.* Illinois, 343 U.S. 250, 268; p. 66, l. 4, 332 U.S. 46, 64-65; p. 66, l. 25, 347 U.S. 128, 138; p. 66, l. 30, 359 U.S. 121, 128; p. 67, l. 4, 96 U.S. 97; p. 67, l. 5, 347 U.S. 128, 143; p. 67, l. 11, 96 U.S. at 104; p. 67, l. 12, 302 U.S. 319, 325, 326; p. 67, l. 21, 297 U.S. 278; p. 67, l. 22, 309 U.S. 227; 356 U.S. 560, 561; p. 67, l. 28, Harris *v.* South Carolina, 338 U.S. 68; Turner *v.* Pennsylvania, 338 U.S. 62; Watts *v.* Indiana, 338 U.S. 49. It was in the Watts case that Justice Frankfurter said: "Ours is the accusatorial as opposed to the inquisitional system." At 54; p. 67, l. 30, For other cases where confessions were found violative of the due process clause see Spano *v.* New York, 360 U.S. 315; Fikes *v.* Alabama, 352 U.S. 191; Leyra *v.* Denno, 347 U.S. 556; Haley *v.* Ohio, 332 U.S. 596; Malinski *v.* New York 324 U.S. 401; Ashcraft *v.* Tennessee, 322 U.S. 143; Ward *v.* Texas, 316 U.S. 547; Vernon *v.* Alabama, 313 U.S. 547; Lomax *v.* Texas, 313 U.S. 544; White *v.* Texas, 310 U.S. 530; White *v.* Texas, 309 U.S. 631; Canty *v.* Alabama, 309 U.S. 629; *cf.* Lee *v.* Mississippi, 332 U.S. 742; p. 67, l. 30, For cases where confessions were sustained see, *e.g.*, Cicenia *v.* LaGay, 357 U.S. 504; Crooker *v.*

California, 357 U.S. 433; Ashdown v. Utah, 357 U.S. 426; Stroble v. California, 343 U.S. 181; Stein v. New York, 346 U.S. 156; Gallegos v. Nebraska, 342 U.S. 55; Lyons v. Oklahoma, 322 U.S. 596; Lisenba v. California, 314 U.S. 219; p. 67, l. 31, *E.g.*, compare Stein v. New York, 346 U.S. 156, with Leyra v. Denno, 347 U.S. 556, Fikes v. Alabama, 351 U.S. 191, and Payne v. Arkansas, 356 U.S. 560; p. 67, l. 35, The same thing was true in Haley v. Ohio, 332 U.S. 596, and Gallegos v. Nebraska, 342 U.S. 55; p. 67, l. 39, 287 U.S. 45; p. 67, l. 40, 348 U.S. 3, 10; p. 68, l. 5, 287 U.S. at 69, 53, 59; p. 68, l. 17, Hawk v. Olson, 326 U.S. 271; House v. Mayo, 324 U.S. 42; see White v. Ragen, 324 U.S. 760, 764; Avery v. Alabama, 308 U.S. 444, 446; p. 68, l. 20, Powell v. Alabama, 287 U.S. 45, 71; Hawk v. Olson, 326 U.S. 271; Tomkins v. Missouri, 323 U.S. 485; Williams v. Kaiser, 323 U.S. 471. *But cf.* Carter v. Illinois, 329 U.S. 173; p. 68, l. 23, Pennsylvania ex rel. Herman v. Claudy, 350 U.S. 116, 118. Other like holdings are: Cash v. Culver, 358 U.S. 633; Moore v. Michigan, 355 U.S. 155; Massey v. Moore, 348 U.S. 105; Palmer v. Ashe, 342 U.S. 134; Gibbs v. Burke, 337 U.S. 773; Uvegas v. Pennsylvania, 335 U.S. 437; Townsend v. Burke, 334 U.S. 736; Wade v. Mayo, 334 U.S. 672; De Meerleer v. Michigan, 329 U.S. 663; Rice v. Olson, 324 U.S. 786; *cf.* Smith v. O'Grady, 312 U.S. 329; p. 68, l. 27, The Court did not find fundamental unfairness in Quicksall v. Michigan, 339 U.S. 660; Gryger v. Burke, 334 U.S. 728; Bute v. Illinois, 333 U.S. 640; Gayes v. New York, 332 U.S. 145; Foster v. Illinois, 332 U.S. 134; Betts v. Brady, 316 U.S. 455; see Gallegos v. Nebraska, 342 U.S. 55, 64; *cf.* Canizio v. New York 327 U.S. 82; p. 68, l. 30, 287 U.S. 45; p. 68, l. 34, 110 U.S. 516; p. 68, l. 39, 166 U.S. 226; p. 69, l. 4, 211 U.S. 78, 99; p. 69, l. 18, 287 U.S. at 68; p. 69, l. 24, 338 U.S. 25, 27–28. In Stefanelli v. Minard, 342 U.S. 117, the Court adhering to Wolf v. Colorado, held that federal courts would not give equitable relief to prevent the fruits of an unlawful search by New Jersey police from being used in evidence in a state criminal trial. But the Court sustained an injunction by a federal court against a federal agent to prevent him from testifying in a state court prosecution about the fruits of an illegal search. Rea v. United States, 350 U.S. 214; p. 69, l. 34, 291 U.S. 97, 105; p. 70, l. 1, 333 U.S. 257, 261, 270; p. 70, l. 12, 349 U.S. 133, 136. In Tumey v. Ohio, 273 U.S. 510, 532, the Court invalidated a state procedure which permitted a village mayor to try certain offenses and in the event of conviction, but not otherwise, to receive his costs. Chief Justice Taft for a unanimous court said: ". . . but the requirement of due process of law in judicial procedure is not satisfied by the argument that men of the highest honor and the greatest self-sacrifice could carry it on without danger of injustice. Every procedure which would offer a possible temptation to the average man as a judge to forget the burden of proof required to convict the defendant, or which might lead him not to hold the balance nice, clear and true between the State and the accused, denies the latter the due process of law."; p. 70, l. 29, 291 U.S. 97, 106; p. 70, l. 38, See Hoag v. New Jersey, 356 U.S. 464, 466–71; p. 70, l. 39, Louisiana ex rel. Francis v. Resweber, 329 U.S. 459, 463. In that case the court held that Louisiana could try a second time to execute a defendant when a first attempt failed because of a mechanical difficulty with the electric chair.; p. 70, l. 42, 342 U.S. 165; p. 71, l. 10, Recently in Hoag v. New Jersey, 356 U.S. 464, 470, the Court thus described this aspect of judicial finality: "A common statement of the rule of collateral estoppel is that 'where a question of fact essential to the judgment is actually litigated and determined by a valid and final judgment, the determination is conclusive between the parties in a subsequent action on a different cause of action.' . . . As an aspect of the broader doctrine of *res judicata,* collateral estoppel is designed to eliminate the expense, vexation, waste, and possible inconsistent results of duplicatory litigation."; p. 71, l. 13, 355 U.S. 184, 188; see Peters v. Hobby, 349 U.S. 331, 344–345; United States v. Ball, 163 U.S. 662, 671; *cf.* Kepner v. United States, 195 U.S. 100; Sanges v. United States, 144 U.S. 310; p. 71, l. 23, See Kepner v. United States, 195 U.S. 100, 128. *But cf.* Wade v. Hunter, 336 U.S. 684.; p. 71,

l. 25, 356 U.S. 464, 470–71. The leading federal case is Sealfon v. United States, 332 U.S. 575; accord: United States v. De Angelo, 139 F.2d 466; see Yates v. United States, 354 U.S. 298, 335–336; United States v. Adams, 281 U.S. 202, 205; Frank v. Mangum, 237 U.S. 309, 333–334; cf. United States v. Oppenheimer, 242 U.S. 85. The federal courts have also applied the doctrine of collateral estoppel to prosecutions for perjury concerning controverted issues which constituted the basis of the alleged offenses. Yawn v. United States, 244 F.2d 235; Cosgrove v. United States, 224 F.2d 146; Ehrlich v. United States, 145 F.2d 693; Allen v. United States, 194 Fed. 664; Chitwood v. United States, 178 Fed. 442; see Kuskulis v. United States, 37 F.2d 241, 242; Youngblood v. United States, 266 Fed. 795, 797; United States v. Butler, 38 Fed. 498, 499–500. But cf. Williams v. United States, 341 U.S. 58.; p. 71, l. 35, The Supreme Court of Washington followed the Green case. State v. Schoel, 341 P.2d 481. But cf. Stroud v. United States, 251 U.S. 15; Trono v. United States, 199 U.S. 521; p. 71, l. 38, 302 U.S. 319; p. 71, l. 40, 344 U.S. 424; p. 72, l. 4, 356 U.S. at 471; p. 72, l. 9, In an earlier case, Brantley v. Georgia, 217 U.S. 384, where the defendant, who was convicted of manslaughter under an indictment for murder, obtained a reversal, the Court sustained a murder conviction on a retrial. However, the defendant based his writ of error, not on the due process clause of the Fourteenth Amendment, but on the double jeopardy provision of the Fifth; p. 72, l. 17, Cf. Gore v. United States, 357 U.S. 386, involving a narcotics indictment in six counts based on two sales. The Court sustained a conviction on all six counts. The decision, announced in June on the last day of the term, was five to four. Justices Douglas and Black based their dissent on the double jeopardy ground. But in Ladner v. United States, 358 U.S. 169, the Court held that a single discharge of a shotgun even if it wounded two federal officers constituted but a single violation of the applicable federal statute. In Abbate v. United States, 359 U.S. 187, 197, where the Court in a six to three decision sustained a state prosecution after an acquittal in a federal court based on the same acts, Justice Brennan after delivering the Court's opinion said in an additional concurring opinion: "However, whatever the case under the Fourteenth Amendment as to successive state prosecutions, . . . or under the Fifth Amendment as to consecutive federal sentences imposed upon one trial, . . . I think it clear that successive federal prosecutions of the same person based on the same acts are prohibited by the Fifth Amendment even though brought under federal statutes requiring different evidence and protecting different federal interests."; p. 72, l. 18, 356 U.S. 464; p. 72, l. 19, 356 U.S. 571; p. 72, l. 27, 110 U.S. 516; p. 72, l. 29, 332 U.S. 46; 211 U.S. 78; p. 72, l. 30, 291 U.S. 97, 105, quoted with approval in Adamson v. California, 332 U.S. 46, 52; p. 73, l. 3, 357 U.S. 504; p. 73, l. 4, 357 U.S. 433, 439; p. 73, l. 13, 352 U.S. 330; p. 73, l. 18, 355 U.S. 225; p. 73, l. 19, Shevlin-Carpenter Co. v. Minnesota, 218 U.S. 57, 68. John Selden (1584–1654), English jurist, antiquary, and chosen patron of the Selden Society, observed: "Ignorance of the Law excuses no man, not that all men knowe the Law, but tis an excuse every man will plead & no man can tell how to confute him." TABLE TALK 68 (Pollock ed.); p. 73, l. 23, 355 U.S. at 228. When the case returned, the California District Court of Appeals held that the defendant could be retried under the ordinance in question. 343 P.2d 8; p. 73, l. 24, 351 U.S. 12, 19; p. 73, l. 25, 357 U.S. 214; p. 73, l. 28, The Griffin case rested on equal protection as well as due process. This case was applied in United States ex rel. Westbrook v. Randolph, 259 F.2d 215, where the court held that the state's loss of a transcript necessary for an appeal required the granting of a new trial.; p. 73, l. 32, 351 U.S. at 20–21. In another recent case, Sweezy v. New Hampshire, 354 U.S. 234, 266, Justice Frankfurter, in a concurring opinion in which Justice Harlan joined, wrote similarly: ". . . The implications of the United States Constitution for national elections and 'the concept of ordered liberty' implicit in the Due Process Clause of the Fourteenth Amendment as against the States . . . were not frozen as of 1789 or 1868, respectively. While the language of the Constitution does not change, the changing circumstances of a progressive society for which it was designed yield new and fuller import to its meaning. * * *"; p. 73, l. 35, 360 U.S. 252, 258; p. 74, l. 2, 355 U.S. 184. The earlier leading case on double jeopardy, Kepner v. United States, 195 U.S. 100, was also decided by a five to four vote; p. 74, l. 4, 357 U.S. 371, 381, 382, 384, affirming 2 N.Y. 2d 913, affirming 2 App. Div. 2d 579, 586, 157 N.Y.S. 2d 158, 166; p. 75, l. 13, In Feldman v. United States, 322 U.S. 487, 492, 494, the Court was careful to point out: "The Constitution prohibits an invasion of privacy only in proceedings over which the Government has control. There is no suggestion of complicity between Feldman's creditors and federal law enforcing officers. . . . If a federal agency were to use a state court as an instrument for compelling disclosures for federal purposes, the doctrine of the Byars case, supra, as well as that of McNabb v. United States, * * * afford adequate resources against such an evasive disregard of the privilege against self-incrimination. * * * Nothing in this record brings either doctrine into play."; p. 75, l. 24, Selden complained: "Equity is a Roguish thing, for Law wee have a measure know what to trust too. Equity is according to the conscience of him that is Chancellor, and as it is larger or narrower soe is equity. Tis all one as if they should make the standard for the measure wee call A foot, to be the Chancellors foot; what an uncertain measure would this be; One Chancellor has a long foot another A short foot a third an indifferent foot; tis the same thing in the Chancellors Conscience." TABLE TALK 43 (Pollock ed.).

CHAPTER V

P. 76, l. 16, 5 Stat. 304; p. 76, l. 17, The Court in its opinion in Roth v. United States, 354 U.S. 476, 485, listed 20 such acts; p. 76, l. 19, 5 Stat. 566; p. 76, l. 21, 9 Stat. 237; p. 76, l. 23, 13 Stat. 507; p. 76, l. 24, 14 Stat. 81; p. 76, l. 26, 15 Stat. 196; p. 76, l. 28, 17 Stat. 302; p. 76, l. 33, 17 Stat. 598; p. 76, l. 36, 19 Stat. 90; p. 76, l. 37, 28 Stat. 963; p. 76, l. 38, 188 U.S. 321; p. 76, l. 39, 96 U.S. 727; p. 76, l. 40, 143 U.S. 110; p. 76, l. 42, 96 U.S. at 736; p. 77, l. 1, 194 U.S. 497, 507–8; p. 77, l. 11, 27 Stat. 531, 45 U.S.C. §§1 to 8; p. 77, l. 13, 34 Stat. 674; p. 77, l. 14, 34 Stat. 768; p. 77, l. 15, 35 Stat. 420; p. 77, l. 17, 39 Stat. 675; p. 77, l. 18, 40 Stat. 960; p. 77, l. 19, 261 U.S. 525; p. 77, l. 20, 300 U.S. 379; p. 77, l. 22, 36 Stat. 825, 18 U.S.C. §§2421 to 2424; p. 77, l. 26, 227 U.S. 308; 242 U.S. 470; p. 77, l. 29, 37 Stat. 240; p. 77, l. 30, 37 Stat. 554, 39 U.S.C. §234 (This provision was sustained in Lewis Publishing Co. v. Morgan, 229 U.S. 288); p. 77, l. 31, 41 Stat. 324, 18 U.S.C. §§2311 to 2314 (For a recent case under this act, see United States v. Turley, 352 U.S. 407); p. 77, l. 33, 47 Stat. 70, 29 U.S.C. §§101 to 107; 47 Stat. 326, 18 U.S.C. §1201; p. 77, l. 38, 48 Stat. 74, 15 U.S.C. §§77a to 77aa; 48 Stat. 881, 15 U.S.C. §§78a to 78o, 78o–3, 78p to 78hh; p. 77, l. 39, 49 Stat. 803, 838, 15 U.S.C. §§79 to 79z–6; p. 77, l. 40, 49 Stat. 449, 29 U.S.C. §§151 to 166; p. 77, l. 41, 52 Stat. 1054, 21 U.S.C. §§361 to 364 (part of the Federal Food, Drug, and Cosmetic Act); 48 Stat. 979, 18 U.S.C. §1951; p. 78, l. 1, 56 Stat. 1087, 18 U.S.C. §1821; p. 78, l. 3, 303 U.S. 419; 327 U.S. 686; p. 78, l. 5, 301 U.S. 1; p. 78, l. 7, 65 Stat. 529, 26 U.S.C. §§4411 to 4413 (Supp. IV, 1957); p. 78, l. 8, United States v. Kahriger, 345 U.S. 22, 35–36 (as to persons in the states); Lewis v. United States, 348 U.S. 419 (as to persons in the District of Columbia) (Whatever else this act may have accomplished, it has not been successful as a revenue measure. This bears out the doubts which Justice Jackson expressed in his concurring opinion in the Kahriger case); p. 78, l. 9, 359 U.S. 385; p. 78, l. 21, Act of Feb. 25, 1799, §1, 1 Stat. 619; p. 78, l. 24, Act of Feb. 28, 1803, §3, 2 Stat. 206; p. 78, l. 28, S. Rep. 118, 24th Cong., 1st Sess. 6 (49 NILES WEEKLY REGISTER 408, 410); p. 78, l. 40, 12 Stat. 284; 62 Stat. 808, 18 U.S.C. §2384 (Supp. IV, 1957); p. 78, l. 42, 35 Stat. 1088, 1096 (It is now 62 Stat. 701, 18 U.S.C. §371); p. 79, l. 2,

35 Stat. 1152; p. 79, l. 6, Goldman v. United States, 245 U.S. 474; p. 79, l. 14, 40 Stat. 219; 249 U.S. 47; 249 U.S. 204; 249 U.S. 211; p. 79, l. 28, 40 Stat. 553; Abrams v. United States, 250 U.S. 616; p. 79, l. 29, 41 Stat. 1359; p. 79, l. 31, 40 Stat. 230 (These provisions were involved in Milwaukee Pub. Co. v. Burleson, 255 U.S. 407, and Masses Pub. Co. v. Patten, 246 Fed. 24); p. 79, l. 35, 40 Stat. 554; p. 79, l. 39, 61 Stat. 136, codified in scattered sections of 2, 29, 50 App., U.S.C.; p. 79, l. 42, 64 Stat. 987, codified in scattered sections of 8, 18, 22, 50 U.S.C.; p. 80, l. 1, 68 Stat. 775, 50 U.S.C. §§841 to 844, 782, 784(a)(1)(E), 789, 790, 791(e)(3), 792a, 793(a)(b) (Supp. IV, 1957); p. 80, l. 23, 339 U.S. 382; p. 80, l. 24, 341 U.S. 494; p. 80, l. 27, 351 U.S. 115. The Subversive Activities Control Board struck the testimony of Matusow, Crouch and Johnson but again found that the Communist party had to register as a subversive organization. This time the Court of Appeals remanded the case, with the direction that the Board order the government to produce the reports to the F.B.I. of one of its witnesses, citing the Jencks case. 254 F.2d 314. Once again the Board reaffirmed its former finding.

CHAPTER VI

P. 81, l. 18, Judge Herbert F. Goodrich of the United States Court of Appeals for the Third Circuit, while he was a law teacher, wrote that Justice Holmes's "test is similar to the common law liability for attempt to commit a crime—the act done by the wrongdoer must have come dangerously near to success." Judge Hastie in his dissenting opinion, in which Judge Maris joined, in United States v. Mesarosh, 223 F.2d 449, 461, reversed, 352 U.S. 1, quoted this statement with approval. Judge Goodrich in that case voted with the majority; p. 81, l. 20, 341 U.S. 494, 503; 249 U.S. 47, 52; p. 81, l. 25, FREE SPEECH IN THE UNITED STATES 81; p. 81, l. 26, *The First Amendment and Evils That Congress Has a Right to Prevent,* 26 IND. L. J. 477; p. 81, l. 29, FREE SPEECH AND ITS RELATION TO SELF-GOVERNMENT 50; p. 81, l. 30, 183 F.2d at 212; p. 81, l. 33, HAND, THE BILL OF RIGHTS 58; p. 81, l. 38, 318 U.S. 101, 104. See also United States v. Gradwell, 243 U.S. 476; United States v. Hudson, 11 U.S. (7 Cranch) 31. Cf. Knapp v. Schweitzer, 357 U.S. 371, 375; Pennsylvania v. Nelson, 350 U.S. 497, 519 (dissenting opinion of Justice Reed in which Justices Burton and Minton joined); Rochin v. California, 342 U.S. 165, 168; Malinski v. New York, 324 U.S. 401, 412–13 (concurring opinion of Justice Frankfurter); Marcello v. United States, 196 F.2d 437, 443; p. 81, l. 41, In re Guayde, 112 Fed. 415 (Attempt to import women into the United States for the purposes of prostitution). But see United States v. Galleanni, 245 Fed. 977, 978–79; p. 82, l. 3, Calc. Magis. Cases 397, 399, 400 (The defendant was in possession of the house, and thus it was not a felony at common law for him to burn it); p. 82, l. 19, 170 Mass. 18, 20, 22; p. 82, l. 20, 177 Mass. 267, 272; p. 83, l. 7, 185 F.2d 629, 633, cert. denied, 342 U.S. 920; p. 83, l. 14, For other federal cases holding that the conduct in question amounted to a criminal attempt, see Lemke v. United States, 211 F.2d 73, cert. denied, 347 U.S. 1013 (attempt to obtain money under false pretenses); Daniel v. United States, 127 F.2d 1 (attempt to transport liquor into Kansas, a dry state); Gregg v. United States, 113 F.2d 687, reversed on other grounds on rehearing, 116 F.2d 609 (same); United States v. Baker, 129 F.Supp. 684 (attempt to rob a bank); United States v. Duane, 66 F.Supp. 459 (attempt to transport liquor into Kansas).

For federal cases holding conduct to amount to preparation falling short of an attempt, see Seiden v. United States 16 F.2d 197 (manufacture of spirits did not constitute attempt to defraud United States of taxes on liquor while engaged as a distiller); Wooldridge v. United States 237 Fed. 775 (arranging with a girl under 16 years of age to meet her at a particular place and meeting her at the appointed place held not to be an attempt to commit rape); United States v. Stephens, 12 Fed. 52 (transmitting from Alaska to a firm in San Francisco a letter ordering whiskey to be sent to Alaska held not to amount to an attempt to introduce spirituous liquors into Alaska); p. 84, l. 4, HOLMES, THE COMMON LAW 66–69, 65, 68; p. 84, l. 7, 196 U.S. 375, 396; p. 84, l. 41, 2 East 5, 21; p. 85, l. 14, 135 Mass. 545, 549; p. 85, l. 38, Sayre, *Criminal Attempts*, 41 HARV. L. REV. 821, 857–58; p. 86, l. 7, Arnold *Criminal Attempts—The Rise and Fall of an Abstraction*, 40 YALE L. J. 53, 76–77; p. 86, l. 16, See United States v. Stephens, 12 Fed. 52; p. 86, l. 18, But see HAND, THE BILL OF RIGHTS 58; p. 86, l. 34, Vol. 1, §218 (12th ed. Ruppenthal); p. 87, l. 6, Dennis v. United States, 341, U.S. 494, 511, quoted with approval in Yates v. United States, 354 U.S. 298, 317; p. 87, l. 16, At 110. Justice Jackson set forth this comment in his concurring opinion in the Dennis case. See also Pinkerton v. United States, 328 U.S. 640, 643–44; Frohwerk v. United States, 249 U.S. 204, 210; Goldman v. United States, 245 U.S. 474, 477; United States v. Rabinowich, 238, U.S. 78, 88; p. 87, l. 18, See Hogan v. O'Neill, 255 U.S. 52, 55; Nash v. United States, 229 U.S. 373, 378; p. 87, l. 18, 62 Stat. 701, 18 U.S.C. §371; p. 87, l. 19, 14 Stat. 484; p. 87, l. 20, 62 Stat. 808, 18 U.S.C. §2384 (Supp. IV, 1957); p. 87, l. 21, 12 Stat. 284; p. 87, l. 21, 26 Stat. 209, 15 U.S.C. §§1 to 7. In sustaining this provision in Nash v. United States, 229 U.S. 373, 378, Justice Holmes wrote for the Court: "Coming next to the objection that no overt act is laid, the answer is that the Sherman Act punishes the conspiracies at which it is aimed on the common law footing—that is to say, it does not make the doing of any act other than the act of conspiring a condition of liability."; p. 87, l. 22, 54 Stat. 671. With the revision of the criminal code in 1948 Smith Act conspiracy cases were brought under the general federal conspiracy statute, 62 Stat. 701, 18 U.S.C. §371, and an overt act is now necessary. See Yates v. United States, 354 U.S. 298; p. 87, l. 25, 225 U.S. 347, 387–88; p. 88, l. 4, 354 U.S. 298, 334; p. 88, l. 15, Dennis v. United States, 341 U.S. 494, 572–78. Charles Holt, one of those imprisoned under the Sedition Act of 1798, after he got out of prison, continued writing, but under the pseudonym, Nathan Sleek. This was one of the things he wrote: "Punishment only hardens printers. . . . They come out of jail holding their heads higher than if they had never been persecuted. Finally they assume the appearance of innocent men who have suffered wrongfully." Quoted in SMITH, FREEDOM'S FETTERS 384; p. 88, l. 38, 326 U.S. 273; p. 88, l. 39, 245 U.S. 474; p. 89, l. 9, 135 Mass. 545; p. 89, l. 15, 236 U.S. at 277–78; p. 89, l. 21, See Roth v. United States, 354 U.S. 476, 498, 501, 503, 505–7 (concurring and dissenting opinion of Justice Harlan); Beauharnais v. Illinois, 343 U.S. 250, 288, 294–95 (dissenting opinion of Justice Jackson); Gitlow v. New York, 268 U.S. 652, 672 (dissenting opinion of Justice Holmes in which Justice Brandeis joined). Cf. Palko v. Connecticut, 302 U.S. 319; p. 89, l. 32, 245 U.S. at 477; p. 89, l. 33, 249 U.S. 47, 204, 211. In Schaefer v. United States, 251 U.S. 466, 482–83, Justice Brandeis, in a dissenting opinion in which Justice Holmes joined, quoted Justice Holmes's clear and present danger test in the Schenck case and explained: "This is a rule of reason. . . . The question whether in a particular instance the words spoken or written fall within the permissible curtailment of free speech is, under the rule enunciated by this court, one of degree. . . . If the words were of such a nature and were used under such circumstances that men, judging in calmness, could not reasonably say that they created a clear and present danger that they would bring about the evil which Congress sought and had a right to prevent, then it is the duty of the trial judge to withdraw the case from the consideration of the jury; and if he fails to do so, it is the duty of the appellate court to correct the error. . . ." In a concurring opinion for himself and Justice Holmes in Whitney v. California, 274 U.S. 357, 376–77, he stated: ". . . The wide difference between advocacy and incitement, between preparation and attempt, between assembling and conspiracy, must be borne in mind. . . . No danger flowing from speech can be deemed clear and present, unless the incidence

of the evil apprehended is so imminent that it may befall before there is opportunity for full discussion. If there be time to expose through discussion the falsehood and fallacies, to avert the evil by the processes of education, the remedy to be
applied is more speech, not enforced silence. . . "; p. 90, l. 37, In the Schenck
case Justice Holmes said with reference to the Goldman case: "Indeed that case
might be said to dispose of the present contention if the precedent covers all
media concludendi. But as the right to free speech was not referred to specifically,
we have thought fit to add a few words." The Fox case, since it arose before
Gitlow v. New York, 268 U.S. 652, confined its discussion to the Fourteenth
Amendment; p. 91, l. 2, 2 HOLMES-POLLOCK LETTERS 7 (Howe ed.); p. 91, l. 6,
Dennis v. United States, 341 U.S. 494, 503, 504, 506; p. 92, l. 10, Crim. No.
73,086, D.D.C., Jan. 4, 1944. When the writer took over this prosecution in
February 1943 there had already been two indictments. United States v. Winrod,
Crim. Nos. 70, 153, and 71, 203, D.D.C., July 21, 1942 and Jan. 4, 1943; p. 92,
l. 37, 322 U.S. 680, 683; p. 93, l. 9, 325 U.S. 478; p. 93, l. 20, United States v.
McWilliams, 163 F.2d 695; p. 93, l. 33, 250 U.S. 616, 629, 627–28. At the
same term as the Abrams case they dissented in two cases in which the Court
sustained convictions under the Espionage Act of 1917. Schaefer v. United States,
251 U.S. 468 and Pierce v. United States, 252 U.S. 239; p. 94, l. 39, CHAFEE,
FREE SPEECH IN THE UNITED STATES 50–51; p. 95, l. 23, At 421–22; p. 95, l. 29,
255 U.S. 407. In Masses Pub. Co. v. Patten, 246 Fed. 24, the court sustained
the postmaster of the city of New York in seeking to bar from the mails a particular
issue of a monthly magazine called *The Masses*.; p. 95, l. 37, 254 U.S. 325; 268
U.S. 652; p. 95, l. 38, 274 U.S. 357. See also Burns v. United States 274 U.S. 328;
p. 96, l. 11, 2 HOLMES-POLLOCK LETTERS 163 (Howe ed.,).

CHAPTER VII

P. 97, l. 11, 341 U.S. 494, 510; p. 97, l. 17, 183 F.2d 201, 212. In the Roth
case Circuit Judge Frank in his concurring opinion suggested that in the light "of
the Supreme Court's opinion in the Dennis case" he "would stress the element of
probability in speaking of a 'clear danger.'" 237 F.2d at 826; p. 98, l. 17, 216
F.2d 354, 367, cert. denied, 348 U.S. 909; p. 98, l. 22, 223 F.2d 449, 456, rev'd
on other grounds, 352 U.S. 1; p. 98, l. 23, 227 F.2d 757, 764, judgment vacated
and case remanded, 354 U.S. 931; p. 98, l. 25, 228 F.2d 861, 870, rev'd, 355
U.S. 2; p. 99, l. 19, 341 U.S. at 570; p. 99, l. 28, 251 U.S. 466, 483; p. 100,
l. 1, 252 U.S. 239, 244, 250. Justice Brandeis in his concurring opinion in Whitney
v. California, 274 U.S. 357, 379, in which Justice Holmes joined, wrote: "Whether,
in 1919, when Miss Whitney did the things complained of, there was in California
such clear and present danger of serious evil, might have been made the important
issue in the case. She might have required that the issue be determined either by
the court or the jury. She claimed below that the statute as applied to her violated
the Federal Constitution; but she did not claim that it was void because there
was no clear and present danger of serious evil, nor did she request that the
existence of these conditions of a valid measure thus restricting the rights of free
speech and assembly be passed upon by the court or a jury. . . ."; p. 100, l. 29,
341 U.S. at 512, 514–15, 587; p. 100, l. 42, The Court of Appeals for the Fourth
Circuit recently followed this ruling in Scales v. United States, 260 F.2d 21, 28, a
membership case; p. 101, l. 3, 283 U.S. 359; 283 U.S. 697; 299 U.S. 353; p. 100,
l. 5, 357 U.S. 449; p. 100, l. 6, Staub v. City of Baxley, 355 U.S. 313 (invalidating
an ordinance which prohibited solicitation for membership in an organization
without a permit); Sweezy v. New Hampshire, 354 U.S. 234 (reversing contempt
conviction of a socialist who lectured at the University of New Hampshire and
who refused to answer the inquiries of the attorney general of New Hampshire);

Fowler v. Rhode Island, 345 U.S. 67 (invalidating an ordinance which as applied was used to interrupt and terminate a meeting of Jehovah's Witnesses in a public park); Kunz v. New York, 340 U.S. 290 (invalidating an ordinance which as construed required a permit from the police commissioner before speaking on religious subjects at a street meeting); Niemotko v. Maryland, 340 U.S. 268 (invalidating municipal practice requiring a permit from the police commissioner for holding a public meeting in a public park where such meetings were permitted); Terminiello v. Chicago, 337 U.S. 1 (invalidating a Chicago ordinance which as interpreted by the Illinois courts applied to speech which "stirs the public to anger"); Saia v. New York, 334 U.S. 558 (invalidating an ordinance which forbade the use of sound amplification devices directed towards the streets and public places without permission of the chief of police); Craig v. Harney, 331 U.S. 367 (reversing a contempt conviction of a publisher, an editorial writer, and a news reporter); Pennekamp v. Florida, 328 U.S. 331 (ibid.); Tucker v. Texas, 326 U.S. 517 (invalidating a Texas statute to the extent that it was construed to apply to one who refused to refrain from distributing religious tracts); Marsh v. Alabama, 326 U.S. 501 (ibid.); Thomas v. Collins, 323 U.S. 516 (holding unconstitutional a Texas statute requiring labor union organizers operating in that state to obtain an organizer's card before soliciting for members); Follett v. Town of McCormic, 321 U.S. 573 (annulling a South Carolina ordinance which exacted a fee for distributing religious tracts on the public streets); West Virginia Board of Education v. Barnette, 319 U.S. 624 (holding unconstitutional compulsory flag salute legislation), overruling Minersville School District v. Gobitis, 310 U.S. 586; Taylor v. Mississippi, 319 U.S. 583 (holding invalid a state statute which made it unlawful to urge people on religious grounds, to refuse to salute the flag); Martin v. City of Struthers, 319 U.S. 141 (invalidating an ordinance which prohibited the ringing of doorbells by itinerants who went from door to door distributing religious tracts); Murdock v. Pennsylvania, 319 U.S. 105 (annulling an ordinance which exacted a fee for the distribution of religious tracts on the public streets); Jones v. Opelika, 319 U.S. 103, adopting per curiam on rehearing the dissenting opinions in 316 U.S. 584 (ibid.); Largent v. Texas, 318 U.S. 418 (invalidating an ordinance which required a permit from the mayor for the distribution of religious pamphlets); Jamison v. Texas, 318 U.S. 413 (invalidating an ordinance which forbade the distribution of handbills); Bridges v. California, 314 U.S. 252 (reversing a contempt conviction of a newspaper publisher and an editor); Cantwell v. Connecticut, 310 U.S. 296 (holding invalid a statute which required a certificate for one soliciting funds for a religious, charitable or philanthropic cause, and reversing a conviction of one proselytizing on a public street of the common law offence of inciting a breach of the peace); Schneider v. State, 308 U.S. 147 (invalidating ordinances of Los Angeles, California, Milwaukee, Wisconsin, and Worcester, Massachusetts which prohibited the distribution of handbills, and an ordinance of Irvington, New Jersey which banned door to door advocacy without a permit from the chief of police); Hague v. CIO, 307 U.S. 496 (annulling two ordinances of Jersey City, one of which prohibited assemblies "in or upon the public streets, highways, public parks or public buildings" without a permit from the director of public safety, and the other of which prohibited the distribution of pamphlets); Lovell v. City of Griffin, 303 U.S. 444 (invalidating an ordinance which prohibited the distribution of "circulars, handbooks, advertising or literature of any kind" without a permit from the city manager); Grosjean v. American Press Co., 297 U.S. 233 (holding unconstitutional a Louisiana license tax on certain gross receipts of publications having a circulation of more than 20,000 copies a week). In McCollum v. Board of Education, 333 U.S. 203, the Court required the states to observe a separation of church and state; p. 101, l. 11, 343 U.S. 250; p. 101, l. 12, 357 U.S. 449; p. 101, l. 14, 268 U.S. 652; p. 101, l. 25, 343 U.S. at 295; p. 101, l. 33, 283 U.S. at 715; p. 101, l. 36, 315 U.S. 568, 571–72; p. 102, l. 5, 312 U.S. 569. In Smith v. New York, 292 U.S. 606, the Court approved the ordinance which it later invalidated in Kunz v. New York, 340 U.S. 290. The ordinance required a permit for street speaking. However, the earlier appeal, by one convicted of preaching atheism in the street without a permit, was only on the ground of unreasonable classification; p. 102, l. 7, 336 U.S. 77; p. 102, l. 8, 316 U.S. 52; p. 102, l. 9, 341 U.S. 622. There is a distinction between this case and Martin v. City of Struthers, 319 U.S. 141, where the Court invalidated an ordinance prohibiting door to door advocacy, albeit a narrow one; p. 102, l. 12, 321 U.S. 158. In the field of education see Zorach v. Clauson, 343 U.S. 306 (sustaining New York City's released time program), and Everson v. Board of Education, 330 U.S. 1 (permitting reimbursements to parents for payments made for transporting children to parochial schools); p. 102, l. 13, 345 U.S. 395; p. 102, l. 14, 340 U.S. 315; p. 102, l. 19, It is only on this narrow ground that this case is distinguishable from various of the decisions cited previously; p. 102, l. 26, 340 U.S. at 317. Prior to Gitlow v. New York, 268 U.S. 652, the Court in Fox v. Washington, 236 U.S. 273, sustained a statute of the state of Washington which made the advocacy of the commission of any crime an offense, and in Davis v. Massachusetts, 167 U.S. 43, affirming 162 Mass. 510, a Boston ordinance which required a permit from the mayor in order to make a speech on public grounds. In the latter case Justice Holmes, then a member of the Supreme Judicial Court of Massachusetts, wrote the state court's opinion; p. 102, l. 37, In the concluding paragraph of his dissenting opinion in Truax v. Corrigan, 257 U.S. 312, 344, Justice Holmes commented: ". . . There is nothing that I more deprecate than the use of the Fourteenth Amendment beyond the absolute compulsion of its words to prevent the making of social experiments that an important part of the community desires, in the insulated chambers afforded by the several States, even though the experiments may seem futile or even noxious to me and to those whose judgment I most respect. * * *" Justice Brandeis in the concluding paragraph of his dissenting opinion in New State Ice Co. v. Liebmann, 285 U.S. 262, 311, pointed out: "To stay experimentation in things social and economic is a grave responsibility. Denial of the right to experiment may be fraught with serious consequences to the Nation. It is one of the happy incidents of the federal system that a single courageous State may, if its citizens choose, serve as a laboratory; and try novel social and economic experiments without risk to the rest of the country. * * *"; p. 103, l. 18, 354 U.S. 476, 485; p. 103, l. 29, 354 U.S. 436, 447; p. 103, l. 38, 354 U.S. 931; p. 104, l. 15, 357 U.S. 371, 375; p. 104, l. 23, 342 U.S. 165, 168. Or as Justice Douglas put it for the Court in Jerome v. United States 318 U.S. 101, 104–5: ". . . Since there is no common law offense against the United States, the administration of criminal justice under our federal system has rested with the states, except as criminal offenses have been explicitly prescribed by Congress. * * *" In Malinski v. New York, 324 U.S. 401, 412–13, Justice Frankfurter in his concurring opinion stated: "Apart from permitting Congress to use criminal sanctions as means for carrying into execution powers granted to it, the Constitution left the domain of criminal justice to the States." In Marcello v. United States, 196 F.2d 437, 443, the court, in supstaining a claim of privilege before a subcommittee of the Kefauver Committee, although the claim was really based on a fear of state prosecution, adverted to this point: "It must be remembered also that, in our federal system, the administration of criminal justice rests preponderantly with the states."; p. 104, l. 35, 350 U.S. at 519; p. 104, l. 41, 354 U.S. at 505–7; p. 106, l. 2, C. 1, §15. The Court referred to the declaration of rights in the Vermont constitution of 1777, c. 1, §14, which did not contain this restricting identification; p. 106, l. 9, Art. IX, §7. The Delaware constitution of 1792 contained a similar provision. Art. I, §5. Again, in the case of Pennsylvania, the Court referred to the declaration of rights in an earlier constitution, that of 1776, art. 12, which again was more broadly drawn; p. 106, l. 13, Art. VIII, §1, p. 106, l. 16, Art. XXXIII. Of the remaining five there were two whose constitutions provided that freedom of the press was to remain inviolate. GA. CONST., art. LXI (1777), art. IV, §3

(1789); N.H. CONST., art. I, §22 (1784). The remaining three provided that the liberty of the press was not to be restrained. MASS CONST., Declaration of Rights, art. XVI (1780); N.C. CONST., Declaration of Rights, art. XV (1776); VA CONST., Declaration of Rights, §12 (1776); p. 106, l. 24, 1 ANNALS OF CONG. 439; p. 107, l. 4, 335 U.S. 848. There the Court evenly divided, Justice Frankfurter not sitting, affirmed a holding that Edmund Wilson's *Memoirs of Hecate County* was obscene; p. 107, l. 5, Justice Jackson said: "Does your argument mean that we would have to take every obscenity case and decide the constitutional issues on the merits of the literary work? It seems to me that would mean we would become the High Court of Obscenity." 17 U.S. LAW WEEK 3119; p. 107, l. 7, Times Film Corp. v. City of Chicago, 355 U.S. 35; p. 107, l. 8, Sunshine Book Co. v. Summerfield, 355 U.S. 372; p. 107, l. 9, One, Inc. v. Olesen, 355 U.S. 371; p. 107, l. 14, Mounce v. United States, 355 U.S. 180; p. 107, l. 28, Kingsley International Pictures Corp. v. Board of Regents, 360 U.S. 684; p. 107, l. 40, Joseph Burstyn, Inc. v. Wilson, 343 U.S. 495; p. 108, l. 1, Holmby Productions, Inc. v. Vaughn, 350 U.S. 870; Commercial Pictures Corp. v. Board of Regents, 346 U.S. 587; p. 108, l. 2, Gelling v. Texas, 343 U.S. 960; p. 108, l. 15, 352 U.S. 380, 383–84; p. 108, l. 28, 92 U.S. 214, 220; p. 108, l. 31, 333 U.S. 507, 515, p. 109, l. 3, Id. at 509; accord, Thornhill v. Alabama, 310 U.S. 88; Herndon v. Lowry, 301 U.S. 242; Stromberg v. California, 283 U.S. 359; p. 109, l. 6, 350 U.S. 870; p. 109, l. 8, 346 U.S. 587; p. 109, l. 10, 346 U.S. 587; p. 109, l. 11, 343 U.S. 960; p. 109, l. 13, 343 U.S. 495. In an earlier decision, Mutual Film Corp. v. Industrial Comm'n, 236 U.S. 230, the Court, in approving the same language which it later invalidated in Superior Films v. Dept. of Education, 346 U.S. 587, expressed the view that motion pictures were not entitled to the same measure of protection as other forms of utterance. In the Burstyn case the Court overruled its earlier position: ". . . To the extent that language in the opinion in *Mutual Film Corp.* v. *Industrial Comm'n, supra,* is out of harmony with the views here set forth, we no longer adhere to it." This result was forecast in United States v. Paramount Pictures, 334 U.S. 131, 166, where the Court said: ". . . We have no doubt that moving pictures, like newspapers and radio, are included in the press whose freedom is guaranteed by the First Amendment. . . "; p. 109, l. 14, 333 U.S. 507; p. 109, l. 15, 333 U.S. 95. For legislation in other areas than that of utterance which was held not sufficiently definite to meet due process requirements see, e.g., Lanzetta v. New Jersey, 306 U.S. 451; Champlin Refining Co. v. Corporation Comm'n., 286 U.S. 210; Smith v. Cahoon, 283 U.S. 553; Cline v. Frink Dairy Co. 274 U.S. 445; Connally v. General Construction Co., 269 U.S. 385; United States v. Cohen Grocery Co., 255 U.S. 81; Collins v. Kentucky, 234 U.S. 634; International Harvester Co. v. Kentucky, 234 U.S. 216; cf. Watkins v. United States, 354 U.S. 178; United States v. Cardiff, 344 U.S. 174; Kraus & Bros. v. United States, 327 U.S. 614; p. 109, l. 20, State v. Musser, 118 Utah 537; p. 109, l. 24, 354 U.S. at 487 n. 20; p. 110, l. 17, Frankfeld v. United States, 198 F.2d 679, cert. denied, 344 U.S. 922; p. 110, l. 24, United States v. Flynn, 216 F.2d 354, cert. denied, 348 U.S. 909; p. 110, l. 29, United States v. Flynn, 130 F.Supp. 412. In United States v. Flynn, 131 F.Supp. 742, the court denied a motion of the remaining eleven for reargument of their motion for a new trial; p. 110, l. 30, See Scales v. United States, 260 F.2d 21, 31. Mrs. Hartle was formerly a leading communist party organizer in the Pacific northwest. She served twenty and a half months of a five year sentence. On February 1, 1956 Assistant Attorney General William F. Tompkins in announcing her release from prison praised her for her cooperation. He said that of all the 88 American Communist party leaders who had been convicted up to that point in Smith Act prosecutions she was the only one who had "exhibited remorse for her past activities and offered to cooperate with the Government." In June 1954 she was the star witness before the House Committee on Un-American Activities and identified more than 400 persons she had known as party members; p. 110, l. 38, Huff v. United States, 251 F.2d 342;

p. 111, l. 2, Mesarosh v. United States, 352 U.S. 1; p. 111, l. 10, 350 U.S. 497; p. 111, l. 14, 354 U.S. 298. On a previous petition the Court gave relief as to bail requirements. Stack v. Boyle, 342 U.S. 1. Schneiderman was involved in another well-known case in which the Court refused to invalidate his naturalization certificate. Schneiderman v. United States, 320 U.S. 118. The Court divided five to three in that case (Justice Jackson did not participate) with Justice Murphy writing the majority opinion and Chief Justice Stone the dissenting one. Wendell L. Willkie, the Republican candidate for president in 1940, successfully argued the case for Schneiderman. In the Dennis case the defendants relied on the majority opinion in this case and the government on the dissenting one. Yates further received various contempt sentences, some of which were reversed and some affirmed on appeal. One of those which was affirmed went to the Supreme Court, and the Court, although sustaining the conviction on one specification, vacated the sentence and remanded the case to the district court for resentencing. Yates v. United States, 355 U.S. 66. Subsequently the district court, after reconsidering the matter in the light of the Supreme Court's opinion, again imposed a sentence of one year on the defendant. 158 F.Supp. 480. The Court of Appeals for the Ninth Circuit again affirmed. 252 F.2d 568. But the Supreme Court again vacated the judgment. 356 U.S. 363. This time the Court remanded the case to the district court with directions to reduce the sentence on the petitioner to the time already served; p. 111, l. 26, See United States v. Yates, 158 F.Supp. at 481; p. 111, l. 28, 354 U.S. 931; p. 111, l. 36, 248 F.2d 201 (six of the seven defendants have been retried and again convicted); p. 111, l. 41, Patricia Blau v. United States, 340 U.S. 159, and Irving Blau v. United States, 340 U.S. 332; p. 112, l. 1, 248 F.2d 671, cert denied, 355 U.S. 942; p. 112, l. 4, 249 F.2d 619; p. 112, l. 9, 251 F.2d 342. In the Honolulu case the Supreme Court before the trial denied a motion for leave to file a petition for a writ of prohibition or mandamus. Fujimoto v. Wiig, 344 U.S. 852; p. 112, l. 24, 253 F.2d 310; p. 112, l. 29, 253 F.2d 601. In another case which involved Wellman the Court of Appeals for the District of Columbia Circuit held that Communist party membership, even though active and meaningful, did not work a forfeiture of a veteran's service connected disability benefits. Wellman v. Whittier, 259 F.2d 163; p. 112, l. 33, 256 F.2d 79; p. 112, l. 36, 257 F.2d 830. Stein, who was also known as Steinberg, was at one time held in bail of $125,000. This was for two prosecutions, one of them this one. In one his bail was $75,000 and in the other, $50,000. The Court of Appeals for the Second Circuit reduced the $50,000 bail to $30,000. United States v. Stein, 231 F.2d 109, cert. denied, 351 U.S. 943. Justice Douglas reduced the $75,000 amount first to $45,000, with the consent of the government, and then to $10,000. Stein v. United States, 76 S.Ct. 822. But Stein's total bail was still $40,000. Stein's other prosecution was for harboring and conspiring to harbor Thompson, one of the convicted defendants in the Dennis case, and one of the eight who decamped. He won a reversal here too. Kremen v. United States, 353 U.S. 346. The ground was the admission into evidence of material unreasonably seized; p. 113, l. 11, Scales v. United States, 355 U.S. 1; p. 113, l. 12, Lightfoot v. United States, 355 U.S. 2; p. 113, l. 21, Jencks v. United States, 353 U.S. 657, 668; p. 113, l. 23, Scales v. United States, 260 F.2d 21, cert. granted, 358 U.S. 917. Argued and set for reargument. 360 U.S. 924; p. 113, l. 27, United States v. Noto, 262, F.2d 501. The remaining five cases are: United States v. Blum (D.S.D. Ind.); United States v. Dr. Albert Emanuel Blumberg (D.E.D. Pa.); United States v. Hellman (D. Mont.); United States v. Russo (D. Mass.); United States v. Max Morris Weiss (D.N.D. Ill.). Blumberg and Hellman have been tried and convicted and their cases are pending on appeal. In Noto v. United States, 76 S.Ct. 255, Justice Harlan fixed bail at $10,000 after the district court had fixed it at $30,000 and the Court of Appeals for the Second Circuit had refused to change it. The Supreme Court confirmed his ruling. Noto v. United States, 351 U.S. 902; p. 113, l. 41, 356 U.S. 670; 356 U.S. 660; p. 114, l. 4, 355 U.S. 115, 120; p. 114, l. 7, 353 U.S. 194, 202;

353 U.S. 963; p. 114, l. 17, 354 U.S. 178, 183, 185; p. 114, l. 30, 354 U.S. 234, 262–63; p. 115, l. 11, Flaxer v. United States, 354 U.S. 929; p. 115, l. 12, Barenblatt v. United States, 354 U.S. 930, p. 115, l. 13, Sacher v. United States, 354 U.S. 930, p. 115, l. 23, 355 U.S. 16, p. 115, l. 32, Sacher v. United States, 356 U.S. 576, p. 115, l. 33, Flaxer v. United States, 358 U.S. 147; p. 115, l. 38, Speiser v. Randall, 357 U.S. 513, and First Unit. Church v. Los Angeles, 357 U.S. 545; p. 116, l. 7, Miller v. United States, 259 F.2d 187, p. 116, l. 15, Singer v. United States, 244 F.2d 349 (Singer at some points claimed his right of silence, but both courts held that he had waived it); p. 116, l. 17, 247 F.2d 535; p. 117, l. 3, United States v. Peck, 154 F.Supp. 603, 605, 606; p. 117, l. 12, Even before the Watkins decision, witnesses before the Permanent Subcommittee on Investigations of the Committee on Government Operations, usually known as the McCarthy Committee during the chairmanship of Senator Joseph R. McCarthy of Wisconsin, fared moderately well at the hands of the courts. See, e.g., O'Connor v. United States, 240 F.2d 404 (Harvey O'Connor, an author); United States v. Lamont, 236 F.2d 312 (Corliss Lamont; Abraham Unger, a New York attorney; and Albert Shadowitz, whose refusal was based on the advice of Dr. Albert Einstein); United States v. Diantha Hoag, 142 F.Supp. 667; United States v. Kamin, 136 F.Supp. 791 (Leon J. Kamin, a research assistant in Harvard's Department of Social Relations). After the judge directed Kamin's acquittal, the government dropped its case against Prof. Wendell H. Furry of Harvard. For a witness in this group after the Watkins decision, see Brewster v. United States, 255 F.2d 899 (Frank W. Brewster, former chairman of the Western Conference of Teamsters); p. 117, l. 17, 359 U.S. 535 and 360 U.S. 474, 709 (The Greene case was followed in Cafeteria and Restaurant Workers Local v. McElroy, 28 U.S.L. WEEK 2091); p. 118, l. 17, 360 U.S. 684; p. 119, l. 41, 360 U.S. 315, 252, 264, 622; p. 120, l. 1, 360 U.S. 72, 423, 109; p. 120, l. 9, 350 U.S. 497.

CHAPTER VIII

P. 122, l. 21, 354 U.S. 284, 289; p. 122, l. 23, 315 U.S. 769, 776; p. 122, l. 39, 257 U.S. 312; p. 123, l. 1, 47 Stat. 70, 29 U.S.C. §§101 to 107; p. 123, l. 2, 301 U.S. 468; p. 123, l. 10, 310 U.S. 88, 102; p. 123, l. 16, 312 U.S. 321, 326; p. 123, l. 33, 315 U.S. 722; p. 123, l. 38, 336 U.S. 490; p. 123, l. 39, 339 U.S. 470; 345 U.S. 192; p. 124, l. 29, Professor Paul Freund in his, ON UNDERSTANDING THE SUPREME COURT 18 says: "Picketing is indeed a hybrid, comprising elements of persuasion, information, and publicity together with elements of non-verbal conduct, economic pressure and signals for action."; p. 124, l. 34, 358 U.S. 270; p. 124, l. 38, 356 U.S. 341; p. 125, l. 19, 355 U.S. 131, 138, 139. Chief Justice Warren and Justices Black and Douglas were "of opinion that Congress has given the National Labor Relations Board exclusive jurisdiction of this controversy."; p. 126, l. 1, In Day-Brite Lighting, Inc. v. Missouri, 342 U.S. 421, 423, Justice Douglas wrote for the Court: ". . . But the state legislatures have constitutional authority to experiment with new techniques; they are entitled to their own standard of the public welfare; they may within extremely broad limits control practices in the business-labor field, so long as specific constitutional prohibitions are not violated and so long as conflicts with valid and controlling federal laws are avoided. * * *" There the Court sustained the validity of a Missouri statute which permitted an employee to absent himself from his employment for four hours between the opening and the closing of the polls without penalty; p. 126, l. 4, 345 U.S. 192. Prof. Frederic Meyers, who made a study of Texas' right to work law, concluded (in a report for the Fund for the Republic) that the law, although loaded with symbolism, had little actual direct effect.

CHAPTER IX

P. 127, l. 20, 350 U.S. 497; p. 127, l. 26, Braden v. Commonwealth, 291 S.W. 2d 843 (Ky.); Commonwealth v. Gilbert, 334 Mass. 71; cf. Commonwealth v. Hood, 334 Mass. 76; p. 127, l. 28, Albertson v. Millard, 345 Mich. 519; p. 127, l. 37, 358 U.S. 270; p. 128, l. 3, 355 U.S. 131, 137–38; p. 128, l. 10, 358 U.S. 283, 296; p. 128, l. 19, 359 U.S. 236, 247–48; p. 128, l. 40, 359 U.S. 434; p. 129, l. 1, 359 U.S. 498; p. 129, l. 3, 359 U.S. 354; p. 129, l. 9, 351 U.S. 225, 231–32; p. 129, l. 15, Amalgamated Assn. v. Wisconsin Employment Relations Bd., 340 U.S. 383; p. 129, l. 16, United Automobile Workers v. O'Brien, 339 U.S. 454; p. 129, l. 19, Plankington Packing Co. v. Wisconsin Employment Relations Bd., 338 U.S. 953; p. 129, l. 20, LaCrosse Telephone Corp. v. Wisconsin Employment Relations Bd., 336 U.S. 18; p. 129, l. 22, Bethlehem Steel Co. v. New York State Labor Relations Bd., 330 U.S. 767; p. 129, l. 23, Hill v. Florida, 325 U.S. 538; p. 129, l. 29, 339 U.S. at 457. This language was quoted with approval in Amalgamated Assn. v. Wisconsin Employment Relations Bd., 340 U.S. 383, 390; p. 129, l. 30, 354 U.S. 476. P. 129, l. 40, 4 ELLIOT, DEBATES 545, 542 (2d ed.); p. 130, l. 9, 99 CONG. REC. 2459; p. 130, l. 14, 67 Stat. 145; p. 133, l. 27, 358 U.S. 272; p. 133, l. 32, 356 U.S. 634; p. 133, l. 35, 356 U.S. 617; p. 133, l. 38, 347 U.S. 656; p. 134, l. 7, See United States v. Texas, 339 U.S. 707, United States v. Louisiana, 339 U.S. 699, United States v. California, 332 U.S. 19; Submerged Lands Act, 67 Stat. 29, 43 U.S.C. §§1301 to 1315 (Supp. IV, 1957), Alabama v. Texas, 347 U.S. 272. For a collection of instances in which Congress passed legislation to avoid the effect of Supreme Court decisions see Note, *Congressional Reversal of Supreme Court Decisions: 1945–1957*, 71 HARV. L. REV. 1324; p. 134, l. 12, The Conference of Chief Justices' Committee on Federal-State Relationships as affected by Judicial Decisions in its report in 1958 said: "We are now concerned specifically with the effect of judicial decisions upon the relations between the Federal Government and the State governments. Here we think the over-all tendency of decisions of the Supreme Court over the last 25 years or more has been to press the extension of Federal power and to press it rapidly."; p. 134, l. 24, Guss v. Utah Labor Relations Board, 353 U.S. 1, Amalgamated Meat Cutters v. Fairlawn Meats, Inc., 353 U.S. 20, San Diego Building Trades Council v. Garmon, 353 U.S. 26; p. 134, l. 25, H.R. 9678, 85th Cong., 2d Sess.; p. 134, l. 32, N.Y. Times, June 7, 1958, p. 18, col. 1. However, the Labor-Management Reporting and Disclosure Act of 1959 provides, 73 Stat. 541, 29 U.S.C.A. §164(c)(2) (Supp. 1959): "Nothing in this Act shall be deemed to prevent or bar any agency or the courts of any State or Territory (including the Commonwealth of Puerto Rico, Guam, and the Virgin Islands), from assuming and asserting jurisdiction over labor disputes over which the Board declines, pursuant to paragraph (1) of this subsection, to assert jurisdiction."; p. 134, l. 41, 102 CONG. REC. 2023; p. 136, l. 13, The vote led Arthur Krock to conclude a column on the subject, *The Question of Congress "Intent"*, with the comment: "And it belongs in the same general category as those 'election returns' which, as Mr. Dooley once noted, the Supreme Court does not ignore." N.Y. Times, July 22, 1958, p. 26, col. 4; p. 136, l. 36, 360 U.S. 72; p. 136, l. 37, 350 U.S. 497.

CHAPTER X

P. 138, l. 33, 350 U.S. 422, 449, affirming 221 F.2d 760, affirming 128 F.Supp. 617 (Ullmann spelled with one "n" by the district court); p. 138, l. 38, 161 U.S. 591, 632; p. 139, l. 12, *Nemo Tenetur Seipsum Prodere*, 5 HARV. L. REV. 71. He enlarged upon his study in *The Privilege Against Self-Incrimination; Its History*, 15 HARV. L. REV. 610. This material was embodied in §2250 of his work on evidence; p. 139, l. 17, *Attack of the Common Lawyers on the Oath Ex Officio*

as Administered in the Ecclesiastical Court in England in ESSAYS IN HISTORY AND
POLITICAL THEORY IN HONOR OF CHARLES HOWARD MCILWAIN 199; Morgan, The
Privilege Against Self-Incrimination, 34 MINN. L. REV. 1; p. 139, l. 22, 8 WIGMORE,
EVIDENCE §2250, n.1 (3d ed.); p. 139, l. 27, Watts v. Indiana, 338 U.S. 49, 54;
p. 140, l. 4, Apparently trial by battle did not at first exist in England. The
Normans under William the Conqueror brought it over in 1066. But then it had
its day.; p. 141, l. 34, Esmein finds the earliest instance of the inquisitio procedure
in a decretal of 1198. See 5 CONTINENTAL LEGAL HISTORY SERIES 80 (1913). But
Wigmore, Pollock and Maitland, Tanon, and Hinschius are of the opinion that
the first reference to the inquisitio procedure as a generic method was in a decretal
of 1199. 8 WIGMORE, EVIDENCE §2250, n.28 (3d ed.,); 2 POLLACK AND MAITLAND,
THE HISTORY OF ENGLISH LAW 657, n.4 (2d ed.,); p. 141, l. 35, This phrase, which
became identified in England with the inquisitio procedure of the church, ap-
parently derives from one of Innocent's decretals of 1199.; p. 143, l. 29, 1
PUBLICATIONS OF THE SELDEN SOCIETY, SELECT PLEAS OF THE CROWN 118 (Maitland ed.); 4 id., THE COURT BARON 64–65 (Maitland ed. 1891); p. 144, l. 25,
NEILSEN, TRIAL BY COMBAT 42–45; 1 PUBLICATIONS OF THE SELDEN SOCIETY,
SELECT PLEAS OF THE CROWN 92, 123, 128–29 (Maitland ed.); p. 145, l. 12, 3
Edw. 1, c. 12; 1 PUBLICATIONS OF THE SELDEN SOCIETY, SELECT PLEAS OF THE
CROWN 99–101, 134 (Maitland ed.); 59 id., ROLLS OF THE JUSTICES IN EYRE
332, 346 (Stenton ed), Y.B. 30 & 31 Edw. 1, p. 543; p. 146, l. 15, At 51 (Chrimes
transl.); p. 146, l. 33, MATTHAEI PARIS MONACHI ALBANENSIS ANGLI, HISTORIA MAJOR
716 (1640 ed.); p. 146, l. 36, AN EXACT CHRONOLOGICAL VINDICATION AND HIS-
TORICAL DEMONSTRATION OF OUR BRITISH, ROMAN, SAXON, NORMAN, ENGLISH KINGS
SUPREAM ECCLESIASTICAL JURISDICTION, The Second Tome 699, 705 (1665);
p. 147, l. 8, 7 SELDEN SOCIETY PUBLICATIONS, THE MIRROR OF JUSTICES 172 (Whittaker ed.); p. 147, l. 23, 2 POLLOCK AND MAITLAND, THE HISTORY OF ENGLISH
LAW 604, 658 (2d ed.); p. 147, l. 39, 1 STATUTES OF THE REALM 209; p. 147,
l. 41, 2 INST. *600; p. 147, l. 42, 1 STATUTES OF THE REALM 171; p. 148, l. 3, 2
ROTULI PARLIAMENTORUM 168, item 28 (1347); p. 148, l. 8, 25 Edw. 3, stat.
5, c.4; p. 148, l. 15, 43 Edw. 3, c.3; p. 148, l. 23, 5 Rich. 2, stat. 2, c.5; p. 148,
l. 25, 3 ROTULI PARLIAMENTORUM 141, item 53; p. 148, l. 28, 2 Hen. 4, c.15;
p. 148, l. 32, 2 Hen. 5, Stat. 1, c.7; p. 148, l. 36, 2 Hen. 5, stat. 1, c.3; p. 148,
l. 42, 2 Hen. 5, Stat. 1, c.4. (1414); 2 Hen. 6, c.18 (1423); 6 Hen. 6, c.3 (1427);
8 Hen. 6, c.4, (1429); 11 Hen. 6, c.12 (1433); 18 Hen. 6, c.19 (1439); 23 Hen.
6, c.12 (1444–45); 33 Hen. 6, c.7 (1455); 3 Edw. 4, c.1 (1463); 4 Edw. 4, c.1
(1464–65); 8 Edw. 4, c.2, (1468); 17 Edw. 4, c.4 (1477–78); 22 Edw. 4, c.1
(1482–83); 1 Hen. 7, c.7, (1485); 11 Hen. 7, c.3 (1495); 19 Hen. 7, c.11,
(1503); 19 Hen. 7, c.14, 2 STATUTES OF THE REALM 658 (1503); p. 149, l. 32,
A Treatise concernying the diuision betwene the spiritualtie and temporalitie
in THE APOLOGYE OF SYR THOMAS MORE, KNYGHT 203, 220–21, 147 (Early English Text Society, original ser. no. 180, Taft ed.); p. 149, l. 39, SALEM AND
BIZANCE, f. 49b, 50a (1533); p. 149, l. 42, 25 Hen. 8, c.14, 3 STATUTES OF THE
REALM 454, 455; p. 150, l. 22, From a letter to his daughter written in June 1535
in the Tower of London. THE CORRESPONDENCE OF SIR THOMAS MORE 557 (Rogers
ed.); p. 150, l. 28, 1 & 2 P. & M., c.6, 4 STATUTES OF THE REALM 244. The repudiated statute of 1382, which had remained on the books, and the act of 1414
had been repealed in the reign of Edward III. 1 Edw. 6, c.12, §2, 4 id. at 19;
p. 150, l. 37, 1 & 2 P. & M., c.13, §4; p. 150, l. 39, 2 & 3 P. & M., c.10; p. 151,
l. 22, 1 Eliz. 1, c.1, §37; p. 151, l. 25 BURN, THE STAR CHAMBER 50; 4 COKE, INST.
*63, *65; FRENCH, CHARLES I AND THE PURITAN UPHEAVAL 94, 211–22, 256–79;
3 HOW. ST. TR. 374, 519, 562, 711; Pollard, Council, Star Chamber and Privay
Council Under the Tudors, 37 ENG. HIST. REV. 516, 529; RUSHWORTH, HISTORICAL
COLLECTIONS, The Second Part [268] (misnumbered 270) (1680); SCOFIELD,
COURT OF STAR CHAMBER 36; 16 SELDEN SOCIETY PUBLICATIONS, SELECT CASES
BEFORE THE KING'S COUNCIL IN THE STAR CHAMBER (Leadam ed.); 25 id. (Leadam

ed.); SMITH, THE COMMON-WEALTH OF ENGLAND 118–20 (1594 ed.); LAMBARDE, ARCHION; OR, A COMMENTARY UPON THE HIGH COURTS OF JUSTICE IN ENGLAND 215 (1635); p. 154, 1. 39, FRENCH, CHARLES I AND THE PURITAN UPHEAVAL 280–307; USHER, THE RISE AND FALL OF THE HIGH COMMISSION; p. 156, 1. 30, 1 Eliz. 1, c.1, §§17 and 18; p. 157, 1. 21, A BRIEFE TREATISE OF OATHES 10, 11, p. 157, 1. 33, 1 HOW. ST. TR. 1271, 1274, 1275; p. 157, 1. 40, 1 STRYPE, THE LIFE AND ACTS OF JOHN WHITGIFT *338. P. 158, 1. 3, Vol. 1, at 194, 196, 162–63 (Toulnim's ed., with additional notes by Choules); p. 158, 1. 31, THE EXPANSION OF THE COMMON LAW 85; p. 159, 1. 4, 1 HOW. ST. TR. 1277, 1282; p. 159, 1. 18, 3 STRYPE, THE LIFE AND ACTS OF JOHN WHITGIFT, app. at *136, *137; p. 159, 1. 39, Skrogges v. Coleshil, Dy. 175a; p. 159, 1. 40, Reported in a note, Dy. 175b; p. 160, 1. 1, Burrowes v. High Commission, 3 Buls. 48, 49–50. Concerning Hynde, Coke is reported as saying parenthetically "some love money, and he loved usury well", and about Leigh, "he loved mass as well as he loved his life."; p. 160, 1. 6, Caudrey's Case, 5 Co. Rep. 1a; p. 160, 1. 34, Collier v. Collier, Cro. Eliz. 201, (spelled Cullier); Moo. K.B. 906, 4 Leon. 194; p. 160, 1. 37, Morice in his tract against the oath used the phrase separately and also in its full context. At 17, 21–22. He could not understand why even under the *inquisitio* procedure a person should not be advised in advance of the charges against him; p. 161, 1. 10, 1 HOW. ST. TR. 1271, 1274; p. 161, 1. 13, Cro. Eliz. 262; p. 162, 1. 13, 3 COKE INST. *29; p. 164, 1. 17, Garland v. Jekyll, 2 Bing. 273, 296–97; p. 167, 1. 11, 2 HOW. ST. TR. 69, 86; p. 167, 1. 20, 2 id. 131, 155; p. 167, 1. 26, 2 id. 217, 244; p. 167, 1. 31, 12 Co. Rep. 26; p. 168, 1. 12, 12 Co. Rep. 63; p. 169, 1. 6, BOWEN, THE LION AND THE THRONE 304–5; p. 169, 1. 12, 8 Coke 113b, 118a; p. 169, 1. 31, Edward's Case, 13 Co. Rep. 9, 10; p. 169, 1. 33, 2 INST. *658; p. 169, 1. 36, Huntley v. Cage, 2 Brownl. 14, 15; p. 169, 1. 42, Burrowes v. High Commission, 3 Bulst. 48; p. 170, 1. 28, Hob. 84; p. 170, 1. 35, Noy 151; p. 171, 1. 15 3 HOW. ST. TR. 1315.

P. 173, 1. 18, 16 Chas. 1, c.10, §8; 16 Chas. 1, c.11, §4; 13 Chas. 2, c.12, §4; 3 HOW. ST. TR. 1315, 1342, 1349, 1358; JARDINE, A READING ON THE USE OF TORTURE IN THE CRIMINAL LAW OF ENGLAND 70; p. 175, 1. 9, 4 HOW. ST. TR. 63, 76; p. 175, 1. 14, 4 id. 989, 1101; p. 175, 1. 16, 4 id. 1269, 1292–93, 1342; p. 175, 1. 22, 5 id. 1034, 1039; p. 175, 1. 32, 6 id. 951, 957–58, 966; p. 176, 1. 5, 6 id. 1189, 1194; p. 176, 1. 19, 4 id. 1269, 1342; p. 176, 1. 25, 3 CAMPBELL, LIVES OF THE CHIEF JUSTICES OF ENGLAND 9 (3d ed.). See, e.g., Reg. v. Baynton, 14 HOW. ST. TR. 597, 620–5; Reg. v. Swendsen, 14 id. 559, 580–81; p. 176, 1. 27, Rex v. Reading, 7 HOW. ST. TR. 259, 296; Rex v. Whitebread, 7 id. 311, 361; Rex v. Langhorn, 7 id. 417, 435; Rex v. Castlemaine, 7 id. 1067, 1096; Rex v. Stafford, 7 id. 1293, 1314; Rex v. Plunket, 8 id. 447, 480–1; Rex v. Rosewell, 10 id. 147, 169; Rex v. Oates, 10 id. 1079, 1098–1100, 1123; p. 176, 1. 35, 161 U.S. 591; p. 176, 1. 37, 350 U.S. 422, 445, 454. Compare Chief Judge Magruder's statement in Maffie v. United States, 209 F.2d 225, 227 (one of the cases arising out of a grand jury investigation into the Brink's robbery in Boston in 1950): ". . . If it be thought that the privilege is outmoded in the conditions of this modern age, then the thing to do is to take it out of the Constitution, not to whittle it down by the subtle encroachments of judicial opinion."; p. 177, 1. 5, 8 ENGLISH HISTORICAL DOCUMENTS 86; Vaugh. 135; p. 177, 1. 36, 3 INST. *162. In Semayne's Case, 5 Co. Rep. 91a, 91b, the court stated: "That the house of every one is to him as his castle and fortress, as well for his defence against injury and violence as for his repose. . . ."; p. 178, 1. 1, At *176–*77; p. 178, 1. 9, 2 THE STORY OF THE PLEAS OF THE CROWN 113 (published by Emlyn from the original manuscripts, Wilson ed. 1778); p. 178, 1. 33, Entick v. Carrington, 2 Wils. K. B. 275, 291; 19 HOW. ST. TR. 1029, 1066; p. 178, 1. 37, 116 U.S. 616, 626; p. 179, 1. 2, 1 BROUGHAM, HISTORICAL SKETCHES OF STATESMEN WHO FLOURISHED IN THE TIME OF GEORGE III 42 (1858); p. 179, 1. 23, ANTINOMINIANISM IN THE COLONY OF MASSACHUSETTS BAY, 194, 195 (Charles Francis Adams ed.); p. 179, 1. 29, 1 CHANDLER, AM. CRIM. TRIALS 1, 10, 11; p. 179, 1. 35, BRADFORD'S HISTORY "OF PLIMOTH PLANTATION"

465, 466, 467, 472, 473 (1928); p. 180, l. 20, 2 LAWS OF VIRGINIA 422 (Hening);
p. 181, l. 4, John William Wallace, *An Address Delivered at the Celebration by
the New York Historical Society* 49–52 (1863); p. 181, l. 14, See NARRATIVES
OF THE INSURRECTIONS 237, 246 (Andrews ed.); p. 181, l. 19, 1 CHANDLER, AM.
CRIM. TRIALS 144; p. 181, l. 30, JOURNALS OF THE HOUSE OF BURGESSES OF VIRGINIA
1773–1776, at 22 (1905); p. 181, l. 39, 21 VA. MAG. OF HIST. AND BIOG. 370
(1913); p. 182, l. 20, 8 COLL. OF THE MASS. HIST. SOC. 4th Ser. 394 (1868); p.
182, l. 28, COLONIAL LAWS OF MASSACHUSETTS 43 (Whitmore 1890); p. 182, l.
41, 3 ELLIOT, DEBATES ON THE FEDERAL CONSTITUTION 447–48 (2d ed.); p. 183,
l. 29, Letter to William Tudor, March 29, 1817, printed in 8 OLD SOUTH LEAF-
LETS 57, 60; p. 185, l. 5, State v. Height, 117 Iowa 650; see Koenck v. Cooney,
244 Iowa 153, 157; State v. Fary, 19 N.J. 431; In re Pillo, 11 N.J. 8; In re
Vince, 2 N.J. 443; State v. Grundy, 136 N.J.L. 96, 97; State v. Miller, 71 N.J.L.
527; State v. Zdanowicz, 69 N.J.L. 619, 622; p. 185, l. 9, In re Willie, 25 Fed.
Cas. 38, 40. The Supreme Court applied this rule in Hoffman v. United States,
341 U.S. 479, and Blau v. United States, 340 U.S. 159; p. 185, l. 13, 142 U.S.
547, 562; p. 185, l. 19, 349 U.S. 190 and 155; United States v. Costello 198
F.2d 200, cert. denied 344 U.S. 874; Starkovich v. United States, 231 F.2d 411;
Jackins v. United States, 231 F.2d 405; United States v. Doto (Joe Adonis), 205
F.2d 416; Aiuppa v. United States, 201 F.2d 287; Accardo v. United States, 196
F.2d 1021; Marcello v. United States, 196 F.2d 437; Poretto v. United States,
196 F.2d 392; United States v. Fischetti, 103 F.Supp. 796; United States v.
Pechart, 103 F.Supp. 417; United States v. Nelson, 103 F.Supp. 215; United
States v. Licovali, 102 F.Supp. 607; United States v. DiCarlo, 102 F.Supp. 597;
United States v. Cohen, 101 F.Supp. 906; United States v. Jaffe, 98 F.Supp. 191;
United States v. Raley, 96 F.Supp. 495; United States v. Fitzpatrick, 96 F.Supp.
491; United States v. Yukio Abe, 19 U.S. Law Week 2321; see Carlson v.
United States, 209 F.2d 209, 212; Cohen v. United States, 201 F.2d 386, 390,
cert. denied 345 U.S. 951; United States v. Yukio Abe, 95 F.Supp. 991, 992; cf.
Emery's Case, 107 Mass. 172; Matter of Doyle, 257 N.Y. 244; Ex parte Johnson,
187 S.C. 1; see State v. James, 36 Wash. 2d 882, 897; p. 185, l. 33, 203 F.2d
at 23. Fitzpatrick was held properly to have claimed his Fifth Amendment privilege.
United States v. Fitzpatrick 96 F.Supp. 491; p. 186, l. 3, 350 U.S. 551, 557, 559.
Sixteen days after his reinstatement, Slochower was suspended again. This time
he was charged with making false statements under oath. However, on the eve of
his hearing he submitted his retirement or resignation; p. 186, l. 14, Grunewald v.
United States, 353 U.S. 391, 421–22, 425–26. A second trial ended with a hung
jury. Thereafter Grunewald died. Halperin and Bolich were tried a third time,
and this time acquitted; p. 187, l. 15, 116 U.S. 616, 631–32; p. 187, l. 26, 128
F.2d 265, 278–79; p. 187, l. 37, In addition to those already cited see Curcio v.
United States, 354 U.S. 118 (petitioner was secretary-treasurer of one of John
Dioguardi, Johnny Dio's, paper locals in the Teamsters Union); Trock v. United
States, 351 U.S. 976; Singleton v. United States, 343 U.S. 944; Brunner v. United
States, 343 U.S. 918; Greenberg v. United States, 343 U.S. 918; Greenberg v.
United States, 341 U.S. 944; Hoffman v. United States, 341 U.S. 479; Irving
Blau v. United States, 340 U.S. 332; Patricia Blau v. United States, 340 U.S.
159; Estes v. Potter, 183 F.2d 865, cert. denied 340 U.S. 920; Kasinowitz v.
United States, 181 F.2d 632, cert. denied 340 U.S. 920; Isaacs v. United States,
256 F.2d 654; United States v. DeLucia, 256 F.2d 493; United States v. Trigilio,
255 F.2d 385; United States v. Miranti, 253 F.2d 135; Ballantyne v. United States,
237 F.2d 657; United States v. Courtney, 236 F.2d 921; United States v. Gordon,
236 F.2d 916; United States v. Rosen, 174 F.2d 187, cert. denied 338 U.S. 851;
Powell v. United States, 226 F.2d 269; Krogmann v. United States, 225 F.2d
220; Carroll v. Savoretti, 220 F.2d 910; Daly v. United States, 209 F.2d 232;
Maffie v. United States, 209 F.2d 225; Kiewal v. United States, 204 F.2d 1;
United States v. Coffey, 198 F.2d 438; United States v. Girgenti, 197 F.2d 218;

Doran v. United States, 181 F.2d 489; Alexander v. United States, 181 F.2d 480; United States v. Guterma, 174 F.Supp. 581; United States v. Cleary, 164 F.Supp. 328; In the matter of Harnik, 151 F.Supp. 504; Application of House, 144 F.Supp. 95; United States v. Hoag, 142 F.Supp. 667; Application of Daniels, 140 F.Supp. 322; Federal Deposit Ins. Corp. v. Logsdon, 18 F.R.D. 57; United States v. Vadner, 119 F.Supp. 330; United States v. Malone, 111 F.Supp. 37; In Friedman, 104 F.Supp. 419; United States v. Steffen, 103 F.Supp. 415; p. 188, l. 5, United States v. Yukio Abe, 19 u.s.l. week 2321, 2322; p. 188, l. 11, United States v. Girgenti, 197 F.2d 218, 221; p. 188, l. 29, United States v. Gordon, 236 F.2d 916, 920; p. 188, l. 33, United States v. Bando, 244 F.2d 833, cert. denied, 355 U.S. 844; p. 188, l. 40, See United States v. Dioguardi, 20 F.R.D. 10; p. 189, l. 8, In re Bando, 20 F.R.D. 610, 619, p. 189, l. 19, United States v. Miranti, 253 F.2d 135, 139, 141; p. 189, l. 30, The statutes are collected in McNabb v. United States, 318 U.S. 332, 342 n.7; p. 189, l. 32, Id. at 344, quoted with approval in Upshaw v. United States, 335 U.S. 410, 412; p. 190, l. 8, 11 & 12 Vic. c. 42, §18; p. 190, l. 17, They are set out in a note to Rex v. Voisin, [1918] 1 K.B. 531, 539 n.3; p. 190, l. 22, report of the royal commission on police powers and procedures 71 n. (Cmd. 3297) (1929); p. 190, l. 32, Id. at 118; p. 191, l. 2, trial of rattenbury and stoner 126–27 (Jesse ed.); p. 191, l. 6, forsyth, hortensius the advocate 282 n. 1 (1882); p. 191, l. 14, 255 U.S. 298, 309; 285 U.S. 452, 464–65; p. 191, l. 35, It provides: "A warrant may be issued under this rule to search for and seize any property;

(1) Stolen or embezzled in violation of the laws of the United States; or

(2) Designed or intended for use or which is or has been used as the means of committing a criminal offense; or

(3) Possessed, controlled, or designated or intended for use or which is or has been used in violation of Title 18, U.S.C., §957." (Section 957 relates to the possession of property or papers in aid of a foreign government.); p. 191, l. 39, 353 U.S. 346, 347–48 (But cf. United States v. Rabinowitz, 339 U.S. 56; Harris v. United States, 331 U.S. 145); p. 192, l. 10, Jones v. United States, 357 U.S. 493; Miller v. United States, 357 U.S. 301. See also Giordenello v. United States, 357 U.S. 480; p. 192, l. 28, Benge v. Commonwealth, 231 S.W. 2d 248, 250 (In People v. Gonzales, 97 N.W. 2d 16, the Michigan Supreme Court held that a policeman's search of an automobile after stopping it to give the driver a traffic ticket was unreasonable); p. 192, l. 40, The Court heard argument and set the case for reargument on October 12, 1959. Abel v. United States, 359 U.S. 940; p. 193, l. 4, 232 N.S. 383; p. 193, l. 13, Hanna v. United States, 260 F.2d 723, 727; p. 193, l. 27, Lady Ivy's Trial, 10 how. st. tr. 555, 628; p. 193, l. 37, 1 publications of the selden society, select pleas of the crown 128 (Maitland ed.); p. 193, l. 40, The statutes are collected in 8 wigmore, evidence §2395 (3d ed.); p. 193, l. 42, The statutes are collected in 8 id. §2380; p. 194, l. 13, Mullen v. United States, 263 F.2d 275, 280; p. 194, l. 15, Alabama and California had such a statute since 1935. Ala. Gen. Acts, No. 253, at 649; Cal. Stat. c. 532, at 1608, 1610. For a recent case under the California statute see Application of Howard, 136 Cal. App. 2d 816, 289 P.2d 537; p. 194, l. 34, Garland v. Torre, 259 F.2d 545, 548, 549, cert. denied, 358 U.S. 910; p. 195, l. 3, 340 U.S. 367; p. 195, l. 4, 356 U.S. 148; p. 195, l. 10, Accord: United States v. St. Pierre, 132 F.2d 837 cert. granted 318 U.S. 751, case dismissed as moot, 319 U.S. 41; Singer v. United States, 244 F.2d 349, affirming 139 F.Supp. 847, reversed after the Watkins decision, 247 F.2d 535; p. 195, l. 31, United States v. Field, 193 F.2d 109, cert. denied, 342 U.S. 894; United States v. Field, 193 F.2d 92, cert. denied, 342 U.S. 894, and petition for cert. dismissed on motion of counsel for petitioner, 342 U.S. 908; p. 195, l. 36, Curcio v. United States, 354 U.S. 118, 126–27, 122; p. 196, l. 5, Rogers v. United States, 340 U.S. 367, 371; p. 196, l. 12, Slochower v. Board of Education, 350 U.S. 551, 557–58, quoted with approval in Grunewald v. United States, 353 U.S. 391, 421; p. 196, l. 26, Vol. 1 at 282–83 (Reeve text as

rev. by Bowen, Bradley ed.); p. 195, l. 36, 318 U.S. 332; p. 196, l. 41, 309 U.S. 227. One should similarly be able to argue in a federal court proceeding that the introduction in evidence of a confession so obtained would be violative of the due process clause of the Fifth Amendment. Compare Watts *v.* Indiana, 338 U.S. 49 with Ashcraft *v.* Tennessee, 322 U.S. 143, 154, n. 9, and McNabb *v.* United States, 318 U.S. 332, 339, 340. But in Gallegos *v.* Nebraska, 342 U.S. 55, 63–64, Justice Reed writing for the Court went out of his way to explain that the rule in the McNabb case was not a limitation imposed by the due process clause. In United States *v.* Carignan, 342 U.S. 36, 41, he said: "Whether involuntary confessions are excluded from federal criminal trials on the ground of a violation of the Fifth Amendment's protection against self-incrimination, or from a rule that forced confessions are untrustworthy, these uncontroverted facts do not bar this confession as a matter of law." In Bram *v.* United States, 168 U.S. 532, the Court did place its exclusion of a confession on the Fifth Amendment's provision against self-incrimination. Wigmore argued vehemently that the right to remain silent and the admissibility of confessions were two different things. 3 WIGMORE, EVIDENCE §§821, 823, 844 (3d ed.). He severely criticized the opinion of Justice, later Chief Justice, White in Bram *v.* United States, supra, and Chief Baron Kelly in Regina *v.* Jarvis, 10 Cox Cr. Cas. 574, for tying the two together. He stated that the Bram case "reached the height of absurdity in misapplication of the law." §821 n.2. Justice White said: "In criminal trials, in the courts of the United States, wherever a question arises whether a confession is incompetent because not voluntary, the issue is controlled by that portion of the Fifth Amendment . . . commanding that no person 'shall be compelled in any criminal case to be a witness against himself.'" At 542. Chief Baron Kelly commented: "I have always felt that we ought to watch jealously any encroachment on the principle that no man is bound to criminate himself, and that we ought to see that no one is induced either by a threat or a promise to say anything of a criminatory character against himself." At 576. It would seem however, that rather than being two different things, the right to remain silent and the admissibility of confessions are different sides of the same thing. Justices Black and Douglas in recent dissenting opinions in Stein *v.* New York, 346 U.S. 146, 197, 198, 208, the Reader's Digest case, both supported Chief Justice White's view. Accord: Brock *v.* United States, 223 F.2d 681; p. 196, l. 41, Haley *v.* Ohio, 332 U.S. 596; Mallory *v.* United States, 354 U.S. 449; Upshaw *v.* United States, 335 U.S. 410; People *v.* Snyder, 297 N.Y. 81; p. 196, l. 42, Ashcraft *v.* Tennessee, 322 U.S. 143; People *v.* Munniani, 258 N.Y. 394; p. 197, l. 1, 354 U.S. 449; p. 197, l. 2, 352 U.S. 191; p. 197, l. 8, Rex *v.* Bennett, 2 Leach, Crown Cas. 553 n.(a) (4th ed. 1815); p. 197, l. 12, Rex *v.* Wilson, Holt, N.P. 597; p. 197, l. 20, Reg. *v.* Pettit, 4 Cox Cr. Cas. 164, 165; p. 197, l. 24, Reg. *v.* Gavin, 15 Cox Cr. Cas. 656, 657; p. 197, l. 25, Reg. *v.* Male and Cooper, 17 Cox Cr. Cas. 689, 690; p. 197, l. 28, Reg. *v.* Histed, 19 Cox Cr. Cas. 16, 17; p. 197, l. 35, Rex *v.* Knight and Thayne, 20 Cox Cr. Cas. 711, 713; p. 197, l. 36, L.R. [1918] 1 K.B. 531, 539, 540; p. 198, l. 2, Rex *v.* Grayson, 16 Cr. App. 7, 8; p. 199, l. 25, Fikes *v.* Alabama, 352 U.S. 191, 198–99; p. 199, l. 35, Haley *v.* Ohio, 332 U.S. 596, 605–6; p. 199, l. 40, Harris *v.* South Carolina, 338 U.S. 68; Turner *v.* Pennsylvania, 338 U.S. 62; Watts *v.* Indiana, 338 U.S. 49; p. 200, l. 8, At 54. The following week these three cases were cited and language from two of them was quoted in State *v.* Cooper, 2 N.J. 540, reversing a conviction of six Negroes in Trenton, New Jersey, based on alleged confessions of five of them. Another case in accord with the McNabb and Upshaw decisions was Anderson *v.* United States, 318 U.S. 350. But cf. United States *v.* Mitchell, 322 U.S. 65; p. 200, l. 13, Stein *v.* New York, 346 U.S. 156, 184, 197–98, 201, 208n; Devita *v.* New Jersey, Grillo *v.* New Jersey, 11 N.J. 173, cert. denied, 345 U.S. 976; Burns *v.* Wilson, 346 U.S. 137; p. 200, l. 29, Gallegos *v.* Nebraska, 342 U.S. 55, 73–75; United States *v.* Carignan, 342 U.S. 36, 46; p. 201, l. 40, See *e.g.*, Reg. *v.* Joyce, [1957] 3 All E.R. 623; Reg. *v.*

Bass, [1953] 1 All E.R. 1064; Reg. v. Straffen, [1952] All E.R. 657; Rex v. Mills and Lemon, [1946] 2 All E.R. 776; p. 202, l. 5, 347 U.S. 556; 352 U.S. 191; 354 U.S. 449; p. 202, l. 6, 360 U.S. 315; p. 202, l. 28, United States ex rel. Caminito v. Murphy, 222 F.2d 698, cert. denied, 350 U.S. 896. Cf. Brock v. United States, 223 F.2d 681. In United States ex rel. Wade v. Jackson, 256 F.2d 7, 9, 16, cert. denied, 357 U.S. 908, the same court set "aside a seventeen year old jury verdict which until now, has been unanimously affirmed by the New York appellate courts, both on the original appeal and in subsequent proceedings." The reason was the admission into evidence of a confession obtained during a twenty-three hour incommunicado period. The court through Circuit Judge J. Edward Lumbard said: "* * * When law enforcement officials create a situation where those in their custody have no means of communicating with the outside world and no way of calling their plight to the attention of any disinterested persons for as long as 23 hours, common sense requires that we conclude that the observance of the constitutional rights of their prisoners was secondary to obtaining incriminating statements from those so isolated. Such methods are inherently coercive." Subsequently Wade went free. The district attorney moved for the dismissal of the first degree murder indictment against him, and the court granted the motion. The district attorney explained that the case could not be tried again successfully, for witnesses had died in the interim and most of the evidence had vanished. In United States v. Coppolo, 28 U.S.L. WEEK 2038, this court invalidated a confession obtained by federal officials to a federal crime while a defendant was held without arraignment by state officials from 9:00 A.M. one day until 2:00 P.M. the next. Article 31(b) of the Uniform Code of Military Justice provides: "No person subject to this chapter may interrogate, or request any statement from, an accused or a person suspected of an offense without first informing him of the nature of the accusation and advising him that he does not have to make any statement * * *." This was held to apply to a request for a sample of handwriting. United States v. Minnefield, 9 USCMA 373; p. 203, l. 7, 3 WIGMORE, EVIDENCE §§822, 844, 847–51 (3d ed.); p. 203, l. 10, See FROEST THE MAELSTROM, c.34; p. 203, l. 34, Haley v. Ohio, 332 U.S. 596, 601, 607. See also Harris v. South Carolina, 338 U.S. 68; Turner v Pennsylvania, 338 U.S. 62; Upshaw v. United States, 335 U.S. 410; Ashcraft v. Tennessee, 322 U.S. 143. But cf. United States v. Carignan, 342 U.S. 36, 42, where Justice Reed in writing the opinion of the Court said that the rule in the McNabb case was not intended as a penalty or sanction for violation of a commitment statute or Rule 5 of the Federal Rules of Criminal Procedure.

CHAPTER XI

P. 204, l. 16, See, e.g., Rex v. Reading, 7 HOW. ST. TR. 259, 296; Rex v. Earl of Shaftesbury, 8 HOW. ST. TR. 759, 817 (1681). In the next century Lord Chief Justice Camden commented in Entick v. Carrington, 19 HOW. ST. TR. 1030, 1074; "Nay, if the vengeance of the government requires a production of the author, it is hardly possible for him to escape the impeachment of the printer, who is sure to seal his own pardon by his discovery." In Queen v. Boyes, 1 B. & S. 311, the queen's bench held that a pardon took away the right of silence, and this in spite of the fact that under the Act of Settlement, 1700, the pardon was not pleadable to an impeachment by the House of Commons; p. 204, l. 25, 3 COLONIAL RECORDS OF CONNECTICUT *296. See also an act of 1703, 3 id. at *409–10, and one of 1711, 4 id. at *154; p. 204, l. 36, 9 Anne c. 14, §4; 18 COLONIAL RECORDS OF GEORGIA 608, 613 (Candler 1911) (an act of 1764, §4); 2 ACTS AND RESOLVES OF THE PROVINCE OF THE MASSACHUSETTS BAY 836, 837 (Boston, 1874) (an act of 1736–37, §4); 3 id. at 45, 47 (Boston, 1878) (an act of 1742–43, §4); 5 COLONIAL LAWS OF NEW YORK 621, 623 (an act of 1774); 6 LAWS OF VIRGINIA

76, 78 (Hening, 1819) (an act of 1748, §4). South Carolina in 1712 by legislative enactment provided that statutes made in England since the eighth year of Queen Anne were to be in force there. THE PUBLIC LAWS OF SOUTH CAROLINA 100, app. 20–21 (Grimke 1790). The Georgia statute was held to be constitutional in Higdon v. Heard, 14 Ga. 225. The colony of New York also had an immunity provision in an act against private lotteries. 5 COLONIAL LAWS OF NEW YORK 639, 642 (an act of 1774); p. 204, l. 38, United States v. Dixon, 25 Fed. Cas. 872, 873; KILTY, A REPORT OF ALL SUCH ENGLISH STATUTES 268 (1811) (Maryland); p. 204, l. 41, See e.g., 2 CAL. CODES AND STAT. par. 13, 334 (1876); CONN. STATE STAT. c.22, §2 (1854) (answers not admissible in evidence against one); ILL. REV. STAT. c.46, §5 (1845); 2 IND. REV. STAT. 372, §89 (1852); MD. CODE Art. 30, §65 (1860); 1 MO. REV. STAT. §3819 (1889) (testimony may not be used against one); 1 N.Y. REV. STAT. 668 (2d ed. 1836) (answers not admissible in subsequent proceedings); 2 N.C. CODE, §2843 (1883) (answers not admissible in any criminal prosecution); VA. CODE, c.195, §20 (3d ed. 1873) (immunity provision for witnesses). The Missouri provision was held valid in Ex parte Buskett, 106 Mo. 602. The Virginia provision was held not applicable to a lottery prosecution in Temple v. Commonwealth, 75 Va. 892; p. 204, l. 42, See, e.g., 1 IND. REV. STAT. §1799 (1888); 4 IND. STAT. ANN. §9–1604 (Burns 1942); KY. REV. STAT. §436. 510 (3) (1953) (testimony not to be used in any prosecution); p. 204, l. 42, See, e.g., 1 IND. REV. STAT. c.57, §8 (1852) (answers not to be used in any criminal proceeding); 1 N.Y. REV. STAT. 761 (2d ed. 1836); N.Y. Laws 1837, c.430, §8, pp. 487–88 (answers not to be used before any grand jury or on the trial of any indictment). These provisions were held constitutional. Wilkins v. Malone, 14 Ind. 153; Henry v. Bank of Salina, 5 Hill (N.Y.) 523; Stevens v. White, 5 Hill (N.Y.) 548; Perrine & Pixley v. Striker, 7 Paige (N.Y.) 598; p. 204, l. 42, N.Y. Laws (1853) c.539, §14, pp. 1012–13 (testimony not to be used in any subsequent proceeding); N.Y. Penal Code (Donnan, 5th ed. 1886) §79; Mass. Acts and Resolves (1871) c.91, §1, p. 490. Both New York acts were sustained. People v. Kelly, 24 N.Y. 74; People v. Sharp, 107 N.Y. 427. The Massachusetts act was declared unconstitutional. Emery's Case, 107 Mass. 172; p. 205, l. 1, Ark. Stat. (1884) §1792 (testimony not admissible in any subsequent proceeding); 2 Cal. Codes and Stat. (1876). par. 13.232 (testimony not admissible in any subsequent proceeding); 2 N.Y. Rev. Stat. (2d ed. 1836) 572 (testimony not admissible in any subsequent proceeding); Va. Laws (1869–1870) c.355, §1 (testimony not admissible in any subsequent proceeding). In Cullen v. Commonwealth, 24 Gratt. (Va.) 624, the court held that the Virginia statute was not broad enough to take away the right of silence; p. 205, l. 1, N.Y. Code of Civil Procedure §292(5) (Townshend, 10th ed., 1870) (answers not to be used in any criminal proceeding); 1 N.C. Code (1883) §488(5) (answers not to be used in any criminal proceeding). The New York provision was assumed to be constitutional in Lathrop v. Clapp, 40 N.Y. 328 and the North Carolina provision was held constitutional in La Fontaine v. Southern Underwriters Assn., 83 N.C. 132; p. 204, l. 2, N.H. Gen. Stat. (1867) c.99, §20 (limited immunity provision for employee). This section was held constitutional in State v. Nowell, 58 N.H. 314.

In addition there were a few miscellaneous immunity provisions. Both Arkansas and California gave a limited grant of immunity to one of two or more conspirators. A DIGEST OF THE STATUTES OF ARKANSAS, c.52, §72 (English, 1848); Cal. Laws (1855) c.82, §5, p. 106. Indiana provided a limited immunity to a witness whose answer showed the commission of a misdemeanor. Ind. Rev. Stat. (1881) §1800. All these provisions were held constitutional. State v. Quarles, 13 Ark. 307 (indictment for gaming at poker); Ex parte Rowe, 7 Cal. 184; Bedgood v. State, 115 Ind. 275; p. 205, l. 13, United States v. James, 60 Fed. 257, 261, 263; p. 205, l. 28, 350 U.S. at 440, 445, 446, 450; p. 205, l. 38, CONG. GLOBE, 34th Cong., 3d Sess., 403–11, 435–44; p. 206, l. 3, 11 Stat. 156. In the same year California adopted a similar statute. Cal. Laws c.95, p. 97; p. 206, l. 6, CONG GLOBE

37th Cong., 1st Sess., 449; CONG. GLOBE, 37th Cong. 2d Sess., 56, 228, 364; p. 206, l. 12, 12 Stat. 333; p. 206, l. 19, L.R. 4 Eq. 327, affirmed, L.R. 3 Ch. 79; p. 206, l. 23, CONG. GLOBE, 40th Cong., 2d Sess., 1334. In Boyd v. United States, 116 U.S. 616, 632, Justice Bradley stated that the act of 1868 was passed to alleviate the search and seizure provisions in the revenue acts of 1863 and 1867, but he in no way documented his statement; p. 206, l. 25, 284 U.S. 141; p. 206, l. 26, CONG. GLOBE, 40th Cong., 2d Sess., 845; p. 206, l. 30, 15 Stat. 37; p. 206, l. 34, United States v. McCarthy, 18 Fed. 87; United States v. Williams, 28 Fed. Cas. 670; United States v. Brown, 24 Fed. Cas. 1273; In re Strouse, 23 Fed. Cas. 261; In re Phillips, 19 Fed. Cas. 506, No. 11,097; p. 206, l. 36, 142 U.S. 547; p. 206, l. 39, 24 Stat. 379; p. 206, l. 40, §§9 and 12 (". . . but such evidence or testimony shall not be used against such person on the trial of any criminal proceeding"); p. 207, l. 9, 27 Stat. 444, 49 U.S.C. §46; p. 207, l. 10, 161 U.S. 591; p. 207, l. 11, See, e.g., 56 Stat. 30, §202(g) (Emergency Price Control Act of 1942); Shapiro v. United States, 335 U.S. 1, 3, n.2, 4; p. 207, l. 13, See, e.g., 32 Stat. 828; 42 Stat. 1002, 7 U.S.C. §15 (Grain Futures Act); 56 Stat. 30 (Emergency Price Control Act of 1942); 56 Stat. 297, 49 U.S.C. §1017(a) (Freight Forwarders Act); 60 Stat. 770, 771, 42 U.S.C. §1812(a) (3) (Atomic Energy Act of 1946); 63 Stat. 8, 50 U.S.C. Appx. §2026(b) (Export Control Act of 1949); 63 Stat. 27, 28–29, 50 U.S.C. Appx. §1896(f)(6) (Housing and Rent Act of 1949); 68 Stat. 948, 42 U.S.C. §2201(c) (Supp. III, 1956) (Atomic Energy Act of 1954); p. 207, l. 18, 30 Stat. 548; 39 Stat. 906; 52 Stat. 1057, 21 U.S.C. §373 (1952); 61 Stat. 168, 7 U.S.C. §135(c); 64 Stat. 991–992, 50 U.S.C. §783(f); p. 207, l. 22, McCarthy v. Arndstein, 266 U.S. 34; McCarthy v. Arndstein, 262 U.S. 355; Arndstein v. McCarthy, 254 U.S. 71; p. 207, l. 25, 52 Stat. 847, 11 U.S.C. §25(a)(10); p. 207, l. 31, 32 Stat. 828; 32 Stat. 848–49, 49 U.S.C. §43; p. 207, l. 33, 32 Stat. 904, 15 U.S.C. §32, 49 U.S.C. §47; p. 207, l. 40, United States v. Armour & Co., 142 Fed. 808; p. 208, l. 2, H.R. Doc. No. 706, 59th Cong., 1st Sess., 3; p. 208, l. 6, 34 Stat. 798, 15 U.S.C. §33, 49 U.S.C. §48; p. 208, l. 8, 36 Stat. 352; p. 208, l. 9, Counselman v. Hitchcock, 142 U.S. 547; p. 208, l. 10, H.R. Rep. 266, 61st Cong., 2d Sess., 2; p. 208, l. 15, 36 Stat. 827, 18 U.S.C. §2424(b); 38 Stat. 723, 15 U.S.C. §49; p. 208, l. 21, 39 Stat. 737, 46 U.S.C. §827; 39 Stat. 797; 41 Stat. 317; 42 Stat. 168, 7 U.S.C. §222; 42 Stat. 1002, 7 U.S.C. §15; 46 Stat. 536–37, 7 U.S.C. §499m(f); 46 Stat. 700, 19 U.S.C. §1333(e); p. 208, l. 24, 48 Stat. 86, 15 U.S.C. §77v(c); p. 208, l. 27, 48 Stat. 900, 15 U.S.C. §78u(d) (Securities Exchange Act of 1934); 48 Stat. 1097, 47 U.S.C. §409(1) (Communications Act of 1934); 48 Stat. 1114 (an act to amend the Air Commerce Act of 1926); 49 Stat. 456 (1935), 29 U.S.C. §161(3) (National Labor Relations Act); 49 Stat. 832, 15 U.S.C. §79r(e) (Public Utility Holding Company Act of 1935); 49 Stat. 858, 16 U.S.C. §825f(g) (Federal Power Act); 49 Stat. 1991, 46 U.S.C. §1124(c) (Merchant Marine Act); 50 Stat. 87 (Bituminous Coal Act of 1937); 52 Stat. 828–29, 15 U.S.C. §717m(h); 52 Stat. 1022–23, 49 U.S.C. §644(i) (Civil Aeronautics Act of 1938); 52 Stat. 1107, 45 U.S.C. §362(c) (Railroad Unemployment Insurance Act); 53 Stat. 1370, 42 U.S.C. §405(f) (Social Security Act Amendments of 1939); 54 Stat. 853–54, 15 U.S.C. §80b–9(d) (Investment Company Act of 1940); 56 Stat. 30 (Emergency Price Control Act of 1942); 56 Stat. 297, 49 U.S.C. §1017(a) (Freight Forwarders Act); 56 Stat. 179, 50 U.S.C. §1152(a)(4) (Second War Powers Act); 60 Stat. 770–71, 42 U.S.C. §1812(a)(3) (Atomic Energy Act of 1946); 61 Stat. 150–51 (Labor Management Relations Act, 1947); 62 Stat. 106–07, 50 U.S.C. Appx. §1931(b); 63 Stat. 8, 50 U.S.C. Appx. §2026(b) (Export Control Act of 1949); 63 Stat. 27, 28–29, 50 U.S.C. Appx. §1896(f)(6) (Housing and Rent Act of 1949); 64 Stat. 816–17, 50 U.S.C. Appx. §2155(b) (Defense Production Act of 1950); 64 Stat. 882–83 (1950), 12 U.S.C. §1820(d) (Federal Deposit Insurance Act); 68 Stat. 948, 42 U.S.C. §2201(c) (Supp. III, 1956) (Atomic Energy Act of 1954); 70 Stat. 574, 18 U.S.C.A. §1406 (Supp,

1958) (Narcotic Control Act of 1956); p. 208, l. 28, 49 Stat. 550 (Motor Carrier Act of 1935); 49 Stat. 875, 53 Stat. 363, 26 U.S.C. §3119 (Liquor Law Repeal and Enforcement Act); 52 Stat. 1065, 29 U.S.C. §209 (Fair Labor Standards Act of 1938); p. 208, l. 31, 317 U.S. 424. The history of federal immunity provisions has been a topic of discussion on several occasions in Supreme Court opinions. There are such discussions in the Monia case in the majority opinion of Justice Roberts, at 427–30, as well as the minority one of Justice Frankfurter, at 432–38. For further such discussions see Smith v. United States, 337 U.S. 137, 146–48; United States v. Bryan, 339 U.S. 323, 327, 335–40. A partial catalog of federal immunity provisions may be found in Shapiro v. United States, 335 U.S. 1, 6, 7, n.4; p. 209, l. 18, United States v. James, 60 Fed. 257, 264; p. 209, l. 22, H.R. Rep. 2606, 83d Cong., 2d Sess., p. 13; p. 209, l. 35, 5 RATIONALE OF JUDICIAL EVIDENCE, bk. 9, pt. 4, c.3, pp. 241–45 (1827); 8 EVIDENCE §2250 (3d ed.); p. 210, l. 6, 161 U.S. 591; p. 210, l. 18, United States v. Ullmann, 221 F.2d 760, 763; p. 210, l. 30, Kovacs v. Cooper, 336 U.S. 77, 95; p. 210, l. 38, H.R. Rep. 2606, 83d Cong., 2d Sess., p. 12, 15; p. 211, l. 8, THE FIFTH AMENDMENT TODAY 8–9, 58–59; p. 212, l. 30, Lawson v. United States, 176 F.2d 49, cert. denied 339 U.S. 934; Barsky v. United States, 167 F.2d 241; cert. denied 334 U.S. 843; United States v. Josephson, 165 F.2d 82, cert. denied 333 U.S. 838; p. 212, l. 42, United States v. Dennis, 183 F.2d 201; p. 213, l. 5, Blau v. United States, 340 U.S. 159; p. 213, l. 8, Dennis v. United States, 341 U.S. 494; p. 213, l. 17, Hearings before the House Committee on Un-American Activities, Communist Infiltration of Hollywood Motion-Picture Industry, 82d Cong., 2d Sess., pt. 8, at 3546; p. 214, l. 12, Hearing before the Permanent Subcommittee on Investigations of the Committee on Government Operations, 83d Cong., 1st Sess., pt. 4, at 272, pt. 5, at 306–7; p. 215, l. 14, Should Teachers Testify?, SAT. REV., Sept. 26, 1953, pp. 22, 23; p. 215, l. 20, How to Make Gangsters Talk, THIS WEEK MAGAZINE, Feb. 1, 1953, pp. 7, 34–35; p. 216, l. 4, REPORT ON ORGANIZED CRIME AND LAW EN-FORCEMENT, vol. 1, pp. 59–60; p. 216, l. 22, S. Rep. 153, 83d Cong., 1st Sess., 15; p. 216, l. 33, 100 CONG. REC. 13997; p. 217, l. 8, 18 U.S.C. §3486 (Supp. III, 1956); p. 218, l. 15, 100 CONG. REC. 13323–24; p. 219, l. 3, Ullmann v. United States, 350 U.S. 422. Cf. Regan v. New York, 349 U.S. 58 (state criminal contempt conviction sustained because of broad state immunity statute); p. 220, l. 17, Carter v. Carter Coal Co., 298 U.S. 238; Utah Power & Light Co. v. Pfost, 286 U.S. 165; Williams v. Standard Oil Co. of La., 278 U.S. 235; Dorchy v. Kansas, 264 U.S. 286; p. 220, l. 19, In Family Security Life Ins. Co. v. Daniel, 79 F.Supp. 62, 65–66, rev'd, 336 U.S. 220, the majority of a three-judge statutory court stated: "In view of the modern form of legislative drafting, the omission of such a provision evidences clearly the legislative intent that this statute must stand or fall as a whole." State cases to this effect are Maury County v. Porter, 195 Tenn. 116; Life and Casualty Inc. Co. v. McCormack, 174 Tenn. 327; Burroughs v. Lyles, 142 Tex. 704; p. 220, l. 21, 298 U.S. 238, 312; p. 221, l. 10, H.R. Rep. 2606, 83d Cong., 2d Sess. 8; p. 221, l. 19, 128 F.Supp. at 626; p. 222, l. 6, 100 CONG. REC. 13323, 13324, 13997–98; p. 222, l. 35, 100 CONG. REC. 13325 (Congressman Javits was not a member of the House Judiciary Committee. He was one of the 55 who voted against the measure. 100 CONG. REC. 13333; p. 223, l. 28, See In re McElrath, 248 F.2d 612, 615; p. 224, l. 7, 2 AMERICAN BAR ASSOCIATION COMMISSION ON ORGANIZED CRIME AND LAW ENFORCEMENT 161, 168–69; p. 224, l. 33, 15 STAT. 37; p. 224, l. 35, 142 U.S. 547; p. 224, l. 39, 36 STAT. 352; p. 224, l. 40, H.R. Rep. No. 266, 61st Cong., 2d Sess. 2; p. 225, l. 5, See Whiskey Cases, 99 U.S. 594; United States v. Shotwell Mfg. Co., 225 F.2d 394, judgment vacated for other reasons on review, 355 U.S. 233; United States v. Marzec, 249 F.2d 941, cert. denied, 356 U.S. 913; King v. United States, 203 F.2d 525; p. 225, l. 6, 317 U.S. 424, 434; p. 225, l. 26, 154 U.S. 447, 487. Of course judicial proceedings can retain their adversary character even though they in fact involve no contest in a particular case. A criminal case may end with a guilty plea, and often does. A civil suit may go by default. All that is necessary is that there be provision and an opportunity for the presentation of opposing views should the parties concerned deem it in their best interests to follow such a course. As the Supreme Court, speaking through Justice Brandeis, observed in Tutun v. United States, 270 U.S. 568, 577, in holding naturalization proceedings to be cases or controversies within the meaning of art. III, §2: "The United States is always a possible adverse party."; p. 225, l. 34, 350 U.S. at 434; p. 225, l. 35, 128 F.Supp. at 626 n.22; p. 226, l. 21, Isaacs v. United States, 256 F.2d 654, 661; p. 226, l. 32, United States v. Fitzgerald, 235 F.2d 453, cert. denied, 352 U.S. 842; p. 226, l. 35, Corono v. United States, 250 F.2d 578, cert. denied, 356 U.S. 954; Tedesco v. United States, 255 F.2d 35; p. 226, l. 35, 359 U.S. 41. This case was followed in United States v. Levine, 267 F.2d 335; p. 226, l. 37, 161 U.S. 591; p. 227, l. 7, He felt that the petitioner should have been proceeded against on notice and hearing under Rule 42(b) of the Federal Rules of Criminal Procedure rather than summarily under Rule 42(a); p. 228, l. 26, 2 ENGLISH HISTORICAL DOCUMENTS 479–481, 482 (Douglas and Greenaway ed.); p. 230, l. 2, THE FEDERALIST, No. 47; p. 230, l. 22, Bk. 11, cc.4–6; p. 230, l. 33, THE FEDERALIST, No. 47. Adams in a letter of November 1775 to Richard Henry Lee commented: ". . . It is by balancing each of these three powers against the other two, that the efforts in human nature towards tyranny can alone be checked and restrained, and any degree of freedom preserved in the Constitution." 4 THE WORKS OF JOHN ADAMS 186 (Chas. F. Adams ed.). Jefferson in his Notes on the State of Virginia observed: "The concentrating these in the same hand is precisely the definition of despotic government. It will be no alleviation that these powers will be exercised by a plurality of hands, and not by a single one. 173 despots would surely be as oppressive as one."; p. 231, l. 2, As quoted in 1 GSOVSKI, SOVIET CIVIL LAW 74; p. 231, l. 8, At 318; p. 231, l. 22, BERMAN, JUSTICE IN RUSSIA 134–35, 303; p. 233, l. 1, H.R. REP. No. 2606, 83d Cong., 2d Sess. 12 (1954). On the power of Congress to investigate, Chief Justice Warren in the Court's opinion in Quinn v. United States, 349 U.S. 155, 161, wrote: "Similarly, the power to investigate must not be confused with any of the powers of law enforcement; those powers are assigned under our Constitution to the Executive and the Judiciary." In Irvine v. California, 347 U.S. 128, where the Court sustained a state court conviction based upon evidence obtained by an illegally secreted microphone, Justice Jackson and Chief Justice Warren were in favor of directing the clerk of the Court to forward a copy of the record in the case together with a copy of the Court's opinion to the Attorney General of the United States. However, they were alone in this view. On this point Justice Black in a dissenting opinion in which Justice Douglas concurred commented:

"It has been suggested that the Court should call on the Attorney General to investigate this record in order to start criminal prosecutions against certain California officers. I would strongly object to any such action by this Court. It is inconsistent with my own view of the judicial function in our government. Prosecution, or anything approaching it, should, I think, be left to government officers whose duty that is."

P. 233, l. 29, 32 Fed. 241, 255; p. 233, l. 31, 219 U.S. 346, 356–57; 300 U.S. 227, 239; p. 233, l. 38, 2 U.S. (2 Dall.) 409; p. 233, l. 38, Unreported, 1794. Chief Justice Taney in a note to United States v. Ferreira, 54 U.S. (13 How.) 40, 52, inserted at the direction of the Court, gave the substance of the decision; p. 234, l. 12, 2 U.S. (2 Dall.) at 410n.(a); p. 234, l. 33, 3 CORRESPONDENCE AND PUBLIC PAPERS OF JOHN JAY 488–89 (Johnston ed.). The reference is to Art. II, §2 of the Constitution, which provides that the president may require the Opinion, in writing, of the principal Officer in each of the executive Departments, upon any Subject relative to the Duties of their respective Offices."; p. 235, l. 4, 54 U.S. (13 How.) at 53. This case thus becomes the first one in which the Court declared an act of Congress to be unconstitutional, antedating

Marbury v. Madison, 5 U.S. (1 Cranch) 137, by almost a decade; p. 235, l. 5, 219 U.S. 346, 361–62. Other cases to the same effect are Chicago & Southern Air Lines v. Waterman S.S. Corp., 333 U.S. 103; Coffman v. Breeze Corporations, Inc., 323 U.S. 316; Alabama v. Arizona, 291 U.S. 286; Gordon v. United States, 69 U.S. (2 Wall.) 561, 117 U.S. 697 App.; United States v. Ferreira, 54 U.S. (13 How.) 40; Great Northern Ry. Co. v. Lumber and Sawmill Workers, 232 F.2d 628; United States v. Carrollo, 30 F.Supp. 3. In Great Northern Ry. Co. v. Lumber and Sawmill Workers, supra, the court stated that the issuance of an advisory opinion was "a 'consummation' devoutly to be avoided, for that is the way bad law is made." In United States v. Carrollo, supra, the court refused to act under a statutory provision empowering it to make a recommendation to the Secretary of Labor, which would be mandatory, against the deportation of an alien convicted in this country of a crime involving moral turpitude. But cf. Gubbels v. Hoy, 261 F.2d 952; p. 235, l. 25, 319 U.S. 302; p. 236, l. 2, Lord v. Veazie, 49 U.S. (8 How.) 251, 255; p. 236, l. 6, South Spring Hill Gold Mining Co. v. Amador Medean Gold Mining Co., 145 U.S. 300, 301; p. 236, l. 17, International Longshoremen's and Warehousemen's Union v. Boyd, 347 U.S. 222, 224; p. 236, l. 18, 330 U.S. 75; p. 236, l. 21, 325 U.S. 450; p. 237, l. 3, Other cases to the same effect are United States v. Appalachian Electric Power Co., 311 U.S. 377; Electric Bond & Share Co. v. Securities and Exchange Comm'n, 303 U.S. 419; p. 237, l. 5, 319 U.S. 41, 42; p. 237, l. 12, 360 U.S. 709. Other cases refusing to rule on moot questions are United States v. Alaska S.S. Co., 253 U.S. 113; Campbell Soup Co. v. Martin, 202 F.2d 398; Harris v. Texas & Pacific Ry. Co., 196 F.2d 88; p. 237, l. 21, A Modern Evolution in Remedial Rights,—The Declaratory Judgment, 16 MICH. L. REV. 69, 89; p. 237, l. 24, 300 U.S. 227; p. 237, l. 26, See, e.g., MASS. CONST. c.3, art. 2; N.H. CONST. [art.] 74; R.I. CONST. art. 10, §3, amend. 12, §2; p. 237, l. 32, A Note on Advisory Opinions, 37 HARV. L. REV. 1002, 1006, 1008; p. 237, l. 38, JUDICIAL POWER OF THE UNITED STATES 23; p. 238, l. 4, Lawson v. United States, 176 F.2d 49, cert. denied, 339 U.S. 934; Barsky v. United States, 167 F.2d 241, cert. denied, 334 U.S. 843; United States v. Josephson, 165 F.2d 82, cert. denied, 333 U.S. 858; p. 238, l. 6, See, e.g., Holmes v. Atlanta, 350 U.S. 879; Baltimore v. Dawson, 350 U.S. 877; Brown v. Board of Education, 349 U.S. 294; Bolling v. Sharpe, 347 U.S. 497; Brown v. Board of Education, 347 U.S. 483; p. 238, l. 7, See, e.g., Slochower v. Board of Higher Education, 350 U.S. 551; Emspak v. United States, 349 U.S. 190; Quinn v. United States, 349 U.S. 155; p. 238, l. 8, Pennsylvania v. Nelson, 350 U.S. 497; p. 238, l. 10, Cole v. Young, 351 U.S. 536; p. 238, l. 18, Colorado Interstate Gas Co. v. Federal Power Comm'n, 324 U.S. 581; Keller v. Potomac Electric Power Co., 261 U.S. 428; Prentis v. Atlantic Coast Line Co., 211 U.S. 210. But see Canada Southern Ry. Co. v. International Bridge Co., 8 Fed. 190; p. 238, l. 19, In re MacFarland, 30 App. D.C. 365, appeal dismissed sub nom. Washington Gas Light Co. v. MacFarland, 215 U.S. 614, on motion of counsel for appellants; p. 238, l. 20, Federal Radio Comm'n v. General Electric Co., 281 U.S. 464; p. 238, l. 21, See Postum Cereal Co. v. California Fig Nut Co., 272 U.S. 693, 698–701; Frash v. Moore, 211 U.S. 1; United States v. Duell, 172 U.S. 576, 587; Butterworth v. United States, 112 U.S. 50, 60; Baldwin Co. v. R. S. Howard Co., 256 U.S. 35; E. C. Atkins & Co. v. Moore, 212 U.S. 285; p. 238, l. 22, Application of L.B. & W. 4217, 238 F.2d 163; Boggess v. Berry Corp., 233 F.2d 389; Bordenelli v. United States, 233 F.2d 120; p. 238, l. 23, In re Annexation to City of Anchorage, 146 F.Supp. 98; p. 238, l. 42, 46 Stat. 845; p. 239, l. 5, Federal Radio Comm'n v. Nelson Bros. Bond & Mortgage Co., 289 U.S. 266, 276–77; p. 239, l. 27, 233 F.2d at 125; p. 239, l. 30, 338 U.S. 632, 640–41. In a recent state case, State v. Boone Circuit Court, 236 Ind. 202, 211–12, the court stated that "a review or appeal to the courts from an administrative order or decision is limited to a consideration of whether or not the order was made in conformity with proper legal procedure, is based upon substantial evidence, and does not violate any constitutional, statutory, or legal principle."; p. 240, l. 17, See, *e.g.,* Schwartz, *Legal Restriction of Competition in the Regulated Industries: An Abdication of Judicial Responsibility,* 67 HARV. L. REV. 436; p. 240, l. 22, COMMISSION ON ORGANIZATION OF THE EXECUTIVE BRANCH OF THE GOVERNMENT, REPORT ON LEGAL SERVICES AND PROCEDURE 85–86. The Hoover Commission further stated that the proposed Administrative Court "would serve as an intermediate stage in the evolution of administrative adjudication and the transfer of judicial activities from the agencies to courts of general jurisdiction." At 87; p. 240, l. 26, Cromwell *v.* Jackson, 188 Md. 8; p. 240, l. 27, Close *v.* Southern Md. Agr. Ass'n, 134 Md. 629; p. 240, l. 28, Hodges *v.* Public Service Comm'n, 110 W. Va. 649; p. 240, l. 28, Staud *v.* Sill, 114 W. Va. 208; p. 240, l. 29, State *v.* Huber, 129 W. Va. 198; p. 240, l. 30, Sims *v.* Fisher, 125 W. Va. 512; p. 240, l. 31, In re City of Phoenix, 52 Ariz. 65; State *v.* Town of Riverdale, 244 Iowa 423; Ruland *v.* City of Augusta, 120 Kan. 42; p. 240, l. 31, Brenke *v.* Borough of Belle Plaine, 105 Minn. 84; Winkler *v.* City of Hastings, 85 Neb. 212; p. 240, l. 32, North *v.* Board of Education, 313 Ill. 422; p. 240, l. 33, Potter County Commissioners' Salary Case, 350 Pa. 141; State *v.* County Court, 138 W. Va. 885; p. 240, l. 33, Henderson County *v.* Wallace, 173 Tenn. 184; p. 240, l. 34, State *v.* Barker, 116 Iowa 96; Prince George's County *v.* Mitchell, 97 Md. 330; Beasley *v.* Ridout, 94 Md. 641; Application of O'Sullivan, 117 Mont. 295; p. 240, l. 35, City of Enterprise *v.* State, 156 Ore. 623; p. 240, l. 36, Gandy *v.* Elizabeth City County, 179 Va. 340; p. 240, l. 37, State *v.* Police Civil Service Comm'n, 253 Minn. 62; p. 240, l. 39, Funkhauser *v.* Randolph, 287 Ill. 94; p. 240, l. 41, Tyson *v.* Washington County, 78 Neb. 211; p. 240, l. 42, Verdigris Conservancy District *v.* Objectors, 131 Kan. 214; p. 240, l. 42, Searle *v.* Yensen, 118 Neb. 835; p. 241, l. 1, State *v.* Johnson, 61 Kan. 803; p. 241, l. 1, Daniel *v.* Tyrrell & Garth Investment Co., 127 Tex. 213; p. 241, l. 2, Oklahoma Cotton Ginners' Ass'n. *v.* State, 174 Okla. 243; p. 241, l. 3, Boston *v.* Chelsea, 212 Mass. 127; p. 241, l. 4, Silver *v.* Osage County, 76 Kan. 687; p. 241, l. 4, Robey *v.* Prince George's County, 92 Md. 150; p. 241, l. 5, Norwalk Street Ry. Co.'s Appeal, 69 Conn. 576, 594; p. 241, l. 13, Dearborn Township *v.* Township Clerk, 334 Mich. 673; p. 241, l. 22, People ex rel. Christiansen *v.* Connell, 2 Ill. 2d 332, 349; p. 241, l. 31, Guaranty Trust Co. *v.* United States, 304 U.S. 126; p. 241, l. 32, United States *v.* Pink, 315 U.S. 203; Oetjen *v.* Central Leather Co., 246 U.S. 297; Kennett *v.* Chambers, 55 U.S. (14 How.) 38; p. 241, l. 33, Harisiades *v.* Shaughnessy, 342 U.S. 580; Chicago & Southern Air Lines *v.* Waterman S.S. Corp., 333 U.S. 103 (determination as to which citizen carrier was to be granted a certificate of convenience and necessity for an overseas air route); United States *v.* Curtiss-Wright Corp., 299 U.S. 304; Foster *v.* Neilson, 27 U.S. (2 Pet.) 253; In re Cooper, 143 U.S. 472, 503; Namkung *v.* Boyd, 226 F.2d 385; p. 241, l. 35, Wilson *v.* Girard, 354 U.S. 524; p. 241, l. 36, Clark *v.* Allen, 331 U.S. 503; p. 241, l. 37, Luther *v.* Borden, 48 U.S. (7 How.) 1; p. 241, l. 37, Cockran *v.* Board of Education, 281 U.S. 370; Ohio ex rel. Bryant *v.* Akron Park Dist., 281 U.S. 74; Mountain Timber Co. *v.* Washington, 243 U.S. 219; Ohio ex rel. Davis *v.* Hildebrant, 241 U.S. 565; Marshall *v.* Dye, 231 U.S. 250; Pacific State Tel. & Tel. Co. *v.* Oregon, 223 U.S. 118; Luther *v.* Borden, 48 U.S. (7 How.) 1; p. 241, l. 39, South *v.* Peters, 339 U.S. 276; Cooke *v.* Fortson, 329 U.S. 675; p. 241, l. 40, Dennis *v.* United States, 171 F.2d 986, aff'd on other grounds, 339 U.S. 162; Saunders *v.* Wilkins, 152 F.2d 235, cert. denied, 328 U.S. 870; p. 241, l. 41, Colegrove *v.* Green, 328 U.S. 549; p. 241, l. 42, White *v.* Howard, 347 U.S. 910; Illinois ex rel. Sankstone *v.* Jarecki, 346 U.S. 861; MacDougall *v.* Green, 335 U.S. 281; p. 242, l. 1, Coleman *v.* Miller, 307 U.S. 433; Leser *v.* Garnett, 258 U.S. 130; p. 242, l. 3, Harwood *v.* Wentworth, 162 U.S. 547; Field *v.* Clark, 143 U.S. 649; Flint *v.* Stone Tracy Co., 220 U.S. 107, 143; p. 242, l. 3, Ludecke *v.* Watkins, 335 U.S. 160; Commercial Trust Co. *v.* Miller, 262 U.S. 51; p. 242, l. 5, Matter of Yamashita, 327 U.S. 1; p. 242, l. 6, United States *v.* California,

332 U.S. 19. In Alabama v. Texas, 347 U.S. 272, the Court in sustaining the validity of the Submerged Lands Act ruled that the power of Congress over the public land was unlimited; p. 242, 1. 29, At 54–55. In Panama Canal Co. v. Grace Line, 356 U.S. 309, 317 the Court held that an action for compelling the revision of Panama Canal tolls was "not one appropriate for judicial action." In Gomillion v. Lightfoot, 28 u.s.l. week 2115, the court used the precept of not reviewing political action as a basis for refusing to rule on a contention that an Alabama statute reducing the area of a municipality was enacted in order to bar Negroes from municipal elections. One judge dissented; p. 242, 1. 35, Mins v. McCarthy, 209 F.2d 307; Fischler v. McCarthy, 117 F.Supp. 643; Hutner v. McCarthy, Civil No. 89–364, s.d.n.y.; p. 243, 1. 6, Methodist Federation for Social Action v. Eastland, 141 F.Supp. 729. See also Hearst v. Black, 87 F.2d 68, where the courts denied aid to William Randolph Hearst, who sought to enjoin the members of the Senate Committee headed by Senator, later Justice, Black from publishing telegrams alleged to have been obtained in violation of his constitutional rights. In Dayton v. Hunter, 176 F.2d 108, cert. denied, 338 U.S. 888, and Dalton v. McGranery, 201 F.2d 711, the courts refused to interfere with the regulations of the Bureau of Prisons relating to the communications of inmates of federal penitentiaries with the outside world and their application to a particular prisoner. In the latter case the plaintiff, a prisoner, also requested the removal from the files of prison officials certain letters which he claimed were false and malicious. The court refused this request on the ground that "the courts have no inherent power of disposition over internal documentary data of the executive branch of the Government."; p. 243, 1. 18, Highway Truck Drivers and Helpers Union, Local 107 v. McClellan, cert. denied, 358 U.S. 947; p. 243, 1. 25, Lanza v. New York State Joint Legislative Committee on Government Operations, 3 N.Y.2d 92, 100, cert. denied, 355 U.S. 856; p. 243, 1. 30, 111 F.Supp. 858, 861, 869; p. 243, 1. 39, People v. McCabe, 148 Misc. 330, 333. State cases expunging such documents and other authorities condemning them are collected in Application of United Electrical Radio and Machine Workers, 111 F.Supp. 858, 866, 867 n.26, 868 n.35. See also Ex parte Burns, 261 Ala. 217; In re Report of Grand Jury, 260 P.2d 521; p. 243, 1. 42, 28 u.s.l. week 2266; p. 244, 1. 12, vanderbilt, the doctrine of the separation of powers and its present-day significance 117–19; p. 244, 1. 34, 145 F.2d 316, 318–20, cert. denied, 325 U.S. 867. In United States v. Morton Salt Co., 338 U.S. 632, 641–42, Justice Jackson, writing for the Court, stated: "Federal judicial power itself extends only to adjudication of cases and controversies and it is natural that its investigative powers should be jealously confined to these ends." But cf. MacAlister v. Guterma, 263 F.2d 65, where the court stated that under Rule 42(a) of the Federal Rules of Civil Procedure a federal district court had authority to consolidate stockholders' derivative suits against the same corporation for pre-trial proceedings and to designate general counsel to supervise and coordinate prosecution of the case; p. 245, 1. 15; 153 Ore. 100, 109. In Kauble v. Haynes, 64 F.Supp. 153, a conscientious objector in a civilian public service camp sought release on habeas corpus on the ground that he was suffering from excessive nervousness and depression. The court in denying relief, commented: "Administrative powers, with which courts should not interfere, involve carrying of laws into effect—their practical application to current affairs by way of management and oversight, including investigation, regulation and control in accordance with and in execution of the principles prescribed by the law-makers."; p. 246, 1. 7, 347 U.S. 483; p. 246, 1. 8, 350 U.S. 497; p. 246, 1. 9, 351 U.S. 536; p. 246, 1. 12, 353 U.S. 657; p. 246, 1. 14, 354 U.S. 178; p. 246, 1. 18, 354 U.S. 298; p. 246, 1. 20, 354 U.S. 449; p. 246, 1. 22, 357 U.S. 116; p. 246, 1. 34, 102 cong. rec. 6383–85; p. 250, 1. 9, 71 Stat. 595, 18 U.S.C.A. §3500 (Supp. 1958); p. 250, 1. 17, 207 F.2d 134, cert. denied, 346 U.S. 885; p. 250, 1. 19, 62 Stat. 831, 18 U.S.C. §3432; p. 251, 1. 24, 355 U.S. 96. Senator Keating's bill would make evidence obtained by state authorized wire-

tapping admissible in federal and state courts. Benanti held that such evidence was not admissible in federal court; p. 251, l. 25, S. 1292, 86th Cong., 1st Sess.; p. 251, l. 31, 142 U.S. 547; p. 252, l. 8, 227 U.S. 131, 142, 144. In Mason v. United States, 244 U.S. 362, the Court ruled that a valid claim of privilege must be based on a real danger of prosecution; p. 252, l. 34, 26 U.S. (1 Pet.) 100; p. 252, l. 35, 200 U.S. 186; p. 253, l. 8, 201 U.S. 43; p. 253, l. 10, 199 U.S. 372, affirming 69 Kan. 387; p. 253, l. 30, 161 U.S. at 608; p. 253, l. 32, 284 U.S. 141. In United States ex rel. Vajtauer v. Commissioner of Immigration, 273 U.S. 103, 113, the Court, after holding that a claim of privilege had not been made in that case, went on to say that this conclusion made it unnecessary "to consider the extent to which the 5th Amendment guarantees immunity from self-incrimination under state statutes. . . .". A number of lower federal courts sustained a claim of privilege where the basis for it was the danger of state prosecution. United States v. Lombardo, 228 Fed. 980, aff'd on another ground, 241 U.S. 73; In re Gasteiger, 290 Fed. 410; In re Hooks Smelting Co., 138 Fed. 954; In re Hess, 134 Fed. 109; In re Kanter, 117 Fed. 356; In re Nachman, 114 Fed. 995; In re Franklin Syndicate, 114 Fed. 205; In re Feldstein, 103 Fed. 269; In re Scott, 95 Fed. 815; In re Graham, 10 Fed. Cas. 913; Buckeye Powder Co. v. Hazard Powder Co., 205 F.827, 829. District Judge Woolsey in sustaining a claim of privilege in 1930, in In re Doyle, 42 F.2d 686, made a careful review of the authorities, quoting the opinion in United States v. Saline Bank and two pertinent paragraphs from Ballmann v. Fagin. However, he was reversed on appeal, without opinion. United States v. Doyle, 47 F.2d 1086. Shortly after the decision on appeal the federal government nolprossed an indictment against Doyle. The Doyle in this case was the same one who was involved in Matter of Doyle, 257 N.Y. 244; p. 254, l. 13, 1 B. & S. 311; p. 254, l. 19, 19 L.J. (n.s.) (Ch.) 202 (1850), 20 L.J. (n.s.) (Ch.) 417 (1851); p. 254, l. 32, L.R. 4 Eq. 327 (1867), affirmed on the point of the claim of privilege, L.R. 3 Ch. 79 (1867). Cf. East India Co. v. Campbell, 1 Ves. Sr. 246, 27 Eng. Rep. 1010 (1749). But see In re Atherton, [1912] 2 K.B. 251, 253–54, a case arising out of the public examination of a bankrupt, an area in which the English courts have not given a due regard to the right of silence; p. 255, l. 18, Murdock was subsequently convicted, but his conviction was reversed for the double reason that the judge in the circumstances of that case expressed an opinion as to the defendant's guilt and refused to give a requested charge on willfulness. United States v. Murdock, 290 U.S. 389; p. 255, l. 20, Although the government in its brief (at 15–16) quoted at length from the opinion in King of the Two Sicilies v. Willcox, it in no way indicated that the quoted language had been qualified and restricted in the later case of United States v. McRae; p. 255, l. 25, Feldman v. United States, 322 U.S. 487 (testimony given by a debtor in a discovery proceeding in a state court in New York, most of which was given under a limited immunity provision which simply forbade the use of such testimony in a subsequent criminal proceeding against the debtor, held admissible against him in a federal court on the trial of a mail fraud indictment); United States v. Kahriger, 345 U.S. 22 (federal occupational tax on gamblers sustained as to persons in the states); Irvine v. California, 347 U.S. 128 (federal wagering tax stamp and documentary evidence from federal internal revenue collector's office permitted in evidence in state court criminal proceedings); Lewis v. United States, 348 U.S. 419 (federal occupational tax on gamblers upheld as to persons in the District of Columbia); Regan v. New York, 349 U.S. 58 (state criminal contempt conviction sustained because of broad state immunity statute); Knapp v. Schweitzer, 357 U.S. 371 (ibid.); Mills v. Louisiana, 360 U.S. 230 (ibid.); p. 255, l. 41, 196 F.2d 437, 443; p. 256, l. 13, 102 F.Supp. 597, 604; p. 256, l. 26, See, e.g., Notes, 22 UNIV. CIN. L. REV. 193; 26 TEMP. L. Q. 64; 66 HARV. L. REV. 185; 31 TEX. L. REV. 433. Contra: Comment, 4 STAN. L. REV. 594; p. 256, l. 30, 293 Mich. 263, 284–86; p. 257, l. 11, 318 Mich. 645, 651; p. 257, l. 21, 303 S.W. 2d 301, 304; p. 257, l. 33, 27 U.S.L. WEEK 2319. Accord: State v.

Dominguez, 228 La. 283; State v. Doran, 215 La. 151; People v. Hoffa, 318 Mich. 656; Frad v. Columbian Nat. Life Ins. Co., 37 N.Y.S.2d 250, affd. without opinion, 264 App. Div. 836, 35 N.Y.S.2d 756; p. 258, l. 3, 257 N.Y. 244, 267; p. 258, l. 9, 357 U.S. 371; p. 258, l. 12, 2 A.D. 2d at 586, 157 N.Y.S.2d at 166. For other cases to the same effect see, e.g., Lorenzo v. Blackburn, 74 S.2d 289; State v. Kelly, 71 S.2d 887; People v. Butler Street Foundry, 201 Ill. 236; Koenck v. Cooney, 244 Iowa 153; Republic of Greece v. Koukouras, 264 Mass. 318, (foreign state); In re Cohen, 295 Mich. 748; In re Ward, 295 Mich. 742; In re Schnitzer, 295 Mich. 736; In re Pillo, 11 N.J. 8; State v. March, 46 N.C. *526; In re Greenleaf, 28 N.Y.S.2d 28, aff'd, 266 App. Div. 658, 41 N.Y.S.2d 209, aff'd, 291 N.Y. 690; In re Cappeau, 198 App. Div. 357, 190 N.Y.S. 452; In re Werner, 167 App. Div. 384, 152 N.Y.S. 862; Matter of Herlands (Carchietta), 124 N.Y.S.2d 402; Ex parte Copeland, 91 Tex. Cr. 549; State v. Wood, 99 Vt. 490. In People v. Butler Street Foundry, supra, the court said: "But if it be conceded that there is a bare possibility that the affidavit might contain disclosures which would furnish evidence of a violation of the Anti-trust statute of some other State of the Union or of the United States, we think, within the meaning of the authorities, that such disclosure is not a real and probable danger, and does not fall within the danger which the constitutional privilege was intended to obviate." In Ex parte Copeland, supra, the court ruled: "The further reason urged that relator should not answer the questions because the State court and district attorney had no right to guarantee immunity from Federal prosecution has such a shadowy and uncertain basis that we scarcely deem it necessary to discuss it." In Gould v. Gould, 201 App. Div. 674, 194 N.Y.S. 742, prosecution in a foreign jurisdiction had already been concluded; p. 258, l. 18, People v. Costello, 6 A.D. 2d 385, 178 N.Y.S.2d 432; p. 258, l. 19, Commission of Investigation v. Lombardozzi, 180 N.Y.S.2d 496; p. 258, l. 21, See, e.g., Tedesco v. United States, 255 F.2d 35; In re Reina, 170 F.Supp. 592; United States v. Eramdjian, 155 F.Supp. 914, 925–26; George v. Lindberg, 138 F.Supp. 77, 80; Cabot v. Corcoran, 332 Mass. 44; State v. Morgan, 164 Ohio St. 529; p. 258, l. 28, 128 F.Supp. at 622; p. 258, l. 34, 5 N.Y. 2d 1026, cert. denied, 360 U.S. 930; p. 258, l. 34, 6 N.Y. 2d 761; p. 258, l. 36, 360 U.S. 230; p. 259, l. 18, 322 U.S. 487; p. 260, l. 3, United States v. Bonanno, 178 F.Supp. 62, 68; p. 261, l. 42, 350 U.S. 497; p. 262, l. 37, Fla. Stat. (1955) §§876.22 to 876.31; Ga. Code Ann. (1953) (Supp. 1955) §§26–901a to 26–914a; La. Rev. Stat. (Supp. 1954) §§14.366 to 14.380; Miss. Code (Supp. 1954) §§4046–01 to 4064–12; N.H. Rev. Stat. (1955) §§588.1 to 588.16 and (Supp. 1955) §§588.3-a, 588.3-b; Ohio Rev. Code (Baldwin, Supp. 1956) §§2921.21 to 2921.27; Pa. Stat. Ann. (Purdon, Supp. 1955) tit. 65, §§211 to 225; Wash. Rev. Code (1951; Supp. July 1953) §§9.81.010 to 9.81.130; p. 262, l. 39, Ala. Code (Supp. 1955) tit. 14, §§97(1) to 97(8); Ark. Stat. Ann. (Supp. 1955) §§41–4125 to 41–4127; Cal. Corp. Code (Deering, 1953) §§35000 to 35302; Del. Code Ann. (Supp. 1954) tit. 20, §§3501 to 3503; La. Rev. Stat. Ann. (Supp. 1954) §§14–358 to 14–365; Mich. Comp. Laws (Supp. 1954) §§752.321 to 752.332; Mont. Rev. Code Ann. (Supp. 1955) §§94–4411 to 94–4427; N.M. Stat. Ann. (1953) §§4–15–1 to 4–15–3; S.C. Code (1952) §§16–581 to 16–589; Tex. Civ. Stat. (Vernon, Supp. 1956) §§6889–3, 3A; p. 263, l. 3, Ind. Stat. Ann. (Burns, 1956) §§10–5201 to 10–5209; Mass. Ann. Laws (1956) c.264, §§16 to 23; Pa. Stat. Ann. (Purdon, Supp. 1955) tit. 18, §3811; Tex. Civ. Stat. (Vernon, Supp. 1956) §6889–3A. Sections 16A and 17 of the Massachusetts act provide: "The Communist Party is hereby declared to be a subversive organization" and "A subversive organization is hereby declared to be unlawful."; p. 263, l. 41, Pennsylvania v. Nelson, 350 U.S. 497 (Pennsylvania sedition act); Wieman v. Updegraff, 344 U.S. 183 (Oklahoma statute prescribing loyalty oath for state officers and employees); Herndon v. Lowry, 301 U.S. 242 (Georgia statute against insurrection as applied); DeJonge v. Oregon, 299 U.S. 353 (Oregon criminal syndicalism law as applied); Stromberg v. California, 283 U.S. 359 (California red flag law); Fiske v. Kansas, 274 U.S. 380 (Kansas criminal syndicalism statute as applied); p. 263, l. 42, 350 U.S. 497, 500; p. 264, l. 14, 268 U.S. 652; p. 264, l. 15, 278 U.S. 63; p. 264, l. 16, 342 U.S. 485; p. 264, l. 17, 254 U.S. 325; p. 264, l. 18, 274 U.S. 357; p. 264, l. 19, 274 U.S. 328; p. 264, l. 19, 341 U.S. 716; p. 264, l. 22, 341 U.S. 56; p. 264, l. 24, 360 U.S. 72; p. 264, l. 28, 360 U.S. 423; p. 265, l. 4, The States were Arizona, Connecticut, Florida, Georgia, Indiana, Kansas, Louisiana, Maine, Maryland, Massachusetts, Michigan, Mississippi, Montana, Nebraska, Nevada, New Mexico, New York, North Carolina, Ohio, South Carolina, Tennessee, Virginia, Washington and Wisconsin; p. 265, l. 37, N.H. Rev. Stat. (1955) §§588.1 to 588.16 (Subversive Activities Act of 1951); N.H. Laws 1953, c.307 at 524, 525 (joint resolution directing the attorney general "to make full and complete investigation with respect to violations of the subversive activities act of 1951 and to determine whether subversive persons as defined in said act are presently located within this state," and "to proceed with criminal prosecutions under the subversive activities act whenever evidence presented to him in the course of the investigation indicates violations thereof," and "to report to the 1955 session on the first day of its regular session the results of this investigation, together with his recommendations, if any, for necessary legislation"); p. 265, l. 38, See, e.g., Nelson v. Wyman, 99 N.H. 33, sustaining the validity of the legislation just cited; p. 266, l. 37, 351 U.S. 934; p. 266, l. 40, The states were Alabama, Arizona, Arkansas, Colorado, Connecticut, Florida, Georgia, Idaho, Illinois, Indiana, Iowa, Kansas, Kentucky, Louisiana, Maine, Maryland, Massachusetts, Mississippi, Missouri, Nebraska, New Hampshire, New Mexico, North Carolina, Tennessee, Texas, Utah, Vermont, Virginia, Washington, Wisconsin and Wyoming; p. 267, l. 27, 62 Stat. 826, 18 U.S.C. §3231; p. 267, l. 34, Cf. Sexton v. California, 189 U.S. 319; In re Dixon, 41 Cal. 2d 756; Nastasi v. Aderhold, 201 Ga. 237; People v. Fury, 279 N.Y. 433; People v. Welch, 141 N.Y. 266; p. 267, l. 39, International Union v. Wisconsin Employment Relations Board, 336 U.S. 245, 253. For further illustrations see Allen-Bradley Local v. Wisconsin Employment Relations Board, 315 U.S. 740; Kelly v. Washington, 302 U.S. 1; Reid v. Colorado, 187 U.S. 137. In Kelly v. Washington, the Court said, speaking through Chief Justice Hughes: "The principle is thoroughly established that the exercise by the State of its police power, which would be valid if not superseded by federal action, is superseded only where the repugnance or conflict is 'so direct and positive' that the two acts cannot 'be reconciled or consistently stand together.' " In Reid v. Colorado, the Court ruled: "It should never be held that Congress intends to supersede or by its legislation suspend the exercise of the police powers of the States, even when it may do so, unless its purpose to effect that result is clearly manifested." In Schwartz v. Texas, 344 U.S. 199, 202–3, where the Court sustained the use of wiretap evidence in a state court proceeding, the Court said: ". . . If Congress is authorized to act in a field, it should manifest its intention clearly. It will not be presumed that a federal statute was intended to supersede the exercise of the power of the state unless there is a clear manifestation of intention to do so. The exercise of federal supremacy is not lightly to be presumed."; p. 268, l. 12, 274 U.S. 328, 331; p. 268, l. 19, White v. Hart, 80 U.S. (13 Wall.) 646, 650–51; p. 268, l. 21, See Gerende v. Board of Supervisors, 341 U.S. 56; p. 268, l. 22, See Garner v. Board of Public Works, 341 U.S. 716; p. 269, l. 5, 195 F.2d 583, cert. denied, 344 U.S. 838, stay of execution granted 346 U.S. 313 (Justice Douglas), stay of execution vacated, 346 U.S. 273; p. 270, l. 2, Washington v. McGrath, 341 U.S. 923 (loyalty investigation); Bailey v. Richardson, 341 U.S. 918 (ibid.); Joint Anti-Fascist Refugee Committee v. McGrath, 341 U.S. 123 (attorney general's blacklist of organizations, compiled without any hearings); Adler v. Board of Education, 342 U.S. 485 (Feinberg Law of New York, relating to the public school system, which provided that the board of regents was to establish its own blacklist of organizations and in so doing to make use of any similar authorized blacklist of any federal agency or authority); Shaughnessy *v.* United States ex rel. Mezei, 345 U.S. 206 (alien resident of this country seeking to return after a trip abroad held entitled to no hearing at all); United States ex rel. Knauff *v.* Shaughnessy, 338 U.S. 537 (alien war bride held entitled to no hearing); Ludecke *v.* Watkins, 335 U.S. 160 (alien ordered banished without a hearing); Carlson *v.* Landon, 342 U.S. 524 (alien denied bail without a hearing); United States *v.* Nugent, 346 U.S. 1 (draft status of conscientious objector); Jay *v.* Boyd, 351 U.S. 345 (exercise of attorney general's discretionary power of suspension of deportation of an alien); Leifer *v.* United States, 260 F.2d 648, cert. denied, 358 U.S. 946 (conscientious objector); Blalock *v.* United States, 247 F.2d 615 (ibid.); p. 270, l. 39, H.R. Rep. 2606, 83d Cong., 2d Sess. 12; p. 271, l. 40, In subsequent court proceedings one obtained his release but the other had to stay in jail. People ex rel. Valenti *v.* McCloskey, 6 N.Y. 2d 390; p. 272, l. 10, In re McElrath, 248 F.2d 612; p. 272, l. 16, S. Rep. 1477, 85th Cong., 2d Sess. 18, 19; p. 273, l. 17, 73 Stat. 539, 29 U.S.C.A. §521(b) (Supp. 1959); p. 273, l. 24, 335 U.S. 1; p. 273, l. 28, Is this decision applicable to records which income tax regulations require a taxpayer to keep for the determination of the amount of his tax liability? See Falsone *v.* United States, 205 F.2d 734, 739; United States *v.* Willis, 145 F.Supp. 365, 368; p. 273, l. 34, Communist Party *v.* Subversive Activities Control Bd., 223 F.2d 531. Cf. Lewis *v.* United States, 348 U.S. 419 (federal occupational tax on gamblers upheld as to persons in the District of Columbia); Irvine *v.* California, 347 U.S. 128 (federal wagering tax stamp and documentary evidence from federal internal revenue collector's office permitted in evidence in state court proceeding); United States *v.* Kahriger, 345 U.S. 22 (federal occupational tax on gamblers sustained as to persons in the states); p. 274, l. 1, Communist Party *v.* Subversive Activities Control Bd., 351 U.S. 115; p. 275, l. 1, 3 EVIDENCE §851 (3d ed.) (Supp. 1949); p. 275, l. 37, 7 WORKS 452–55 (Bowring ed.); p. 276, l. 10, 8 WIGMORE §2251 (3d ed.); p. 276, l. 20, Vol. 1 at 441; p. 276, l. 26, People *v.* Arrighini, 122 Cal. 121, 126; p. 276, l. 36, 350 U.S. 422; p. 276, l. 37, 161 U.S. 591; p. 276, l. 38, 359 U.S. 42; p. 276, l. 38, 340 U.S. 367; p. 276, l. 39, 335 U.S. 1; p. 278, l. 6, Board of Education *v.* Allen, 6 N.Y. 2d 127. Commissioner Allen also annulled the dismissal of Charles W. Hughes, an associate professor of music at Hunter College, by the Board of Higher Education, but required Hughes to give numbers, if not names, of faculty members who were or had been communists. Hughes gave the numbers and was returned to his post.

CHAPTER XII

P. 279, l. 25, At 74–75; p. 280, l. 3, 3 ELLIOT, DEBATES ON THE FEDERAL CONSTITUTION 661 (2d ed.); p. 280, l. 9, 1 id., at 327; p. 280, l. 13, Virginia's seventeenth proposed amendment became North Carolina's eighteenth. 4 id. at 246. North Carolina and Rhode Island ratified the Constitution in 1790. Rhode Island in doing so made a declaration similar to that of New York. 1 id. at 334; p. 280, l. 21, 1 ANNALS CONG. 434, 754, 432–33, 439, 437, 441; p. 282, l. 33, The preceding year he had written in The Federalist, No. 44: "Had the convention attempted a positive enumeration of the powers necessary and proper for carrying their other powers into effect, the attempt would have involved a complete digest of laws on every subject to which the Constitution relates; accommodated too, not only to the existing state of things, but to all possible changes which futurity may produce, for in every new application of a general power, the *particular powers*, which are the means of attaining the *object* of the general power, must always necessarily vary with that object, and be often properly varied whilst the object remains the same."; p. 282, l. 42, See 5 THE WRITINGS OF JAMES MADISON 431, 432 (Hunt ed.); p. 283, l. 3, 4 SPARKS, CORRESPONDENCE OF THE AMERICAN REVOLUTION 298; p. 284, l. 1, 2 ANNALS CONG. 1748, 1899, 1960; p. 284, l. 13,

6 THE WORKS OF THOMAS JEFFERSON 201 (fed. ed. by Ford). Washington signed the bill, although he held it almost to the last hour allowed him.; p. 284, l. 15, 4 THE WORKS OF ALEXANDER HAMILTON 70 (fed. ed. by Lodge); p. 284, l. 21, Letter of Jan. 1, 1792. 6 THE WRITINGS OF JAMES MADISON 81 n. (Hunt ed.); p. 284, l. 34, 6 id. at 383–84 (Hunt ed.); 4 ELLIOT, DEBATES ON THE FEDERAL CONSTITUTION 567–68 (2d ed.); p. 284, l. 37, 6 id. at 347; 4 ELLIOT at 547; p. 284, l. 38, 6 THE WORKS OF THOMAS JEFFERSON 198 (fed. ed. by Ford); p. 284, l. 41, 17 U.S. (4 Wheat.) 316, 421. In that case the Court held that Congress had power to incorporate a bank and that a Maryland statute which taxed a branch of that bank was unconstitutional; p. 285, l. 19, 8 THE WRITINGS OF JAMES MADISON 447, 448, 451–52 (Hunt ed.,); p. 285, l. 36, 9 id. at 434; p. 285, l. 40, 79 U.S. (12 Wall.) 457, 534, 535. Recently in Franklin Nat. Bank v. New York, 347 U.S. 373, the Court applied the principal case to invalidate an act of New York which forbade national banks to use the words "saving" or "savings" in their business or advertising; p. 286, l. 9, Perez v. Brownell, 356 U.S. 44; Savorgnan v. United States, 338 U.S. 491; United States v. Curtiss-Wright Export Corp., 299 U.S. 304; Mackenzie v. Hare, 239 U.S. 299; p. 286, l. 19, 356 U.S. 44, 57. In United States v. Curtis-Wright Export Corp., 299 U.S. 304, 315–16, 318, the Court gave a greater latitude to federal powers in the foreign field than in the domestic area: "The two classes of powers are different, both in respect of their origin and their nature. The broad statement that the federal government can exercise no powers except those specifically enumerated in the Constitution and such implied powers as are necessary and proper to carry into effect the enumerated powers, is categorically true only in respect of our internal affairs. * * * The powers to declare and wage war, to conclude peace, to make treaties, to maintain diplomatic relations with other sovereignties, if they had never been mentioned in the Constitution, would have vested in the Federal government as necessary concomitants of nationality. * * *"; p. 286, l. 41, Palko v. Connecticut, 302 U.S. 319, 325; p. 287, l. 4, See, e.g., Roth v. United States, 354 U.S. 476; United Public Workers v. Mitchell, 330 U.S. 75; Tennessee Electric Power Co. v. TVA, 306 U.S. 118; Ashwander v. TVA, 297 U.S. 288; Kape v. Home Bank & Trust Co., 370 Ill. 170; p. 287, l. 7, 277 U.S. 438; p. 287, l. 12, 330 U.S. 75; p. 287, l. 22, Kent v. Dulles, 357 U.S. 116; p. 287, l. 32, Warren and Brandeis, The Right to Privacy, 4 HARV. L. REV. 193; p. 287, l. 34, 277 U.S. 438, 478; p. 287, l. 37, Pavesich v. New England Life Insurance Co., 122 Ga. 190; p. 287, l. 39, To the cases collected in Hazlitt v. Fawcett Publications, 116 F.Supp. 538, add Bremmer v. Journal-Tribune Pub. Co., 247 Iowa 817; Biederman's of Springfield, Inc. v. Wright, 322 S.W. 2d 892; Housh v. Peth, 165 Ohio St. 35; Roach v. Harper, 105 S.E. 2d 564; Gouldman-Taber Pontiac v. Zerbst, 213 Ga. 682, 683; p. 287, l. 40, To the cases collected in Hazlitt add Brunson v. Ranks Army Store, 161 Neb. 519; Yoeckel v. Samonig, 272 Wis. 430; p. 288, l. 17, 48 Stat. 1103, 47 U.S.C.A. §605 (Supp. 1958); p. 288, l. 20, 277 U.S. 438, 470; p. 288, l. 36, See statement of March 13, 1940 of Attorney General Jackson. 86 Cong. Rec. App. 1471–72; p. 288, l. 40, 9 A Mass. Anno. Laws (1956) c.272, §99; p. 289, l. 2, N.Y. Code of Crim. Proc. (McKinney Supp. 1958) §813-a, as amended. The New York constitutional and statutory provisions providing for warrants to wiretap were held not to violate Section 605. People v. Feld, 305 N.Y. 322; People v. Stemmer, 298 N.Y. 728, aff'd without opinion by an evenly divided court, 336 U.S. 963; Matter of Harlem Check Cashing Corp. v. Bell, 296 N.Y. 15. In an excellent recent case, Matter of Interception of Telephone Communications, 136 N.Y.S. 2d 612, Justice Samuel H. Hofstadter, who had signed orders permitting wiretapping with "much misgiving", refused to enter the order there requested; p. 289, l. 5, Nardone v. United States, 302 U.S. 379; p. 289, l. 6, Nardone v. United States, 308 U.S. 338; p. 289, l. 7, Weiss v. United States, 308 U.S. 321; p. 289, l. 16, Hearings before Subcommittee No. 1 of the House Committee on the Judiciary on H.R. 2266 and H.R. 3099, 77th Cong. 1st Sess. 18; p. 289, l. 31, Westin,

The Wire-Tapping Problem: An Analysis and a Legislative Proposal, 52 COLUM.
L. REV. 165, 167–68; p. 289, l. 41, 344 U.S. 199, 205; p. 290, l. 19, United
States v. Noce, 5 U.S.C.M.A. 715; United States v. DeLeon, 5 U.S.C.M.A. 747;
United States v. Gopaulsingh, 5 U.S.C.M.A. 772. But cf. United States v. Coplon,
185 F.2d 629, cert. denied, 342 U.S. 920, where the court reversed her conviction
for the double reason that the prosecution did not show in open court that none
of the wiretaps led to any of the evidence there involved, and that the defense
was unduly prevented from learning whether the information which originally
led to the tracking of her movements was itself the result of a wiretap; p. 290,
l. 20, 351 U.S. 916 (per curiam); p. 290, l. 24, Massicot v. United States, 254
F.2d 58; United States v. Gris, 247 F.2d 860; p. 290, l. 25, Commonwealth v.
Publicover, 327 Mass. 303; People v. Broady, 5 N.Y. 500, appeal dismissed and
cert. denied, 80 S. Ct. 57. In State v. Spindel, 24 N.J. 395, the court sustained
a wiretapping complaint; p. 290, l. 32, 355 U.S. 96. New York courts have
divided on the effect of this decision on state proceedings. Justice Hofstadter, in
In the Matter of Interception of Telephone Communications, 170 N.Y.S. 2d
84, ruled that under it no state wiretap order could lawfully be issued. But cf.
People v. Dinan, 6 N.Y.2d 715, cert. denied, 80 S. Ct. 71 (wiretap evidence
admissible); People v. Grant, 179 N.Y.S.2d 384 (ibid.). The Pennsylvania Supreme
Court likewise ruled that wiretap evidence was admissible in a state criminal proceeding. Commonwealth v. Voci, 393 Pa. 404, cert. denied, 358 U.S. 885;
Commonwealth v. Chaitt, 380 Pa. 532. In Burack v. State Liquor Authority,
160 F.Supp. 161, the court held that a New York liquor retailer was entitled to
have the State Liquor Authority enjoined from using wiretap evidence in a proceeding to revoke or suspend the plaintiff's license.; p. 290, l. 42, 277 U.S. 438;
p. 291, l. 37, 6 THE WRITINGS OF JAMES MADISON 119 (Hunt ed.); p. 291, l. 38,
Brant, JAMES MADISON FATHER OF THE CONSTITUTION 348; p. 291, l. 42, 354 U.S.
234, 265. The Court upset the conviction; p. 292, l. 19, 330 U.S. 75, 96, 101;
p. 293, l. 41, 357 U.S. 116 and 144. Others who went to court were Dr. Nathan,
Mr. Boudin and former Judge William Clark. In Dulles v. Nathan, 225 F.2d 29 the
court ordered Dr. Nathan's complaint dismissed, but only because the government
advised it that he had gotten his passport. Previously District Judge Henry A.
Schweinhaut had denied the government's motion to dismiss Dr. Nathan's complaint. Nathan v. Dulles, 129 F.Supp. 951. Judge Schweinhaut had made a
similar ruling with reference to a similar complaint of Judge Clark. Clark v.
Dulles, 129 F.Supp. 950. In Boudin v. Dulles, 136 F.Supp. 218, 222, District
Judge Luther W. Youngdahl ruled that in a passport hearing all the evidence upon
which the passport office relied for its decision "must appear on record so that
the applicant may have the opportunity to meet it and the court to review it."
However, the Court of Appeals for the District of Columbia Circuit did not find
it necessary to reach this question. Boudin v. Dulles, 235 F.2d 532; p. 294, l. 2,
Worthy v. Herter, 270 F.2d 905, cert. denied, 80 S. Ct. 255; Frank v. Herter, 269
F.2d 245, cert. denied, 80 S. Ct. 256; p. 294, l. 9, Porter v. Herter, cert. denied,
80 S. Ct. 260; p. 295, l. 8, The State Department denied visas to a number of
well-known foreigners who wanted to visit us, for examples, Nobel Prize-winning
physicist Professor P.A.M. Dirac of Cambridge University, England, and the
Dean of Canterbury, Dr. Hewlett Johnson. There were many more visa rebuffs
that did not become public knowledge. According to a report from the Federation
of American Scientists visa difficulties blocked or seriously delayed 100 foreign
scientists invited to the United States by Harvard, Princeton, Stanford and other
leading universities, medical institutions and, in several instances, prominent
business concerns; and led seven international scientific organizations to prefer
meeting abroad; p. 295, l. 26, *Availability of Information From Federal Departments and Agencies, Twenty-Fifth Intermediate Report of the Committee on Government Operations*, H.R. Rep. No. 2947, 84th Cong. 2d Sess. 81–83, 88–89;
p. 296, l. 39, OHIO REV. CODE §121.22 (Page Supp. 1958); p. 296, l. 42, Stat. of

Cal. (1957) cc.2170–2235; Conn. Public Acts (1957) No. 468, at 688; 2 ILL. REV. STAT. c.102, §41–44 (State Bar Ass'n ed., 1957); Laws of Pa. (1957) no. 213, at 392–93, PA. STAT. ANN. §§251–54 (Purdon, Supp. 1957); p. 297, 1. 5, 72 STAT. 547, 5 U.S.C.A. §22 (Supp. 1958); p. 297, 1. 8, Act of July 27, 1789, c.4, §4, 1 STAT. 29; Act of Aug. 7, 1798, c.7, §4, 1 STAT. 50; Act of Sept. 2, 1789, c.12, 1 Stat. 65; Act of Sept. 15, 1789, c.14, §7, 1 Stat. 69; p. 297, 1. 22, N.Y. Times, Aug. 17, 1958, p. 66, col. 1; p. 297, 1. 31, REPORT OF THE COMMISSION ON GOVERNMENT SECURITY 737. In Halpern v. United States, 258 F.2d 36, 44, arising under the Invention Secrecy Act of 1951, the court held: "We conclude that the district court has jurisdiction to entertain the action during the pendency of the secrecy order; and we further conclude that a trial *in camera* in which the privilege relating to state secrets may not be availed of by the United States is permissible, if, in the judgment of the district court, such a trial can be carried out without substantial risk that secret information will be publicly divulged." But cf. New York Post Corp. v. Leibowitz, 2 N.Y.2d 677, where the court ruled that a newspaper was entitled to a transcript of a trial judge's charge to the jury in a criminal case which had been concluded; p. 297, 1. 37, Not only Mr. Worthy but also Edmund Stevens and Phillip Harrington of *Look* magazine went to Communist China in violation of passport restrictions. Thereafter the State Department announced that it would revoke their passports and refer their cases to the Treasury Department for possible action under the Trading with the Enemy Act; p. 298, 1. 34, 136 F.Supp. 218; p. 298, 1. 39, Dayton v. Dulles, 237 F.2d 43; Boudin v. Dulles, 235 F.2d 532; p. 298, 1. 40, Dayton v. Dulles, 146 F.Supp. 876; p. 299, 1. 7, 254 F.2d at 76–77. But in a criminal case the government either produces relevant confidential information or the defendant goes free. United States v. Coplon, 185 F.2d 629, cert. denied, 342 U.S. 920; United States v. Beekman, 155 F.2d 580; United States v. Andolschek, 142 F.2d 503. In the Coplon case Chief Judge Learned Hand said for the court: ". . . the prosecution must decide whether the public prejudice of allowing the crime to go unpunished was greater than the disclosure of such 'state secrets' as might be relevant to the defense." In Roviaro v. United States, 353 U.S. 53, the Court held that the government had to disclose the identity of a confidential informant even though such person was not called as a witness by the government. The confidential informant had been present with the defendant at the time of the alleged commission of the offense. The Court reasoned:

"* * * Where the disclosure of an informer's identity, or of the contents of his communication, is relevant and helpful to the defense of an accused, or is essential to a fair determination of a cause, the privilege must give way. In these situations the trial court may require disclosure and, if the Government withholds the information, dismiss the action. * * *" For a recent state case where the court ruled a search and seizure to be illegal because of the prosecution's refusal to reveal the identity of informers whose information furnished the basis for a search without a warrant see Priestly v. Superior Court, 330 P.2d 39; p. 299, 1. 29, 341 U.S. 918; p. 299, 1. 29, 341 U.S. 923; p. 299, 1. 31, Peters v. Hobby, 349 U.S. 331; p. 299, 1. 32, 346 U.S. 1. The principal case was followed in Leifer v. United States, 260 F.2d 648, cert. denied, 358 U.S. 946; Blalock v. United States, 247 F.2d 615; p. 299, 1. 34, 351 U.S. 345; p. 299, 1. 36, 359 U.S. 35 and 360 U.S. 474 and 709. In the Greene case the Court of Appeals for the District of Columbia Circuit took occasion to state that the right to knowledge was not involved: "We are not dealing here with the vexed questions of the right of Congress, or the press, or the public, to be informed of defense operations generally, or to inspect particular documents." For other employee cases where the federal district court in the District of Columbia denied confrontation see Coleman v. Brucker, 156 F.Supp. 126, reversed and remanded, 257 F.2d 661; Dressler v. Wilson, 155 F.Supp. 373. Both district court decisions were by Judge Alexander Holtzoff. In Dressler v. Wilson, supra, Judge Holtzoff declared: ". . . To be sure, he was not confronted with the witnesses against him, but as the Court has just stated, there is no constitutional requirement of confrontation with witnesses outside of the criminal courts." In Coleman v. Brucker, supra, he asserted: ". . . In other words, procedural due process, in the opinion of this Court, obviously is inapplicable to removals of employees from the Government service." In that case he not only ruled against confrontation but also held that letters of notification which simply advised employees that their continued employment "would not be clearly consistent with the interests of national security" constituted findings under the applicable regulation. It was on the latter point that he was reversed.

For what the writer predicts will become the leading article on the subject see McKay, Confrontation, WASH. U.L.Q. 122 (1959); p. 300, l. 22, 351 U.S. 345, 372, 374; p. 300, l. 33, 227 F.2d 708, 720–21. Subsequently the courts ruled that the seamen were entitled to their sailing papers before rather than after a hearing which measured up to due process. Lester v. Parker, 235 F.2d 787. Thereafter the Court of Appeals denied a petition for rehearing. Lester v. Parker, 237 F.2d 698. But the federal Court of Claims held that a shipmaster to whom the Coast Guard refused to issue a certificate of loyalty while it had the procedure which the court condemned in Parker v. Lester, did not have the basis for a claim against the United States which was within the class of cases cognizable in that court. Dupree v. United States, 141 F.Supp. 773. Then the Court of Appeals for the Third Circuit, affirming the court below, ruled that the shipmaster could not make out a claim under the Federal Tort Claims Act either. Dupree v. United States, 264 F.2d 140 and 247 F.2d 819; p. 301, l. 31, 71 Stat. 634, codified in scattered sections in 5, 28, and 42 U.S.C.A. (Supp. 1958); p. 302, l. 6, Dennis v. United States, 341 U.S. 494; p. 302, l. 9, United States v. Flynn, 216 F.2d 354, cert. denied, 348 U.S. 909; p. 302, l. 18, Green and Winston v. United States, 356 U.S. 165; United States v. Thompson, 214 F.2d 545, cert. denied, 348 U.S. 841; United States v. Hall, 198 F.2d 726, cert. denied, 345 U.S. 905. Thompson subsequently moved to vacate his conviction or correct his sentence. It was denied. Thompson v. United States, 261 F.2d 809, cert. denied, 359 U.S. 967; p. 303, l. 11, 354 U.S. 476, 504 n.5; p. 303, l. 14, 255 U.S. 407, 437. Justice Brandeis also wrote a dissenting opinion. The dissenting opinions of Justices Holmes and Brandeis in that case have been cited with approval in subsequent Supreme Court decisions. See e.g., Speiser v. Randall, 357 U.S. 513, 518; Reilly v. Pinkus, 338 U.S. 269, 277; Hannegan v. Esquire, 327 U.S. 146, 156; p. 303, l. 20, 338 U.S. 269, 277. In Stanard v. Olesen, 74 S. Ct. 768, 771, involving an application to Justice Douglas, he said: "Impounding one's mail is plainly a 'sanction', for it may as effectively close down an establishment as the sheriff himself. * * *"; p. 303, l. 21, 121 F.2d 37, 39, cert. denied, 314 U.S. 625. In Walker v. Popenoe, 149 F.2d 511, 513, Associate Justice Thurman W. Arnold, in a concurring opinion in which the court joined, added: ". . . To deprive a publisher of the use of the mails is like preventing a seller of goods from using the principal highway which connects him with his market. In making the determination whether any publication is obscene the Postmaster General necessarily passes on a question involving the fundamental liberty of a citizen. This is a judicial and not an executive function. It must be exercised according to the ideas of due process implicit in the Fifth Amendment. * * *" Cf. Rudder v. United States, 226 F.2d 51, 53, where the court held that the government as landlord nevertheless had to comply with the requirements of due process: "* * * The government as landlord is still the government. It must not act arbitrarily, for, unlike private landlords, it is subject to the requirements of due process of law * * *"; p. 304, l. 3, 17 U.S. (4 Wheat.) 316, 407, 415; p. 304, l. 7, 19 U.S. (6 Wheat.) 264, 387; p. 304, l. 10, 217 U.S. 349, 373; p. 304, l. 32, See e.g., his dissenting opinion in Adamson v. California, 332 U.S. 46, 68–123; p. 304, l. 34, See e.g., his dissenting opinion in Green v. United States, 356 U.S. 165, 193–219; p. 305, l. 3, Dunbar, James Madison and the Ninth Amendment, 42 VA. L. REV. 627, 640.

351